URBAN AND REAL ESTATE ECONOMICS

R1B30016

ACKNOWLEDGEMENTS

The UBC Real Estate Division gratefully acknowledges the generous financial support of the Real Estate Foundation of BC. The UBC Real Estate Division also wishes to acknowledge the contributions of the following persons and organizations who acted as contributors, authors, editors, and reviewers:

- Robert W. Helsley, BS, MA, PhD, Dean & Grosvenor Professor of Cities, Business Economics and Public Policy, UBC Sauder School of Business
- Ian Saxon, BCom
- Wes Gentle, BCom, RI
- Aviad Pe'er. MSc, PhD
- Justin Tyndall MA, MUP

- John Bridal, BCom, MEd, RI
- Sharon Gulbranson, MBA
- Shawn Davis, BCom
- Steve Dunford, BCom
- Devon Willits, BCom
- Tony Yu, BA

DISCLAIMER: This publication is intended for EDUCATIONAL purposes only. The information contained herein is subject to change with no notice, and while a great deal of care has been taken to provide accurate and current information, UBC, their affiliates, authors, editors and staff (collectively, the "UBC Group") makes no claims, representations, or warranties as to accuracy, completeness, usefulness or adequacy of any of the information contained herein. Under no circumstances shall the UBC Group be liable for any losses or damages whatsoever, whether in contract, tort or otherwise, from the use of, or reliance on, the information contained herein. Further, the general principles and conclusions presented in this text are subject to local, provincial, and federal laws and regulations, court cases, and any revisions of the same. This publication is sold for educational purposes only and is not intended to provide, and does not constitute, legal, accounting, or other professional advice. Professional advice should be consulted regarding every specific circumstance before acting on the information presented in these materials.

AUTHOR'S NOTE:

Robert W. Helsley, Dean & Grosvenor Professor of Cities, Business Economics and Public Policy Sauder School of Business, University of British Columbia

As a graduate student, I was very fortunate to have studied under one of the founders of the field, Professor Edwin S. Mills, then of Princeton University, who made seminal contributions to both urban economic theory and policy. If I can pass on just a tiny fraction of the many insights that Ed has imparted to me, then my time on this project will have been well spent.

In writing this book, a few comments about other resources are in order. There are many fine books on urban economics, but none finer than Mills (1972). This small masterpiece has been superseded by Mills and Hamilton (1994), which is also very good, but if you happen across a copy of the original in some dusty bookstore, I strongly encourage you to buy it. It is the best book ever written on the subject. The dominant U.S. text in the field currently is by O'Sullivan (in its 8th edition as of 2012). Another common text used in undergraduate courses is City Economics by O'Flaherty (2005).

Current developments in urban and real estate economics may be found in the academic journals in the fields. In urban economics, the top journals are the Journal of Urban Economics (Academic Press) and Regional Science and Urban Economics (North-Holland). In real estate, the top academic journals are Real Estate Economics, the journal of the American Real Estate and Urban Economics Association, and The Journal of Real Estate Finance and Economics (Kluwer). You will find many references to articles in these and other journals in the references at the end of the book. Searchable indices of journal articles (and in most cases the articles themselves) are available online. An up-to-date synthesis of academic literature in the field can be found in the Handbook of Regional and Urban Economics, edited by Duranton, Henderson, and Strange (five volumes, 1987-2015).

My thanks to:

- Cynthia Holmes for helping with data collection and library work early in the project and Aviad Pe'er for finishing these jobs and preparing the SimCity exercises that accompany the text.
- Tsur Somerville kindly provided the data behind many of the graphs and charts in Chapter 11.
- André Gravelle, who let many, many deadlines pass without so much as a harsh glance.
- UBC Centre for Urban Economics and Real Estate for its guidance, and the Real Estate Foundation of British Columbia and Appraisal Institute of Canada for financial support.

TABLE OF CONTENTS

Chapter 8: Urban Growth Over Time

Chapter 9: Transportation and Congestion

Chapter 10: Housing and Housing Markets

Chapter 11: Modelling Real Estate Markets

Chapter 12: Local Government and Land Use Regulation

CHAPTER 1
THEMES AND VARIATIONS

INTRODUCTION TO URBAN AND REAL ESTATE ECONOMICS

This book's main objectives are to introduce the key economic principles that govern the operation of urban land markets and the development of cities, and to show how these principles can be used to gain a deeper understanding of real estate markets and the increasingly urban world in which we all live.

Value Matters: Connecting Theory and Practice

Many readers of this book are studying towards becoming real estate valuation professionals. You will find that this course's in-depth review of property economics provides basis for all market value considerations for real property. This also presents a foundation for real estate appraisal. In fact, in some parts of the world, appraisers are known as "land economists" or "applied economists". Reading this book, you may find at times that the concepts seem too theoretical to be useful in practice. But rest assured, all of the concepts covered are applicable, so your task as the reader is to approach these topics with an open-mind. As you proceed through the book, try to step back and thoughtfully consider how the discussion may apply to your market realities. Talk it over with your classmates and colleagues and seek out these links. You will hopefully find these Value Matters boxes helpful in making the connection between theory and practice.

Although philosophers and social scientists have been studying cities since antiquity, the field of urban economics is only about 50 years old. Two events during the 1960s combined to give birth to this relatively new branch of applied microeconomics. The first, and by far the most important, was the realization that many of the pressing social problems and public policy issues of that time were closely tied to cities. Poverty, ghettos, racial discrimination and segregation in labour and housing markets, riots, crime, and education are all both economic problems and urban problems to some degree. There was a need for rigorous economic analysis of these issues, and the resulting research and policy analysis formed part of the core of the young field of urban economics. This is not to imply that urban economics has solved the problems of the cities — far from it. Many of these problems are just as pressing now as they were 40 or 50 years ago. However, the tools of urban economics can help us understand these and other difficult problems, and help us evaluate the consequences of different policies designed to combat them.

The second important formative event in the brief history of urban economics was the significant advancement of the economic modelling of spatial structure, spurred by the urgent social events of the 1960s. These models of *urban spatial structure*, many of which you will encounter in the pages that follow, gave the field a strong theoretical foundation and have led to countless advances in our understanding of urban phenomena.

What is a Model?

"Essentially, all models are wrong, but some are useful." - George Box, Statistician

A model – in this course, at least – is just a diagram or equation that seeks to describe or illuminate some small part of our world.

Models are often criticized for being too simplistic, for stripping away a great deal of complexity, and for being downright wrong – but in a way, that is the whole point. We can never hope to describe all of the messiness and detail of the real world, but models can help us isolate some very interesting and useful urban land economics insights.

The field of real estate economics did not have much in the way of rigorous academic research until the 1980s. There were certainly important papers written on real estate issues prior to this time, but as an academic or intellectual pursuit, the field was methodologically wanting. This picture has changed, and changed for the good. Real estate economics and real estate finance are now well-regarded specializations within applied economics and business studies. The best research in real estate economics and real estate finance meets the highest standards of scholarship and intellectual rigour.

THEMES IN URBAN AND REAL ESTATE ECONOMICS

The theme that unifies all of urban and real estate economics is location. Throughout this course, you will study how business and residential location decisions are made and how these decisions impact housing prices, land values, the allocation of land between competing uses, city sizes, and many other aspects of cities. You will also examine how public policies on transportation pricing, investment, and local government regulation impact location decisions, land values, and urban development patterns.

> The three most important factors affecting real estate value: location, location, location

A key concept underpinning all of the chapters in this book is that markets are important. There are, of course, many non-economic issues that influence the development of cities and real estate markets. Law, political science, sociology, history, urban planning, and even engineering and the environmental sciences all have insights to offer about how cities function and how they affect the quality of our lives. However, urban land economics is built on the contention that market forces are dominant, or at least that market forces have profound impacts on the structure and operation of urban areas. This text is largely an attempt to identify these forces, explain how they work (or how we think they work), and explore their implications for cities.

These general themes appear in a number of different variations throughout the study of urban and real estate economics. The following sections introduce some of the key questions that will be considered throughout the text.

Agglomeration and City Size

Perhaps the most basic question in urban economics is, "Why do cities form?"

The obvious answer is that cities form because people have found it advantageous to carry on activities in a spatially concentrated fashion. What are the advantages of spatial concentration? Clustering saves transportation costs — it economizes on the costs of moving goods and people. Clustering may also help us exploit scale economies — making it possible for us to produce goods and services in large quantities, which may in turn result in lower average costs.

> **Agglomeration Economies**
>
> Clustering of firms and business that promotes economies of scale and efficient networking channels; this can include the sharing of input suppliers, decreased transportation costs, and easier access to a diverse workforce

Perhaps the most important advantage associated with spatial concentration is that it promotes interactions between people and firms. For example, firms may be able to share a common pool of workers if they locate together, resulting in a better labour force or lower training costs. Economists use the term *agglomeration economies* to refer to these (and other) advantages arising from spatially concentrated production.

Of course, there are also costs associated with spatial concentration. Housing and commercial property prices, commuting and shipping costs, and the costs associated with congestion, pollution, and social problems like crime and poverty are all higher in large urban areas. What is the best size for a city? Are the cities of North America too large or too small? What about the very large cities of Asia and Latin America, some of which have populations nearly equal to that of Canada? These are some of the issues and questions that we will discuss in Chapters 3 and 4.

Bid Rent, Land Rent, and Land Allocation

How is the value of a particular parcel of land determined? How is the best use of a particular parcel of land determined? The key to answering both of these questions is the concept of bid rent. Bid rent is the maximum amount that a firm or household is willing to pay to occupy a particular parcel of land. Consider an auction where people and firms offer a seller an annual rent in exchange for the right to occupy a parcel of land. The value of the winning bid would correspond to the bid rent of that parcel.

> **Key Concept**
>
> **Bid rent** is the most a firm or household is willing to pay for a particular parcel of land.
>
> **Highest and best use:** The idea that land should be developed (and properties improved) in order to provide the greatest value to society and promote economic efficiency, within legal regulations.

Other things being equal, we expect land to be rented to the highest bidder. For example, if condominiums are the highest bidder for a particular parcel, then, provided government regulations permit it, the land will most likely be used for condominiums; this is the highest and best use of the land under these conditions.

Bid rent is one of the most important concepts in urban and real estate economics; we will use it repeatedly, especially in Chapters 5, 6, and 8. Should land always be allocated to the highest bidder? Is it always the case that the use that maximizes land value is the best use for a parcel, taking society's broad interests into account? The answer is no: like all markets, land markets can fail to produce an efficient allocation of resources. This, as we will see in Chapter 12, is one of the justifications for government land use regulations.

Value Matters: Highest and Best Use, Appraisal, and Urban Land Economics

In order to find a property's market value, you must first understand the maximally productive use of the property. The Appraisal Institute of Canada defines highest and best use as follows: "the reasonably probable use of property, that is physically possible, legally permissible, financially feasible and maximally productive, and that results in the highest value" (Canadian Uniform Standards of Professional Appraisal Practice).

This determination of maximal productivity involves a blend of disciplines:

Law: what is legally allowable, e.g., zoning bylaws, building codes

Construction/engineering: what is physically possible

Finance/economics: what is financially feasible and economically advantageous in the marketplace

In real estate appraisal, economic/financial analysis may be considered the heart of the matter, since ultimately most property use decisions will be driven by potential for profit. However, considering the economics alone is insufficient, as this must be tempered by the legal and physical constraints (and opportunities) of the situation and environment.

Much like economic models, appraisers attempt to make sense of complex markets by using simplified models. However, the real test of a simple model comes with building in the messy complications of the real world, to see if the model's themes still hold true. Highest and best use analysis is one of these tests for appraisers. Appraisers (and economists) are cautioned to continually step back from the numbers and critically analyze the context: do the model's underlying assumptions make sense when considering the "bigger picture"? Only once the highest and best use is confirmed can an appraiser apply the traditional approaches to valuation.

Urban Spatial Structure

Anyone who has ever looked out of the window of an airplane can tell you that cities in all countries have a common *spatial structure*: the tallest buildings are located downtown and building heights decline in a gradual fashion as one moves away from the city centre. Land values and employment and population densities, or the number of jobs or people per unit land area, also follow this decreasing pattern. Why is this?

The answer has to do with bid rent. As we will see, the bid rent for a particular parcel is closely tied to its access characteristics — how easy it is to get from this location to jobs, shops, parks, schools, etc. For a variety of reasons, access tends to be best in the city centre – this was especially true in the *core dominated* cities of the 19th century. This explains why land values tend to be highest in the downtown core. High land values encourage builders to substitute capital for land, and this naturally results in taller structures downtown. In contrast, the capital-to-land ratio in structures is generally much smaller in the suburbs, where land prices are lower. We examine these and related issues in Chapter 6.

Of course, many cities now have very large clusters of commercial and high-density residential development outside of the downtown. What accounts for the recent growth in these suburban subcentres or so-called *edge cities*? Are our cities now too spread out or too decentralized, as the pejorative *urban sprawl* seems to suggest? We will discuss suburbanization and the development of *polycentric* cities in detail in Chapter 7.

Dynamic Nature of Urban Growth

Bid rent can explain how land rent is determined and how land is allocated among competing uses. However, some aspects of modern cities don't seem to fit the paradigm of highest and best use. For example, why is some land skipped over by suburban development, leaving vacant tracts of land inside the boundary of an urban area? Or, if land is allocated to the highest bidder, why are there parking lots on the busiest streets in the middle of the downtown? Can a parking lot really be the highest and best use of this land?

The answer is: yes and no. This is certainly not the highest and best use of the land today, but it may be part of a transition to different highest and best use in the future. Surface parking lots in central cities exist because they are a convenient way to reserve land for some more valuable future use. Parking lots in the downtown, like many other aspects of cities, are a dynamic phenomenon.

Another dynamic phenomenon is a result of the durability of capital. Because the capital that makes up a city lasts so long, decisions that were made in the past have important implications for the present. For example, past decisions about the locations of commercial centres or roads have critical impacts on land values today. We will examine the dynamics of urban growth and its implications for urban spatial structure and property values in Chapter 8.

Unique Features of Real Estate Markets

What are the unique features of real estate markets and how do they affect the ways that these markets function?

Real estate is both a commodity and a financial asset, and there are separate but related markets for real estate services (or space) and real estate assets. A basic economic principle in all markets is that the price of an asset is generally equal to the stream of net income that the asset will generate (with income generated in the future discounted to present value terms). This present value relationship is what ties the market for real estate services and the market for real estate assets together. Chapter 5 explores these concepts of present values, income/rent, and future values.

Also, because real estate is durable and long-lasting, most real estate services are supplied from the existing stock. This means that the supply of real estate is nearly fixed in the short run, and, as a result, changes in demand may cause wide fluctuations in real estate prices. This demand and supply relationship is illustrated in Figure 1.1. These graphs show the impact of *elasticity* of supply, or the ability of supply to respond to changes in price from P_0 to P_1 in the short term and long term. Elasticity will be examined in detail in Chapter 2.

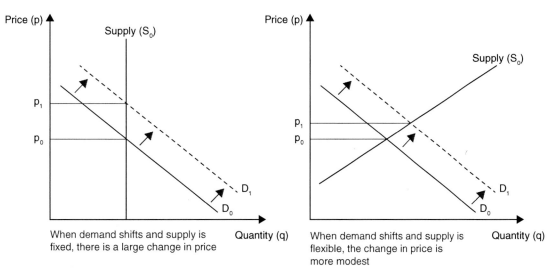

FIGURE 1.1

How Elasticity of Supply Affects Prices When Demand Increases

When demand shifts and supply is fixed, there is a large change in price

When demand shifts and supply is flexible, the change in price is more modest

Because real estate is heterogeneous, with no two properties being exactly the same, real estate transactions generally involve a costly search process for both buyers and sellers. Heterogeneity also makes it difficult to measure the price of real estate. When a property sells, all we observe is its value — the product of price and quantity — we do not observe either price or quantity independently. To compare prices in different areas or across time, we need some method of controlling for differences in property characteristics. Chapter 10 examines these and other issues in the context of housing markets, while Chapter 12 focuses on commercial real estate.

Heterogeneity

A type of good that may perform a similar function to another good in the same market, but differs in location, physical composition, age, etc.

Questions

To summarize, these are the key urban and real estate economics questions that will concern us throughout the text:

1. Why is economic activity clustered in just a few locations?
2. What are the key determinants of location decisions by firms and households?
3. How is the size and economic structure of a city determined? Are cities too large or too small?

4. What determines land rent (or value) within an urban area? What determines how different parcels of land are used?
5. How do cities respond to changes in the economic environment?
6. How are housing rents and values influenced by variables like dwelling and lot size, structural quality, schools, crime, amenities, rent control, and taxes?
7. How can we solve the problem of urban road congestion? Can and should we discourage auto use and encourage public transit? Is rapid transit (e.g., subway, light rail) more or less efficient than other transit modes?
8. How do government actions like taxation, spending, and regulatory policies affect cities? What are the costs and benefits of zoning and other forms of land use regulation?
9. What are the unique features of real estate and how do these features affect the operation of real estate markets?

Preview: Market Areas and Central Places

To give you a preview of some of the techniques that we will employ throughout this book, the following section discusses a basic location problem: the determination of market areas. The market area of a firm is the geographic region in which the firm's customers reside. In some cases, the market area of a firm is as small as a neighbourhood (think of a corner store). In other cases, the market area of a firm is as large as the world (think of Google).

Figure 1.2 demonstrates a simple model of market area determination. The figure displays a firm whose potential customers are evenly spread along a horizontal line. Suppose that there are N potential customers at every point along the line — N is the density of consumers at a given point along the line. The firm is located at the centre of this line, where distance is zero. The points on the line are spaced at one kilometre increments, and the d at the end of the line represents distance from the firm.

FIGURE 1.2

The Determination of Market Area: Location Decisions

The Determination of Market Area: Location Decisions

The question to be answered is: how far from the firm's location does it still make economic sense for a consumer to buy the firm's product? If there were no transportation costs, there would be no limit to the market, e.g., a software vendor with worldwide sales of a downloadable product. However, that is not realistic for most goods-producing businesses because there are costs to the business to transport the product to the sales location, and there are costs to the consumer to travel to the store to buy the product. Looking at it from the consumer's perspective, there is a limit to how far the consumer will travel to buy the item. The key determinant of whether the consumer will buy the product offered by the firm is the price of the product. If the price is low enough, the consumer will travel to purchase the product. If the price is too high, the consumer will not travel to purchase the product. Thus, the consumer will compare the cost of travel to purchase the product to the price of the product and the benefit received from the product. There is a point where the consumer will be unwilling to travel to buy the item, as the total cost becomes too high. In other words, the cost of the product and the cost of travel are greater than the benefit the consumer would receive from the product. The point where the costs exceed the benefit to the consumer is the consumer's reservation price – which we will call p^0.

Reservation Price (p^0)

The price for a good or service where a rational consumer determines that the costs of consumption are equal to the utility benefits

Think of yourself and your shopping habits. Do you drive the extra kilometres to get your groceries at a big box store or are you willing to pay more for the same groceries at your local store in order to save this travel time and expense? How far are you willing to drive to save money on a new car? Of course the answer depends on how much you save! If you could get a car for half price, you might travel quite far – but for only 5% off, you probably would buy locally. If we are to assume that most humans also follow the same rational decision making model, we can see how market area is determined and how cities form.

Let's add this price and travel cost relationship to our simple line graph. The price of the item at the store is p. The consumer must also pay for his or her round-trip travel cost, which we can specify as t per unit of distance: for each unit of distance, the consumer must pay a cost equal to t, e.g., the cost of gas. Therefore, if the consumer travels d units of distance to shop, the total price paid for one unit of the good is equal to $p + (t \times d)$, the price of the good plus the cost to travel to the sales location.

With this information, we can now answer the question: what is the maximum distance a consumer will travel to shop at this firm? We will review this on our revised graph, Figure 1.3.

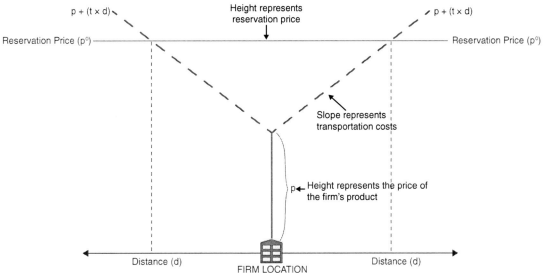

FIGURE 1.3

The Determination of Market Area: Impact of Price and Cost

Visit the course website to see a video explaining the step-by-step derivation of this figure.

This graph has three inputs or working parts and one output. The three working parts are:

1. **Price.** The vertical line extending upward from the Firm location shows the price at the store. This price line can be adjusted longer or shorter depending on how high the price is.
2. **Transportation costs.** The diagonal lines show how total price increases when travel cost is built in — note how it increases the further away from the firm that the consumer lives. The higher the transportation costs, the greater the slope of the two diagonal lines; the lower the transportation costs, the shallower these diagonal lines will be.
3. **Reservation price.** The horizontal line labelled reservation price (p^0) shows the maximum price a consumer will pay when considering the item's price plus travel cost. Above p^0, we can assume a consumer would find it too expensive and not buy the item. The greater the consumer's reservation price, the higher this line.

With these three model inputs illustrated, the model's output is what we are ultimately looking for: how far from the firm's location can the firm still draw customers? This is illustrated in Figure 1.3 as the intersection point between the diagonal line (total cost) and p^0 (reservation price). Drawing a dashed line downward from this intersection to the horizontal axis (distance line) gives us d*. This is the maximum distance that consumers will travel to buy the firm's product. Consumers located more than d* units of distance away from the store do not buy the good since the total price exceeds their reservation price.

Mathematically, the maximum distance that a consumer will travel to shop at the firm is d*, where:

EQUATION 1.1

$$p^0 = p + (t \times d^*)$$

Reminder: in this equation:

p = Product price

t = Travel cost

d* = Maximum distance a consumer will travel

p^0 = Reservation price

Solving for d*, the result is as follows:

EQUATION 1.2

$$d^* = \frac{p^0 - p}{t}$$

FIGURE 1.4

**The Determination
of Market Area:
Two-Dimensional
Model**

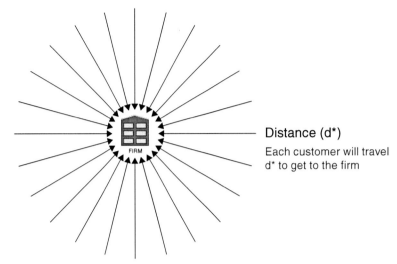

Distance (d*)

Each customer will travel
d* to get to the firm

FIGURE 1.5

**The Determination
of Market Area**

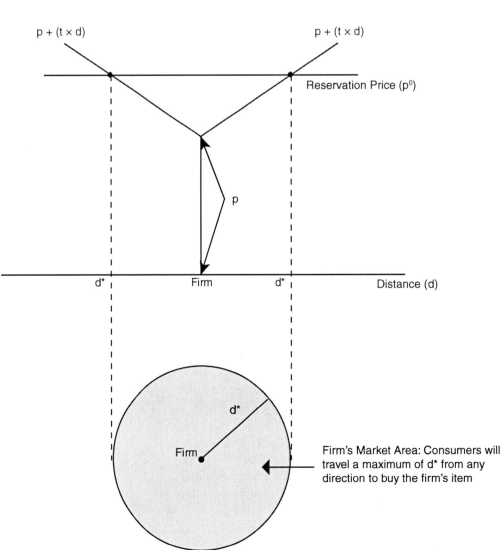

$p + (t \times d)$ $p + (t \times d)$

Reservation Price (p^0)

p

d*   Firm   d*   Distance (d)

d*

Firm

Firm's Market Area: Consumers will
travel a maximum of d* from any
direction to buy the firm's item

What Does It Mean?

We have illustrated algebraically what d* means and shown this on a simple graph. Let's substitute in some numbers and see if we can make more concrete sense of this concept. Say the product's price (p) is $20. Travel costs (t) are $2 per kilometre and the reservation price (p^0) is $40 – that is the maximum total price, including travel cost, a consumer will pay.

Therefore, the maximum distance a consumer will travel is 10 kilometres. Ten kilometres of travel would cost the consumer $20 ($2 per km × 10 km = $20). Add this cost to the price of the product ($20) and the total cost is $40, which is equal to the consumer's reservation price of $40. The market area is a circle 20 km wide, with the firm at the center.

Figures 1.2 displays a highly simplified one-dimensional world, where d* is the distance on the d line on either side of the firm's location. Of course, firms do not exist in one-dimensional space. We can make the model more realistic by adding a second dimension. A consumer can travel d* in any direction towards the firm's location – like the spokes of a wheel, as shown in Figure 1.4.

Thus, as shown in Figure 1.5, the market area is a circle, with the radius d* or a diameter of 2 × d*. The calculation above shows the width of the market area, but what is the *area* of the market? This requires some algebra and geometry in one additional calculation. The market area of the store is a circle with radius d*. Recall that the area of a circle with a radius r is πr^2, where π is the constant 3.14159. Since the firm sells one unit to every customer in the circle of radius d*, then the area of the circle would be equal to πd^{*2} or:

EQUATION 1.3

$$\text{Market Area} = \pi \left(\frac{p^0 - p}{t} \right)^2$$

What Does It Mean?

Applying this area calculation concept with our same numbers as above, if the maximum travel distance for a customer is 10 km, then the market area =

$\pi \times (10)^2 = 314.159 \, \text{km}$

Using this equation:

$\text{Market Area} = \pi \left(\dfrac{\$40 - \$20}{2} \right)^2 = 314.15$

Now we can examine how the firm's market area changes as the parameters of the problem change.

1. Increase in the density of consumers: this increases sales, but it does not change the market area.
2. Increase in the price, p: this lengthens the vertical price line in Figure 1.5, which shortens the diagonal Y shape, and effectively shortens the distance d* — this reduces both the market and total sales.
3. Increase in consumers' reservation price, p^0: this raises the horizontal reservation price line in Figure 1.5, which lengthens the diagonal Y-shape, and widens the distance d* — this increases the market area and total sales.
4. Increase in transportation costs: this steepens the diagonal lines in Figure 1.5, narrowing the Y-shape, and shortening the distance d* — this decreases the market area and total sales.

A problem with the outcome shown in Figure 1.5 is that many potential consumers beyond a distance of d* are not served by the firm. This suggests that there may be room for more firms to enter the market. Assuming firms will locate to maximize their sales, they will prefer to avoid competing with each other, so they will locate just far enough apart that their market area just touches that of their neighbour, but does not intrude into their area. This is illustrated in the top half of Figure 1.6. However, notice that there are gaps between the circles, meaning consumers fall between the market areas and are unserved.

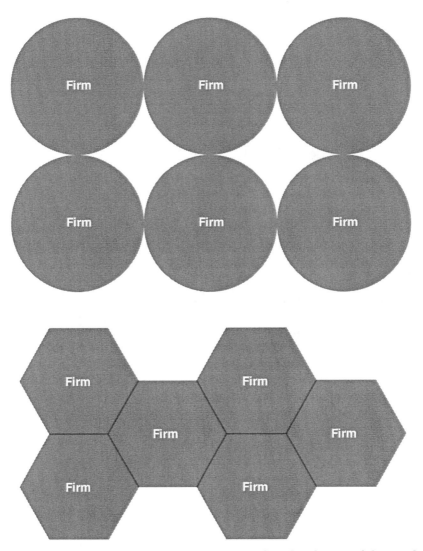

FIGURE 1.6

Market Areas with Many Firms

A possible extension to the concept would be to assume that the shapes of the market areas will adjust so that all consumers are served, resulting in the hexagonal market areas shown in bottom half of Figure 1.6. However, this complicates the calculations substantially.

Suffice it to say, a fundamental principle flowing from this analysis is that if there are many firms in a region competing for market area, the price chosen by any one will depend on the prices chosen by its neighbours. That is a result of the price versus transportation cost relationship in how market areas develop.

Economies of Scale

The cost advantages that a firm obtains due to its size, where the larger the firm becomes, the lower the cost per unit

These ideas are the foundation of *central place theory* – a very old theory associated with Christaller (1933) and Losch (1940) that explains the sizes and functions of cities. The basic idea behind central place theory is that there is a hierarchy of cities in terms of the diversity of the economic activities that they contain. Small cities contain only activities with small market areas. These turn out to be economic activities where scale economies are small and the density of demand is high, so the market can support many such firms in a given region. Large cities contain all of these activities too, but also activities with very large market areas as well. These turn out to be activities where scale economies are large and the density of demand is low, so the market can support only one or a few firms in a given region. This implies that large cities contain a much more diverse set of economic activities than small cities, which is of course true. Every small city has gas stations, but few of them have opera houses or highly specialized medical centres. This is just one example of how we use microeconomics to study location decisions. We will examine many other location problems in the chapters that follow.

Value Matters: Economies of Scale

Economies of scale have a number of real estate market applications:

Consider the hierarchy of retail centres, from small convenience corner malls, to strip malls, neighbourhood centres, regional malls, and then super-regional malls. The latter become large enough that they become a recreation destination beyond just an assortment of stores. As well, there are structural and operational savings in locating together.

The big-box outlet mall is a similar application of economies of scale. With several giant speciality stores, consumers will drive a fair distance from neighbouring municipalities for convenient and inexpensive shopping. As well, a large complex like this may be able to generate sufficient political pressure to gain advantages like highway interchanges, zoning variances, and property tax relief.

Have you ever noticed how car sales lots tend to congregate together? This may be partially due to zoning regulations, but it is also agglomeration and a form of scale economies. By locating close together, the firms benefit from each others' marketing, as shoppers may come to one lot but are likely to cross the street to competing lots too.

SUMMARY

Urban land economics can be thought of as the interaction of individuals in an urban setting. The choices that these individuals make (i.e. where to sell products, where to live, and where to work) are the basis of how cities form. The study of urban land economics allows us to understand why cities form the way they do, and how to manage the attributes that accompany this growth, i.e. poverty, pollution, and transportation. This chapter touched on major topics and tools used in urban land economics that will be explored in detail throughout the book.

The way in which cities form and how they are spatially concentrated is essentially based on the needs of people. The ability to be in close connection with others allows for lower costs of doing business through agglomeration economies; however, spatial concentration can also lead to congestion, pollution, and other detrimental effects. Thus, studying the spatial structure of cities allows us to find the optimal use of specific land located in a city. One way to find this optimal use is by using the concept of bid rent. Bid rent is a concept that explains how land rent is determined and how land is allocated among competing uses; this is a major focus throughout this book.

This chapter introduced a basic location problem: how a firm determines its market area. This problem presented the concept that consumers have trade-offs that impact how much they will spend to purchase a product from a firm. The techniques used to solve this problem will be built on throughout the book.

The next chapter will review fundamental concepts in microeconomics and present more problems that will be solved using techniques presented in this chapter.

CHAPTER 2
MICROECONOMIC ANALYSIS

INTRODUCTION

The chapter has three basic objectives:

1. Refresh your problem solving skills by introducing techniques and concepts that will be used later in the course.
2. Review several fundamental concepts and tools from microeconomics.
3. Show how microeconomics can be used to frame and analyze issues that arise in the study of cities and the markets that they contain.

The chapter begins with a discussion of the fundamentals of demand and supply. The next section reviews the concept of market equilibrium, illustrating the use of demand and supply curves for predicting how prices and quantities respond to changes in the economic environment. Following this is a discussion of the efficiency of market outcomes, using the basic tools of welfare analysis to examine the economic consequences of rent control and land taxes. Finally, there is a discussion of market failure, with particular emphasis on problems involving externalities such as congestion and pollution.

Value Matters: First Principles of Value

The Appraisal Institute of Canada published the *First Principles of Value* as an aid for appraisers and appraisal clients to better understand the basis for real estate value. This brief document presents a straightforward overview of valuation fundamentals, breaking down an immensely complicated field of practice into a handful of basic tenets. The introduction states: "a common thread in each real property discipline is the need to understand the interrelationships between forces of economics, law and the marketplace on real property". Given our focus on economics, let's see what the document specifies for this:

Economic Variables

To understand what is meant by Economic Variables, it is first necessary to understand what economics means. In essence, economics is the study of the allocation of scarce resources. Land and market inputs all have limitations. Wasn't it Will Rogers who said of land, "They ain't making any more of it"?

Economic Variables is an all-encompassing term that catches tangible and intangible inputs to the real property market. Tangible examples might be the supply of land in an identifiable area, or the availability of labour. Intangible examples might be the cost of money (interest) or inflation rates.

First Principles specifies the need to research property content, property rights, economics, land use regulations, and legal issues, towards addressing a client's purpose and the function of an assignment. Economics arguably plays the most crucial role in dictating a property's highest and best use and ultimately its market value – though the other considerations will temper or constrain some opportunities in achieving the economically optimal outcome.

DEMAND AND SUPPLY

Demand and supply analysis is probably the most basic and widely applied methodology in economics. It is a simple and intuitive tool for analyzing the operation and performance of markets, including the markets for land, housing, and other forms of real estate.

When we use demand and supply curves to analyze the operation of a market, we are implicitly assuming that the market in question is competitive. Competition has a particular meaning in this context. To be competitive, a market must satisfy three basic requirements.

1. The product traded on the market must be **homogeneous**, i.e., the products of different sellers must be identical, at least in the eyes of consumers. This implies that there can be only one price for a good in a competitive market.
2. There must be **many buyers and sellers**, each of whom is relatively small. Under these conditions, it is reasonable to suppose that no individual buyer or seller has any influence over the market price. Buyers and sellers are *price takers* in a competitive market.
3. It must be **easy for new firms to enter the industry**. Under perfect competition, new firms enter an industry whenever they can profit from doing so. Consequently, all firms in a competitive market earn *normal profits*, but no more. Normal profit infers that firms only create the minimum level of profit to remain competitive in the market; in other words, when revenue minus total cost equals zero.

Normal Profit

The minimum level of profit for a company to remain competitive in the market

Perfect Competition

Under perfect competition, there are many buyers and sellers and prices are determined by forces of supply and demand. There are no barriers to entry into and exit from the market; therefore, consumers have many substitutes available to them and firms earn normal profit levels

Very few markets are perfectly competitive, but all markets are competitive to some degree. As we will see, real estate markets differ in important ways from the ideal competitive market. However, even when a market is not perfectly competitive in the formal sense described above, demand and supply analysis can often be used to highlight the key issues that affect the market's operation, and lay the groundwork for more complex and realistic treatments.

The Demand Curve

A demand curve shows the relationship between the price per unit p and the quantity demanded q^D (see Figure 2.1). There are two ways to interpret the information contained in an individual demand curve:

1. Choosing a particular price and tracing this across to the curve gives the number of units of the good that the consumer is willing to purchase at that price. Therefore, in Figure 2.1, the consumer is willing to purchase q^D_0 units at the price p_0.
2. Alternatively, choosing a particular quantity and tracing this up to the curve gives the maximum amount that the consumer is willing to pay to purchase that one additional unit. This maximum price is the marginal benefit received by the consumer for that final unit purchased.

Demand Curve

Shows the relationship between the price per unit and the quantity demanded

Marginal Benefit

The change in total benefit from consuming one more unit of a good

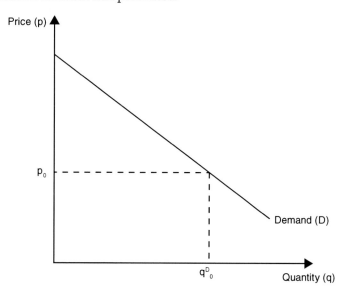

FIGURE 2.1

Demand Curve

The marginal benefit is the benefit to the consumer of consuming one additional unit. In Figure 2.1, the marginal benefit at q^D_0 units is p_0. This analogy between demand and marginal benefit will prove useful later on. We generally assume that demand curves slope downward: if the price rises, the quantity demanded falls, and vice versa. This will be the case if the consumer's marginal benefit declines as consumption rises, a reasonable assumption.

Key Concept: Demand Curve

You can think of the demand curve as providing two key insights:

A description of consumer behaviour: the demand curve specifies the number of units a consumer will buy at a particular price, i.e., at a price of p, a consumer will by q units.

A description of perceived benefits: the benefit that a consumer gets by purchasing the next unit, i.e., at q units, a consumer will get p worth of benefits.

There are a large number of factors that can influence the position of the demand curve, including income, the prices of other goods, and the demographic characteristics of consumers. A change in any one of these factors will shift the curve, and such a shift in the curve is called a change in demand. It is important to distinguish a change in demand from a change in the quantity demanded.

- A *change in the quantity demanded* is a movement along the curve and arises solely from a change in the price per unit.
- A *change in demand* results in a shift of the entire demand curve and arises from changes in particular variables, including changes in income, prices of other goods, and demographics.

Key Concept: Change in Demand vs. Change in Quantity Demanded

Imagine that you have $500,000 to invest in condominiums. You are viewing condominiums at a new development called Orchid Garden. The current price of a condo is set at $250,000. Given your assessment of the quality and price of Orchid Garden condos, you determine them to be an extremely valuable investment, and aim to invest as much as possible in these assets. So, you decide that you would like to purchase two condos at $250,000 each and contact the seller to arrange a deal.

Just then the seller drops the price of the condos by 50%, with each condo now selling for $125,000. Your $500,000 can now purchase up to four condo units, and seeing the condos as a great deal at this price, your preference is to purchase four. The price of the condo units decreased, and the quantity you demanded changed – in this case, the quantity demanded increased. There is no change in demand (no shift in the demand curve) because there was only a change in the price of a condo unit. However, before you can act, the seller realizes this was a mistake, and sets the price of the units back to $250,000 each.

Then, another unexpected event occurs; your boss calls you with some good news. For all your great work, you are being given a $500,000 bonus! You can now invest $1,000,000. Each condo is priced at $250,000, thus you can purchase four condo units if you wish, and given your strong demand for these condos you decide to purchase four units. The quantity you can purchase has increased, but this was not due to a change in price, rather an external factor that increased your income. The increase in your income thus increased your willingness to buy more condos, shifting the demand curve outwards.

A change in income may increase or decrease demand (shift the demand curve). A good is normal if an increase in income leads to an increase in demand, or a right or outward shift in the curve. A good is inferior if an increase in income leads to a decrease in demand, or a left or inward shift in the curve.

A change in the prices of other goods may also shift the demand curve. Two goods x and y are called *substitutes* if an increase in the price of x leads to an increase in the demand for y. In other words, if x and y are substitutes, then an increase in the price of x leads to an outward shift in the demand curve for y.

Examples of substitute goods would include identical houses in two adjacent neighbourhoods. If the price of a house in one neighbourhood rises, the demand for housing in the other neighbourhood will likely shift outward as consumers adjust their location choices.

Two goods x and y are called *complements* if an increase in the price of x leads to a decrease in the demand for y. In other words, if x and y are complements, then an increase in the price of x leads to an inward shift in the demand curve for y. Examples of complements would include personal computers and printers, or other pairs of products that are commonly used together.

The demographic characteristics of the consumer, such as age, marital status, and family size, can also influence the position of the demand curve. Demographic factors are especially important determinants of the demand for housing, as we will see in Chapter 10.

Normal Good

A good or service that experiences changes in demand that are positively correlated with changes in the real income of consumers in the market or economy, e.g., designer clothes.

Inferior Good

A good or service that experiences changes in demand that are negatively correlated with changes in the real income of consumers in the market or economy, e.g., public transportation.

Substitute

A good or service that can replace a similar good or service, while still satisfying the needs of the consumer. If the price of a good increases, demand for its substitute also increases.

Complement

A good or service that provides more benefit when consumed with another good or service. If the price of a good increases, demand for its complement decreases.

Value Matters: Principle of Substitution

The principle of substitution is the basis for real estate appraisal's approaches to value. *The Appraisal of Real Estate, 3ʳᵈ Canadian Edition* outlines this as follows: "The price of acquiring an equally desirable substitute property tends to set property value. The principle of substitution recognizes that buyers and sellers of real property have options, in that other properties are available for similar uses. The substitution of one property for another may be considered in terms of use, structural design, or earnings. The cost of acquisition may be the cost to purchase a similar site and construct a building of equivalent utility, assuming no undue cost due to delay; this is the basis of the cost approach. On the other hand, the cost of acquisition may be the price of acquiring an existing property of equal utility, again assuming no undue cost due to delay; this is the basis of the direct comparison approach.

The principle of substitution is equally applicable to properties such as houses, which are purchased for their amenity-producing attributes, and properties purchased for their income-producing capabilities. The amenity-producing attributes of residential properties may include excellence of design, quality of workmanship, or superior construction materials. For an income-producing property, an equally desirable substitute might be an alternative investment property that produces equivalent investment returns with equivalent risk. The prevailing prices, rents, and rates of equally desirable substitutes tend to set the limits of property prices, rents, and rates. The principle of substitution is fundamental to all three traditional approaches to value: direct comparison, cost, and income." (p. 3.6-7)

Working with Demand Curves

There will be many occasions throughout this course when you will have to solve or manipulate a simple economic model involving a demand curve. Doing so is often made easier by graphing the problem, so let's work through an example. Suppose you are given the following equation for demand:

$$q^D = 100 - 2p$$

In words, the equation translates to: the quantity demanded is equal to 100 units minus two times the price. In graphing this demand curve, our first task is finding the x-axis and y-axis intercepts. Note that a demand curve will always have intercepts on both the x-axis and y-axis, as shown on the right hand side of Figure 2.2, although they are sometimes drawn without the demand curve explicitly crossing either axis, as shown on the left hand side of Figure 2.2.

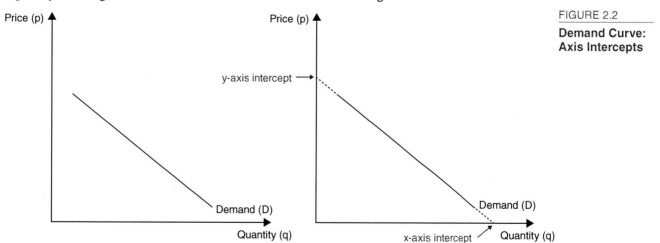

FIGURE 2.2

Demand Curve: Axis Intercepts

Let's start with the y-axis intercept. The key to finding the y-axis intercept is to notice that it represents a unique position with respect to quantity demanded: quantity demanded is always zero at the y-axis intercept! Since we have an equation that only has two variables, price (p) and quantity (q^D), then we can solve for p at the y-axis intercept by setting q^D equal to zero as follows:

Start with our original equation: $q^D = 100 - 2p$

Set q^D equal to zero: $0 = 100 - 2p$

Add 2p to both sides of the equation: $2p = 100$

Divide both sides of the equation by 2: $p = 50$

In other words, at a price of $50, there is no demand for the product and quantity demanded is zero.

Now let's find the x-axis intercept. Again, this will require that we notice that it represents a unique position on our graph: price is always zero at the x-axis intercept! Since we know that p is equal to zero at this position, we can solve for q at the x-axis intercept:

Start with our original equation: $q^D = 100 - 2p$

Set p equal to zero: $q^D = 100 - 2(0)$

Demand is found to be: $q^D = 100$

Thus, at a price equal to zero, quantity demanded is equal to 100 units.

Now we have enough information to label our graph of the demand curve, as shown in Figure 2.3.

FIGURE 2.3

Demand Curve:
$q^D = 100 - 2p$

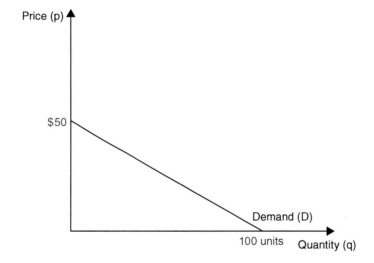

Helpful Hint: Straight-Line "Curves"

In Figure 2.3, notice that when p is increased by 1, q^D always decreases by the same amount – 2 units. This is called a *linear* relationship. Graphically, this means the demand "curve" is drawn as a straight line connecting the y-axis intercept to the x-axis intercept. Linear demand makes analysis simpler and is often a reasonable assumption. We will apply this assumption throughout this chapter and in much of the book. Also note it is common in economics for the demand and supply functions to be called "curves" – even when the relationship is linear and the curve is a straight line!

Manipulating the Demand Equation

While the first step to solving many problems is graphing them, you will also need to manipulate the equations algebraically. Let's point out a few useful things about our demand equation by rearranging it. We started with the original form of the equation:

$q^D = 100 - 2p$

This expresses the quantity demanded as a function of price. This seems to be naturally aligned with the *description of consumer behaviour* interpretation of the demand curve discussed earlier: the number of units a consumer will purchase is dependent on the price per unit.

But suppose you want to express the demand equation in a way that naturally aligns with the *description of perceived benefits* interpretation: at a given quantity, a consumer receives a certain benefit. Recall from earlier that this benefit is expressed in terms of p. We need to rearrange the equation to have it express what p is equal to.

Start with our original equation: $q^D = 100 - 2p$

Add 2p to both sides: $q^D + 2p = 100$

Subtract q^D from both sides: $2p = 100 - q^D$

Finally, divide both sides by 2: $p = 50 - \frac{1}{2}q^D$

This expresses the willingness to pay (the *price*) as a function of the next unit that is purchased. In other words, the 50th unit translates to a willingness to pay of $25 (verify this by plugging 50 into q^D in the equation above).

Helpful Hint: Demand and Marginal Benefit

Try plugging in different quantities and see what p results – this "price" shows the marginal benefit to the buyer of the next unit purchased.

- At 20 units, a buyer is willing to pay $40 for the next unit.
- At 30 units, a buyer is willing to pay $35 for the next unit.
- At 60 units, a buyer is willing to pay $20 for the next unit.
- At 80 units, the buyer will pay only $10 for the next unit.
- At 100 units, the marginal benefit is zero – the buyer doesn't want any more no matter what the price.

The marginal benefit declines as the quantity increases – this illustrates the downward sloping nature of the demand curve, which we will see in more detail shortly. Think of it like eating sushi at a Japanese restaurant ... with each round you get less hungry, and the benefit to you drops – until you reach a point where you are full and wouldn't eat more even if it was free.

From a mathematical perspective, note that the revised equation for p contains identical information to the original form of the equation. It has simply been rearranged so that we can look at it from a slightly different perspective.

Also note that this latter form is how the majority of linear equations are written. The generalized version of any linear equation is:

$Y = b + mX$

Where *b* is always the y-axis intercept and *m* is always the slope of the equation. Writing our demand equation as:

$p = 50 - \frac{1}{2}q^D$

allows us to very quickly see that 50 is our y-axis intercept and the slope of our line is $-\frac{1}{2}$.

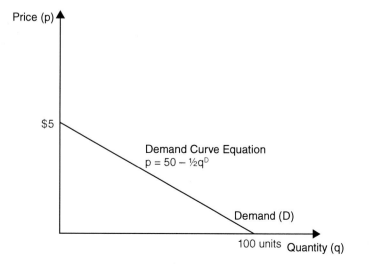

FIGURE 2.4

Demand Curve Equation

Income and Demand

A variation on this linear demand curve adds in the income of the consumer, I:

$$q^D = 50 + I - 2p$$

Consumer income is one of the underlying factors that determines the level of demand. For I equal to 50, this demand curve is identical to the one discussed above ($q^D = 50 + I - 2p = 100 - 2p$). However, it might be important to consider how demand changes as I changes; specifying this in the equation allows us to explore this relationship. Rewriting this demand curve in the conventional form gives:

$$p = 25 + (\tfrac{1}{2})I - (\tfrac{1}{2})q^D$$

Therefore, the y-axis intercept of this demand curve is $25 + (\tfrac{1}{2})I$. Thus, an increase in income leads to an upward shift in the curve or an increase in demand — the good in question is thus a normal good. Figure 2.5 shows this demand curve for two values of the underlying factor I, I = $50 and I = $100.

FIGURE 2.5

The Demand Curve with Income Considered

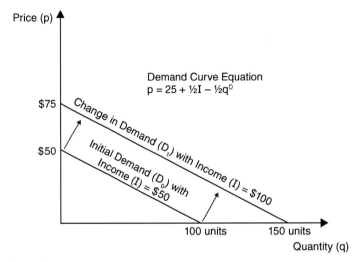

Market Demand Curve

Recall the "Think of yourself and your shopping habits" box in Chapter 1, where we described how many millions of individual buying decisions add up to create a market area. The characteristics of the market area determine the optimal location for firms to position themselves. The sum of all these individual consumer demand decisions adds up to form the market demand curve.

Market Demand Curve

The sum of the demands of all the consumers in a market

Consider two individuals that have the demand curves D_1 and D_2. The horizontal distance at any price shows us how much that one individual would consume at that price. If we add the demand curves horizontally, it shows us how much the two of them would buy at that price. In other words, we add the individual demand curves horizontally. Figure 2.6 illustrates how two individual demand curves D_1 and D_2 are added to give a market demand curve D_{1+2}.

FIGURE 2.6

Market Demand

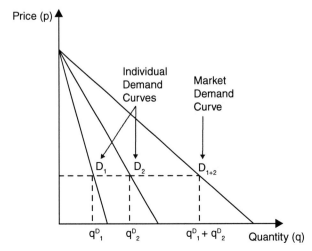

The Supply Curve

A supply curve shows the relationship between the price per unit p and the quantity supplied q^s – see Figure 2.7. Just as with the demand curve, there are two ways to interpret the information contained in an individual supply curve.

1. The curve shows the amount the producer is willing to sell at every price. In Figure 2.7, the producer is willing to sell q^s_0 units at the price p_0.

2. Alternatively, the curve shows the minimum amount the producer is willing to accept to supply each quantity. This minimum amount is the *marginal cost* of that quantity to the producer, or the change in total cost from producing one more unit of the good. In Figure 2.7, the marginal cost at q^s_0 units is p_0. This analogy between supply and marginal cost will prove useful later on.[1]

> **Supply Curve**
>
> Shows the relationship between the price per unit and the quantity supplied

> **Marginal Cost**
>
> The change in total cost from producing one more unit of a good

We generally assume that supply curves slope upward: if the price rises, the quantity supplied rises, and vice versa. This will be the case if the marginal cost of production increases as output expands — a logical assumption.

It is important to distinguish between a change in the quantity supplied and a change in supply (similar to the conceptual difference between the change in quantity demanded and a change in demand discussed earlier).

- A *change in the quantity supplied* is a movement along the supply curve, which arises only from a change in the price.
- A *change in supply* is a shift in the curve, which arises from a change in some underlying factor such as the state of the firm's technology, the productivity of its inputs, the prices of these inputs, and taxes and other government policies. Generally speaking, an increase in productivity will lead to an increase in supply, or an outward or right shift in the supply curve. Conversely, an increase in input prices or taxes will lead to a decrease in supply, or an inward or left shift in the supply curve.

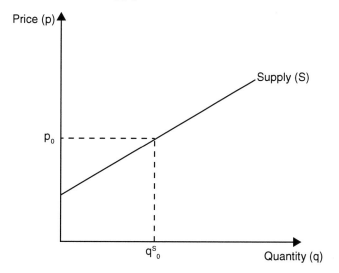

FIGURE 2.7

Supply Curve

---

[1] The supply curve of a competitive firm arises from the process of profit maximization. In the simplest terms, the profit of the firm is $p = (p \times q) - C_q$, where $p \times q$ (price times quantity) is total revenue, and C_q is total cost. The firm chooses q to maximize profit, and for a competitive firm, this implies that the firm should set price equal to marginal cost, or $p = MC$. In other words, the firm supplies the quantity such that $p = MC$. This is why the supply curve of a competitive firm represents the marginal cost of producing each quantity.

Key Concept: Supply Curve

You can think of the supply curve as providing two key insights:

A description of producer behaviour: the supply curve specifies the number of units a producer will supply at a particular price, i.e., at a price of p, a producer will supply q units.

A description of perceived costs: the marginal cost that a seller incurs by supplying the next unit, i.e., at q units, a producer will incur p worth of costs, both monetary and non-monetary.

Working with Supply Curves

An example of a very simple supply curve is $q^S = 25$. In this case, the quantity supplied is a constant; the supply curve is a vertical line at 25 units. A vertical supply line infers that the quantity will always stay fixed no matter what the price is set to. Vertical supply curves may be realistic in some settings. If the time period under consideration is very short, for example, an hour or a day, then the supplier may not be able to change the quantity supplied. This suggests that as the time period under consideration increases in length, the supply curve should become flatter. Alternatively, the product may be non-reproducible. Some economists have argued that the supply of land is essentially fixed ("The great thing about land is that they are not making it anymore"). This observation has played an important role in historical debates about the desirability and efficacy of land taxation. We will consider the implications of fixed supply for taxation later in the chapter.

FIGURE 2.8

Vertical Supply

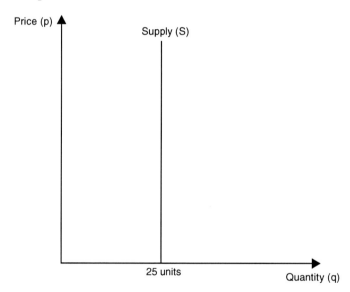

Consider another supply curve example that considers the impact of price: with a little more complexity:

$q^S = -50 + 2p$

Apart from the fixed supply curve example above, most supply curves we will encounter in this text will have a y-axis intercept and a slope that we need to discover in order to graph them.

Let's start with the y-intercept. Just as in the case of the demand curve, the y-intercept for the supply curve is a unique point. It will always occur where q^S is equal to zero. Using the equation above, we can solve for the y-intercept as follows:

Start with original equation: $q^S = -50 + 2p$

Set to q^S to zero: $0 = -50 + 2p$

Add 50 to both sides: $50 = 2p$

Divide both sides by 2: $25 = p$

The y-axis intercept is a price of $25.

Now let's find the slope, so that we know how steep or shallow the supply curve is. Remember that the slope is:

EQUATION 2.1

$$\text{Slope} = \frac{\text{Rise}}{\text{Run}}$$

Or, to make it specific to our supply curve:

EQUATION 2.2

$$\text{Slope} = \frac{\text{Change in Price}}{\text{Change in Quantity Supplied}}$$

We can find this ratio using our original equation: $q^S = -50 + 2p$. We simply need to know how much q^S increases by when p increases by one. In this case, increasing p by one dollar increases q^S by two units; therefore, the slope must be ½. The change in q^S is the denominator of our ratio, while the change in p is the numerator of our ratio.

Using the information that we now have about the y-axis intercept and the slope, we can now graph the supply curve as in Figure 2.9.

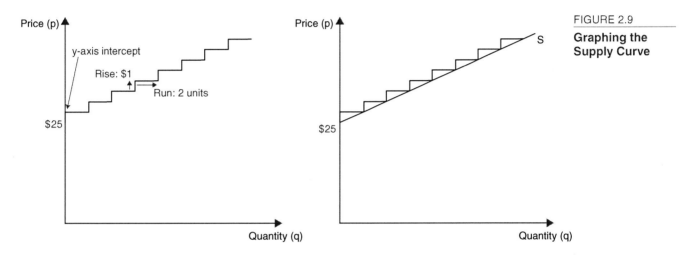

FIGURE 2.9

Graphing the Supply Curve

If we want, we can also express our supply equation in the "generic linear line" format of $Y = b + mX$.

Start with original equation: $q^S = -50 + 2p$

Add 50 to both sides: $q^S + 50 = 2p$

Divide both sides by 2: $\frac{1}{2}q^S + 25 = p$

Rewrite this as: $p = 25 + \frac{1}{2}q^S$

Remember that in the generic line $Y = b + mX$, b is the y-axis intercept and m is the slope, which means that for our equation the y-axis intercept is 25 and the slope is ½. Those are the same figures we have already solved for. Both methods result in the same answer – this is an example where students can use whichever method they feel more comfortable with.

Now let's see what happens when we consider the impact of the cost of inputs, which can shift the supply curve. If we add in a new variable W to represent the wages of workers or the price of some other input that is used to produce the good, then the revised supply curve equation is:

$q^S = 100 - W + 2p$

If W = $150, then $q^S = \$100 - \$150 = -\$50$ — meaning this supply curve would be identical to the simple one given above. Rewriting our new supply curve in its conventional form gives:

$p = (\frac{1}{2})W - 50 + (\frac{1}{2})q^S$

Solving for the vertical intercept of this supply curve, where $q^S = 0$, is:

$p = (\frac{1}{2})W - 50$

If the cost of inputs W decreases, this will shift the supply curve down (outward or right), which has the effect of increasing the quantity supplied at any given price. This is illustrated in the supply curves in Figure 2.10, which shows the supply curves for W = $150 (S$_0$) and W = $100 (S$_1$).

FIGURE 2.10

Supply Curve with Input Costs

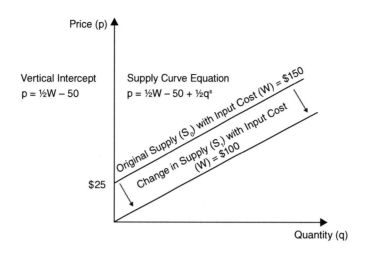

Market Supply Curve

A market supply curve is the sum of the individual supply curves of all firms in the market, exactly like the market demand curve is for consumers. To find this sum, we add the curves horizontally, that is, we add the amounts that each firm is willing to supply at each price.

Figure 2.11 illustrates how two individual supply curves S$_1$ and S$_2$ are added to arrive at a market supply curve S$_{1+2}$.

FIGURE 2.11

Market Supply

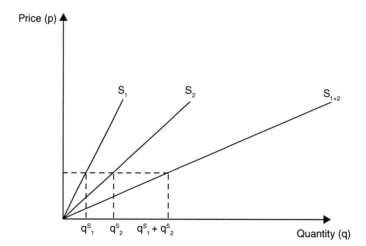

Market Equilibrium

The concept of an *equilibrium* is central to all of economics. Economists generally presume that economic processes tend toward states of equilibrium. In general, a system is in equilibrium if it is at rest or in balance. When a system is in equilibrium, it shows no inherent tendency toward change. The concept of an equilibrium can be applied to almost any economic choice. In this chapter, we will review the characteristics and properties of equilibrium prices and quantities in competitive markets. Later on in the course, we will consider other types of equilibriums, including equilibrium location choices and equilibrium allocations of land between competing uses.

Equilibrium

In economics terms, a state of balance between market forces of supply and demand that result in an efficient price level and quantity of goods supplied

A market is in equilibrium if demand and supply are in balance. This equilibrium occurs at the intersection of the demand and supply curves. The intersection gives the equilibrium price and quantity in the market. In Figure 2.12, the equilibrium price and quantity are labelled p* and q*, respectively.

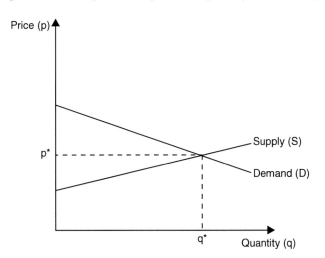

FIGURE 2.12

**Market
Equilibrium**

When price equals p*, there is neither a shortage nor a surplus on the market, and consequently there is no pressure on the price to change. Conversely, if p is less than p* (p < p*), then the quantity demanded exceeds the quantity supplied ($q^D > q^S$), and there is a shortage on the market. In this case, we imagine that consumers bid up the price to eliminate the shortage.

On the other hand, if p is greater than p* (p > p*), then the quantity demanded is less than the quantity supplied ($q^D < q^S$), and there is a surplus on the market. In this case, we imagine that sellers lower the price to eliminate the surplus. Figure 2.13 graphically illustrates a surplus and shortage.

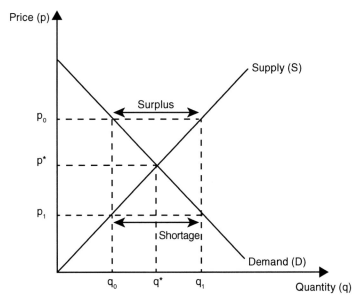

FIGURE 2.13

**Shortage and
Surplus**

Solving for the equilibrium price and quantity involves solving for the point of intersection of the demand and supply curves. Earlier we considered the linear demand and supply curves $q^D = 100 - 2p$ and $q^S = -50 + 2p$. To solve for the equilibrium price:

Start with equilibrium condition: $q^D = q^S$

Substitute in equations: $100 - 2p = -50 + 2p$

Add 2p to both sides: $100 = -50 + 4p$

Add 50 to both sides: $150 = 4p$

Divide both sides by 4: p* = $37.5

To find the equilibrium quantity, replace p in either the demand or supply curve with p*=37.5. The resulting quantity is q*. Using the demand curve:

$$q^* = 100 - 2(37.5) = 25$$

Using the supply curve, we should get the same result:

$$q^* = -50 + 2(37.5) = 25 \text{ units}$$

The solution for market equilibrium is shown in Figure 2.14.

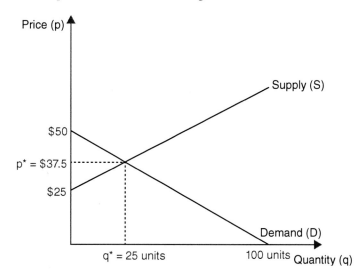

FIGURE 2.14

Market Equilibrium

Comparative Statics

One of the most useful applications of demand and supply analysis is predicting how prices and quantities respond to changes in the economic environment. To do this we change one of the factors that underlies demand or supply and then examine the resulting changes in equilibrium price and quantity. Economists refer to the resulting change in price and quantity as the *comparative static effect* of a change in the underlying factor.

Comparative Statics

The resulting changes in equilibrium price and quantity as a result of changes in the economic environment

For example, an increase in income, an increase in the price of a substitute good, a decrease in the price of a complement good, population growth, or a favorable change in demographics will lead to an increase in demand (shifting the demand curve outward/right) – and consequently an increase in the equilibrium price and quantity. This is illustrated in Figure 2.15. The opposite changes in any of these underlying factors should give rise to opposite comparative static effects, e.g., a decrease in after-tax income should cause demand to fall and lead to decreases in prices and quantities.

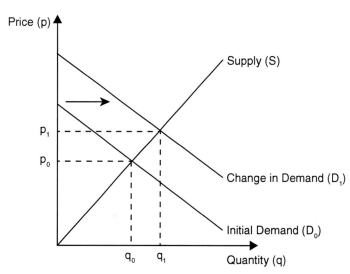

FIGURE 2.15

The Comparative Statics of an Increase in Demand

Consider a more concrete and perhaps controversial example. As the baby boom generation moved into their 30s and 40s, the prime home buying years, the demand for single-family residences increased. This change occurred during the 1980s, which was also a period of rising house prices in many markets in North America. This is very consistent with a basic demand and supply analysis of demographics and housing demand. Now, suppose that as the baby boom generation reaches retirement, its demand for single-family housing falls. What would a basic demand and supply analysis imply about future house prices in this case? We will return to this question in Chapter 10.

On the supply side, increases in wages and other input prices should decrease supply (move supply left/inward), leading to a higher equilibrium price and a lower equilibrium quantity. Conversely, a technological improvement that increases productivity should increase supply and have opposite comparative static effects – see Figure 2.16. Note how the sizes of these effects will vary depending on the slopes of the curves – this is related to the concept of *elasticity*.

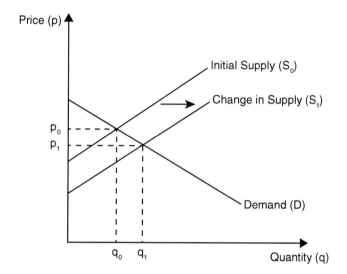

FIGURE 2.16

The Comparative Statics of an Increase in Supply

Elasticity

Within comparative statics, the concept of elasticity helps further our analysis of how quantities change in response to different prices. Elasticity is a measure of how much one economic variable responds to changes in another economic variable. If the price of gas increased by 10 cents, by how much would your gas consumption decrease? Perhaps you would reduce the days you drove your car and instead would take public transit. Or, perhaps this price change does not impact your gas consumption at all. The first instance means demand is more elastic, while the latter is less elastic or even inelastic.

The gas example illustrates the *price elasticity of demand* – the responsiveness of a change in quantity demanded (the first variable) to a change in price (the second variable). Mathematically, the price elasticity of demand can be expressed as:

Elasticity

A measure of how much one economic variable responds to changes in another economic variable

Price Elasticity of Demand

The responsiveness of a change in quantity demanded, relative to a change in price

EQUATION 2.3

$$\text{Price Elasticity of Demand} = \frac{\text{Percentage Change in Quantity Demanded}}{\text{Percentage Change in Price}}$$

When the percentage change in quantity demanded is greater than the percentage change in price, we can say that the demand is elastic. On the other hand, when the percentage change in quantity demanded is less than the percentage change in price, we can say that the demand is inelastic. For example, if a 10% increase in the price of gas results in a 20% decrease in the quantity demanded of gas, the elasticity is equal to:

$$\text{Price Elasticity of Demand} = \frac{-20\%}{10\%} = -2$$

Price Elasticity of Supply

The responsiveness of a change in quantity supplied, relative to a change in price

In general, demand is considered elastic if the calculated price elasticity is greater than 1, in absolute terms (meaning you do not take the negative or positive sign into account). If the calculated price elasticity is less than 1, price elasticity is considered inelastic.

From the supply side, we could also analyze how a change in price of oil that a producer pays (as the primary ingredient in gas refining) will impact the quantity of gas supplied. This is known as the *price elasticity of supply*. Mathematically, the price elasticity of supply can be expressed as:

EQUATION 2.4

$$\text{Price Elasticity of Supply} = \frac{\text{Percentage Change in Quantity Supplied}}{\text{Percentage Change in Price}}$$

Suppose that the cost of oil dropped by 10%, resulting in a 5% increase in the quantity of gas supplied. The elasticity is equal to:

$$\text{Price Elasticity of Supply} = \frac{5\%}{-10\%} = -0.5$$

In this example, the supply of gas is considered to be inelastic as the calculated price elasticity is less than 1 in absolute terms. Whether analyzing supply or demand, when the percentage change in quantity is greater than the percentage change in price, we can say that the supply or demand is elastic. When the percentage change in quantity is less than the percentage change in price, we can say that the supply or demand is inelastic.

Figure 2.17 illustrates the price elasticity of supply. If supply is very steep (i.e., the price elasticity of supply is low), then an increase in demand has a large effect on the equilibrium price, but a small effect on the equilibrium quantity. This might be the effect of a change in demand over a short time interval. Conversely, if supply is very flat (i.e., the price elasticity of supply is high), then an increase in demand has a small effect on the equilibrium price, but a large effect on the equilibrium quantity. This might be the effect of a change in demand over a longer time interval — over a longer interval there is a greater supply response, and consequently a smaller change in price. In the first graph of Figure 2.17, $p_1 - p_0 > q_1 - q_0$ and in the second graph, the opposite is true where $q_1 - q_0 > p_1 - p_0$.

Elasticity

When the percentage change in quantity is greater than the percentage change in price, the supply or demand is *elastic*.

When the percentage change in quantity is less than the percentage change in price, the supply or demand is *inelastic*.

FIGURE 2.17

Price Elasticity of Supply

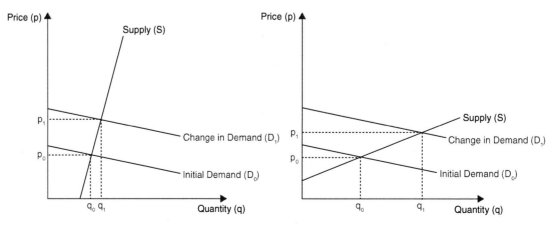

Quantity demanded or supplied can also be measured against other variables, such as income or the price of other goods. In Chapter 10, we will examine how income elasticity relates to quantity demanded for housing (Spoiler alert! The relationship is inelastic).

Value Matters: Price Elasticity

Price elasticity offers important insights for real estate, when attempting to forecast how the market might react to changes. Consider a residential developer who needs to determine absorption rates (how quickly units will sell) in order to carry out cash flow projections and plan future building phases. As a part of this, the developer also needs strategic advice on pricing, in terms of how various price points will likely affect this absorption.

The real estate consultant hired to carry out this study must undertake research and market analysis to gain a comprehensive understanding of the relationship between price and demand; specifically, how demand changes in response to price, i.e., price elasticity! This study will be complicated by potential concurrent changes in the market: the current supply of competing properties (short run), the anticipated trends in supply (long run), and an analysis of demand factors and how these might vary over time. Macroeconomics, demographics, and social attitudes will all influence price elasticity for real estate.

Consumer and Producer Surplus

In addition to helping us understand how prices and quantities are determined, demand and supply analysis can help us evaluate market outcomes from a broader perspective. This evaluation is known as *welfare analysis*. Welfare analysis asks how a particular market outcome impacts the economic well-being of consumers and producers as groups. Two concepts are crucial to this analysis: consumer surplus and producer surplus.

As discussed previously, a demand curve describes the maximum amount that consumers are willing to pay for each quantity. However, a consumer rarely pays a price equal to the maximum that he or she is willing to pay for every unit. In a competitive market, the consumer pays the equilibrium price, which, for all but the "last" unit, is smaller than the maximum amount that the consumer is willing to pay. For example, in Figure 2.18, the consumer is willing to pay up to p_0 for the quantity q_0, but actually pays the market price p^*. Thus, the consumer earns a surplus on this unit equal to $p_0 - p^*$. If we add the surpluses that the consumers earn on all units consumed, we see that the consumer's total surplus is equal to the entire area beneath the demand curve, above the market price, and to the left of q^*. This area is total consumer surplus in the market, labeled CS in the figure.

Welfare Analysis

An analysis of the current and optimal allocation of resources within a market, and how social welfare is impacted by these scenarios

Consumer Surplus

On an individual level, consumer surplus is the maximum amount a consumer would be willing to pay to buy a unit of some good, minus the amount the consumer actually pays. Total consumer surplus in a market is the surplus earned by all consumers in the market across all units they buy.

Producer Surplus

On an individual level, producer surplus is the amount received by a producer to provide a unit of output, minus the minimum amount the producer would be willing to accept for that unit of output. Total producer surplus in a market is the surplus earned by all producers in the market across all units they sell.

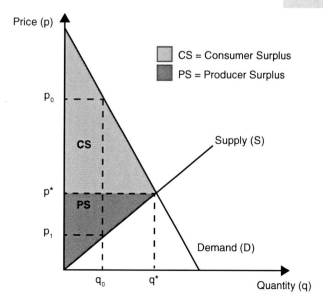

FIGURE 2.18

Consumer and Producer Surplus

EXERCISE 2.1: Calculating the Welfare Effects of a Price Change

Imagine a single consumer's demand curve for trips on public transit per week, specified as follows:

$$q^D = 5 - p$$

The fare or price of a trip is currently $2. However, suppose that the consumer can purchase a special "fare saver" card that will reduce the transit fare to $1 per trip. The fare saver card costs $5. Should he purchase the card?

Solution:

To answer this question, we must determine how purchasing the fare saver card impacts this consumer's surplus. First, let's graph what we know: the demand curve and the price per trip (for a single consumer, this represents the supply curve).

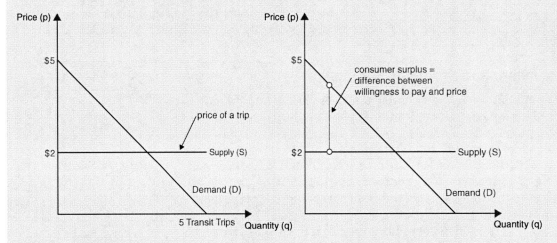

Next, we need to recognize that the consumer surplus for each trip is the difference between the willingness to pay for each trip (as represented by the demand curve) minus the price the consumer actually has to pay for each trip. In this case, the maximum a consumer is willing to pay is $5 (at $5 or above, the quantity demanded is zero). At the current fare of $2, that consumer's surplus is $3.

To calculate the consumer surplus for all trips, we need to find the difference between willingness to pay and the price for all trips, which happens to be the area under the demand curve and above the price.

At the original $2 fare, the total consumer surplus equals the area of the triangle above p = $2 and under the demand curve.

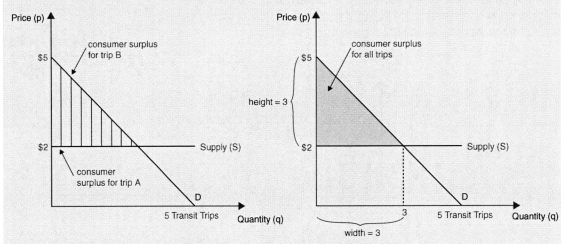

Recall that the area of a triangle is: Area = (½)(Height)(Width)

Thus, the consumer surplus is: $(½)($3)(3) = 4.50

continued on next page

On the other hand, if the consumer purchases the fare saver card, causing the price per trip to decrease to $1, then we will need to recalculate consumer surplus as shown in the following figure:

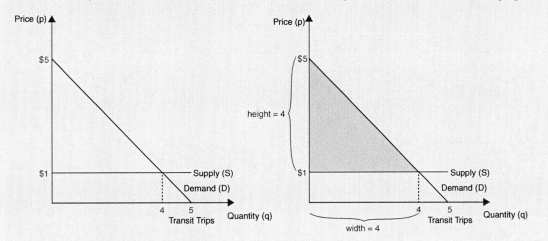

Our consumer will now take 4 trips per week and his consumer's surplus will be:

(½)($4)(4) = $8

Thus, purchasing the card will cause his consumer surplus to rise by $3.50. This is the benefit to him of fare reduction that the card provides. However, the fare card costs $5, which is less than the consumer surplus he gains. Therefore, the consumer is better off declining the card and continuing to purchase his transit trips at $2 each. This is an example of how consumer surplus is used to analyze the welfare effects of price changes.

A similar surplus accrues to the producers of a product. As noted above, a supply curve describes the minimum amount that the producer is willing to accept to supply different quantities. In Figure 2.18, the producer is willing to supply q_0 units at the price p_1.

However, the producer does not receive this price, but rather receives the market price p^*. This means that the producer earns a surplus of $p^* - p1$ on this unit. If we add up the surplus that the producer earns on every unit provided, we arrive at the total producer surplus in the market. This is given by the area above the supply curve but below the market price and to the left of q^*. Producer surplus is the triangular area labelled PS in Figure 2.18.

Consumer surplus is the total value of this good or service to consumers. Producer surplus is the total value of this good or service to producers. Adding these surpluses together gives the total value of the good or service to society, commonly known as aggregate economic welfare, or simply *aggregate welfare*.

Aggregate Welfare

The total welfare generated by consumers and producers participating in a market

The Efficiency of Perfect Competition

One of the most important objectives of any economic system is to allocate resources efficiently. Intuitively, an allocation of resources is efficient if it involves no waste or slack. Formally, an allocation of resources is efficient if it is impossible to increase the well-being of one member of society without reducing the well-being of another. In the present context, an allocation is efficient if it maximizes aggregate welfare, that is, if it maximizes the sum of consumer and producer surplus.

Suppose for a moment that you are an omniscient economic planner with the ability to set the level of output in every market in a competitive economy. Suppose further that you are benevolent (hopefully this is not too unrealistic), and that your objective is to maximize aggregate welfare. What level of output should you choose? Stated in graphical terms, your objective is to maximize the area between the supply and demand curves. Looking at Figure 2.19, the output level that maximizes this area is q^*, the competitive equilibrium output level. In other words, the outcome of a perfectly competitive market maximizes the aggregate economic welfare of society: the outcome of a competitive market is efficient.

FIGURE 2.19

**The Fundamental
Theorem
of Welfare
Economics**

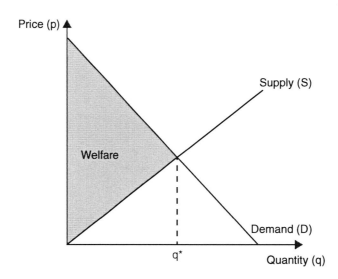

This remarkable result, sometimes called the *fundamental theorem of welfare economics*, is one of the most important ideas in all of economics. It says that under perfect competition, individual consumers and producers, each pursuing only his or her self-interest, arrive at an allocation of resources that maximizes the welfare of society. It is as if they are led by an *invisible hand* to coordinate their actions to achieve a desirable end. The coordinating force is the system of competitive prices. However, there is an important caveat to this happy state of affairs: not all markets are competitive. There are a variety reasons why markets might fail to produce an efficient allocation, and understanding how and why markets fail is nearly as important as understanding how and why markets succeed. We will examine market failures later in the chapter.

Fundamental Theorem of Welfare Economics

Under perfect competition, individual consumers and producers, each pursuing only his or her self-interest, arrive at an allocation of resources that maximizes the welfare of society.

URBAN PUBLIC POLICY APPLICATIONS

The next two sections apply the tools of welfare analysis to two famous issues in urban public policy: rent controls and the economic effects of land taxes.

The Economic Effects of Rent Control

In its most basic form, a rent control policy places an upper limit or ceiling on the rent that landlords can charge tenants.[2] Why do governments impose rent controls? The stated economic objectives usually include improving the quality of life of lower income households by making rental housing more affordable. However, the actual economic effects of a ceiling on housing rents are quite different.

Figure 2.20 uses demand and supply analysis to analyze the economic effects of a rent control policy. With no government intervention, rent would be set at the p^* equilibrium price. Instead, a rent ceiling is set at the price p_0. Note that the rent control policy is only binding when $p_0 <$ p^*. The immediate effect of the rent control policy is to create a housing shortage. With the price artificially lowered, demand will exceed supply – lots of consumers are interested in "cheap" rent, but not many investors are interested in acquiring and renting out housing units if the rents are too low.

---

[2] Actual rent control programs are not simply a ceiling on rents. Rent control or rent regulations usually allow for rent increases when they can be justified by increases in costs or to ensure landlords a "fair" rate of return on their investments. They also often exempt newly constructed rental housing.

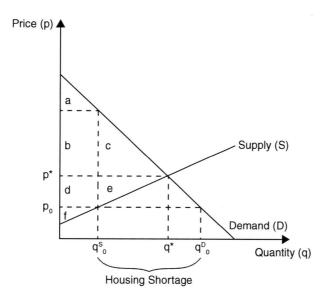

FIGURE 2.20

The Economic Effects of Rent Control

Figure 2.20 shows that the quantity demanded at price p_0 is q^D_0, while the quantity supplied at p_0 is q^S_0, where $q^D_0 > q^S_0$. If we imagine that the market consists of a number of different housing consumers, each of whom demands one rental unit, then $q^D_0 - q^S_0$ consumers are unable to find accommodation at the controlled price. This outcome presumably differs markedly from what the government intended. It is hard to imagine a government announcing that they were imposing rent controls because they want to create a housing shortage, but this is one of the policy's unavoidable effects.

The effects of rent control on economic welfare are also interesting. In Figure 2.20, consumer surplus prior to the imposition of rent control is given by the area a + b + c. Producer surplus prior to the imposition of rent control is given by the area d + e + f. With rent control, consumers purchase q^S_0 units at the controlled price p_0, and consumer surplus is now the area a + b + d. With rent control, producers sell q^S_0 units at the controlled price p_0, and producer surplus equals the area labeled f. Thus, consumers gain the area d, but lose the area c, and firms lose the areas d and e. The area d is transferred from producers to consumers by the policy — consumers who are fortunate enough to find accommodations at the controlled price are better off. However, excluded consumers and all producers are made worse off by rent controls.

The net effect of the policy is that economic welfare, the sum of consumer and producer surplus, decreases by the areas c and e. This is known as the *deadweight loss* of the policy. This loss arises because $q^* - q^S_0$ units are no longer traded. These units were valuable — consumers were willing to pay more for them than what they cost to produce — and their disappearance is a loss to society as a whole. The general lesson here, one that is a corollary to the fundamental theorem of welfare economics, is that any intervention in a competitive market reduces aggregate welfare.

Deadweight Loss

In an inefficient market with a non-equilibrium outcome, consumers or producers may each gain or lose relative to one another, but the deadweight loss is the loss to society as a whole from this inefficiency

EXERCISE 2.2: Calculating the Economic Effects of Rent Control

Suppose the demand for housing is given by: $q^D = 1{,}000 - p$

and that the supply of housing is given by: $q^S = p$

What are the effects of a rent control policy that establishes a maximum price of $p_0 = \$300$?

Solution:

Before analyzing the effect of any market intervention, we need to know what the competitive market equilibrium conditions are, i.e., the conditions that would prevail in the absence of intervention. To do so, we start by solving for the equilibrium price:

Start by setting $q^D = q^S$: $1{,}000 - p = p$

Add p to both sides: $1{,}000 = 2p$

Divide both sides by 2: $500 = p$

continued on next page

Now that we have the equilibrium price (p* = $500), we can solve for the equilibrium quantity by plugging the price into either the demand or the supply equation.

Using the demand equation: q* = 1,000 – p*

Solve for q*: q* = 1,000 – 500 = 500 units

We have solved for p* and q*, the conditions that would prevail in the absence of any intervention. An efficient market leads to an equilibrium rent of $500 and 500 units demanded and supplied. This solution is shown in the following figure.

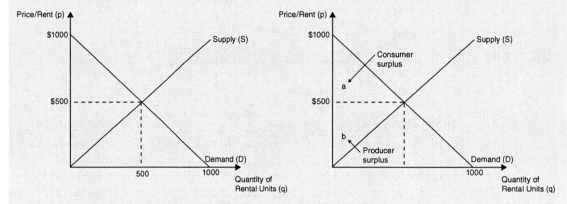

Now that we know what the equilibrium price and quantity are, we can calculate consumer and producer surplus. Consumer surplus is the area above the price and below the demand curve. The area of that triangle is:

Consumer surplus = (½)($500)(500) = $125,000

Producer surplus is the area below the price and above the supply curve. The area of that triangle is:

Producer surplus = (½)($500)(500) = $125,000

In this example, these happen to be equal.

Now let's see the effects of rent control. First, notice in the following figure that the rent control policy sets a price ceiling at p = $300, which creates a disparity between supply and demand. Because the price is so low, demand is 700 (q^D = 1,000 – 300), much higher than in equilibrium; and because the price is so low, supply is merely 300 (q^S = 300), much lower than in equilibrium.

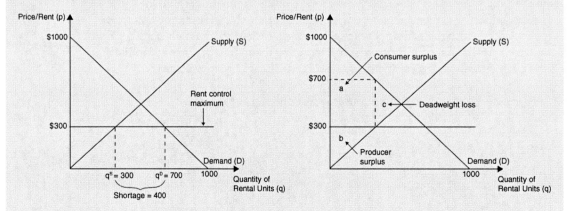

Because supply is just 300 units, fewer transactions take place under rent control than under equilibrium market conditions. Fewer transactions mean fewer opportunities for consumers to capture consumer surplus and fewer opportunities for producers to capture producer surplus; the result is a deadweight loss represented by area c.

continued on next page

How does consumer and producer surplus change under rent control conditions? Consumer surplus is represented by area a. This area is an irregular shape, consisting of a rectangle and a triangle. In order to solve for the consumer surplus, we need to solve for the price if quantity demanded was equal to 300. Substituting 300 as q^S into $q^D = 1,000 - p$, produces a price of $700.

After rent control, consumer surplus = ½($1,000 - $700)(300) + 300($700 - $300)

Therefore, consumer surplus = ½($300)(300) + (300)($400) = $165,000

And producer surplus = (½)($300)(300) = $45,000

Thus, consumers as a group are better off, while producers as a group are worse off.

The deadweight loss of the policy is the difference between total surplus in the market equilibrium scenario and total surplus in the rent control scenario.

Deadweight loss = $125,000 + $125,000 - $165,000 - $45,000 = $40,000

In conclusion, the rent control policy causes consumers to gain at producers' expense, BUT, ultimately, society as a whole is worse off.

The Economic Effects of Taxes

Popular discussions of taxation usually begin and end with the observation that people don't like to pay taxes, especially high taxes. This is certainly true, but it is not particularly insightful. What are the real economic impacts and costs of taxes? Are some taxes better than others? Welfare analysis can be used to uncover deep insights into the economic effects of taxes. In this section, we review these issues and apply them specifically to taxes on land.

Figure 2.21 illustrates the impact of a sales tax that is imposed on purchasers of a product. For simplicity, we will assume that the tax is a constant amount t per unit. Imposing the tax reduces the maximum amount that consumers are willing to pay for every quantity by t. Thus, the tax results in a parallel downward shift in the demand curve (from D_0 to D_1). This decrease in demand naturally changes the equilibrium price and quantity in the market. After the tax is imposed, the equilibrium quantity decreases from q_0 to q_1. The change in the price is a bit more complex. The price that sellers receive for their product falls to p^S. However, this is not the price that buyers pay, as they must also pay the tax. Consequently, the price that a buyer pays is $p^B = p^S + t$. Thus, the tax creates a gap or wedge between the price that a buyer *pays and the price that a seller receives equal to the amount of* the tax: $p^B - p^S = t$.

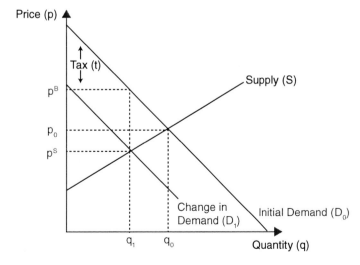

FIGURE 2.21

The Economic Effects of a Tax on Buyers

Figure 2.22 illustrates the impact of the same tax imposed on sellers. The tax effectively increases the marginal cost of supplying each quantity by t, leading to a left parallel shift in the supply curve. This decrease in supply naturally changes the equilibrium price and quantity in the market. Specifically, the equilibrium quantity decreases from q_0 to q_1, while the price that a buyer pays increases to p^B. However, p^B is not the price that sellers receive, as the sellers must pay the tax. The price that a seller receives is $p^S = p^B - t$. Once again, the tax creates a wedge between the price that a buyer pays and the price that a seller receives equal to the amount of the tax. Notice in Figures 2.21 and 2.22 that the effects of the tax on equilibrium prices and quantities are the same in both graphs. This is an important insight: the economic effect of a tax does not depend on whether it is collected from buyers or sellers.

FIGURE 2.22

**The Economic
Effects of a Tax
on Sellers**

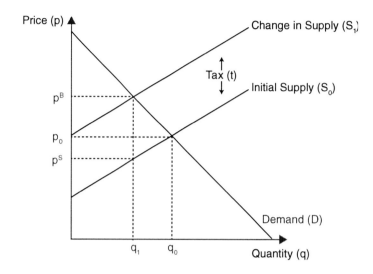

Figure 2.23 illustrates the impact of the tax on economic welfare. For simplicity, the graph shows the economic effects of the tax without shifting the demand or supply curves. The prices and quantities are exactly the same as in Figures 2.21 and 2.22. The government revenue that is raised by the tax is tax per unit times the number of units that are traded or $t \times q_1$. In the figure, government revenue equals the area $b + d$. The revenue collected from buyers is $b = (p^B - p_0)q_1$, while the revenue collected from sellers is $d = (p_0 - p^S)q_1$. Notice that both buyers and sellers pay a part of the tax in this case. Prior to the imposition of the tax, consumer surplus is the area $a + b + c$, and producer surplus is the area $d + e + f$. After imposition of the tax, consumer surplus is equal to the area a, producer surplus is equal to the area f, and the government receives the area $b + d$ in revenue. What about the area $c + e$? This is the true economic cost of the tax. The area c is consumer surplus that disappears because $q_0 - q_1$ units of the good are no longer traded. The area e is producer surplus that disappears for the same reason. The area $c + e$ is the reduction in aggregate economic welfare as a result of the imposition of the tax. This is the deadweight loss of the tax. This loss arises because the units no longer traded, $q_0 - q_1$, were valuable — consumers were willing to pay more for them than they cost to produce — and their disappearance is a loss to society as a whole.

FIGURE 2.23

**The Welfare
Effects of a Tax
on Buyers or
Sellers**

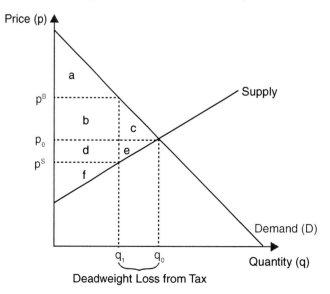

The economic effects of the tax will depend on the slopes of the demand and supply curves. Figure 2.24 depicts a special case that is of interest in the context of urban and real estate economics, namely a tax on a good whose supply is fixed. As noted earlier, the market for land may fit this model reasonably well, with a vertical supply curve, since — at least in some circumstances — producers cannot react to a higher price by supplying more land.[3] Assume the land tax is collected from buyers, shifting the demand curve down by t at every quantity. The price a seller receives falls to p^S and the price a buyer pays is $p^S + t$. However, since the supply curve is vertical, the price that a buyer pays actually does not change from the pre-tax conditions: $p^S + t = p^B = p_0$. While p^S drops, p^B does not change — this implies that the tax is paid entirely by suppliers or landowners. While the tax is imposed on buyers, in effect it is landowners who end up paying the tax through lower land prices.

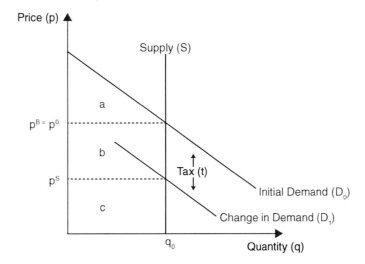

FIGURE 2.24

A Tax on Land

Furthermore, a tax on a commodity that is in fixed supply creates no deadweight loss. In Figure 2.24, consumer surplus before the tax equals the area a, while producer surplus equals the area b + c. After imposition of the tax, consumer surplus is still equal to the area a (since the price that the consumers pay does not change) and producer surplus is equal to the area c. The surplus that producers lose, area b, is exactly equal to the revenue that the government collects, $b = (p_0 - p^S)q_0$. Thus, the tax is simply a shift in surplus from producers to the government, but it does not reduce aggregate welfare. We noted above that the deadweight loss of a tax arises because the tax causes a reduction in the number of units of the good that are traded. Here the number of units that are traded is fixed (since supply is fixed); therefore, the deadweight loss of the tax is zero. In fact, this model implies that the government could completely confiscate land rents without affecting the allocation of resources. The idea that it is efficient to tax land because land is in fixed supply is at the heart of the so-called *single tax* or *site value tax* movement that originated with the American journalist Henry George in the 1870s. This is a good example of how demand and supply analysis can be used to gain fundamental insights into the economic effects of taxes.

> **Single Tax on Land**
>
> A theory that the government should finance all of its projects with proceeds from a single tax on the unimproved value of land

MARKET FAILURE

So far our review has emphasized the efficiency of competitive markets. We have seen that the outcome of a competitive market maximizes the sum of consumer and producer surplus, and that intervention into the operation of competitive markets, in the form of price controls or taxes, generally lowers economic welfare. However, not all markets are competitive. We conclude our review of demand and supply analysis by examining how and why markets can fail to produce an efficient allocation of resources.

> **Market Failure**
>
> Market Failure occurs whenever the outcome of a market is not efficient, or does not maximize the sum of consumer and producer surplus

---

[3] This may not always be the case. Developers can drain swamps, shape terrain, and even infill ocean areas to make available more usable land for buildings.

Generally speaking, a *market failure* occurs whenever the outcome of a market is not efficient, or does not maximize the sum of consumer and producer surplus. There are many sources and types of market failure:

- Monopoly: firms with monopoly market power, who can influence the price at which they sell their output, will generally produce too little and charge a price that is too high.
- Asymmetric information/adverse selection: markets may also fail when some participants have more information than others. For example, if consumers cannot tell the difference between high quality and low quality products, then sellers of high quality products may not be offered an appropriate price (one that reflects the fact that their products are high quality), and consequently only low quality products may be sold (think of the market for used cars).
- Public goods: some goods and services cannot be provided through markets because it is difficult or impossible to charge for their use (think of lighthouses or national defense).
- Externalities: markets may perform poorly when there are interactions between individuals or firms that are not accounted for by the price system. For example, a business that pollutes a river does not have to consider how its action impacts commercial and recreational river users. Externalities are probably the most important source of market failure in urban and real estate economics simply because externalities become more frequent and significant when economic activities are clustered together in relatively small spaces, as they are in cities.

Externality

The cost or benefit that affects a party who is not directly involved in the production of that cost or benefit

Negative Externalities

There are two types of externalities: negative and positive. A negative externality occurs when the actions of a person or firm have a direct detrimental impact on the well-being of others. The polluting firm described above is the source of a negative externality.

We model negative externalities by distinguishing between private, external, and social costs.

- Private costs are the costs that individual consumers or firms incur as a result of their actions, e.g., the costs of inputs for the polluting firm.
- External costs are the costs that are imposed on others — the costs that other firms incur to clean the water before using it or the value of lost recreational opportunities.
- Social costs are the sum of private and external costs.

Figure 2.25 illustrates the impact of externalities. The demand curve measures marginal benefit (MB), while the supply curve measures marginal cost (MC). However, MC to the producer only accounts for the direct private cost, it does not account for external costs to society. The marginal external cost (MEC) line shows this external cost, rising with each unit of output. The marginal social cost (MSC) line adds together MC + MEC to show total costs to society, both private and external.

FIGURE 2.25

A Negative Externality

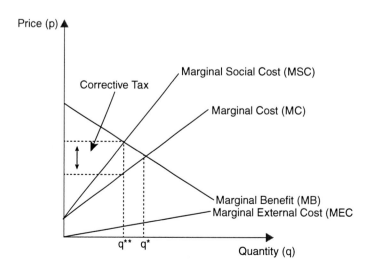

Producing firms, by definition, do not take external costs into account, so they produce where MB = MC, at q*. Efficiency requires that we maximize the net social benefit of the activity in question. This implies that we should set marginal benefit (MB) equal to marginal social cost (MSC), where marginal social cost is the sum of marginal private cost (MC) and marginal external cost (MEC). That is, efficiency requires MB = MSC or MB = MC + MEC. This efficient output level is denoted q**. However, with no requirement to account for social costs, the firms will produce q*. This illustrates how markets generate too many activities that produce negative externalities.

This oversupply could be corrected by taxing the production or consumption of the good or service in question. For example, a per unit tax equal to MEC at q** would raise MC and cause the firms to make efficient choices. This is known as "internalizing" the externality, i.e., effectively converting social cost to private cost.

Key Concept: Taxing Negative Externalities

Linking this topic back to our prior discussion of taxes and economic welfare, the tax here would reduce both the consumer and producer surplus. From the perspective of individual producers/consumers, it would also create deadweight loss equal to the triangular area below the MB line and between the MSC and MC lines. However, from society's perspective, the deadweight loss here is not a loss, since the q* equilibrium was over-production due to firms not considering true social cost. In fact, in this example, the deadweight loss could actually be considered a gain to society, in terms of avoiding costly over-production (from a societal perspective, there was a deadweight loss prior to the corrective tax). An example of this could be the "savings" to society from not having to clean up contaminated rivers or in not permanently losing farmland or greenspace. This may be a somewhat controversial perspective, depending on if you are a private producer or social advocate – more on these topics in Chapter 12.

Positive Externalities

For positive externalities, the situation is reversed. A positive externality exists when the actions of an individual or firm have a direct beneficial impact on others. For example, a firm that does research that benefits other companies is a source of a positive externality. A little closer to home, individuals who improve the appearance of their properties may raise the property values of their neighbors' properties. To model positive externalities, we distinguish between private, external, and social benefits.

- Private benefits are the benefits that the individual undertaking the activity receives, e.g., the value of research to the original firm.
- External benefits are the benefits that are bestowed on others — the value of the research to other firms and individuals.
- Social benefits are the sum of private and external benefits.

Figure 2.26 illustrates positive externalities. Efficiency again requires that we maximize the net social benefit of the activity in question, and this implies that we should set marginal social benefit (MSB) equal to marginal cost (MC), where marginal social benefit is the sum of marginal private benefit (MB) and marginal external benefit (MEB). That is, efficiency requires MSB = MC or MB + MEB = MC. This efficient output level is denoted q**. However, because decision makers, by definition, do not take external benefits into account, they produce where MB = MC, at q*. Thus, markets generate too few activities that produce positive externalities.

This under-supply could be corrected by subsidizing the production or consumption of the good or service in question. For example, a per unit subsidy equal to MEB at q** would raise MB and cause the decision makers to make efficient choices. The gain to society is the triangular area below the MC line and between MSB and MB lines.

FIGURE 2.26

A Positive Externality

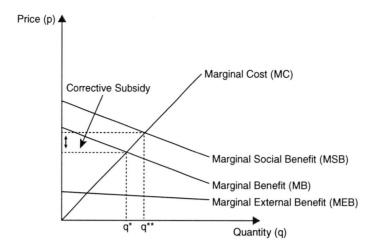

Externalities, both positive and negative, are frequently addressed by governments, developers, and property owners. For example, zoning regulations are often designed to limit the undesirable mixing of land uses — locating the lard rendering plant next to residential areas may be prohibited because the smell of the lard being processed would be too unpleasant for neighbours. That is an attempt to reduce or eliminate a potential negative externality.

Alternatively, consider a developer's choice to build a swimming pool and tennis court as part of a high-rise development. Those amenities will tend to attract those who wish to use them (after all, the rent will likely be higher than for a building without them), filling the building with people who share each other's interests. Since living next to neighbours with similar interests could be considered a positive externality in many housing environments, the high-rise developer has found a way to capture the benefits and thereby "internalize" the positive externality.

Finally, consider a shopping mall owner who offers subsidized rents to a large, anchor tenant. In other locations, this popular firm draws significant traffic to itself as well as to nearby stores but is not compensated for the benefit to nearby stores; as a result, the firm builds fewer stores than is warranted by the total social benefit it brings. The shopping mall owner's offer to subsidize the anchor tenant helps the anchor tenant "internalize" the positive externality it shares with neighbouring stores. As a result, the firm's owners are likely to build more stores. This benefits all stores located next to the anchor tenant and justifies the higher rent they have to pay in order to subsidize the anchor tenant. Society as a whole gains by achieving a more efficient level of production that would otherwise not be provided.

Value Matters: Externalities

The concept of *externalities* is a guiding principle in real property valuation. Externalities are discussed in *The Appraisal of Real Estate, 3rd Canadian Edition*: "The principle of externalities states that factors external to a property can have either a positive or negative effect on its value. Bridges and highways, police and fire protection, and a host of other essential structures and services are positive externalities that are provided most efficiently through common purchase by the government. Negative externalities result when the action of others impose inconveniences on property owners. Externalities may refer to the use or physical attributes of properties located near the subject property or to the economic conditions that affect the market in which the subject property competes." (p.3.10)

In valuing a property, an appraiser must identify and evaluate the property's internal attributes: lot size, topography, view, house size, house quality and condition, etc. However, the appraiser must also consider how external factors may influence its value. For example, if you build your dream house, but the property next door becomes the municipal landfill, this will influence its market value. Similarly, if the house across the street is torn down to make a mark, giving you waterfront access, this also will affect your property's value!

SUMMARY

In this chapter, we reviewed the fundamentals of demand and supply analysis and the insights that demand and supply analysis provides into the efficiency of competitive markets. We also reinforced some basic modeling and problem solving skills. The concepts of elasticity, consumer and producer surplus, and economic welfare were reviewed in general terms and then examined in a real estate context as these economic tools pertain to rent control and land taxes. We also examined different types and sources of market failure, with particular emphasis on the problem of externalities. The next chapter will begin to build on the fundamentals presented in this chapter. We will explore how economic variables influence the development and growth of regions.

CHAPTER 3
THE STRUCTURE AND GROWTH OF REGIONAL ECONOMIES

INTRODUCTION

In the fall of 1973, the Organization of Petroleum Exporting Countries (OPEC) doubled the world price of oil to about $3 US a barrel. Then in January of 1974, following the October Arab-Israeli war and the oil embargo on countries aiding Israel, OPEC increased prices again, to roughly $11.50 a barrel. These events had consequences across the globe, ranging from line-ups at gas stations and reduced speed limits on highways to (some argue) a prolonged period of high unemployment and high inflation in North America and Western Europe. Interestingly, these actions also led to a strong economic expansion in the province of Alberta. Economic growth in Alberta in turn led to substantial immigration from other parts of Canada, and real estate markets in Calgary and Edmonton boomed. Thus, as odd as it may sound, the price of a condominium in Edmonton or Calgary may have a direct link to Middle East politics.

This chapter explores the key variables that influence the development and growth of regions. Our survey of regional economics will address a number of fundamental questions. Why is economic activity clustered in just a few locations? Why do regions tend to specialize in just a few industries? What are the most important factors that influence where industries locate? What are the primary economic determinants of regional growth and decline?

New Economic Geography

A theoretical framework that analyzes the impact of increasing returns to scale and transportation costs on urban development and the growth of large agglomerations

The chapter begins with an overview of data on the spatial distribution of economic activity in Canada, and the industrial structure of Canada's largest regional economies. Then we introduce a model of labour migration and regional growth, and use it to study the simple dynamics of regional economic performance. Following that, we discuss models and evidence about the determinants of firm location. The chapter concludes with a brief statement of the issues raised and insights offered by the *new economic geography*.

THE SPATIAL DISTRIBUTION OF ECONOMIC ACTIVITY

Table 3.1 provides several measures of the spatial distribution of economic activity in Canada. The table shows population, employment, and GDP (subsequently split into three categories: goods production, services production, and construction) for Canada and the provinces in 2012. The GDP data shows that Ontario accounts for about 37% of all economic activity in the country, Quebec about 20%, British Columbia about 12%, and Alberta about 17%. There are some differences between the measures in sub-categories — e.g., Alberta has more than their share of construction activity and Saskatchewan has a proportionately larger share of goods production. However, most of the measures in the sub-categories have similar percentages as total GDP. The results also indicate that spatial distribution of economic activity in Canada is highly uneven, with just two regions — Quebec and Ontario — accounting for over 50% of all economic activity in the country. Of course, this general pattern is repeated in every country; economic activity is not spread evenly across the globe.

Table 3.1: The Spatial Distribution of Economic Activity in Canada, 2012 ($ millions)				
Geography	**Services Production**	**Goods Production**	**Construction**	**GDP ($ millions)**
Nunavut	1,332	667	199	674,485
Yukon	1,748	670	213	357,859
Northwest Territories	2,731	1,544	400	219,994
Prince Edward Island	4,400	819	327	311,898
Newfoundland and Labrador	16,959	14,183	2,675	58,245
New Brunswick	23,742	5,943	1,858	77,929
Nova Scotia	31,420	4,792	2,185	38,397
Saskatchewan	38,606	33,190	6,133	33,817
Manitoba	42,088	11,876	4,281	5,547
Alberta	171,856	103,207	36,835	4,675
British Columbia	169,373	32,845	17,776	2,631
Quebec	259,555	73,218	25,086	2,198
Ontario	520,028	112,909	41,548	674,485

* Employment numbers exclude the self-employed
** Goods production ordinarily includes construction, but it has been disaggregated in this table

Flat, Featureless Plain

An area or land with a central location that extends outward in all directions, without geographical constraints; e.g., Regina, Saskatchewan may be close to a real-world example

To understand why economic activity is concentrated in just a few locations, it is useful to try to imagine the opposite extreme. Imagining a world in which the spatial distribution of economic activity is uniform requires some special assumptions:

- First, we must suppose that all land is homogeneous (i.e., identical) and that natural resources are available in unlimited quantities everywhere. Urban and regional economists sometimes refer to such a mythical landscape as a *flat, featureless plain* — the lack of geographical constraints makes for a simpler model.
- Second, assume that transportation is costly (which it surely is).

- Third, and most important, assume that there are no scale economies in any economic activity. Recall that a scale economy exists when the average cost of production declines as the level of production rises. Intuitively, when there are scale economies, it is cheaper to produce a good in large quantities. By supposing that there are no scale economies, we are assuming that every good can be produced efficiently at any scale, large or small.

Under these conditions, there will be no clustering of economic activity because everyone is better off if they go it alone. Since resources are ubiquitous and there are no scale economies, each of us can produce everything we might want efficiently at home. Further, if some individuals worked together in a firm, then each would produce exactly the same amount that they could produce at home (no scale economies again), but someone would have to bear the costs of transporting workers and their outputs to and from the firm. Clearly, everyone would be better off producing in isolation, and consequently, a uniform spatial distribution of economic activity would be ideal. Because there are no scale economies, there is no advantage to clustering production.

The hypothetical situation above is clearly not realistic, given its fundamental assumptions. In reality, we do have scale economies and this example illustrates why economic activity is clustered in just a few locations. The spatial distribution of economic activity is determined by fundamental economic forces that include economies of scale, the costs of transportation, and the locations of resources. We will consider each of these forces in detail as the chapter unfolds.

THE ECONOMIC STRUCTURE OF CANADA'S REGIONAL ECONOMIES

Table 3.2 gives a rough description of the economic structure of Canada's largest regional economies. Specifically, the table documents the distribution of employment by broad industry groups for Canada, Quebec, Ontario, Alberta, and British Columbia in 2012.

Table 3.2 highlights some similarities among Canada's regions and a number of important differences between them. One obvious similarity is that service industries are the largest employers in every province shown, from 71% in Alberta to 80% in British Columbia. In Canada as a whole, nearly 78% of all employment is in the service sector. Within the service sector, wholesale and retail trade, health care and social assistance, and professional, scientific and technical services are the most significant categories. The goods producing sector accounts for between 20% (British Columbia) and 30% (Alberta) of employment among the provinces shown, with the Canada-wide average standing at 22%.

If we compare the data in Table 3.2 with comparable data from earlier years, we would see that post-World War II, the share of total employment in services has been rising and the share of total employment in manufacturing has been falling. This fundamental shift away from manufacturing employment and toward service employment is the footprint of technical progress. Technical progress has reduced labour requirements in manufacturing far more than it has reduced labour requirements in services. Service industries are, by their nature, difficult to automate. Other things being equal, then, increasing automation should cause service employment to rise over time relative to manufacturing employment. In addition, the demand for services seems to have grown rapidly during the post-World War II period. The net result of these changes is that Canada's economy, like that of other developed countries, is now dominated by the services sector.

Table 3.2 also shows some important differences between the regions. For example, regional economies have specialized in certain industry groups. The third column under each jurisdiction (labelled LQ) gives the *location quotient* for that industry in that region. The location quotient is the percentage of employment regionally in a particular industry divided by the percentage of employment nationally in that industry. A location quotient larger than one indicates that this industry is more important regionally than nationally. For example, logging and forestry accounted for 0.8% of employment in British Columbia and 0.3% of employment in Canada in 2012. Therefore, the location quotient for logging and forestry in British Columbia was 2.59 (0.8 ÷ 0.3) in 2012.[1]

> **Location Quotient**
>
> The percentage of employment regionally in a particular industry divided by the percentage of employment nationally in that industry. A location quotient larger than one indicates that this industry is more important regionally than nationally

In contrast, manufacturing has the highest LQ in Ontario and Quebec, showing their proportionately larger share of the manufacturing sector in Canada relative to other provinces.

---

[1] Readers may notice 0.8/0.3 = 2.67. The difference is due to rounding of the % figures in the table.

Table 3.2: The Distribution of Employment* by Industry Group: Canada and Selected Provinces, 2012

	Canada			Quebec			Ontario			Alberta			British Columbia		
	Employment (000s)	%	LQ	Employment (000s)	%	LQ	Employment (000s)	%	LQ	Employment (000s)	%	LQ	Employment (000s)	%	LQ
Services-producing sector (16)	13,636	77.9	1.00	3,125	78.4	1.01	5,362	79.0	1.01	1,530	71.2	0.91	1,853	80.1	1.03
Wholesale and retail trade	2,644	15.1	1.00	630	15.8	1.05	990	14.6	0.97	322	15.0	0.99	357	15.4	1.02
Health care and social assistance	2,128	12.2	1.00	529	13.3	1.09	762	11.2	0.92	229	10.6	0.87	275	11.9	0.98
Professional, scientific, and technical services	1,299	7.4	1.00	297	7.5	1.00	564	8.3	1.12	158	7.3	0.99	173	7.5	1.01
Educational services	1,288	7.4	1.00	296	7.4	1.01	504	7.4	1.01	129	6.0	0.82	177	7.7	1.04
Hotels and restaurants	1,102	6.3	1.00	237	6.0	0.95	416	6.1	0.97	133	6.2	0.98	172	7.4	1.18
Public administration	956	5.5	1.00	233	5.8	1.07	383	5.6	1.03	89	4.1	0.75	102	4.4	0.81
Transportation and warehousing	849	4.9	1.00	174	4.4	0.90	317	4.7	0.96	116	5.4	1.12	129	5.6	1.15
Other services	795	4.5	1.00	176	4.4	0.97	291	4.3	0.94	106	4.9	1.09	114	4.9	1.08
Information and cultural industries	790	4.5	1.00	186	4.7	1.03	333	4.9	1.09	71	3.3	0.73	116	5.0	1.11
Finance and insurance	783	4.5	1.00	163	4.1	0.92	370	5.4	1.22	72	3.3	0.75	92	4.0	0.88
Business support services	691	3.9	1.00	147	3.7	0.94	294	4.3	1.10	73	3.4	0.86	98	4.2	1.07
Real estate and leasing	310	1.8	1.00	57	1.4	0.81	140	2.1	1.16	32	1.5	0.84	50	2.2	1.23
Goods-producing sector	3,872	22.1	1.00	860	21.6	0.98	1,422	21.0	0.95	619	28.8	1.30	459	19.9	0.90
Manufacturing	1,786	10.2	1.00	499	12.5	1.23	801	11.8	1.16	139	6.4	0.63	179	7.7	0.76
Construction	1,268	7.2	1.00	244	6.1	0.85	434	6.4	0.88	227	10.5	1.46	193	8.3	1.15
Agriculture	309	1.8	1.00	57	1.4	0.81	94	1.4	0.79	56	2.6	1.48	26	1.1	0.64
Mining, quarrying, and oil and gas extraction	299	1.7	1.00	21	0.5	0.30	28	0.4	0.24	174	8.1	4.73	26	1.1	0.66
Utilities	141	0.8	1.00	25	0.6	0.77	56	0.8	1.02	21	1.0	1.20	15	0.6	0.80
Forestry and logging	52	0.3	1.00	13	0.3	1.09	8	0.1	0.41	4	0.2	0.58	18	0.8	2.59
Fishing, hunting, and trapping	18	0.1	1.00	2	0.0	0.45	n/a	n/a	n/a	n/a	n/a	n/a	2	0.1	0.86
Total	17,508	100	1.00	3,984	100	1.00	6,784	100	1.00	2,150	100	1.00	2,313	100	1.00

Source: Statistics Canada
*Measures of "employment" include the self-employed, while measures of the number of "employees" do not.

North American Industrial Classification System (NAICS)

The industries specified in Table 3.2 are grouped together according to the North American Industrial Classification System (NAICS). NAICS was developed jointly by Canada, the United States, and Mexico in order to provide a common statistical framework for economic analysis among the three countries. NAICS is a hierarchical system with categories constructed on a production/process-oriented basis. Codes have 6-digits, starting with "industry codes" and working down to finer categories:

XX	Industry Sector
XXX	Industry Subsector
XXXX	Industry Group
XXXXX	Industry
XXXXXX	Country-Specific Industry Detail

For example, code 53 includes real estate and rental and leasing. It then breaks down as follows:

53	Real estate and rental and leasing
531	Real estate
5313	Activities related to real estate
53131	Real estate property managers (US)
531310	Real estate property managers (Canada)

The industry groups shown in Table 3.2 are the two-digit NAICS code categories. A complete listing of the NAICS classification system for Canada is available at the Statistics Canada website: *www.statcan.gc.ca*

Location quotients are an important tool in regional economics for classifying industries. A location quotient larger than one indicates that the industry is a basic or export industry, while a location quotient smaller than one indicates that the industry is a non-basic industry, or one that produces largely for local consumers. The idea is that if one region has more than the national average share of employment in a particular industry, then the excess workers must be producing for export. It is also traditional to view basic or export industries as the engines of regional growth and decline. At one level, this is perfectly logical: the economic performance of a region is obviously tied to its most important industries. However, it is also important to keep in mind that exports are not necessarily required for growth.[2] For example, regional economies may grow by producing for themselves the products that they used to import from other regions (called import substitution). As well, consider that the world economy as a whole continues to grow despite no exports outside our world!

> **Basic Industry**
>
> An industry within a region that exports the majority of its production, generating new money and growth in the domestic economy

> **Non-Basic Industry**
>
> An industry within a region that provides goods or services domestically, recycling the money that already exists within the economy

Table 3.2 indicates that logging and forestry is a basic or export industry in British Columbia, while mining, quarrying, and oil and gas extraction are basic industries in Alberta. Manufacturing is basic in Quebec and Ontario, while construction, transportation, and warehousing are basic in the western provinces. The finance and insurance industry is basic only in Ontario, while the real estate and leasing industry is basic only in Ontario and British Columbia.

The broad industry groups used in Table 3.2 wash out some of the differences between the regions. Table 3.3 drills down one level further with the same employment data for a selection of four-digit, NAICS classified industry groups. With these finer industry groups, the degree of specialization is more pronounced. For example, the relative importance of sawmills and wood preservation, and pulp and paper mills in British Columbia is clearly evident, as is the importance of the manufacture of basic chemicals, boiler tanks, and shipping containers in Alberta, communication equipment in Ontario, and aircraft parts in Quebec.

---

[2] There is a bit more to the "economic base" or "export base" view of regional economics than is indicated here. If we assume that the size of the non-basic sector can be determined by the size of the basic sector, then employment forecasts in basic industries can be used to generate total employment forecasts.

Table 3.3: The Distribution of Employees in Selected Four-Digit Industries: Canada and Selected Provinces, 2012 (number of people)

SIC Code	Industry group	Canada Emp	%	Quebec Emp	%	LQ	Ontario Emp	%	LQ	Alberta Emp	%	LQ	British Columbia Emp	%	LQ
3116	Meat product manufacturing	56,873	3.8	16,283	4.0	1.05	18,817	2.9	0.75	9,323	7.0	1.84	5,246	3.8	1.00
3211	Sawmills and wood preservation	32,948	2.2	9,249	2.3	1.03	2,862	0.4	0.20	3,841	2.9	1.31	13,976	10.2	4.61
3212	Veneer, plywood and engineered wood product manufacturing	16,753	1.1	4,608	1.1	1.01	3,068	0.5	0.42	2,632	2.0	1.76	4,026	2.9	2.61
3219	Other wood product manufacturing	38,795	2.6	12,925	3.2	1.22	9,486	1.4	0.55	5,612	4.2	1.62	5,957	4.3	1.67
3221	Pulp, paper and paperboard mills	27,046	1.8	10,510	2.6	1.42	4,587	0.7	0.38	2,110	1.6	0.87	6,554	4.8	2.63
3251	Basic chemical manufacturing	12,125	0.8	2,753	0.7	0.83	6,132	0.9	1.15	2,161	1.6	2.00	450	0.3	0.40
3272	Glass and glass product manufacturing	8,118	0.5	2,887	0.7	1.30	3,253	0.5	0.91	613	0.5	0.85	1,059	0.8	1.42
3273	Cement and concrete product manufacturing	28,332	1.9	7,658	1.9	0.99	10,982	1.7	0.88	3,121	2.3	1.23	3,062	2.2	1.17
3323	Architectural and structural metals manufacturing	57,342	3.9	17,292	4.3	1.10	20,741	3.2	0.82	8,493	6.4	1.66	5,061	3.7	0.96
3324	Boiler, tank and shipping container manufacturing	14,221	1.0	2,266	0.6	0.58	5,461	0.8	0.87	4,083	3.1	3.22	758	0.6	0.58
3326	Spring and wire product manufacturing	3,808	0.3	979	0.2	0.94	1,620	0.2	0.96	738	0.6	2.17	258	0.2	0.74
3327	Machine shops, turned product, and screw, nut and bolt manufacturing	33,776	2.3	8,132	2.0	0.88	15,726	2.4	1.06	4,668	3.5	1.55	2,248	1.6	0.72
3332	Industrial machinery manufacturing	13,288	0.9	4,397	1.1	1.21	5,951	0.9	1.01	320	0.2	0.27	1,571	1.1	1.28
3342	Communications equipment manufacturing	20,872	1.4	4,137	1.0	0.73	14,206	2.2	1.54	N/A	N/A	N/A	1,321	1.0	0.69
3344	Semiconductor and other electronic component manufacturing	14,084	0.9	4,798	1.2	1.25	6,866	1.0	1.10	668	0.5	0.53	1,418	1.0	1.09
3362	Motor vehicle body and trailer manufacturing	13,565	0.9	3,414	0.8	0.92	3,645	0.6	0.61	1,417	1.1	1.17	1,569	1.1	1.26
3364	Aerospace product and parts manufacturing	37,112	2.5	19,766	4.9	1.95	8,817	1.3	0.54	751	0.6	0.23	1,826	1.3	0.53
3391	Medical equipment and supplies manufacturing	18,239	1.2	4,805	1.2	0.96	8,475	1.3	1.05	1,483	1.1	0.91	2,184	1.6	1.30
31-33	**All Manufacturing**	1,488,954	100.0	406,497	100.0		657,032	100.0		132,884	100.0		136,996	100.0	

Source: Statistics Canada

*Measures of the number of "employees" do not include the self-employed, while measures of "employment" do.

N/A values suppressed by Statcan to meet the confidentiality requirements of the Statistics Act

A DEMAND AND SUPPLY MODEL OF REGIONAL GROWTH AND DEVELOPMENT

Regional economies are *open economies* in the sense that they are heavily dependent on trade with other external areas. There is a great deal of movement of goods from one region of the country to another. Table 3.4 documents the value of interprovincial trade flows (trade between provinces) in 2009. The flows are substantial. Indeed, for more than half of the provinces, the value of imports from other regions of the country exceeds the value of imports from abroad. In the aggregate, interprovincial trade flows are about 70% as large as trade flows between Canada and other countries.

The magnitude of trade between the provinces varies significantly. Just three provinces – Quebec, Ontario, and Alberta – account for two-thirds of all interprovincial trade. It is interesting to note that the same three provinces are the only three who are net interprovincial exporters; every other province is a net interprovincial importer.

Open Economy

An economy that allows for trade of goods, services, and fund with external areas

Table 3.4: International and Interprovincial Trade Flows: Canada and the Provinces, 2009 (millions $)

	Interprovincial			International		
	Exports	Imports	Net	Exports	Imports	Net
Newfoundland and Labrador	5,459	7,455	1,996	9,205	6,483	2,722
Prince Edward Island	1,240	2,457	1,218	1,022	949	73
Nova Scotia	7,146	12,086	4,941	5,983	9,204	3,221
New Brunswick	9,488	11,816	2,328	11,024	13,101	2,078
Quebec	62,155	60,479	1,676	75,848	94,977	19,129
Ontariot	107,146	82,694	24,452	166,640	191,959	25,319
Manitoba	15,245	19,426	4,181	12,740	12,716	24
Saskatchewan	15,927	21,109	5,182	23,977	12,774	11,202
Alberta	57,505	51,512	5,992	73,936	54,905	19,031
British Columbia	31,603	41,034	9,431	38,117	44,725	6,609
Yukon	397	1,001	603	332	351	19
Northwest Territories	1,091	2,211	1,120	1,611	755	856
Nunavut	221	1,150	929	21	255	234
Canada	314,635	314,635	-	420,458	468,601	48,143

Source: Statistics Canada

There is also a great deal of movement of people between the provinces. Table 3.5 documents interprovincial migration between 1976 and 2011. These figures show dramatic changes in migration patterns over time. For example, Newfoundland, Saskatchewan, and British Columbia were all experiencing net out-migration in the early 2000s, but became net migration recipients by the latter part of the decade. That pattern is reversed for Prince Edward Island and the Northwest Territories. They had been net recipients of migrants in the early 2000s, but by the end of the decade more people were leaving those provinces than entering them.

Migration patterns are heavily influenced by labour market conditions between regions, particularly differences in earnings or job opportunities. Labour market statistics also show that interprovincial migrants tend to be more active in the labour force, which is consistent with migrants being younger and better-educated.[3]

Interprovincial migrants are more likely to be in the labour force (which means they are either employed or actively looking for work) than non-migrants, and they often move to another province because they have found a new job or are looking for work. The employment rate for interprovincial migrants in 2001 was 65.6%, which was higher than for the total working age population at 61% (Statistics Canada, 2001 Census). In addition, the labour force participation rate for migrants, 76%, was higher than that of the total working age population, 66%.

---

[3] Sharpe, A., Arsenault, J., and Ershov, D. 2007. "The Impact of Interprovincial Migration on Aggregate Output and Labour Productivity in Canada, 1987-2006". p. 24. *www.csls.ca*

Table 3.5: Net Interprovincial Migration for Provinces and Territories, 1976/1977 to 2010/2011

	2001/2-2003/4	2004/5-2006/7	2007/8-2010/11	Net since 1976/7
Newfoundland	−7,062	−12,119	2,937	−121,419
Prince Edward Island	371	−1,627	−977	−1,462
Nova Scotia	−1,160	−10,191	−1,974	−30,171
New Brunswick	−2,821	−8,193	−732	−39,753
Quebec	−7,001	−27,239	−27,122	−462,355
Ontario	−944	−48,720	−39,020	65,722
Manitoba	−9,784	−20,608	−12,743	−174,136
Saskatchewan	−18,482	−15,049	9,852	−150,773
Alberta	48,744	114,027	33,673	484,094
British Columbia	−1,728	32,019	36,787	454,371
Yukon	−45	81	11,51	−4,148
Northwest Territories	221	−1,843	−1,527	−17,412
Nunavut	−309	−538	−305	−2,558

Net interprovincial migration equals in-migrants minus out-migrants
Note: Nunavut is included in the Northwest Territories before 1991/1992.
Source: Statistics Canada, Demography Division

Other important determinants of interregional migration patterns include house prices, amenities, and government social policies. A region or province may be more attractive to potential migrants if there are low housing prices, desirable physical and cultural amenities, and generous social programs – or vice versa. For example, Vancouver is considered a desirable place to live for climate and recreation, but housing affordability is a concern.

Value Matters: Immigration to Vancouver via Asian Countries

Interprovincial migration is an important determinant of economic growth within provinces, but international immigration is a major factor as well. Consider the large immigration influx to Vancouver, primarily from Asian countries such as China, India, and the Philippines. This immigration is a large part of Metro Vancouver's doubled population in the last 30 years and it being the third fastest growing city in Canada between 2001 and 2011. Population growth of this kind obviously has a strong impact not only on the economic growth of an area, but on its cultural, social, and political environment.

While immigrants have come from around the globe, Statistics Canada reports that 70% of Metro Vancouver's new immigrants have Asian origins. Motivations behind this strong trend include the high quality of life that can be attained within Vancouver, as well as the fact that Vancouver's west coast Pacific location makes it a relatively quick flight back home to many Pacific Rim Asian countries.

A 2015 MoneySense article, Canada's Best Places to Live, lists three Metro Vancouver locations in its top 10 Best Places for New Immigrants in Canada. Port Moody, Port Coquitlam, and Delta have immigrants as a percent of population at 28%, 27.8%, and 27.2% respectively. The rankings are based on rental market statistics, vacancy rates, accessibility to services, and the ethnic composition of each city.

These growth statistics lead directly to real estate value increases, which then further attract foreign investors. The MoneySense article ranks West Vancouver as the richest place in Canada, with the highest property values. Various news reports in 2016 report that as much as one-third of sales volume in the Vancouver market can be attributed to Mainland China buyers.

Source: www.moneysense.ca

Economists use demand and supply analysis to model how changes in the performance of a region's basic industries influence migration patterns. This will be illustrated here in three steps:

- First, we derive the demand for labour from the profit maximizing choices of firms and show how labour demand depends on conditions in the market for the region's basic or export goods.
- Second, we examine how changes in labour demand impact migration and regional populations.
- Third, we investigate how our simple model of regional development can be made more realistic by integrating real estate market considerations into the markets for the basic goods and labour.

Like any input or factor of production, the demand for labour is derived from the value of the goods that labour can produce. Intuitively, firms hire additional workers as long as doing so adds more to the firm's revenues than it adds to the firm's costs. As long as this condition is satisfied, hiring additional workers increases the firm's profit. Therefore, the demand for labour is closely related to the process of profit maximization.

Let's be a little more precise. Consider a firm that has labour as its only variable input. The firm presumably also employs other inputs like land, capital, and materials, but we will assume that these inputs are fixed for now. The firm's production function can be described in equation format as $Q = F(L)$. This means that the firm's output level Q is a function of, or depends on, the number of units of labour (L) that the firm employs. L could be defined as a certain number of employees or a certain number of labour hours. In any case, we will assume that L can be changed smoothly. Based on the assumption that more labour leads to more output, we can assume that the function is increasing; therefore, more labour leads to more output. This is illustrated in Figure 3.1. However, the relationship between Q and L is not constant or linear. If the firm only has one worker who is very over-worked, then adding a second worker L may dramatically improve the firm's output Q. On the other hand, if the firm has so many workers that they are not all that productive all the time, then adding another worker L may have little impact on output Q. This relationship is seen in Figure 3.1 as the curving line in the left graph — at low levels of L, the line is steep; as Q increases, the line flattens.

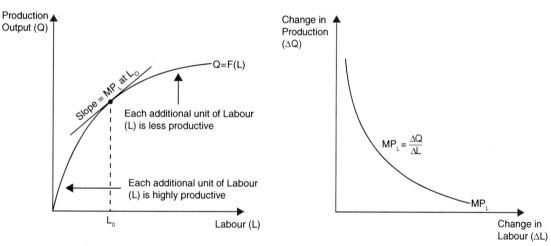

FIGURE 3.1

Production Function and the Marginal Product of Labour

Helpful Hint: What is a Function?

A *function* may sound like a complicated thing, but it is really just an equation that contains one or more variables. For example, consider the equation $y = 2x$. The value of y depends on the value of x – or, in other words, *y is a function of x*. This is standard economic jargon for describing relationships between data – in particular where changes in one input are related to changes in another output.

Notice that this is similar to the notation we will use for our bid rent functions, where we might have $r(d) = 2{,}000 - 50d$. That would be read "r is a function of d" or "bid rent is a function of distance."

The slope of the $Q = F(L)$ function represents the additional output Q that could be achieved by adding one more worker L. Thus, the slope at any given point on the curve represents the *marginal product of labour* (MP_L). Since the function is a curving line, its slope or MP_L, changes as we move along the curve. The shape of the curve also embodies the assumption that the marginal product of labour is decreasing. This means that as L increases, the MP_L gets smaller. In other words, the amount that each additional worker adds to output gets smaller as the number of workers grows. The right side of Figure 3.1 shows the associated marginal product of labour — as discussed above, the MP_L decreases as L increases.

Again, the marginal product of labour determines the value to the firm of hiring another worker. If the output produced can be sold for a price p, this means the amount that another worker adds to the firm's total revenue is $p \times MP_L$. This revenue increment from employing one more unit of labour is commonly known as the value of the marginal product of labour, or VMP_L.

EQUATION 3.1

$$VMP_L = p \times MP_L$$

It is obvious that an increase in worker productivity will increase the VMP_L. However, note that an increase in the price of the firm's output will also increase the VMP_L. This makes sense intuitively: if the price of the output rises, then the value of the output that an additional worker creates rises as well (even with no change in worker productivity). This is key to the impact of basic industries on regional growth. The more valuable the output, the greater the value of hiring new workers. The investors who own the industries demand profit maximization, so the management will choose the produce the most valuable output possible. The more profitable firms can then compete with higher wages. And we begin to see how cities form.

Figure 3.2 illustrates the relationship of labour demand with the price of output. When the price of output is p_0, then the firm's demand for labour is $D_0 = p_0 \times MP_L$. However, if the price of output rises to p_1, then the firm's labour demand rises to $D_1 = p_1 \times MP_L$. The value of the marginal product of labour VMP_L increases at all levels of labour.

FIGURE 3.2

Labour Demand and Employment

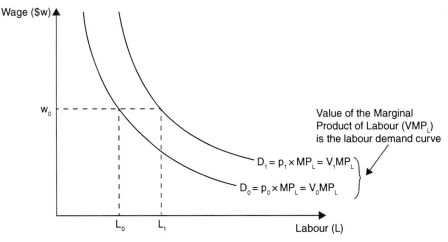

So how does this price increase affect the firm's demand for labour? The cost to the firm of hiring another worker is given by the workers' wage w. This wage should be broadly interpreted to include all the costs of hiring an additional unit of labour. The firm's VMP_L is the marginal benefit of labour. The firm's marginal cost of labour is the wage, w. Thus, to increase profit, the firm should hire additional workers as long as $VMP_L > w$. In other words, new workers add benefit as long as the value they produce is more than their wages. Conversely, if $VMP_L < w$, then adding more workers is counter-productive, as the value they add is less than their wages.

The firm's employment level is profit maximizing if $p \times MP_L = w$, or if the value of the marginal product of labour equals the wage. In other words, whatever the wage w, the firm should choose the level of labour, L, such that $VMP_L = w$. This means that VMP_L is the firm's demand

Marginal Product of Labour

The increase in productivity or output due to one additional unit of labour

Marginal Benefit of Labour

The increase in revenue due to one additional unit of labour = $VMP_L = p \times MP_L$ (demand for labour)

Marginal Cost of Labour

wage (w)

Profit Maximizing Demand for Labour

where $VMP_L = w$

curve for labour. Figure 3.2 illustrates that a wage of w_0 will mean the firm hires L_0 workers. However, if the price of output rises to p_1, then the demand curve moves outward to $D_1 = p_1 \times MP_L$, and employment rises to L_1. What about labour supply? In general, the amount of labour that individuals are willing to supply is determined by a tradeoff between labour (income) and leisure. This choice generally results in an upward sloping labour supply curve — the higher the wage, the more people are willing to work, at least up to a point.

In the context of regional development, the labour supply decision also involves a location choice. Clearly wage w is a key consideration in a worker's willingness to supply his or her labour. As noted earlier, in a market economy wages will tend to be highest for the most productive output. Workers will migrate between regions in response to differences in wages or employment opportunities. Considering the intensity of production, a factory can produce more profitable output than rural activities, so the wages are higher and people begin to congregate around the factories. In its simplest format, we have a classic model for urban development.

There may be confounding variables in this simple model of labour supply and urban development. For example, workers may be willing to accept a lower wage to live in an area where physical or cultural amenities are plentiful, other things being equal. Perhaps 100 years ago these location decisions were more wage-based, reflecting people's concerns for shelter and basic needs, and seen worldwide in rapid urbanization. And perhaps today we are seeing the first glimmers of a cultural reversal, where people are attracted to the simpler rural life and increasingly willing to forego personal wealth to pursue it. But this is jumping ahead to the subject of a later chapter!

A Simple Regional Development Model

The discussion above has alluded to urban development trends and processes for regional economics. Let's examine this more formally, in developing a simple model for regional development.

We start with the assumption that workers migrate into (out of) a region whenever the wage that it offers is higher (lower) than the wage that is available elsewhere. As noted above, other factors might enter into this decision, such as amenities and house prices, but we will ignore these confounding factors for now to keep the model simple.

Figure 3.3 shows the labour demand curves for two regions, A and B. The demand curves show the amount of labour demanded at different wages (and further simplifying the model, we'll assume the demand relationship is linear/constant at all wages). Remember the assumption that firms will choose their optimal labour supply based on their profit maximizing decisions.

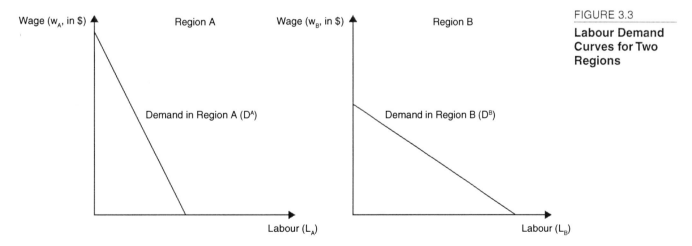

FIGURE 3.3

Labour Demand Curves for Two Regions

Suppose that the workers in each region are identical, which will allow us to combine the two demand curves into a single graph. To do so, we flip the demand curve for Region B about its vertical axis as in Figure 3.4. Note that the graph is still showing the same relationship between wages and the number of workers — we haven't done anything but change our visual perspective and then merge the two demand graphs into one.

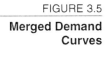

FIGURE 3.4

**Merging Labour
Demand Curves**

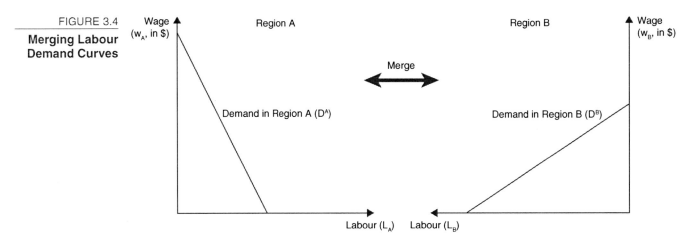

The result is Figure 3.5, which combines the x-axes from each graph into one (representing the number of workers in Region A and Region B).

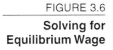

FIGURE 3.5

**Merged Demand
Curves**

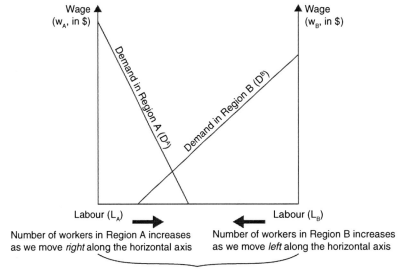

The final result is shown in Figure 3.6, which shows workers allocating themselves between the regions such that all wage differentials are eliminated, i.e., workers in both regions earn the same wage. In this figure, $w_A^* = w_B^*$. At this optimal equilibrium wage, the labour quantity demanded in Region A is L_A^* and in Region B is L_B^*. The demand curves in Figure 3.6 are based on the MP_L relationships and prices in each region. If these underlying equations were known, we could solve for the optimal wage and equilibrium labour amounts. This is illustrated in Exercise 3.1.

FIGURE 3.6

**Solving for
Equilibrium Wage**

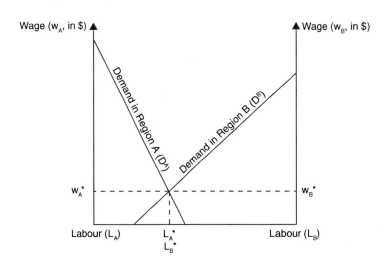

EXERCISE 3.1: Solving for a Regional Equilibrium

Assuming the following facts, determine the equilibrium allocation of workers to regions A and B and the equilibrium wage:

- The marginal product of labour in region A is $MP_L^A = 20 - (1/2)L^A$ and the marginal product of labour in region B is $MP_L^B = 10 - (1/12)L^B$.
- Let $p^A = \$2$ and $p^B = \$3$.
- The national labour force is $L = 100$ (workers, in 1000s).

Solution:

Since $D = p \times MP_L$, we can obtain the demand curves for region A and B by substituting the prices into the MP_L curves:

$D_A = \$2[20 - (1/2)L^A]$ and

$D_B = \$3[10 - (1/12)L^B]$

Therefore,

$D_A = \$40 - \$L^A$

$D_B = \$30 - (\$1/4)L^B$

Equilibrium is where $w^A = w^B$ (or $D^A = D^B$) and $L^A + L^B = 100$.

To solve for the equilibrium wages, combine $L^A + L^B = 100$ and $D^A = D^B$ into one equation:

Given: $L^A + L^B = 100$, solve for L^B:

Subtract L^A from both sides: $L^B = 100 - L^A$

Substitute L^B into D_B: $\$30 - (\$1/4)(100 - L^A)$

and set the two demand equations equal to one other:

$\$40 - L^A = \$30 - (\$1/4)(100 - L^A)$

Then, solve for L^A:

Expand brackets: $\$40 - L^A = \$30 - \$25 + (\$1/4)L^A$

Simplify: $\$40 - L^A = \$5 + (\$1/4)L^A$

Subtract 5 from both sides: $\$35 - L^A = (\$1/4)L^A$

Add L^A to both sides: $\$35 = L^A + (1/4)L^A$

Combine like terms: $\$35 = (\$5/4)L^A$

Divide both sides by $\$5/4$: $28 = L^A$

Since $L^A = 28$ and $L^A + L^B = 100$:

$L^B = 100 - 28 = 72$

Substituting $L^A = 28$ into $D_A = \$40 - \$L^A$

And substituting $L^B = 72$ into $D_B = \$30 - (\$1/4) L^B$

Results in D_A and $D_B = 12$

continued on next page

Since $D_A = D_B$ is equivalent to $w^A = w^B$, the equilibrium wage = \$12.

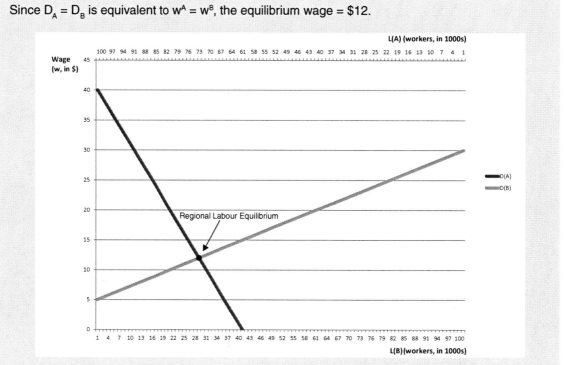

Reality Check

This intensive calculation was needed to solve for the equilibrium wage and labour quantities in the two regions. This is a theoretical model that begins to explain patterns of labour mobility between regions, depending on the value of production in each (which is a function of labour productivity and prices) and relative wages between them. The next sections will examine the impact of changing prices, product demand, and other variations.

Dynamics of the Regional Development Model

The previous section introduced a basic model for regional development, which allowed us to solve for the equilibrium wage and equilibrium allocation of workers between the two regions. The usefulness of this model lies in the dynamics — what happens when something in the two regions changes? This is where economic models can help us to better understand the ever-changing urban development patterns, and ideally predict future changes in a region.

As one example, what will happen to our simple model's wages and worker allocation if the price of the product produced in region B increases? The answer can be broken down into two distinct effects: short-run and long-run.

Short-Run Effects

An assumption of perfect, immediate labour mobility is great in theory, but is not realistic. In the short run, the number of workers in each region remains fixed. In fact, the short term can be defined in this model as the amount of time that passes before workers begin to re-allocate themselves between regions. Given the current allocation of workers, we need to think about what the labour demand curve in each region implies for the wage that employers have to offer.

The first diagram in Figure 3.7 shows the original equilibrium wages and quantities for each region (based on initial demand $D_A{}^0$ and $D_B{}^0$). The wages in both regions are the same: $w_A{}^* = w_B{}^*$. If the price of the product in Region B increases, the demand curve for Region B shifts left and outward (to $D_B{}^1$). The increase in the value of the marginal product of labour in Region B causes industry to demand more workers in order to capture this additional profit, but because there are no extra workers available; the increased competitiveness for labour simply leads to increased wages (new higher $w_B{}^*$). Employers in Region B can and will pay more for employees because labour becomes more valuable and each unit produced can be sold for more as shown in the second diagram in Figure 3.7.

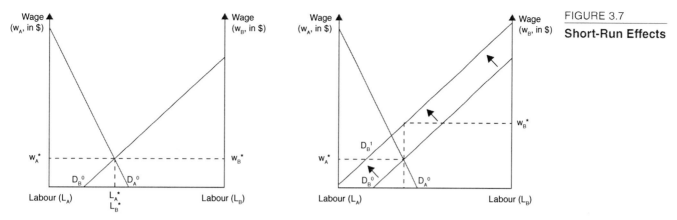

FIGURE 3.7

Short-Run Effects

In Region A, the labour demand curve is unchanged. There is no reason for employers to pay a higher wage because workers cannot migrate to Region B. Region A's same wage will prevail, leading to a short-run disparity between regions.

Long-Run Effects

In the long run, workers are able to make location decisions and can re-allocate themselves between the two regions. The natural tendency is to move from the low-wage region to the high-wage region, and this movement continues until wages in both regions are once again equal as in the right side of Figure 3.8.

Thus, the net effects of the increase in price of the good produced in Region B are:

- More workers in Region B and fewer workers in Region A relative to the initial equilibrium.
- Higher wages in both regions. In the short run, wages in Region B spiked to a very high level. As more workers migrate from Region A, the increased supply forces wages down. At the same time, wages increase in Region A to keep workers from leaving. Eventually an equilibrium wage is reached once again.

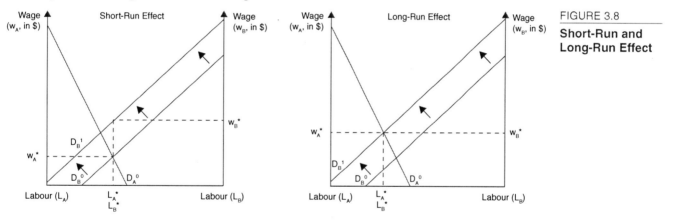

FIGURE 3.8

Short-Run and Long-Run Effect

This simple model illustrates a few basic points. A region's labour market conditions are tied to conditions in the region's product markets. An increase in the demand for a region's export good will increase the price of the good, and increase the value of the marginal product of labour and the demand for labour in that activity. If workers migrate between regions in response to differences in earnings or employment opportunities, then a favorable shock in export demand will lead to a regional expansion, as workers are attracted from other areas.

This helps us understand the relationship between OPEC and Alberta discussed in the introduction of this chapter. Alberta is a major producer and exporter of oil. When OPEC policies caused the world price of oil to rise in the early 1970s, this encouraged oil firms in Alberta to increase production, which in turn caused employment opportunities in Alberta to increase. The improvement in job opportunities caused some workers and their families to move to Alberta from other regions of the country. During the 1976-81 period, the population of Edmonton increased by 17%, while the population of Calgary increased by almost 26%. The most important component of population growth in both cities was immigration from other regions of the country. That interprovincial migration is closely tied to differences in economic performance between provinces seems evident from the data.

In the first decade of the 2000s, this pattern was repeated. As world oil and mineral prices rose, so did migration to regions producing those items (illustrated in Figure 3.9). Alberta was the primary beneficiary of net interprovincial migration.

FIGURE 3.9

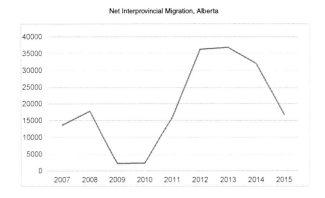

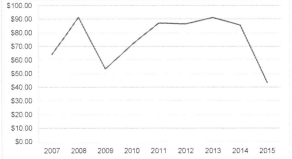

This model also illustrates a subtler point. To the degree that the regions are "open" and labour flows freely between them, there will be a tendency for differences in earnings or job opportunities between regions to dissipate over time. Consider the tales in the early 2010s of Fort McMurray fast-food workers earning $30 per hour — from an economist's point-of-view, this is not likely sustainable over the long term, as demonstrated in Figure 3.9. This movement towards equilibrium in regional economic conditions is known as convergence.

Value Matters: Convergence of Regional Economies

A 2008 study by James and Krieckhaus focuses on the degree to which economic convergence occurs in Canadian provinces, as well as the implications for provincial policy. The findings are that interprovincial convergence and nationwide trends are the two factors most responsible for provincial economic growth (90% variation explained by these two factors). A 2013 study by Desjardins reveals that recent trends of interprovincial disparities in GDP per capita are decreasing, specifically for the three Maritime Provinces. Consider the relationship between convergence and real estate values. On the one hand, real estate demand (and thus prices) will be directly influenced by these changing economic conditions between regions. But on the other hand, these price variations may in themselves become a convergence influence, if buyers are fleeing expensive real estate and migrating to areas offering the optimal combination of jobs and affordability.

Furthermore, economic shocks in any one region will affect all regions in the economy. Part of a favorable shock to a regional economy will be dissipated by migration from other areas. Conversely, part of an unfavorable shock to a regional economy will be dissipated by migration to other areas. This could have important implications for provincial economic policies. For example, regional economic development programs could be made ineffective by migration — if the program succeeds in raising earnings or improving job prospects, it might attract workers from other regions. Rosenbluth examined this issue in the context of Canadian interprovincial migration and concluded that migration is "relatively muted and slow" and as a result, "the effects of interprovincial migration do not eliminate the potential for growth-oriented policies".[4]

Our basic model of regional growth and development is highly simplified, dealing only with regional product markets and regional labour markets. Adding other considerations would increase the model's realism (but also its complexity). A natural addition in this course would be considering a market for land or real estate in each region. How would this impact our analysis? Regional shocks will now have an effect on real estate prices. A change in economic conditions that leads to a decrease in labour demand, a decrease in earnings or employment opportunities, and a consequent out-migration and reduction in the labour force will also be associated with a decrease in the demand for real estate and falling real estate prices. Conversely, a favorable economic shock will eventually lead to an increase in the demand for real estate and rising prices. We will explore the link between economic growth and real estate prices in detail later in the text.

APPLICATIONS FOR REGIONAL DEVELOPMENT MODELS

The model of regional development presented above is a highly simplistic representation of land economics, but it provides the theoretical foundation for many more complex models. The work of land economists often uses existing models as a jumping off point to examine the impact of different assumptions or contexts. In this section, we examine theories related to regional multipliers, firm location decisions, and impact of firm scale on economic geography.

Regional Multipliers

It is often important to be able to measure the cumulative impact of some economic event on a local or regional economy. For example, in recent years, many jurisdictions in North American have embraced legalized gambling as a tool for economic development. Opponents have argued that gambling is associated with increases in crime and a variety of other economic and social problems. Proponents have argued that these problems are overwhelmed by the strong positive impact of legalized gambling on local employment, incomes, and government tax revenues. Furthermore, these claims argue that the positive impacts are typically much larger than the direct spending associated with the activity in question. The concept of a multiplier is a key component to evaluating these and other regional economic events.

The basic idea is simple: one person's (or firm's) expenditure is another person's (or firm's) income. This implies that changes in local spending reverberate through the economy in a circular pattern, with the ultimate impact being a multiple of the initial change. For example, suppose a firm's sales increase unexpectedly by $Y. Some of this additional revenue flows to the government through taxes, some flows to input suppliers in other regions or countries, and some flows to local workers and firms who provide goods and services that the firm requires. The payment to local workers and firms is in turn split between taxes, exports and local spending, and so on. As the process unfolds, the cumulative impact of the initial increase in sales continues to grow — with the end result being economic development of multiples of the $Y initial sales increase.

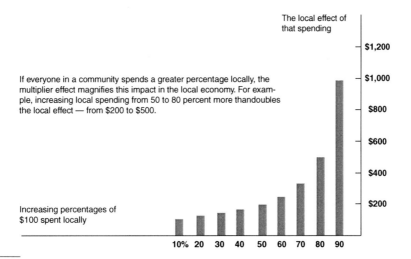

The local effect of that spending

If everyone in a community spends a greater percentage locally, the multiplier effect magnifies this impact in the local economy. For example, increasing local spending from 50 to 80 percent more than doubles the local effect — from $200 to $500.

Increasing percentages of $100 spent locally

FIGURE 3.10

Multiplier Effect: A Little Goes a Long Way

4   Rosenbluth, G. 1996. "Interprovincial Migration and the Efficacy of Provincial Job Creation Policies." *Canadian Business Economics.* 4(2). pp. 22-35.

The *exogenous spending multiplier* is specified as follows:

EQUATION 3.2

$$\text{Cumulative change in local spending} = \Delta Y \times \frac{1}{1 - c(1 - t)(1 - m)}$$

Where:

- ΔY is the initial increase in local spending; this might come from an increase in investment, exports (including tourism), or government spending
- c is the fraction of every dollar of disposable income that is spent (the rest is saved); c is generally known as the *marginal propensity to consume*
- t is the government tax rate
- m is the fraction of every dollar of consumption that is imported to the region; m is sometimes known as the *marginal propensity to import*

Marginal Propensity to Consume

The proportion of an aggregate raise in pay that a consumer uses on the consumption of goods and services, as opposed to saving it

Marginal Propensity to Import

The amount that imports increase or decrease with each unit rise or decline in disposable income; the change in imports induced by a change in income

Let's think of the cumulative change in spending as if it evolves over a number of "rounds". In the first round, local spending rises by Δy. In the second round, local spending also increases by some fraction of Δy, but some of this amount is lost to savings (1–c), as well as to taxes (t) and imports (m). Therefore, in round 2, the increase in local spending is some amount less than Δy. The round 3 impact is less than round 2, and so on. This same pattern will repeat in round after round, with the impact decreasing in each, until the initial spending impact is all used up. The multiplier equation calculations this total cumulative impact. It tells us by how much an initial change in local spending is "factored up" by the circular flow of income in the region.

To apply this spending multiplier in practice, the economist needs to determine the region's marginal propensity to consume (c), the local tax rate (t), and the local propensity to import (m). For example, assume c = 0.8 (people spend 80% of increases of income, saving 20%). If the tax rate is 30% (t = 0.3) and the propensity to import is 20% (m=0.2, meaning 20% of income increase is spent on imports from outside the region), then the multiplier is 1.81. This means every $1 in extra income in the region leads to $1.81 in cumulative economic benefit.

Table 3.6 calculates the spending multiplier for different values of t and m, assuming that c = 0.8. So, for example, if m = 0.7, and t = 0.5, then the exogenous spending multiplier equals 1.14. This implies that a $100,000 initial increase in spending will ultimately increase local spending by $114,000. Note from Table 3.6 that the multiplier gets smaller as m or t increase. This is because both imports and taxes represent a "leakage" from the regional economy. Income that is paid to foreign suppliers or collected in taxes does not circulate through the regional economy.

Table 3.6: The Exogenous Spending Multiplier								
m/t	**0.1**	**0.2**	**0.3**	**0.4**	**0.5**	**0.6**	**0.7**	**0.8**	**0.9**
0.1	2.84	2.36	2.02	1.76	1.56	1.40	1.28	1.17	1.08
0.2	2.36	2.05	1.81	1.62	1.47	1.34	1.24	1.15	1.07
0.3	2.02	1.81	1.64	1.51	1.39	1.29	1.20	1.13	1.06
0.4	1.76	1.62	1.51	1.40	1.32	1.24	1.17	1.11	1.05
0.5	1.56	1.47	1.39	1.32	1.25	1.19	1.14	1.09	1.04
0.6	1.40	1.34	1.29	1.24	1.19	1.15	1.11	1.07	1.03
0.7	1.28	1.24	1.20	1.17	1.14	1.11	1.08	1.05	1.02
0.8	1.17	1.15	1.13	1.11	1.09	1.07	1.05	1.03	1.02
0.9	1.08	1.07	1.06	1.05	1.04	1.03	1.02	1.02	1.01

Note: This table assumes that the marginal propensity to consume is 0.8.

Evaluating Optimal Firm Location

At a very basic level, regional growth is tied to the location of production. To flourish, a region must offer a set of attributes or characteristics that firms and their workers find attractive. By surveying the economic factors that influence firm location and regional success, economists can help make more effective location decisions.

A basic assumption in economic studies of business location is that firms choose locations to maximize profits or minimize costs. Classical location theory emphasizes transportation costs and access to sources of raw materials and markets as determinants of firm location. In the simplest case, if we abstract from variations in production costs, and assume that only transportation costs vary with location, then an optimal location is one that minimizes transport costs. Firms locate near their input sources when transportation costs for inputs are larger than transportation costs for outputs. For example, the lumber and wood products industry is concentrated in forested regions because it is more expensive to ship unfinished than finished lumber. Conversely, firms locate near their markets when transportation costs for outputs are larger than transportation costs for inputs. This helps explain why soft drink bottlers locate near their markets in population centres — they do this to avoid the cost of shipping water. As long as there is only one market and one input source, the optimal location is always at one or the other. If there are many inputs and outputs, then the transportation cost minimizing location involves a tradeoff between access to inputs and access to markets.[5]

Market access may be measured using the *gravity law* of market potential. This equation evaluates potential firm locations by evaluating the purchasing power in various nearby markets as a function of their distance from the potential location.

EQUATION 3.3

$$T_i = \frac{Y_1}{d_{i1}{}^b} + \frac{Y_2}{d_{i2}{}^b} + \frac{Y_3}{d_{i3}{}^b} + ... + \frac{Y_m}{d_{im}{}^b}$$

Where:
- T_i is the market potential of firm location i Y_1, Y_2, Y_3 is the income or purchasing power of each nearby market (the firm may serve up to m different markets)
- d is the distance from location i to that market
- b is a positive constant, typically determined by review of prior research studies[6]

To see how the gravity law works, let's consider a firm that is choosing between a number of different locations.

SPUD, an internet retailer offering domestic delivery of organic groceries, is choosing a location for a new distribution centre. SPUD wants to evaluate the market potential (T) for two possible locations, A and B — so in our gravity law calculation, we are looking for T_A and T_B.

The firm serves three markets, denoted M1, M2 and M3. Figure 3.11 shows the potential locations and the markets served (relative to location A). The table summarizes each market's purchasing power and distance (d) from location's A and B.

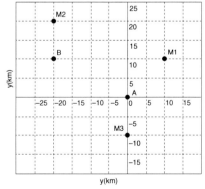

FIGURE 3.11

Spud Location Analysis

---

[5]   The list of potential inputs is nearly limitless. Commonly cited location determinants for manufacturing are access to markets, labour, raw materials, transportation, and a favorable business climate. Favorable labour-related location factors include the availability of a pool of skilled labour, lower labour costs, and lower levels of union activity.

[6]   The parameter b governs how distance enters into the calculation of market potential. If b is large, then it is even more critical for the firm to be near a large concentration of purchasing power. Researchers estimate the coefficient b by finding real world data, then "calibrating" b to fit the data. Coefficients vary by region and industry and what is being predicted, such as firm location, trade, population movement, etc. For any given application of this formula, the analyst will review prior research and choose a commonly accepted range or average for b. Krugman discusses the history of this and many other concepts from spatial economics.

	Distance from A (km)	Distance from B (km)	Purchasing Power t
M1	14	30	$3,000
M2	28	10	$10,000
M3	10	28	$4,000

Assume that b=2. Then:

$$T_A = \frac{3,000}{14^2} + \frac{10,000}{28^2} + \frac{4,000}{10^2} = 68.1$$

$$T_B = \frac{3,000}{30^2} + \frac{10,000}{10^2} + \frac{4,000}{28^2} = 108.4$$

Comparison of these results reveals that the greatest market potential is at location B.

Early research into location decisions were inconclusive, finding economic variables were insignificant and the models had poor explanatory power. However, results have improved with better data on the different components of net employment change: births of new firms, and deaths, relocations, and expansions of existing firms. Since the location decisions of firms in each category are very different, it is not surprising that location studies relying on aggregate data had little success. With more information on the employment and financial characteristics of individual establishments by industry and location over time, researchers can track individual firms through time, and study the location behavior of firms in each category separately. These improvements in data, together with advances in conceptual models of firm location, and applications of sophisticated econometric techniques, have led to investigations that shed a good deal of light on the determinants of manufacturing location.

In one example, Carlton [1983] estimated two models of the regional location decisions of new firms. The first model dealt only with the births of single establishment firms; the second model examined the location of new branch plants. The crucial difference between the two classes of firms is that single establishment firms are typically formed by local entrepreneurs. Individual entrepreneurs do not search across alternative regions for the best site to begin operation. Rather, they establish new firms in industries and areas where they already have some experience.

In Carlton's model, the number of new single establishment firms locating in an area is the product of the number of potential entrepreneurs in the area and the probability that any entrepreneur will start a business. He postulates that the number of potential entrepreneurs depends on the existing level of local economic activity in a particular industry, and that the probability of starting a business depends on expected profitability, which in turn depends on local economic variables. Carlton's model of the location of new branch plants is simpler and more familiar: firms choose among alternative locations to maximize profits, which depend on local economic conditions. The probability that a firm will choose a given location is then a function of that location's attractiveness relative to all others.

Carlton found that economic variables explained over 80% of regional variations in the locations of new firms. He summarized his major findings as follows:

1. Wages matter a great deal in explaining births of single establishment firms. For every 1% decrease in wages, new births increase by 1%.
2. For two of the industries (plastics products and electronic components), energy costs have a large effect on new birth activity, though not as much as wages.
3. The evidence does not provide strong support for the proposition that taxes are a major deterrent to new business activity.
4. The amount of existing activity in an industry within an area exerts a large influence on the number of new births, though it is definitely not the case that areas with the greatest amount of existing activity necessarily have the largest number of births.

5. The more technologically sophisticated an industry is, the more critical the level of technical expertise is in the area. Technical expertise is more important in explaining births of single establishment firms than births of branch plants.

6. The evidence provides little support for the proposition that state or provincial policies which improve the "business climate" will stimulate new births.

Carlton's results are basically consistent with the traditional view of business location. They document the importance of regional variations in the cost and quality of inputs, in this case, labour and energy, and the positive impact of industry size on a region's attractiveness to new firms (we discuss this issue in detail below). The negative findings on the effects of taxes and fiscal inducements are controversial, but are consistent with the views of many urban economists.

While Carlton's study is dated, the results are somewhat timeless — most of the same urban land economic principles remain applicable today. A research article by Artz et al (2015) found the following:

- Proximity to upstream suppliers and downstream customers have the largest impact on decision for most industries
- Proximity to local skilled labour market has the second largest impact of decision for most industries, and is the most important factor for manufacturing firms
- Clusters of local firms attract start-ups in the industry
- The chance for a local monopoly does not attract new entries, but the presence of an established local monopoly deters entry
- Lesser significant factors: local income level, per capital government expenditures, per capita tax burden

This research affirms Carleton's models with respect to factors that determine firm location decisions. Due to agglomeration economies, firms are more likely to locate in areas with greater concentrations of suppliers or customers, and areas where there is adequate skilled labour in the local market. In contrast to Carleton, Artz et al found that fiscal policy, government expenditures, and taxes per capita are significant factors towards firm location decisions.

Another article by Arauzo-Carod (March 2013) found that technical skill of the labour market is also a factor in firms' location decisions, but not strictly at the local level. This places greater importance on transportation infrastructure. This finding also supports the Carleton model.

Increasing Returns and Economic Geography

The field of regional economics enjoyed something of a renaissance under the tutelage of the eminent international trade theorist Paul Krugman. Krugman brought new interest and new insights to the field by strengthening the economic foundations of models of regional location (especially as they relate to market structure), and by cleverly unifying a number of disparate components of the field. The result is the discipline that has become known as *New Economic Geography*.

The central question of the new economic geography is the one which this chapter began: What determines the production locations? Krugman's model of economic geography emphasizes that the process of location and regional development can be self-reinforcing. The key elements of the process include economies of scale, the costs of transportation, and the location (and mobility) of resources.

In Krugman's model, there is an economy with two sectors:

1. Manufacturing – where firms and workers are mobile and there are economies of scale at the level of the individual plant; and
2. Agriculture – where farms are immobile and there are no economies of scale.

Because of scale economies, average production costs fall as output rises. Thus, there is an incentive for firms to concentrate production in just a few places. Since transportation is costly, firms are attracted to locations near their input suppliers and their markets. But, if manufacturing workers migrate to locations offering higher wages (as in our discussion earlier in this chapter), then the locations that will be attractive to firms are precisely those where other manufacturers are located. The model is almost circular — firms are attracted to good locations, and good locations are those that have attracted firms. In this way, the process of regional development can feed upon itself. Krugman refers to this process as cumulative causation.

This analysis has a number of implications:

Cumulative Causation

The tendency for firms and workers to cluster together as economic integration increases; driven by the interaction of labour migration across regions with increasing returns and transport costs. Larger markets attract more firms, which in turn attract more workers. A larger population eases competition in the labour market and attracts more firms.

- The attractiveness of a location depends on the number of other firms there. This is an example of an external scale economy and is consistent with Carlton's study of new firm location. External scale economies play a critical role in the development of cities; we will discuss their sources, measurement, and impacts in the next chapter.
- Regional development may be, in part, the outcome of historical accident. If, for some unknown reason, a region attracts a number of firms in a particular industry, it may become an attractive location for other firms, even when the region possesses no inherent locational advantages. Thus, the region's current development may depend on what has happened in the past.

SUMMARY

This chapter surveyed a number of topics in regional economics. We discussed the spatial distribution of economic activity in Canada and the specialized structure of Canada's regional economies. We developed a simple model of regional growth that highlights the relationship between the performance of a region's basic or export industries and the growth of its labour force.

Flowing from this basic model, we then outlined some related theories in urban land economics. We discussed regional multipliers and how they are derived and calculated. We reviewed the economics of firm location, and presented evidence about the most important factors influencing industrial location patterns. The chapter closed with a brief discussion of how economies of scale, transportation costs, and the location and mobility of resources determine the location of production in the context of the new economic geography.

The next chapter presents the main elements of urban development with a focus on equilibrium and optimal city sizes.

CHAPTER 4

URBAN DEVELOPMENT

INTRODUCTION

Why do economic activities cluster into cities? This is one of the most interesting and important questions in urban and real estate economics. Fortunately, economic analysis offers a simple and compelling account of the forces that encourage spatial concentration:

- Proximity reduces the costs of transporting inputs, outputs, and people; in short, the transportation costs of transactions.
- Proximity increases efficiency in production by enhancing our ability to exploit economies of scale, or agglomeration economies, that arise from spatial concentration.

This chapter explores the basis for theories of urban development. At the heart of this is how the emergence of cities is related to the presence of increasing returns to scale. This leads to a discussion of agglomeration economies in cities and what is considered optimum and equilibrium city sizes. We will see that it is possible in theory to define the optimum size for a city, but in practice real city sizes do not follow this optimal pattern. In this discussion, we will also explore the role of land developers in city formation and examine why cities tend to specialize in certain industries.

WHAT IS A CITY?

Webster's New Collegiate Dictionary defines a city as "an inhabited place of greater size, population, or importance than a town or village". This definition fits well with everyday usage: a city is a large inhabited place. The cities that we will study are best described as metropolitan areas or urban areas. We will use the terms *city*, *metropolitan area*, and *urban area* interchangeably.

Cities are also political and legal entities. The governance, administration, and public finance of cities in Canada is established by provincial legislation. For example, British Columbia's Municipal Act classifies municipalities based on their size:

- an area is incorporated as a *village* if it contains fewer than 2,500 persons,
- as a town if it *contains* between 2,500 and 5,000 persons,
- or a *city* if its population exceeds 5,000.

Though urban or metropolitan areas may not respect these defined legal or political boundaries. Consider the urban sprawl of many Canadian cities, where the city grows outside its defined boundaries into the countryside or amalgamating smaller communities nearby. Windsor/Detroit is and interesting example as this large urban area contains many separate political jurisdictions and spans the border between the United States and Canada.

Census takers have their own notions of how a city should be defined. In Canada, the basic statistical notion of a city is a census metropolitan area (CMA), defined as an urban core with a population of at least 100,000 together with adjacent areas that have a high degree of "social and economic integration with the urban core."[1] Thus, Greater Vancouvers (from Lion's Bay to Langley) is a census metropolitan area; the City of Vancouver is its urban core. Table 4.1 lists Canada's top 35 CMAs and their populations in 2000, 2005, and 2012 — also illustrated in Figure 4.1. The largest CMAs in Canada are Toronto, Montreal, and Vancouver and their relative positions have not changed since 2000. Of the other top CMAs in Canada, their relative positions are largely unchanged over this time.

Table 4.1: Population of Canadian Census Metropolitan Areas (CMAs)					
Census Metropolitan Area	2000	2005	2012	2012 Rank	Change in rank from 2000
Toronto, Ontario	4,764,739	5,250,038	5,941,488	1	0
Montréal, Quebec	3,500,249	3,655,782	3,957,715	2	0
Vancouver, British Columbia	2,040,832	2,160,228	2,463,677	3	0
Calgary, Alberta	950,128	1,087,742	1,309,221	4	1
Ottawa-Gatineau, Ontario/Quebec	1,083,241	1,157,925	1,273,272	5	−1
Edmonton, Alberta	949,819	1,042,464	1,230,056	6	0
Ottawa-Gatineau, Ontario part, Ontario/Quebec	819,973	873,881	957,655	7	0
Winnipeg, Manitoba	692,480	713,101	778,397	8	1
Québec, Quebec	697,027	718,419	769,639	9	−1
Hamilton, Ontario	667,050	713,527	756,630	10	0
Kitchener-Cambridge-Waterloo, Ontario	423,272	463,494	505,104	11	1
London, Ontario	450,871	472,471	499,998	12	−1
Halifax, Nova Scotia	365,947	381,853	413,710	13	1
St. Catharines-Niagara, Ontario	388,097	402,533	405,768	14	−1
Oshawa, Ontario	304,414	337,747	375,639	15	2
Victoria, British Columbia	321,277	336,816	363,113	16	−1

continued on next page

---

[1]   Statistics Canada has detailed criteria for including or excluding areas from a CMA. These criteria involve the location of the area (census block group) relative to the urban core, commuting patterns into and out of the area, spatial contiguity, and whether the area was a part of the CMA in the past.

Table 4.1: Population of Canadian Census Metropolitan Areas (CMAs) (*continued*)

Census Metropolitan Area	2000	2005	2012	2012 Rank	Change in rank from 2000
Windsor, Ontario	312,410	335,395	333,417	17	–1
Ottawa-Gatineau, Quebec part, Ontario/Quebec	263,268	284,044	315,617	18	0
Saskatoon, Saskatchewan	232,597	238,640	284,008	19	0
Regina, Saskatchewan	199,069	199,593	226,312	20	0
Sherbrooke, Quebec	177,830	187,205	203,454	21	1
St. John's, Newfoundland and Labrador	181,006	183,263	200,550	22	–1
Barrie, Ontario	160,497	181,223	196,031	23	1
Kelowna, British Columbia	152,125	163,612	184,744	24	2
Abbotsford-Mission, British Columbia	151,662	161,824	178,055	25	2
Kingston, Ontario	151,303	157,913	165,472	26	2
Greater Sudbury, Ontario	162,091	162,997	163,977	27	–4
Saguenay, Quebec	158,641	152,991	152,646	28	–3
Trois-Rivières, Quebec	141,481	141,765	148,302	29	0
Moncton, New Brunswick	121,662	128,324	142,966	30	3
Guelph, Ontario	121,337	130,962	142,883	31	3
Brantford, Ontario	127,037	134,370	140,507	32	–1
Saint John, New Brunswick	126,662	125,489	128,873	33	–1
Thunder Bay, Ontario	130,115	128,283	127,113	34	–4
Peterborough, Ontario	113,813	119,918	122,439	35	0

Source: Statistics Canada.

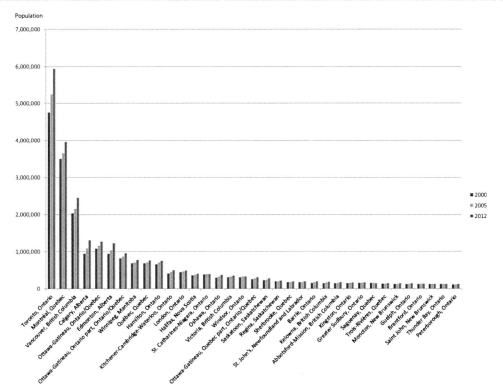

FIGURE 4.1

Population of Canadian Census Metropolitan Areas (CMAs)

In the US, the basic statistical definition of a city is the metropolitan statistical area (MSA). This consists of one or more central cities with a population of at least 50,000, together with adjacent counties that are "metropolitan in character". However, since US MSAs are made up of counties, they may contain a great deal of vacant land. For example, the Eugene-Springfield MSA in Oregon extends all the way from the legal cities of Eugene and Springfield to the Pacific Ocean, a distance of nearly 100 miles. Paradoxically, the vast majority of the land in this particular "city" is farmland and forest.

Economic City

A spatial cluster of economic activity where land is used intensively

In economic terms, a *city* may be defined as a spatial cluster of firms and households, or, even more generally, as a spatial cluster of economic activity. Another important economic characteristic of a city is that it is a place where land is used intensively. In other words, a city is a place where population and employment densities are relatively high. Population density is the number of persons per unit land area (hectares, acres, square kilometres, or square miles) and employment density is the number of jobs per unit land area.

Combining these ideas, we come to a definition of an *economic city*, which is a spatial cluster of economic activity where land is used intensively. This will be our focus in the rest of this chapter.

Value Matters: Geographic Information Systems (GIS)

Before a property can be valued, the real estate professional must first understand the specific asset being appraised. The Appraisal Institute of Canada's *First Principles of Value* require the professional to seek:

Physical understanding, to include size, shape, and topography of land; size, shape, and utility of improvements; and

Location understanding, to understand the socio-economic and geographic context of the assignment.

Appraisers have traditionally relied on paper maps, but with the advent of modern geographic information systems (GIS), analysts now have much greater control over how data is assembled. Maps can be viewed on a computer, focusing in on specific areas, and then data can be assembled for that geographic object. Statistics Canada census data or other applicable data can be illustrated visually with overlays on the GIS map. Property features can be measured and areas calculated on-screen.

INCREASING RETURNS AND ECONOMIC CITIES

Chapter 3 outlined how scale economies lead to economic activities being concentrated in space. The basic idea was that unless there is some advantage to producing in large quantities, there is no reason to bring resources together to produce in just a few locations. Scale economies play an important role in the development of cities. In fact, it is possible to explain the formation of economic cities by simply adding a land market to our earlier illustration about regional development.

First imagine a world in which there are no economic cities. Assume that land is homogeneous, natural resources are ubiquitous, and there are no scale economies in any economic activity. In this hypothetical world, there is no economic benefit to bringing inputs (people and resources) together. The concentration of production offers no productive advantages to offset the costs of transporting inputs or outputs. Think of a prairie full of farms, with each producing enough to meet occupant needs. With nothing else to produce and no potential for trade, there is no economic reason for people to congregate. They live in a uniform distribution of population across space. There is no reason to form economic cities.

Now let's change the story by assuming that there are scale economies in some activity. One of the farmers on the prairie finds a way to multiply crop production and then by processing the crops, he or she can sell the output for other goods, both to residents and nearby areas. This increased productivity spreads across the region. There are strong scale economies, so it makes sense to concentrate production as much as possible in larger production facilities. However, transportation costs must also be considered, for both materials and people and also to get goods to markets. Balancing these factors, it makes sense to concentrate the production of this good in just a few locations. This means there may be areas where employment density is relatively high.

The processing facility needs workers and since workers prefer to live close to their jobs, to minimize the cost of commuting, this gives a reason for people to live closer together.

This implies that the demand for residential land around the job sites will rise, which in turn implies that the price of land will rise there as well. Where the price of land is high, people have an incentive to use land intensively — facing higher prices, manufacturing workers will likely consume less land and more of other goods. In other words, where land prices are high, workers will likely purchase smaller lots. This means that population density (persons per unit land area) will be higher near the job sites than in other places.

Our simple economy now contains economic cities — areas where population and employment densities are relatively high.

This is a simplistic illustration that has a number of loose ends. However, it offers some helpful generalized insights. Scale economies encourage firms to cluster in space. Competition for accessible locations creates differences in land prices that give rise to differences in population density. In this way, increasing returns and the operation of the land market result in the formation of economic cities — spatial clusters of economic activity where land is used intensively.

AGGLOMERATION ECONOMIES

Firms that locate near other firms can achieve a number of advantages. The advantages firms gain from clustering are known as *agglomeration economies* or *external economies* of scale. These scale economies are called *external* because they arise from the external environment, rather than from the internal operation of a particular firm. Agglomeration economies are the result of positive externalities between firms: each firm in the cluster has some characteristic or takes some action that is beneficial to other firms. As a result, the strength of agglomeration economies is determined by the size or scale of the cluster of activity within which a firm operates.

In this section, we discuss the sources and measurement of agglomeration economies. In the next section, we consider their implications for city sizes.

Why do Firms Locate Together?

Economists have been studying the sources of external economies for a long time, beginning with British economist Alfred Marshall's studies in the 1890s. Henderson, in his article, "Efficiency of Resource Usage and City Size", lists four factors that seem to capture the sources of external scale economies in cities:

Economies of intra-industry specialization where greater industry size permits greater specialization among firms in their detailed functions

Labour market economies where industry size reduces search costs for firms looking for workers with specific training relevant to that industry

Scale for "communication" among firms affecting the speed of, say, adoption of new innovations

Scale in providing (unmeasured) public intermediate inputs tailored to the technical needs of a particular industry

Thus, if a firm locates with many other firms:

It may be able to purchase specialized inputs more cheaply than it can produce them internally; for example, the garment district in the New York in the 1950s (Vernon);

It may have access to a pool of skilled labour that is not available elsewhere or better able to match skills of workers with job requirements (Helsley & Strange); and

It may acquire valuable information from other firms regarding technical innovations, marketing practices; for example, the importance of face-to-face contacts in downtown firms (Jacobs).

The importance of these factors will vary from industry to industry and from place to place. In the computer electronics industry, which is heavily localized around Palo Alto, California – Silicon Valley – access to a pool of skilled labour and access to the innovations of other firms are important sources of external economies.

There is also potential agglomeration from a retail perspective. This may seem counter-intuitive, as firms selling similar retail items typically want distance from their competitors. However, if a location gains strength in one particular item or service, it may become a larger draw than any individual store could hope for. Think of car sales lots locating close to each other – or even shopping malls, where a collection of stores makes for a destination shopping experience beyond simply purchasing specific items.

Productive Benefits of Agglomeration

Agglomeration economies make firms more productive. To illustrate this point, let's examine the production function of a firm that enjoys external scale economies — i.e., a firm that benefits from locating near other firms.

Recall the firm's production function from Figure 3.1 in Chapter 3. This firm has just one variable input (say, labour), so the firm's output can be represented by the production function $Q = F(L)$, where Q is output, and L is labour. This means that the firm's output level Q is a function of, or depends on, the number of units of labour L that the firm employs. The production function $Q = F(L)$ tells us how many units of output are produced from L units of labour. The production function $F(L)$ is increasing and concave, reflecting the assumption that the productivity of labour declines over time — adding more labour (L) leads to less and less increases in output (Q). This also means the marginal product of labour (MP_L) is positive (more labour means more output) but diminishing over time (as L increases, the benefit for Q decreases). The MP_L chart in Figure 3.1 shows it as a convex curve with a declining slope.

Now let's consider the impact of external scale economies for this firm. By locating near other firms, this firm's production increases at all levels of labour. Figure 4.2 illustrates the production benefit from agglomeration economies. Q_0 is the original productivity curve with no external scale economies. Q_1 and Q_2 illustrate the benefits to productivity from varying degrees of agglomeration.

FIGURE 4.2

External Scale Economies

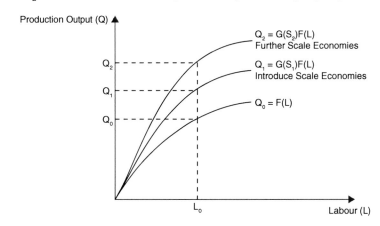

The production function equations with external scale economies considered are rewritten as follows:

EQUATION 4.1

$$Q = G(S)F(L)$$

$G(S)$ is a shift factor that reflects the presence of external scale economies and S is a measure of the size or scale of the cluster within which the firm operates. The agglomeration function $G(S)$ is assumed to be increasing; therefore, if the size of the agglomeration cluster (S) increases, then the production function shifts upward, increasing productivity at all levels of labour. The shifting curves in Figure 4.2 illustrate this. The figure shows that initially, with no scale economies, L_0 units of labour produces Q_0 units of output. When the agglomeration economies are considered, the same L_0 units of labour produce Q_1 units of output. If the size of the cluster increases to S_2, then the same L_0 units of labour produce Q_2 units of output. Thus, the presence of external economies or agglomeration allows a firm to produce more output for a given amount of labour. And when the size of the agglomeration cluster increases, so does the firm's productivity. However, there are practical limits to this agglomeration benefit in reality, as the limitations on space, resources, and markets eventually erode these productivity leaps from external scale economies — the concept of optimal city size will be explored later in this chapter.

Two Types of Agglomeration Economies

There are two types of agglomeration or external scale economies: urbanization economy and localization economy.

In an *urbanization economy*, the external scale economy is mostly determined by the size of the city in which the firm locates. This means resources will be more productive in large cities than in small ones. In this case, the variable S in Equation 4.1 could be measured using city population. The larger the city, the greater the impact of agglomeration — this helps explain the growth of mega-cities like Tokyo, Delhi, and New York.

In a *localization economy*, the external scale economy is mostly determined by the size of the firm's industry at a particular location. This means firms will be more productive when there are many other related firms at the same location. In this case, it is the size of the local industry that matters, not the size of the city. The variable S in Equation 4.1 could be measured by local industry employment. This helps explain why firms tend to locate near others, like in New York's garment district or even Vancouver's collection of snowboard shops in the Kitsilano neighbourhood.

Urbanization Economy

The benefits of agglomeration related to city size

Localization Economy

The benefits of agglomeration related to the size of a firm's industry at a particular location

Urban economists study the nature and strength of external scale economies to better understand city formation and to predict future trends in city growth. A common approach is to rely on output-per-worker as a measure of the productivity of labour and then examine how output-per-worker varies with city or industry size. This analysis can verify the existence of external scale economies and examine their impact. For example, Henderson's analysis of external economies, outlined in his book *Urban Development: Theory, Fact and Illusion*, suggests that doubling the size of an industry in a city increases output-per-worker by roughly 6%. Henderson's study found that size of the industry was more important than size of the city. In other words, his analysis showed localization economies had a stronger impact than urbanization economies.

Value Matters: Agglomeration

Appraisal assignments tend to focus on specific properties in set locations, so it is less likely that an appraiser will directly deal with an urbanization economy. However, localization economies are readily seen throughout all cities, in how office buildings, retail stores, and industrial parks tend to congregate together. Some of this is due to zoning, where specific uses are tied to an intended location by law. But bylaws alone do not explain why all the fashion stores specifically might choose to locate on one given street. Their locating together provides some competitive advantage that would be lost if they were located more distantly. For example, a fashion store may pay a higher rent than other types of retailers for this specific street. By the same token, this fashion store may be willing to pay less for a location on a different street. Therefore, if appraising these properties, the potential benefits of concentration of complementary uses must be considered, above and beyond the typical location attributes.

The Benefits and Costs of Concentration

External economies or agglomeration clusters are one of the primary explanations in urban economics for how and why cities form. The benefits of locating closer to each other leads to both firms and households concentrating their land use decisions into cities.

Of course, the benefits of agglomeration are not limitless. Just as the marginal productivity of labour tends to decline in firms as employee numbers rise, the benefit of adding one more firm to an agglomeration economy may eventually decline as the number of firms increases. In any given location, the benefits from adding more firms will eventually begin to decelerate and ultimately level off or even decline.

As well, there are also costs associated with concentration. From a firm's perspective, there are increasing costs from traffic congestion, from increased government and administrative costs, and also for land and labour, reflecting the higher cost of living in large cities versus smaller ones. There are also indirect costs to society, such as pollution and the social ills (e.g., poverty, drug abuse, crime) that seem to be correlated with city size.

The optimal size of a city occurs when the marginal benefits are equal to the marginal costs of concentration. Let's examine this relationship in both equations and graphical forms to see if we can identify this optimum city size.

Figure 4.2 showed that if a firm enjoys an external scale economy, then labour productivity will rise with the size of the cluster in which the firm is located. However, we also know from Chapter 3 that in a competitive labour market, wages are tied to labour productivity. More specifically, we know that the wage equals the value of the marginal product of labour in a competitive market, $w = VMP_L$ where $VMP_L = p \times MP_L$, and p is the price of the output that firm produces. Thus, when there are external scale economies, wages should rise with city or industry size. This is one of the benefits of living in a large city; other things being equal, wages there are higher.

Expanding the wage equation above to also include the benefit of the scale economies, or G(S), leads to the following:

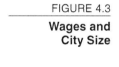
EQUATION 4.2

$$w(S) = p \times G(S) \times MP_L$$

S is the size of the agglomeration cluster and G(S) is the productivity impact of the external scale economies — recall that the external scale economies increased the output produced from any given level of labour input, shifting the production function upward. This reinforces our idea that external scale economies will lead to wage increases.

Let's assume for now that external economies are urbanization economies, so S can be measured by the total population of the city in which the firm resides. We will replace S in Equation 4.2 with N, representing the number of people in the city:

EQUATION 4.3

$$w(N) = p \times G(N) \times MP_L$$

Figure 4.3 illustrates the relationship between wages (w) and city size (N).

As noted, there are also costs associated with concentration. Let's represent these costs of concentration by a function c(N), where the costs of living (c), broadly defined, rise with city size (N). Figure 4.4 illustrates the relationship between living costs and city size.

FIGURE 4.3

Wages and City Size

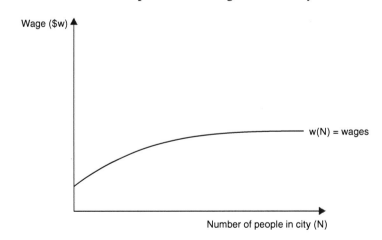

FIGURE 4.4

The Costs of Living and City Size

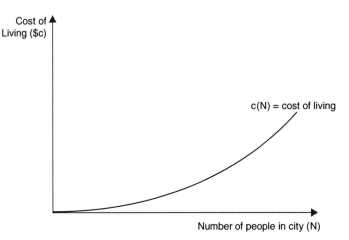

If w(N) is the wage of city residents and c(N) is the cost of living, then w(N) – c(N) is a simple measure of the utility (or satisfaction) that a household can achieve in a city of size N (assuming that all households are identical). This difference is essentially the net benefit of living in a city of size N — the excess of income or wages over the costs of living. Let's denote this utility level by v(N):

EQUATION 4.4

$$v(N) = w(N) - c(N)$$

This utility/satisfaction function v(N) is illustrated graphically in Figures 4.5 and 4.6.
    Figure 4.5 combines the wage, w(N), and costs, c(N) graphs from Figures 4.3 and 4.4.

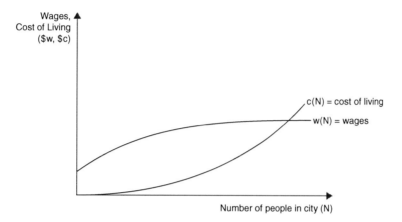

FIGURE 4.5

The Benefits and Costs of Concentration

Figure 4.6 plots the excess of wages over costs, which is the v(N) utility function. The high point of the v(N) curve is where residents have the greatest level of satisfaction. This city size N* represents the optimal city size from the residents' perspective. This concept will be explored in detail in the next section.

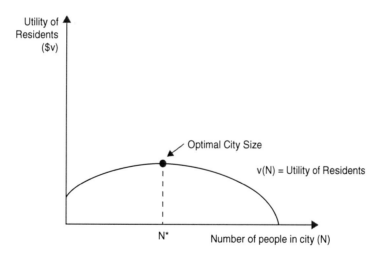

FIGURE 4.6

Optimum City Size

OPTIMUM AND EQUILIBRIUM CITY SIZES

As noted, the best or optimum city size in Figure 4.6 is point N*. This is the city population level that maximizes the utility of a typical resident. You can see from Figure 4.6 that at N* the slope of v(N) is zero, and beyond that point v(N) begins to decline.

    One disappointing aspect of the theory of urban development is that it is difficult or impossible to specify this optimal N* population for any given city. Urban economics cannot say definitively if the city you live in is too large or too small, although they likely have some suspicions, opinions, and theories — discussed further in this section.

    However, we can say a little about the determinants of N*. For example, rapidly increasing external economies tend to be associated with larger optimum city sizes. A city that contains one or more industries with very strong external economies should have a larger optimum size. Conversely, rapidly increasing living costs tend to be associated with smaller optimum city sizes. A city with a highly uneven geography (where much land is lost to bays or mountains) or an inefficient transportation system should have a smaller optimum size. As an example of this, contrast the likely optimal size of Vancouver versus Toronto. Toronto has less physical constraints on growth. Historically, Toronto has more manufacturing firms, which have a higher likelihood of external scale economies — both of which increase optimal city size.

Do cities achieve their optimum sizes? The answer to this question depends on the process through which cities form and grow. Most cities seem to grow through individual migration; their sizes are determined by the location decisions of individual firms and households. Recall from Chapter 3 that there is a considerable amount of migration between regions and cities, and that migration seems to be motivated in part by differences in economic conditions. Continuing our somewhat simplistic example, we can assume that migration is motivated by differences in utility v(N). Let's examine the consequences of individual migration for city sizes.

To begin, let's consider a situation where cities are just starting to emerge from an agricultural economy. To keep matters simple, let's assume that there is just one city. Residents near the city face the decision of whether or not to migrate to it.

Hinterland

The area of land outside of the metropolitan area, often agricultural land

Figure 4.7 can be used to illustrate this situation. Here v(0) is the utility level that is available in the *hinterland* agricultural regions, while the v(N) curve shows the utility level that is available in the metropolitan area based on various population levels. Residents of the hinterland individually decide whether or not they should move to the city. The first migrant has a choice between v(1) and v(0), and since v(1) > v(0), the migrant will choose to move to the city. The second migrant has a choice between v(2) and v(0), and so this migrant should move to the city as well.

FIGURE 4.7

Migration and Equilibrium City Size

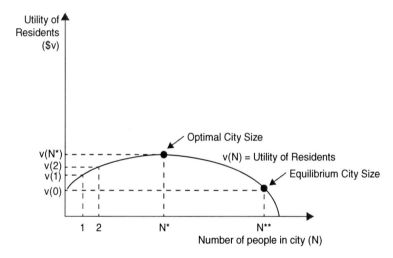

As this process continues, with a collection of individual location decisions, the city's population expands. Eventually, it reaches N*, the optimum city size. It would of course be desirable for the process to stop there, but it won't. The next migrant chooses between v(N*+1) and v(0), and moves to the city as well. Even though their utility is less than the migrant N*, the migrant (N*+1) is still better off than they were in the hinterland, v(0).

When does the process stop? When the population of the city reaches N**. This migrant N** faces the decision of staying in the hinterland with utility of v(0) or moving to the city and achieving utility of v(N**) ... which is also v(0). In other words, the process does not stop until utility in the city is driven all the way down to the utility level that is available in the hinterland. In this model, N* is the *optimal* city size, but N** is the *equilibrium* city size. Thus, individual migration can lead to cities that are too large.

The equilibrium that is shown in Figure 4.7 is inefficient from existing city dwellers' perspectives. Each individual who migrates to the city ignores the impact that he or she has on other residents; each individual migrant considers only his or her own utility v(N). Once the population of the city passes N*, each additional migrant is making all residents of the city worse off. Thus, there is a negative externality in migration that leads to excessive city sizes.

How might one correct this problem? Assuming that we cannot directly control individual migration, there are two approaches:

1. Raise v(0), the utility level that is available in the hinterland. Policies that try to raise rural utility levels to stem urban migration are common in the developing world, especially in

China. Over time, Canada has become more urban than rural – the government offers various incentives for agriculture and rural land ownership.

2. Create more cities, so that even with unrestricted individual migration, all cities are closer to their optimum sizes. In other words, it may be optimal from residents' perspective to have more smaller cities, rather than fewer large ones. For example, consider Metropolitan Vancouver's comprehensive urban planning goals to foster numerous smaller complete urban centres or *nodes* within the larger metropolitan area.

Key Concept: The Sizes and Densities of the World's Largest Cities

The following tables and graphs show the population and proportion of the countries' total populations residing in the world's top 20 cities. This highlights issues related to urban agglomeration, in particular the idea that some urban areas are probably too large. The table shows that the world's largest cities are very large indeed. For example, Tokyo, Delhi, and Mexico City are all projected to have populations larger than 25 million persons by the year 2020. Note also that 8 of the 10 largest cities are in what is sometimes called the *developing world* — in this case, India, Mexico, Brazil, China, and Bangladesh. Our agricultural migration model presumably applies best in these countries. Developing countries are very concerned about urbanization and the emergence of so-called mega-cities. There is also dramatic variation in land areas and densities within this sample. 100% of Hong Kong and Singapore's populations live in an urban setting, while Canada's largest city, Toronto, is host to just 16% of the country's population.

World's Largest Cities by Population				
		Population (000s)		
2010 rank	**Urban Agglomeration**	**2000**	**2010**	**2020 (fcst)**
1	Tokyo, Japan	34,450	36,933	38,707
2	Delhi, India	15,732	21,935	29,274
3	Mexico City, Mexico	13,959	19,554	26,121
4	New York-Newark, USA	16,367	19,422	23,661
5	São Paulo, Brazil	18,022	20,142	23,239
6	Shanghai, China	17,846	20,104	22,487
7	Bombay, India	17,099	19,649	22,243
8	Beijing, China	10,162	15,000	20,781
9	Dhaka, Bangladesh	10,285	14,930	20,064
10	Calcutta, India	10,031	13,500	17,729
11	Karachi, Pakistan	13,058	14,283	16,648
12	Buenos Aires, Argentina	7,281	10,788	15,825
13	Los Angeles-Long Beach-Santa Ana, USA	11,814	13,223	14,907
14	Rio de Janeiro, Brazil	11,847	13,370	14,876
15	Manila, Philippines	9,958	11,654	14,428
16	Moscow, Russian Federation	6,550	10,222	14,221
17	Osaka-Kobe, Japan	7,330	10,486	14,167
18	Cairo, Egypt	8,744	10,953	13,791
19	Istanbul, Turkey	10,170	11,031	13,254
20	Lagos, Nigeria	10,803	11,867	13,020

Source: UN World Urbanization Prospects, the 2011 Revision

continued on next page

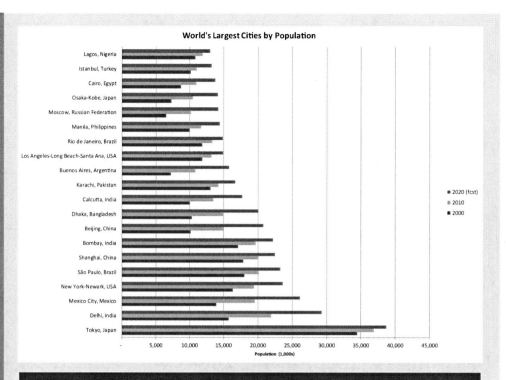

World's Largest Cities by Density

2010 rank	Urban Agglomeration	% of country population living in urban agglomeration		
		2000	2010	2020 (fcst)
1	Hong Kong	100	100	100
1	Singapore	100	100	100
2	Kuwait City, Kuwait	69	85	88
3	San Juan, Puerto Rico	66	66	67
4	Montevideo, Uruguay	48	49	52
5	Beirut, Lebanon	40	47	51
6	Tel Aviv-Jaffa, Israel	46	45	46
7	Ulaanbaatar, Mongolia	32	41	51
8	Panama City, Panama	36	40	44
9	Brazzaville, Congo	33	39	41
10	Yerevan, Armenia	36	36	38
11	Santiago, Chile	34	35	36
12	Buenos Aires, Argentina	32	33	34
13	Auckland, New Zealand	28	32	36
14	Asunción, Paraguay	28	32	37
15	San José, Costa Rica	26	31	36
16	Lima, Peru	28	31	33
17	Athens, Greece	29	30	32
18	Tokyo, Japan	27	29	31
19	Khartoum, Sudan	25	27	29
20	Lisbon, Portugal	26	26	29

Source: UN World Urbanization Prospects, the 2011 Revision

continued on next page

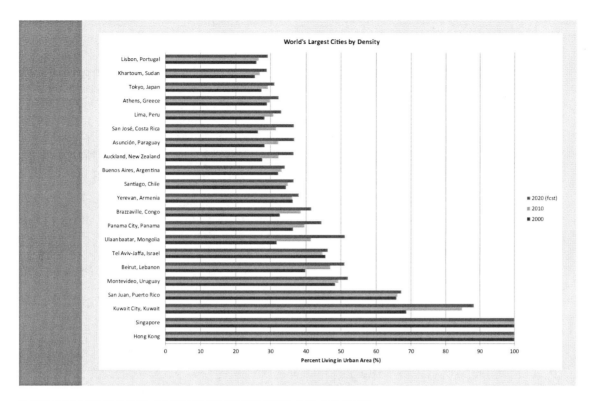

SPECIALIZATION AND THE SYSTEM OF CITIES

The agglomeration discussion so far has focused on urbanization economies. In other words, we have assumed that the productive advantages associated with clustering are determined largely by the population of the city in which a firm locates. However, evidence about external economies indicates that it is the size of the industry that matters — localization economies may be dominant.

The importance of localization economies in city growth implies that cities should specialize in just a few basic industries that complement each other. To see this, suppose that there are localization economies, but that cities are diversified. In other words, suppose that each city contains several different basic industries. The problem with this arrangement is that the basic industries do not help one another — localization economies occur within industries, not between them. This means that placing several different basic industries together in one city increases the city size and therefore the cost of living in the city, but does not add to labour productivity or wages. Thus, workers or residents are better off (their utility is higher) if each metropolitan area contains only basic industries that are related by external economies. This is the pattern that we observed in Chapter 3 when examining the industrial structure of Canada's regions.

The outcome of this process is a *system* of cities. The initial impetus for city formation may be urbanization economies. Firms' productive capacity improves by locating together because of the availability of labour, and this growth attracts even more population. However, the continued city growth is based on optimal efficiency and competitiveness, which is best achieved through specialization in a few basic industries. The city's growth from agglomeration economies arises from the localization or concentration of industry, rather than from the size of the urban population. These specialized cities trade with each other and with cities in other countries. A city's basic industries may be determined by natural resources, locational advantages, or even accidents of history. A city's optimal size is determined by the strength of localization economies in its basic industries and by its ability to accommodate large populations at modest cost.

THE ROLE OF LAND DEVELOPERS

So far we have examined economic models for how cities develop, based on a collection of individual decisions of firms and households taken collectively. Alternatively, there are a fair number of cities in North America whose formation was partly controlled or directed by a few large organizations. In some places, these organizations were governments, who disseminated land around emerging cities through homesteading policies of various sorts. In other places, city formation was heavily influenced by large landowners who directed the process to the advantage of their land holdings. Of course, these landowners did not completely control the formation of the city, but they did have important effects on urban development.

The urban economist J. Henderson studied the role of developers in the process of city formation. His argument was that competitive land developers will correct inefficiencies in city sizes. The basic idea is pretty simple. Referring to Figure 4.7, at the equilibrium size of N^{**}, every resident in the city gets utility level $v(0)$. However, if the city size could be restricted to N^*, every resident would get the higher utility level $v(N^*)$. This presents a profit opportunity: people should be willing to pay up to $v(N^*) - v(0)$ to live in a city of the optimal size. If a developer can form a new city, the developer can capture at least part of this surplus as profit. In this way, developers have an incentive to correct inefficiencies in city sizes.

Of course, developers cannot completely correct the problem of inefficient city sizes. They may lack the organizational skills or capital required for such an enormous undertaking, or they may not be able to control all of the land around a potential city site. However, the idea that developers have an incentive to try to correct inefficiencies in land development patterns is a powerful one. This, in essence, may be a fundamental role of land developers in a market economy. By acting in their own self-interest in pursuing profit opportunities, developers will often indirectly correct market failures.

Value Matters: Developer's Profit

Developers are always seeking opportunities for profitable real estate projects. For example:

- Buying raw land, subdividing it, and selling building lots;
- Buying an improved lot, demolishing the old improvements, and building something new; or
- Buying an existing building, renovating it, and re-selling for a profit.

The key to all of these is the opportunity for profit. *The Appraisal of Real Estate, 3rd Canadian Edition* says that "any building project will include an economic reward (above and beyond direct and indirect costs) sufficient to induce an entrepreneur to incur the risk associated with that project in that market". It further defines developer's profit (or loss) as the difference between the market value and the total cost of development. This is an important appraisal consideration, as it implies that market value includes not only the cost of buying land and building structures, but also compensation to the entrepreneurs who pursue these projects. *Developer's profit* or *entrepreneurial incentive* must be considered as part of the cost approach to appraisal. It is also a factor in the *residual method* or *developer's method*, where the market value of a lot with development potential is a product of the value of the new use less the costs required to pursue the opportunity, including demolition, construction, and developer's profit. The leftover amount, or residual, will be the maximum bid price for that parcel of land – or its market value for redevelopment purposes. An example of this calculation is illustrated in Chapter 5.

Key Concept: How Private Landowners Shaped Vancouver

The Canadian Pacific Railway (CPR) is responsible for much of the design and layout of the City of Vancouver. The CPR decided Granville (the original name of Vancouver) would be the terminus of the trans-Canada railway. For selecting Vancouver as the terminus, CPR received at least two privileges:

- At the suggestion of CPR's president, the settlement was renamed Vancouver, in honour of the British explorer and cartographer.
- CPR received 5,795 acres of forest in the west side of the city, 480 acres of land in and near the downtown, and 175 acres of surrounding privately held lots.

continued on next page

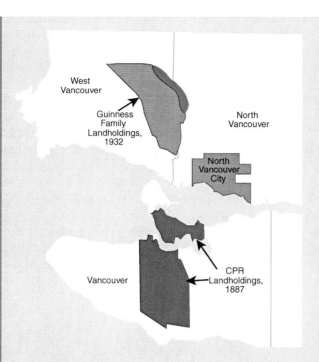

CPR embarked on a policy of extensively servicing its land, in order to raise its price. The neighbourhood of Shaughnessy, named after the CPR president, was developed in the 1920s, following the pattern of *garden cities* developed in England at the same time. Its broad streets, large trees, and elegant houses have made it one of Vancouver's most prestigious neighbourhoods.

The CPR was a powerful landowner, but it was hardly a monopoly. In 1887, CPR owned land worth about $1,000,000 out of a total value in Vancouver of about $3,250,000. However, it controlled more land than any single developers in other Canadian cities, and, as a result, had great influence in shaping its design and character.

Another large developer in the Vancouver metropolitan area was a group of investors led by the Guinness Brewing Company in the 1930s. They purchased 4,000 acres of land on the city's north shore, an area now known as the British Properties. In order to enhance the value of their holdings, in 1938, the investors built a toll bridge between the downtown and the north shore, the Lion's Gate or First Narrows Bridge. However, as with CPR, Guinness did not control all of the land. Landowners in the Municipality of North Vancouver were able to profit from the infrastructure without paying for it. In both cases, the large developers were able to profit by providing infrastructure in Vancouver, but they were not able to internalize all the benefits of their expenditures.

Other cities have examples of private developers playing a significant role in a city's development. For example, The Hudson's Bay Company in Montreal and Toyota in Toyota City played similar roles to CPR and the Guinness Company in Vancouver: dominant but not exclusive.

Source: Helsley, R.W. and Strange, W.C. 1997. "Limited Developers". *Canadian Journal of Economics*. 30(2). pp. 329-348.

SUMMARY

An economic city is a spatial cluster of economic activity where land is used intensively. Economic cities owe their formation to scale economies, in particular, to external scale economies that arise from positive externalities between firms. The evidence suggests that these external economies are such that doubling the size of an industry in a city increases labour productivity by roughly 6%. When labour productivity rises, wages will rise as well, and in this way, external economies make it possible for workers to bear the high costs of living in large urban areas.

A city is at its optimal size when the utility of residents is maximized, measured as the balance point between wages and cost of living. Beyond this optimal point, adding more citizens will lead to wage increases that do not match increased cost of living, leaving all residents worse off. From the firm's perspective, this same equilibrium point is where the marginal benefit of adding one more worker equals the marginal cost of this additional worker.

This optimal size will vary from city to city, depending on differences in industrial structure, geography, and other factors. However, there are strong reasons to suspect that, in reality, cities are larger than they should be. This is because of an externality in migration: each migrant looks at his or her own personal benefit, but ignores the impact of his or her movement on other residents. This leads to migration beyond optimal levels. Land developers have an incentive to try to correct the problem of excessive city sizes. Whether they can actually do so is an open question. However, there is no doubt that developers have played an interesting and sometimes surprising role in the formation of many cities in North America.

The next chapter discusses the important concept of bid rent — the maximum amount that a firm or household is willing to pay to use a particular parcel of land for a given time period. Bid rent helps us understand what determines how much a parcel of land is worth and what determines how a parcel of land is developed.

CHAPTER 5
LAND MARKET FUNDAMENTALS

INTRODUCTION

This chapter examines two very basic questions:

1. What determines how much a parcel of land is worth?
2. What determines how a parcel of land is developed?[1]

The key to answering both of these questions is the concept of *bid rent*. Bid rent is the maximum amount that a firm or household is willing to pay to use a particular parcel of land for a given time period. Since land is generally rented (or sold) to the highest bidder, equilibrium land use is determined by maximum bid rent. For example, if industrial uses outbid all other uses for a particular parcel, then the land in question will be used for industry and the equilibrium rent on that parcel (the rent we actually observe in the market) will be the bid rent of that industry. Equilibrium land rent is the highest of the bid rents for a particular parcel. Therefore, bid rent establishes both the *highest and best use* of the land and the rent that parcel commands. Bid rent also determines the intensity of development, such as how many stories the structures contain, or more generally, how much capital is added to the land, and also the timing of development.

> **Bid Rent**
>
> The maximum amount that a firm or household is willing to pay to use a particular parcel of land for a given time period

---

[1] The discussion in this chapter focuses on how market forces direct land development. However, many aspects of development are in reality controlled by government land use regulations. We will examine the nature and significance of these regulations later in the text.

This chapter discusses the bid rent concept from the firm's perspective, while Chapter 6 discusses the derivation of bid rent from the household's perspective.

- The first section of this chapter discusses the relationship between rent and economic profit. We will see that land rent is a residual — it is what is left over after compensating all other factors of production.
- We will examine the concept of *spatial equilibrium* — showing how bid rents vary between parcels, offsetting the inherent advantage of one site over others.
- We will explore von Thunen's famous model of how location influences land rent, with firms locating around a central market.
- The chapter closes with a discussion of how input substitution impacts the shape of bid rent curves.

Value Matters: What is Highest and Best Use?

The Appraisal Institute of Canada's *First Principles of Value* focuses on highest and best use as a key concept in all value-related assignments. It defines highest and best use as: *"that use which, at the time of appraisal, is most likely to produce the greatest net return, in money or amenities, over a given period of time"*.

It specifies further: *"A practical review of the concept necessitates an understanding of (i) legal permissions and limitations, the permissions that are available to real property, (ii) information about what permissions may practicably be available to real property, and (iii) what uses are not and would likely remain unavailable to real property. Without this knowledge the consultant/user cannot assess the various uses achievable."*

Bearing in mind these legal constraints, the highest and best use of land is not always easily determined. For example, land near urban centres in Greater Vancouver may be profitably developed into housing, but the government has constrained this development by establishing Agricultural Land Reserves (ALRs). In economic terms, the maximum bid rent can be earned by residential or commercial uses, but if these uses are not legal, they are not the land's highest and best use.

RENT AND ECONOMIC PROFIT

Generally speaking, rent is the price or cost of using a physical asset for a given time period. Rent is a payment for a flow of services – the services that an asset provides. Rental payments can be explicit, as when you rent an apartment from someone else, or implicit, as when you occupy a house that you also own. In the latter case, although no one is charging you rent each month, you still incur costs to use the asset (occupy the house). These occupancy costs would include mortgage interest payments, the opportunity cost of any equity that you have invested in the property, the opportunity cost of not renting the property to someone else, property taxes, maintenance expenditures, etc. The sum of these costs constitutes the implicit or imputed rent that you pay as an owner-occupier.

Opportunity Cost

The value someone gives up to get something else

Rent is closely related to the concept of economic profit. Recall that one of the basic characteristics of a competitive industry is that all firms in the industry earn normal profits, or zero economic profits, in the long run. The long-run equilibrium in a competitive industry is illustrated in Figure 5.1. The cost curves of a typical firm in the industry are shown on the top; the industry demand and supply curves are shown on the bottom. As noted in Chapter 2:

$$\text{profit } (\pi) = (p \times q) - C_q$$

Where:

- profit is denoted by the Greek symbol π, or pi
- $p \times q$ (price times quantity) equals total revenue, and
- C_q is total cost

To maximize profit, the firm produces where price equals marginal cost. Recall that marginal cost is the cost of the next unit of production, which tends to increase as production increases; therefore, in the short run the firm will keep increasing production as long as the units produced provide some marginal benefit above cost. However, in the long run, competitive pressures and free entry of new firms will drive economic profits to zero — excess profits are not sustainable. This implies that price must also equal average total cost, p = ATC, where average total cost is the sum of the cost of all units produced, both fixed and variable, divided by the total quantity produced.

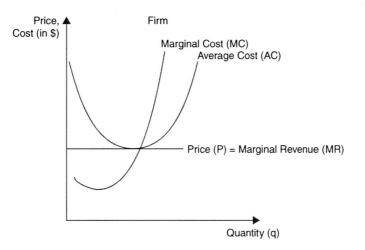

FIGURE 5.1

Long-Run Equilibrium in a Competitive Industry

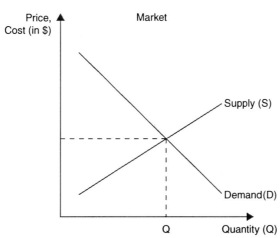

What Does Zero Economic Profit Really Mean?

Expectation of profit is the engine that drives economic activity. To be induced into producing anything, most producers need to earn an accounting profit. However, economists say that in market equilibrium most firms and people are earning zero economic profit, or their revenues are at a break-even level, just covering total costs. This may seem counter-intuitive. Zero economic profit does not mean no profit is earned, but rather *normal profit* is earned, as total costs include a degree of return on investment – otherwise why would an entrepreneur bother? However, competition tends to eliminate *excess profits* … in other words, a zero economic profit equilibrium.

The key difference between accounting profit and economic profit is *opportunity cost*. Opportunity cost is the value someone gives up in order to get something else. For example, if you took a job that paid you $40,000 and your next best offer of employment was for $39,000 then your opportunity cost of the $40,000 job was $39,000. Similarly, if you use your savings for an investment opportunity that nets you $10,000 and your next best opportunity for investing those savings would have netted $6,000, the opportunity cost of achieving the $10,000 return was $6,000. Accounting profits consider only direct cash flows: money spent and earned. Economic profit also includes these implicit amounts for potential values of goods and services.

Zero economic profit, then, is simply a condition where, after accounting for opportunity costs, revenues minus costs equal zero. In other words, a firm making zero economic profit may be making an accounting profit but that accounting profit is no higher than the next best alternative for making profit that the firm has.

continued on next page

We should expect competitive outcomes to lead to zero economic profits for most market participants, including firms, employees, and investors. For example, consider an investor: he or she is unlikely to lend money to anyone who promises a return lower than the investor could get elsewhere for the same risk, i.e., his or her opportunity cost. Similarly, the individual who is borrowing the money is unlikely to agree to pay the investor more than the investor could obtain elsewhere (again, the opportunity cost). Both parties seeking to make the best of their circumstances will tend to lead to the investor getting no less and no more than his or her opportunity cost, resulting in zero economic profits.

Thus, in the long-run equilibrium of a competitive industry, we have p = MC = ATC. This condition reminds us that the outcome of a competitive industry is efficient — the good in question is being produced at minimum cost and consumers are paying the lowest possible price for it. The firm earns normal profits, but excess economic profits are eliminated by competition — there are zero economic profits.

To see how the concepts of rent and economic profit apply to land, consider a competitive agricultural industry where farms differ in land productivity. To simplify, assume that there is just one parcel of highly productive land with excellent soil quality and an unlimited number of parcels of lower productivity land. The long-run equilibrium in this industry is illustrated in Figure 5.2. The cost curves of the high-productivity farm are shown on the far left, the cost curves of a typical low-productivity farm are shown in the centre, and the industry demand and supply curves are shown on the right. The farm that occupies the high-productivity land will face lower costs. However, since any new farm that enters the industry must occupy low-productivity land (all the high-productivity land is already occupied, by assumption), the long-run equilibrium price of the good is determined by the cost of producing on low-quality land. As a result, the high-productivity land earns an economic profit, as seen in Figure 5.2.

FIGURE 5.2

Land Rent and Economic Profit

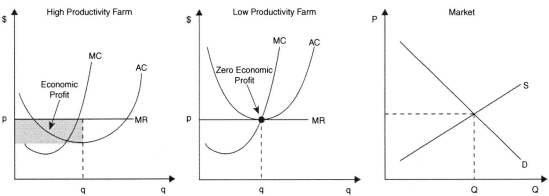

An interesting feature of Figure 5.2 is that the high-productivity farm's economic profit will persist in the long run, even though the industry is perfectly competitive. How is this possible? The answer is that the area we have referred to as profit is not really excess profit; it is a return to the productivity of the land on which this one farm is located. In fact, this profit is related to bid rent: it is the maximum value of the advantage the higher productivity land has over the less productive alternative. This profit is the maximum premium that anyone should be willing to pay to rent this land from its owner. If the farmer is the owner of the land, it is the additional amount that the farmer could receive by renting the high-quality land to someone else, i.e., by subletting the land. If we included this opportunity cost in the farmer's costs, the economic profit (after land rent) would be zero.

Leftover Principle

After non-rent costs are paid, any remaining revenues will go to land, until all economic profit is used up

This example illustrates a very general and important point: all land rent can be considered economic profit. Land rent is what is left over after all other factors of production (labour and capital) are paid their opportunity costs, known as the *leftover principle*. Being more precise, it is sometimes summarized by the phrase, "land is the residual claimant". This idea is central to all models of land markets.

EXERCISE 5.1: Land Rent for Development Land Value

The previous section illustrated how the leftover principle determines land rents and how land rents determine land use. This example demonstrates the application of the leftover principle to estimate the value of a three-acre suburban parcel of land. The process is basically an example of the *residual method* of land appraisal covered in other courses.

A developer is considering purchasing a three-acre parcel in order to develop several residential high-rise buildings with 300 condominium/strata units. In advance of the development, the prospective developer has carried out preliminary research on potential revenues and expenses from this proposed development, towards establishing an offer price for the land.

The developer and the municipality have negotiated a tentative land use contract with the following terms:

1. The developer is permitted to build 100 condominium units per acre in high-rise structures, for a total of 300 units.

2. The developer must pay a fee of $3,800 per unit to the municipality to cover costs that the municipality will incur because of the development. These fees are variously known as development cost charges (DCCs) or impact fees, and are used in many communities throughout North America to defray the public costs of new property development. For example, revenues from DCCs might be used to pay for necessary improvements to sewer lines or local streets.

3. The developer is required to construct a day care facility within the project and improve the existing public open space at the site, at a cost of $1,000 per unit.

Our estimate of value will be based on the following assumptions about the project's revenues and costs:

- Average unit size is 1,200 square feet.
- Expected selling price per square foot is $200 (less 3% market costs).
- Land servicing cost is $1,000 per unit.
- Construction cost is $100 per square foot.

The following table summarizes how a developer would calculate the residual value per unit that is attributable to land. The calculations are explained in more detail below.

Gross Revenue (per unit)		$240,000
Less Marketing Costs @ 3%		-$7,200
Net Revenue (per unit)		$232,800
Less:		
Developer's Profit @ 20%	$46,560	
Construction Costs	$120,000	
Interest (8.5% on construction cost for 6 months)	$5,100	
DCCs and Service Costs	$5,800	-$177,460
Residual (per unit)		$55,340
Total Residual		$16,602,000
Total Residual (per acre)		$5,534,000

Since each unit has 1,200 square feet of living space and the expected selling price per square foot is $200, gross revenue per unit is $240,000. To go from this revenue figure to the residual, we must subtract all the costs that the developer will incur. These fall into several categories:

- Marketing costs (the costs of selling a unit) are assumed to be 3% of gross revenue. Gross revenue minus marketing costs gives net revenue per unit of $232,800.
- The developer's profit is assumed to equal 20% of net revenue per unit. This is based on market experience of the return developers demand to compensate for risk and entrepreneurial effort (while this figure could be researched in practice, it tends to be simply based on a generally accepted rule of thumb). *continued on next page*

- At $100 per square foot, construction cost per unit is $120,000.
- The cost of interim financing for construction costs is $5,100 per unit.
- Development cost charges and servicing costs total $5,800 per unit.

These development costs total $177,460 per unit, leaving a residual of $55,340 per unit, or $5,534,000 per acre. However, this residual is a future value that will not be received until the units are sold. We want to know the land value today.

To go from the future residual to an estimate of current land value, we must consider the timing of the residual payments and discount them appropriately. If the *absorption rate* (the rate at which the units are sold) is 100 units per year, it will take three years for the developer to sell all 300 units in the project. Also assume that the appropriate *discount rate* is 9% (based on inflation, perceived risk, time preferences, and prevailing investment yields rates; prevailing yields reflect the investment's opportunity cost of capital, or the rate of return on the next best potential investment).

The present value of the residual income stream is:

$$PV = \$5,534,000 + \frac{\$5,534,000}{1.09} + \frac{\$5,534,000}{(1.09)^2} = \$15,268,921 \text{ or } \$5,089,640 \text{ per acre}$$

This net present value is the maximum amount that the developer should be willing to pay for the land. In a competitive land market, this will be the equilibrium price of the land (assuming this is indeed the land's highest and best use). This scenario demonstrates how land value is calculated as a residual; it is the revenues left over after compensating all other factors of production. Land is the residual claimant.

Note also that normal profit to the developer is included within the land value calculations. The equilibrium land rent is where economic profit is zero, but the developer still gets paid! In practical terms, land developers undertake considerable efforts with tremendous risk of personal loss – without adequate expectation of profit it is unlikely a developer would pursue these opportunities.

Absorption Rate

The rate at which real estate units are sold in a market during a particular time period

Discount Rate

An interest rate used to adjust a future cash flow to a present value by taking into account the time value of money as well as the uncertainty of the future cash flows

Residual Land Value

The value that is left over after accounting for all other costs of production; the equilibrium land rent for a property in its highest and best use

What is a Present Value?

Suppose you own a condominium that you would like to rent out for a period of five years. For the right to do so, someone offers to pay you $10,000 right now, $15,000 in at the end of year 1, and $40,000 at the end of year 5.

You are also considering an offer from someone else who wants to rent it for the same five-year period. That person has offered $10,000 right now, $16,000 at the end of year 1, and $38,000 at the end of year 5.

Which offer would you prefer?

You may say that you like the first option best, because the total nominal payment over five years is $65,000; that seems better than the second option which yields just $64,000 over five years.

Alternatively, you may say that you like the second option best, because you are impatient and you feel that getting $26,000 within the first two years is better than getting just $25,000.

continued on next page

Which view is correct? Well, it's hard to say – the differing payment timings makes each option a fundamentally different opportunity, and as the options are presently structured, it is impossible to make an informed decision.

This is where the concept of *present value* becomes useful. The present value is the current equivalent of a future dollar amount. The idea is to convert each payment stream into a single number that represents the value of that stream as if it were paid to you as an immediate lump sum. Once that is done, you will have a common metric by which to judge each option.

> **Present Value**
>
> The current equivalent of a future dollar amount

Solution using Present Values

First, assume a discount rate of 5% (the discount rate - which includes considerations for inflation, risk, opportunity cost, and your degree of patience or impatience - is typically unique to each individual and investor). Then, find the present value of each option at the discount rate. Compare the results.

$$\text{PV of Option 1}: \frac{\$10,000}{(1.05)^0} + \frac{\$15,000}{(1.05)^1} + \frac{\$40,000}{(1.05)^5} = \$55,626.76$$

$$\text{PV of Option 2}: \frac{\$10,000}{(1.05)^0} + \frac{\$16,000}{(1.05)^1} + \frac{\$38,000}{(1.05)^5} = \$55,012.09$$

Thus, given a discount rate of 5%, Option 1 is the best since it produces a higher present value. However, changing the discount rate can alter the decision.

For example, if the discount rate increased to 20% (perhaps because you view the future payments as being very risky or you are very impatient), the present values would be as follows:

$$\text{PV of Option 1}: \frac{\$10,000}{(1.20)^0} + \frac{\$15,000}{(1.20)^1} + \frac{\$40,000}{(1.20)^5} = \$38,575.10$$

$$\text{PV of Option 2}: \frac{\$10,000}{(1.20)^0} + \frac{\$16,000}{(1.20)^1} + \frac{\$38,000}{(1.20)^5} = \$38,604.68$$

Now, because our discount rate assumption has changed, Option 2 is preferred since it generates the higher present value.

BID RENT, LAND RENT, AND LAND USE

As noted earlier, bid rent is defined as the maximum amount that a firm is willing and able to pay to use a parcel of land for a given time period. The previous examples explored simple examples of how bid rent represents the economic (excess) profit earned by a firm after accounting for the other factors of production. In a competitive market, the economic rent will flow to the land value in that particular location.

Table 5.1 provides another illustration of how bid rent is determined. In this example, we have two land parcels or potential locations, one in the central city and one in the suburbs, and two types of firms, a law office and a sporting goods store. The upper panel shows each firm's revenues and costs (before land considered) for each of the locations. The leftover, or residual, is economic profit, which can be considered the bid rent for the land.

Table 5.1: Bid Rent Example		
Law Office	**Downtown**	**Suburbs**
Revenue	$500,000	$350,000
Costs (before land)	$450,000	$330,000
Economic Profit	$50,000	$20,000
Bid Rent	$50,000	$20,000
Profit after Land	0	0
Sporting Goods Store	**Downtown**	**Suburbs**
Revenue	$350,000	$600,000
Costs (before land)	$325,000	$560,000
Economic Profit	$25,000	$40,000
Bid Rent	$25,000	$40,000
Profit after Land	0	0
Highest and Best Use	Office	Store
Equilibrium Rent	$50,000	$40,000

If the law office locates downtown, it has as economic profit (before land) of $50,000 per year. If it locates in the suburbs, it has economic profit (before land) of $20,000 per year. Therefore, the downtown location is more profitable for the law firm, so they can afford a higher bid rent for the downtown land — no surprise, the analysis finds the downtown land is more valuable!

In contrast, the sporting goods store's economic profit is higher in the suburbs. The store has economic profit or bid rent of $25,000 at the downtown site and $40,000 at the suburban site. In this case, the suburban location is more profitable for the store. Their maximum bid rent for this land is $40,000.

For both stores, note that the economic profit/bid rent amounts are the maximum amounts that the firm is willing to pay for the parcels annually. Further, note that if the firm actually pays these bid rents for land, then it is indifferent between the sites. Its economic profit after land is

Spatial Equilibrium

A situation where there is no incentive or tendency for a firm to change locations

zero in either case, as it must be in a competitive industry. This is because bid rent varies between the sites to completely offset any advantage that one location may have over another. Stated another way, if the law firm actually pays these bid rents for land, then it has no reason to prefer one site over another. This situation is called a *spatial equilibrium*, since, once located, there is no incentive or tendency for the firm to change locations.

Our assumption that the land market is competitive is critical to this analysis. Literally speaking, competition requires that there be a large number of law firms just like this one competing for these sites. Competition for sites then forces each firm to actually offer the maximum amount that it is willing and able to pay for land (that is, offer its bid rent). If it offers more, it will earn negative economic profit (after land), and go out of business. If it offers less, it will never be successful in bidding for land because some other law firm could bid more for the land and still make zero economic profit (keeping in mind, once again, that zero economic profit does not mean no accounting or normal profit).

If landowners seek to maximize rental income or the value of their landholdings, then they will rent land to the highest bidder. As noted above, this defines the highest and best use of

Highest and best use is established by the highest bid rents among competing uses in a competitive land market

the land, and determines how land is allocated among competing uses. In our example, law offices outbid sporting goods stores for the downtown site, and sporting goods stores outbid law offices for the suburban site. Thus, the highest and best use of the downtown parcel is for offices, while the highest and best use of the suburban parcel is for stores. This is how land is allocated among competing uses by a competitive land market.

Equilibrium land rent is the rent that we actually observe in the market, after the market has allocated sites to their highest and best uses. Thus, equilibrium land rent is the highest of the bid rents for any site. Equilibrium land rent is $50,000 on the downtown site and $40,000 on the suburban site.

This example illustrates all of the basic principles that govern the operation of the market for land. We can summarize the fundamentals of the land market as follows.

- Bid rent is the maximum amount that a firm is willing to pay to use land for a given time period. Bid rent equals economic profit before considering land.
- Bid rent varies between parcels or locations to offset any advantage that one location may have over another. In this way, bid rents enforce a spatial equilibrium, in which firms have no incentive to change locations.
- In general, we expect land to be rented (or sold) to the highest bidder. This defines the highest and best use of the land, the maximally productive use to which land will be put in a competitive market.
- Equilibrium land rent is the highest of the bid rents for a parcel.

> **Equilibrium Land Rent**
>
> The highest bid rent among users competing for land

> **Equilibrium Land Use**
>
> The type of business or land use preferred for the land's highest bidder

Thus, bid rent is the key. It answers both of the questions at the start of this chapter — it determines what land is worth and how land is developed.

What is a Bid Rent Function?

A bid rent function describes a firm's or household's maximum ability to pay to occupy space within an area (could be a city or a market). The value the function takes on varies according to the distance that a firm or household would have to travel to get to the city centre/market. Once constructed, if someone suggests a distance from the city centre/market (say, 10 kilometres), you will be able to identify the maximum ability to pay at that location. This maximum ability to pay is the equilibrium land rent or the value of the land in that location in its highest and best use.

Value Matters: Rent and Real Estate Value

The income approach to appraisal assumes that a property's present value is a function of its capability to generate future benefits for its owner. This is known as the principle of anticipation. A property's future earning capability is usually based on the rents it can command in the marketplace. *The Appraisal of Real Estate, 3rd Canadian Edition* defines market rent as "the most probable rent that a property should bring in a competitive and open market reflecting all conditions and restrictions of the typical lease agreement, including the rental adjustment and revaluation, permitted uses, use restrictions, expense obligations, term, concessions, renewal and purchase options, and tenant improvements (TIs)". This book further distinguishes between other rental variations: contract rent, effective rent, excess rent, deficit rent, percentage rent, and overage rent. In urban appraisals, the rents applied would typically focus on real estate improvements, securing the tenant's use of all or a portion of a building (the land's use is also secured, though indirectly). Land rents are analyzed directly when long-term ground leases are involved, such as the 99-year leases often used with First Nations land.

LAND RENT AND LOCATION

In an urban land market, differences in land rent between parcels arise primarily from differences in location. For households, the most important intra-urban (within city) location factors are access to jobs, schools, and amenities. For firms, the most important factors are access to markets, transportation facilities, workers, suppliers, and other related firms. The link between land rents and location decisions was first seen in the remarkable work of Johann-Heinrich von Thunen (1783-1850).

Von Thunen was a 19th century German businessman and amateur economist. His observations of agricultural practices around his estate near the German town of Tellow led to a number of insights into the economics of location and production. Von Thunen saw that agricultural production followed an orderly geographic pattern that was centred on the local market for agricultural goods. He noticed how production was organized in rings around the town's central market, with the land use, agricultural practices, and land rents varying systematically between the rings. The goods with the highest transportation costs, at that time garden produce and dairy products, were produced in the ring immediately surrounding the market. The next ring had farm land devoted to forestry, whose outputs were less expensive to transport than those of produce and dairy farms, but heavier and more cumbersome than grain or other farm products.

Each successive ring was devoted to lower and lower transport cost goods, out to the point where the distance was so great that it was no longer economical to ship goods to the market. Beyond this *extensive margin*, land was unutilized. Remarkably, von Thunen recognized all of this as the outcome of a competitive land market. He saw that, in this case, location, rather than productivity, was the primary determinant of land rent and land use; this was a fundamental insight.

Extensive Margin

The boundary of the agricultural land area in the von Thunen model

FIGURE 5.3

von Thunen's Model

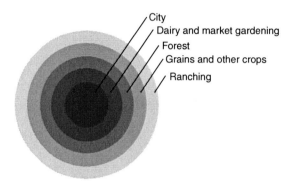

In this section, we add some mathematics and graphs to present a stylized version of *von Thunen's Model* of a spatial land market. This model is based on the following simplifying assumptions:

The von Thunen Model

A model of agricultural land use that determines the location of firms based on transportation costs and bid rents

- There is only one land use — agriculture. Land that is not used for agriculture earns no rent.
- There is a single market for agricultural goods. Everything that is produced in the region is shipped to this central market, which is presumably located in the nearest town. Let p be the price per unit that a seller receives at the market.
- All land is identical except for its distance from the market; the market is located on a flat, featureless plain. Let d represent the distance of a parcel from the market.
- Producers bear the costs of shipping. The cost of shipping one unit of output one unit of distance is t > 0. Thus, the cost of a farmer shipping his or her q units of output the d units of distance to market is (t × q × d). Notice that transport cost depends only on distance; it does not depend on direction. Think of the farms located in concentric rings around the market, like in Figure 5.3. All the farms located in any ring will have the same transport costs.
- Every farm occupies the same amount of land (ℓ), produces the same level of output (i), and incurs the same non-land production cost (c).[2]
- All markets are perfectly competitive.

Under these conditions, the profit of a farm depends on its distance from the market. Profit equals revenue minus costs. In this case costs include production costs (c), shipping costs (t × q × d), and land costs ℓ × r(d), where ℓ is land used and r(d) is the farm's bid rent per unit of land. The profit of the farm (after land is considered) is represented by π(d). In symbols:

EQUATION 5.1

$$\pi(d) = [(p \times q) - c] - [t \times q \times d] - [\ell \times r(d)]$$

Perfect competition requires that π(d) = 0. Or, in other words, the land rent for each use will be the amount that reduces the farm's economic rent to $0.

Imposing this requirement, we can solve for the bid rent function r(d):

---

[2] By assuming that lot or parcel size (ℓ) and non-land production costs (c) are constant, we are effectively assuming that farms cannot substitute other inputs for land. Factor substitution has an important impact on the shape of the bid rent function. We will examine this issue in the next section.

Set equation $= 0 = [(p \times q) - c] - [t \times q \times d] - [\ell \times r(d)]$

Add $[\ell \times r(d)]$ to both sides: $\ell \times r(d) = [(p \times q) - c] - [t \times q \times d]$

Divide all terms by ℓ: $r(d) = \dfrac{[(p \times q) - c] - [t \times q \times d]}{\ell}$

Isolate d and separate terms: $r(d) = \dfrac{(p \times q) - c}{\ell} - \dfrac{t \times q}{\ell} \times d$

EQUATION 5.2

$$r(d) = \frac{(p \times q) - c}{\ell} - \frac{t \times q}{\ell} \times d$$

After some quick algebra, Equation 5.2 gives the bid rent function r(d), which calculates the maximum amount that a farm at distance d from the market is willing to pay for a unit of land.

Figure 5.4 illustrates the r(d) bid rent function. Given the static costs, the bid rent function is a straight line, with a vertical intercept of:

$$\frac{(p \times q) - c}{\ell}$$

and a slope of:

$$-\frac{t \times q}{\ell}$$

Note that the bid rent curve extends on both sides of the market (Y-axis). This reflects the nature of the location analysis — the farm can be any distance d from market. If this were a three-dimensional graph, it would be a sphere, but then the equations would be too complex to decipher. So we will stick to two-dimensional for now.

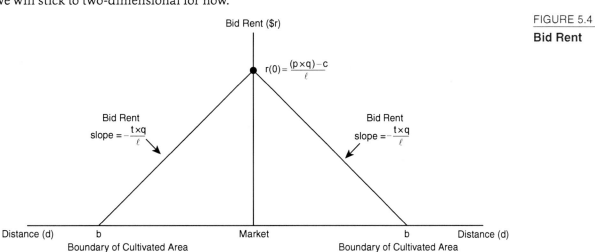

FIGURE 5.4

Bid Rent

The negative slope indicates that bid rent decreases as distance to the market increases — or put another way, land value increases with less distance to market. This makes sense intuitively — as distance d increases, it becomes more expensive to ship goods to the market, leaving a smaller residual that can be paid to land.

If land is rented to the highest bidder, then the equilibrium land rent will be the highest bid rent from any use in any particular parcel. However, in this case, since there is only one land use, r(d) is the equilibrium land rent function. The r(d) line represents the equilibrium land rent at any given location.

Suppose that a farmer moves to a parcel that is a little farther from the market. How does this change affect the farmer's profit (after considering land cost)? Expenditures on land decrease but shipping costs increase. In fact, the slope of the bid rent curve tells us that if the producer moves farther from market, expenditures on land go down by precisely the amount that transport costs go up — or vice versa for locations closer to town. Once again, there is a spatial equilibrium in the sense that producers have no incentive to change locations — economic profit after land is zero everywhere along the bid rent curve. Bid rent varies between locations to offset any advantage that one location may have over another. As noted earlier, this feature is sometimes called the *spatial equilibrium condition*. We will encounter different versions of this fundamental urban economic principle repeatedly over the next few chapters.

How much land in this example will be devoted to agriculture? Since land that is not used for agriculture earns no rent (the opportunity cost of agricultural land is zero), cultivated land extends out to the point where equilibrium land rent is zero. The boundary of the cultivated area is the distance at which r(d) = 0. In Figure 5.4, b represents the boundary of the cultivated area. Beyond this point, the bid rent for land is $0.

Let's illustrate how to solve for this bid rent boundary (b) using Equation 5.2:

$$r(d) = \frac{(p \times q) - c}{\ell} - \frac{t \times q}{\ell} \times d$$

Set r(d) = 0 and solve for d (with ℓ = 1):

Set r(d) = 0: $0 = \frac{(p \times q) - c}{\ell} - \frac{t \times q}{\ell} \times d$

Set ℓ = 1: $0 = \left[(p \times q) - c\right] - \left[t \times q \times d\right]$

Add (t × q × d) to both sides: $t \times q \times d = (p \times q) - c$

Divide both sides by t × q: $d = \frac{(p \times q) - c}{t \times q}$

Therefore, the boundary (b) of the cultivated area is:

EQUATION 5.3

$$b = \frac{(p \times q) - c}{t \times q}$$

EXERCISE 5.2: Drawing the Bid Rent Function for Land

Suppose that the only product produced is wheat; the price of a bushel at the market is $2. Assume that each farm produces 10,000 bushels per year, non-land production costs total $16,000, and each farm occupies 1 acre of land. Finally, assume that the cost of transporting a bushel of wheat to the central market is $0.05 per kilometre.

Determining the bid rent function requires applying Equation 5.2:

$$r(d) = \frac{(p \times q) - c}{\ell} - \frac{t \times q}{\ell} \times d$$

$$r(d) = \frac{[(\$2 \times 10,000) - \$16,000] - [\$0.05 \times 10,000]}{1} \times d$$

$$r(d) = \$20,000 - \$16,000 - \$500d$$

$$r(d) = \$4,000 - \$500d$$

The vertical (Y-axis) intercept is $4,000 and the slope is $500.

continued on next page

Helpful Hint

Notice that if we set d=0, we get the maximum amount a firm would be able to pay for a location at the market.

$r(d) = \$4,000 - \$500(0)$

$r(d) = \$4,000$ at the market area $(\text{vertical } Y - \text{axis intercept})$

Because the bid rent function's slope is negative, as we increase distance from the market areas, the maximum amount that can be bid declines.

This bid rent function is drawn in the figure below:

To repeat, the r(d) bid rent line shows the maximum bid rent at any given location. The boundary for cultivated land is 8 kilometres in any direction from the market. Outside of 8 kilometres, the bid rent is $0, the land has no value. Beyond this distance, transport costs are so high that farms cannot break even, even if they pay no land rent.

What is the boundary of agricultural production in this area? If the bid rent function is r(d) = $4,000 - $500d, the boundary of the cultivated area would satisfy:

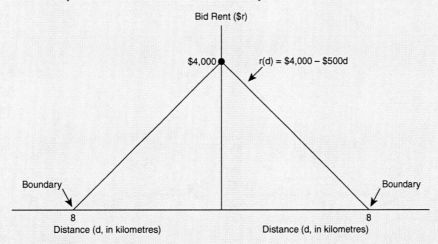

$r(b) = \$4,000 - \$500b = 0$

$0 = \$4,000 - \$500bt$

$\$500b = \$4,000$

$b = \$4,000/\$500 = 8$ kilometres

Alternatively, we could solve for b by inserting the values given for p, q, c, and t into Equation 5.3:

$$b = \frac{(p \times q) - c}{t \times q} = \frac{(\$2 \times 10,000) - \$16,000}{\$0.05 \times 10,000}$$

$$b = \frac{\$20,000 - \$16,000}{\$500} = \frac{\$4,000}{\$500} = 8 \text{ kilometres}$$

In this example, land would be used to produce wheat up to a distance of 8 kilometres from the market. Notice that this is the x-intercept point, the point on the line where it crosses the x-intercept (when y=0).

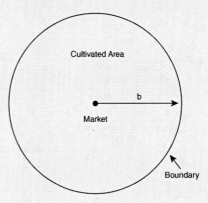

In physical terms, the actual area under cultivation is the area of the circle centred at the market with a radius of b, as shown in the figure provided.

Thus, the actual cultivated area is the area of a circle. Recall from basic geometry that the area of a circle = πr^2 where r = the radius (distance b) and π (pi) equals 3.14159. Therefore, the cultivated area = πb^2 and b is 8 kilometres. Thus, the area under cultivation is:

Area = $b^2 = \pi 8^2 = 201$ square kilometres

Extensions of the Basic Land Rent Model

Now that we have established a basic land rent model, we can begin to investigate how changes in the variables in the model affect the result. Changes to the economic environment will lead to changes in the graphs and equations. These changes can be generalized to real world urban land patterns, explaining forms and themes in city growth.

First, let's examine how changes in the price of output (p) at the market affect the land rent function. Figure 5.5 shows that an increase in p causes the land rent function r(d) to shift up or out in a parallel fashion. Thus, an increase in the price of output causes land rent to rise at every location. The graph also shows an increase in p results in a larger vertical intercept. Since r(d) shifts upward, the outer boundary of the cultivated area b increases as well. Our conclusion is that if the product that land produces becomes more valuable, then land rent and the amount of land under cultivation should increase.

An increase in non-land production cost (c) has exactly the opposite effect: it shifts the land rent function downward. This results in a smaller vertical intercept and moves the outer boundary b inward — leading to a decreased amount of land in cultivation.

FIGURE 5.5

The Effects of an Increase in the Price of Output

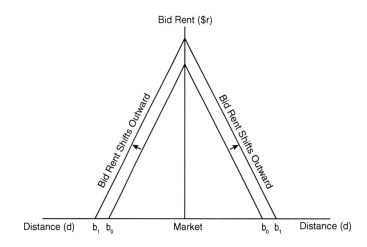

An increase in marginal transport cost (t) makes the rent function steeper, but does not affect its vertical intercept, as shown in Figure 5.6. This causes the outer boundary of the cultivated area to move inward. This makes intuitive sense: if shipping costs rise, then it is no longer feasible to farm locations that are very far from the market. However, locations close the market would experience little impact, since shipping costs are not a major expense. Conversely, a decrease in marginal transport cost (t) makes the rent function flatter, and causes the outer boundary of the cultivated area to move outward.

FIGURE 5.6

The Effects of an Increase in Transport Costs

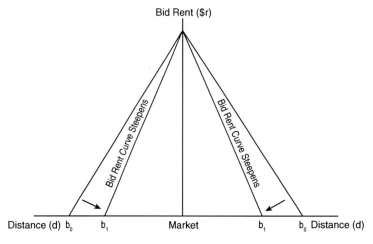

Our land rent model so far is highly simplistic, with only one good in production. Given the diversity of uses in cities, this is clearly not realistic. To examine how the market allocates land between competing uses, we need to introduce a second land use.

Suppose now that there are two economic activities in the region that compete for land around the market. Activity 1 is the production of widgets for sale in the market; Activity 2 is land cultivation for wheat. The widgets produced by Activity 1 sells for a higher price ($p_1 > p_2$). The widgets are also heavy and more expensive to transport ($t_1 > t_2$). Assume all other factors are the same between the two activities.

There are now two bid rent functions for land, reflecting the variations in price and transport cost for widget production (q_1) and wheat cultivation (q_2):

Widgets: $r_1(d) = \dfrac{(p_1 \times q_1) - c}{\ell} - \dfrac{t_1 \times q_1}{\ell} \times d$

Wheat: $r_2(d) = \dfrac{(p_2 \times q_2) - c}{\ell} - \dfrac{t_2 \times q_2}{\ell} \times d$

The higher price for widgets means its bid rent curve has a higher vertical intercept than the bid rent for wheat. As well, the higher transport costs for widgets means that its bid rent function is steeper than for wheat. These bid rent functions are drawn in Figure 5.7.

The graph demonstrates how competition for land impacts location and land rent. Each of the individual bid rent functions shows the land rents for that use at different distances (d) from the market. If each use was isolated in its own location, its bid rent would determine location, rent, and the urban boundary. However, there is only one market area, so the two uses must compete for locations. The two bid rent curves are superimposed on the same location graph, as in Figure 5.7.

Given the higher value for widget production, Activity 1 can outbid Activity 2 for locations close the market. However, widgets are also expensive to transport, so for areas far from the market Activity 2 (wheat cultivation) can outbid widget production (Activity 1). The boundary between Activities 1 and 2 lies at the point where the bid rent functions intersect, labelled b_1 on Figure 5.7.

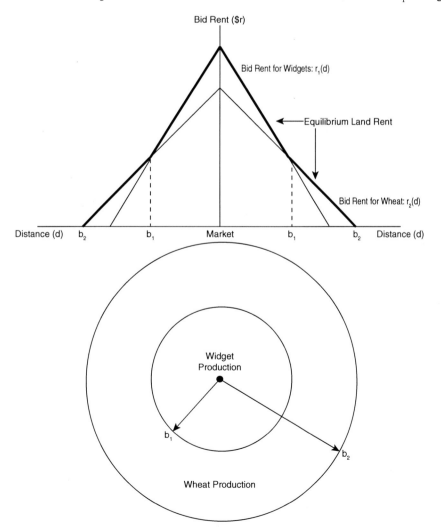

FIGURE 5.7

Equilibrium Land Rent and Land Use

The bottom graph in Figure 5.7 shows the bid rent functions as a map of the market area. There are now two distinct rings around the market. Activity 1 is the highest bidder for all land inside b1, and Activity 2 is the highest bidder for all land between b_1 and b_2. Thus, the activity with higher transport costs locates closer to the market in equilibrium, as in von Thunen's observations. Intuitively, Activity 1 has more to gain from being close to the market, and, as a result, is able to bid more for the land there.

The boundaries for each use, b_1 and b_2, can be found on the graph or by working with the equations:

- The point where the land use changes, b_1, is where the bid rent curves intersect. That means at that point the bid rents curves are equal: $r_1(b_1) = r_2(b_1)$.
- Land beyond b_2 is vacant. b_2 lies at the point where activity 2's bid rent drops to zero. To find this distance we would solve the equation $r_2(b_2) = 0$.

And what about the equilibrium land rent? At any given location, the equilibrium land rent will always be the higher of the two bid rent curves in Figure 5.7. This is intuitive, as the lower bid rent curve will be outbid by the higher bid rent curve at that location. The higher bid rent curve represents the highest and best use at that location. Therefore, for locations between the market and b_1, the equilibrium land rent is based on $r_1(d)$. For locations from b_1 to the b_2 urban boundary, the equilibrium land rent is based on $r_2(d)$.

EXERCISE 5.3: Equilibrium Land Rent with Multiple Uses

Consider a region with three land uses. The three land uses, or agricultural products, are indexed by i = 1, 2, and 3. We will solve for land rent and land use based on the von Thunen bid rent model.

The profit of a type i farm is:

$$\pi_i(d) = [(p_i \times q_i) - c_i] - [t_i \times q_i \times d] - r_i(d)$$

Where:

- $r_i(d)$ is bid rent for type i farm
- d represents distance to the market, in kilometres
- q_i represent output per farm
- p_i represents the price of output
- c_i represents non-land production costs (assumed fixed)
- t_i represents transport cost per unit output and distance
- $\ell_i = 1$; every farm uses exactly one unit of land

Assume that the farm types have equal productivity for output (q) and face uniform prices (p). The primary differences between them are cost of production (c) and transport cost (t). Assume that q_i, p_i, c_i, and t_i take on the following values:

	q_i	p_i	c_i	t_i
Product 1	1	40	10	3
Product 2	1	40	20	1
Product 3	1	40	30	1/3

Based on the above information, answer the following specific questions:

1. Derive the bid rent functions.
2. Graph the bid rent functions and illustrate the equilibrium allocation of land.
3. Solve for the boundaries between the agricultural zones.
4. Illustrate the equilibrium land rent function.
5. Illustrate how the land allocation changes if p_1 decreases to 30.

Solution

1. Derive the bid rent functions

Recall that the equilibrium land rent for any use at any location is where economic profit = $0. Thus, to find the bid rent function for each use i we set $\pi_i(d) = 0$ and then solve for $r_i(d)$:

$$\pi_i(d) = [(p_i \times q_i) - c_i] - [t_i \times q_i \times d] - r_i(d)$$
$$0 = [(p_i \times q_i) - c_i] - [t_i \times q_i \times d] - r_i(d)$$
$$r_i(d) = [(p_i \times q_i) - c_i] - [t_i \times q_i \times d]$$

continued on next page

Plugging in the values from the table above, we determine the following bid rent functions:

$r_1(d) = [(\$40 \times 1) - \$10] - [\$3 \times 1 \times d]$
$r_1(d) = \$30 - \$3d$

$r_2(d) = [(\$40 \times 1) - \$20] - [\$1 \times 1 \times d]$
$r_2(d) = \$20 - \$d$

$r_3(d) = [(\$40 \times 1) - \$30] - [\$1/3 \times 1 \times d]$
$r_3(d) = \$10 - \$(1/3)d$

2. Graph the bid rent functions and illustrate the equilibrium allocation of land

The bid rent functions are drawn in the following figure. Actually, only the right half of the bid rent functions are drawn; this convention simplifies bid rent diagrams and we will follow it from here on. To graph each of these lines, we refer to the functions above and know that the y-intercept values are $30, $20, and $10 for lines 1 to 3, respectively. To graph each line, we can refer to the slopes or solve for the boundary (b_i) on the x-axis by setting $r(d) = 0$ for each function. That will produce the value where each line crosses the x-axis:

$r_1(d) = \$30 - \$3d$
$0 = \$30 - \$3d$
$\$3d = \$30$
$d = 10$ kilometres

$r_2(d) = \$20 - \$d$
$0 = \$20 - \$d$
$d = 20$ kilometres

$r_3(d) = \$10 - \$(1/3)d$
$0 = \$10 - \$(1/3)d$
$\$1/3d = \$10$
$d = 30$ kilometres

Combining the three bid rent functions on one graph show that type 1 farms can pay the highest land rent closest to market, type 3 farms can pay the highest rents for outlying land, and type 2 farms occupy the middle land. This equilibrium land use is illustrated by the dark line on the following figure. This could also be drawn as concentric circles from the market outward, with the type 1 farms occupying land in the bullseye, type 2 in the next circle, then type 3, and then unused land outside this.

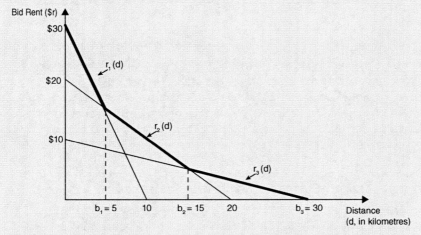

3. Solve for the boundaries between the agricultural zones

To find the boundaries of the rings, we find where the bid rent functions intersect. These intersection points are exact locations where there is a change in who is the highest bidder for the land. These points could be found directly on the graph or by solving with the equations.

At point b_1, the boundary between type 1 and 2 farms, the bid rent will be identical between type 1 and type 2 farms. In equation terms, this means $r_1(b_1) = r_2(b_1)$

continued on next page

Inserting the bid rent functions:	$30 - \$3b_1 = \$20 - \$b_1$
This implies:	$\$2b1 = \$10$
	$b_1 = 5$ kilometres

b_2, the boundary between type 2 and 3 farms, satisfies $r_2(b_2) = r_3(b_2)$

Inserting the bid rent functions:	$\$20 - \$b_2 = \$10 - (\$1/3)b_2$
This implies:	$(\$2/3)b_2 = \$10$
	$b_2 = 15$ kilometres

b_3, the outer boundary of the cultivated area, satisfies $r_3(b_3) = 0$

Inserting the bid rent function:	$\$10 - (\$1/3)b_3 = 0$
This implies:	$\$10 = (\$1/3)b_3$
	$b_3 = 30$ kilometres

4. Illustrate the equilibrium land rent function

Equilibrium land rent is the upper envelope of the bid rent functions of the three types of farms. Equilibrium land rent is indicated by the dark line in the above figure.

5. Illustrate how the land allocation changes if p_1 decreases to 30

If the price of output from the type 1 farm (p_1) decreases from $40 to $30, then the new bid rent function for this type 1 land becomes $r_1(d) = \$20 - \$3d$. The revised $r_1(d)$ bid rent line is shown in the following figure.

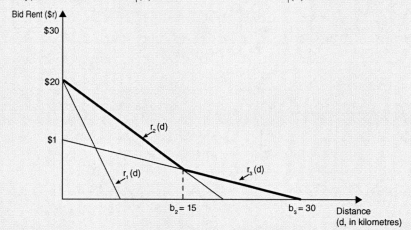

Due to the lower price for its agricultural output, the bid rent curve for type 1 farms is now below the other bid rent curves in all locations – their bid rent is now smaller than that of type 2 farms at every location. This means that type 1 farms now cannot successfully outbid other farm types in any location, meaning type 1 farms can no longer compete for land. The new equilibrium shown indicates that type 2 farms now occupy all land up to the boundary $b_2 = 15$; there are only two land uses in the region in equilibrium. Equilibrium land rent is once again represented by the dark line in the figure.

Value Matters: Von Thunen, Bid Rent, and Highest and Best Use

Returning to this appraisal concept, the highest and best use represents the most profitable legal use of the land. This is reflected by the shaded line from the bid rent curves. As we will see in urban examples coming up soon, the highest value bid rent use near a city's downtown may be office buildings, surrounded by retail, then residential, then agricultural in the outlying areas. Von Thunen's land rent model is one of the primary theories for the development of cities. For the example above, the type 1 farms cannot compete in any location, so that use is never the highest and best use. In our simple city context, this could represent a nuclear power plant or pulp mill – uses that may have value on land somewhere, but that cannot compete for land in the urban area under study.

THE SHAPE OF THE BID RENT FUNCTION

Our presentation of the von Thunen model has been highly simplified, with a number of special assumptions. These assumptions are unrealistic, but are necessary to make the model simple enough to illustrate basic concepts. Reality is much messier — this complexity makes is difficult to discern the patterns. Over the next few chapters, we will relax many of these assumptions, as we build in more realism in describing and explaining urban land markets. However, there is one assumption that we should consider at this early stage.

Our simple von Thunen model assumed that each farm in the region uses the same amount of land regardless of where it locates. This is inconsistent with what we observe in every land market in the world, namely, that where land is expensive, it is used intensively. Rather than using the same amount of land at every location, it is more reasonable to assume that farms will use less land where land is costly. Thus, lot size (ℓ) should not be constant. Rather, since land becomes less expensive as we move away from the market, lot sizes should rise as distance to the market increases. In other words, we should find smaller and more compact farms close to the market and larger farms further away.

Furthermore, if farms (or firms) can substitute a less expensive input, then they will economize on inputs that are relatively more expensive. As we will see in the next chapter, this process of input substitution explains the most basic characteristic of a city, namely, that the tallest buildings are located downtown, where land is expensive. In the downtown, real estate services are produced from structures that combine a great deal of capital with a small amount of land. This is the result of input substitution — substituting the more expensive input (land) with a less expensive input (capital, to build taller buildings). Input substitution changes the shape of the bid rent function for land.

With input substitution, the bid rent function takes the convex shape shown in Figure 5.8. If the firm can substitute other inputs for land, then firms will demand less land near the market, but should use this land more intensively. Farms near the market may produce the same output as outlying farms, but with only a fraction of the land — they are forced to be more productive with this expensive land asset. In contrast, farms in the outlying areas have little incentive to become more productive, since land is inexpensive — they will not need to invest capital as a substitute for land. Land rent will be highest near the market, then should decline very quickly as distance from the market increases. Input substitution will play an important role in our subsequent discussions of urban land markets.

Input Substitution

Where possible, firms will substitute more expensive inputs with less expensive ones; in real estate terms, this means more expensive land is used more intensively, substituting capital investment (e.g., buildings or other assets) for land.

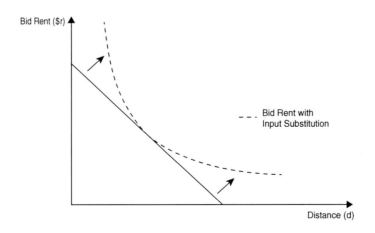

FIGURE 5.8

Bid Rent with Input Substitution

Value Matters: Scope of Work

The Von Thunen bid rent model is an elegantly simple model for illustrating fundamental reasons for how and why cities form. It is easy to understand, largely due to its very strict underlying assumptions. The trade-off for this ease of understanding is its limitations in addressing messy real world complications. Subsequent researchers add twists to the basic model to explore these complications. However, this added realism inevitably comes with a cost of lessened clarity. A researcher is faced with the choice of a simplistic model that is easy to understand, but limited in application, versus a more complex model that better explains complexities, but is more difficult to grasp.

Appraisers face this same conundrum in analyzing market value. Say you are tasked with valuing a large office building in downtown Toronto. You could carry out a simple analysis of capitalization rates that can be summarized on a single page. Or you might present hundreds of pages of discounted cash flow analysis that delves deeply into countless details about the subject property, competing properties, and the marketplace. Which is better? A simple model that is easy to comprehend for the client and other readers, but leaves many avenues unexplored? Or an intensely detailed analysis that explicitly considers all known attributes and imaginable risks, but in a dense report that is difficult to follow?

There is no clear right or wrong answer, as it depends on the circumstances: the needs of the client, the purpose of the assignment, and the intended use of the report. One consideration is the degree of due diligence necessary to support the value estimate, e.g., a report that must be defended in court under vigorous cross-examination. Another is the level of research and analysis the client is willing to pay for! (As well as the related concept of your need to complete *credible* work that fulfills your ethical obligations as a valuation professional). These considerations all combine into the appraiser's need to define the *scope of work* at the start of an assignment: an agreement with the client in advance about the problem to be solved, how you intend to tackle it, the timing expectations, and the compensation involved. For any given assignment, the approach may be highly simplistic or intensely complicated -- what matters most is that you are addressing both the client's expectations and your own professional requirements.

SUMMARY

This chapter developed the basic principles that govern the operation of a land market. The key concept is bid rent — the maximum amount that a firm is willing to pay to use a parcel of land for a given time period. Bid rent determines how land is used and how much land is worth. Bid rent can also be used to explain the pattern of land use over space.

We explored this idea in the context of von Thunen's model of the location of agriculture around a central market (and noted that it will play an important role in the models of cities and urban land markets that follow in subsequent chapters). Most of the illustrations in this chapter used a simplifying assumption that economic activities could not vary the intensity with which they use land. This is inconsistent with the operation of land markets in the real world. We showed that if activities can substitute other inputs for land, then the bid rent function should have a convex shape. The next chapter expands the von Thunen model of an agricultural region into a simple economic model of a city.

Key Concept: Bid Rent and Households

Bid rent is comprised of a residual. Firms earn revenues, pay production costs, and pay transportation costs. The amount that is left over is the residual. That residual represents the maximum amount a firm could bid in an effort to move to a desirable location.

Similarly, households earn income, some of which is used to fund food, recreation, and transportation. Whatever amount remains after those expenses are satisfied can be used to bid for shelter – and the more desirable the location, the higher the bid rent. This will be explored in the next chapter.

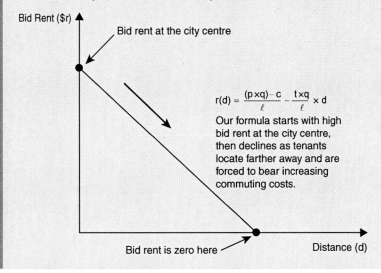

$$r(d) = \frac{(p \times q) - c}{\ell} - \frac{t \times q}{\ell} \times d$$

Our formula starts with high bid rent at the city centre, then declines as tenants locate farther away and are forced to bear increasing commuting costs.

INTRODUCTION

Before 1850, most transportation between cities occurred by water. This is why most of the world's major cities are located at natural harbours or on waterways: manufacturing firms were drawn to locations with easy access to shipping. Also, transportation within cities was slow and cumbersome. Personal transportation was mostly done by horse and wagon. Businesses communicated through individual messengers, even after the development of the telegraph.

The cost and inconvenience of transportation had a profound impact on the way our cities developed — it led to the formation of core-dominated urban areas. Early industrial cities had three common features:

1. Manufacturing activities tended to cluster around a transportation facility (a port or railroad terminal) that was used to export products to other cities and regions.
2. Other ancillary businesses tended to locate near the manufacturing core, to economize on the high cost of moving goods and information within cities.
3. Workers tended to live just outside the manufacturing-commercial core to economize on the high cost of commuting — prior to the development of the street car, walking was the principal means of commuting!

As a result, most employment in 19th century cities was concentrated around the port or railroad terminal, which became the de facto city centre, and most workers commuted from the surrounding residential area to jobs in the downtown.

In this chapter we will examine a simple economic model of such a core-dominated city. This model, building on von Thunen's foundations introduced in Chapter 5, is very important. In fact, it is the cornerstone of modern urban economics. The framework developed in this chapter will let us examine:

- How property values vary within a city;
- How land use varies within a city, including both the type of development (businesses or housing) and the intensity of development (building heights or population density);
- How the geographic size of a city is determined; and
- How property markets respond to changes in the economic environment.

We will use the ideas and concepts developed in this chapter throughout the remainder of the course.

The first section of this chapter lays out the basic assumptions of the "Monocentric City" model. The following section examines the location decisions of households and their implications for land rent. We then derive the bid rent function for residential land (in contrast to Chapter 5, which derived bid rent for firms), and discuss how the boundary of the city is determined. Finally, we extend the model to incorporate competing land uses.

A MONOCENTRIC CITY

In this chapter, we will continue to use von Thunen's insights to study the operation of urban land markets. Our next step is to build on von Thunen's model of an agricultural region, towards the development of a simple economic model of a city. Our model is built on a number of assumptions:[1]

1. The city is located on a flat, featureless plane. Land that is not occupied by the city is the hinterland, used for agriculture. The rent per unit of agricultural land is r^a, a positive constant.
2. The city has a single, predetermined centre. Because of this, the model is generally known as the *monocentric model*. The city centre is where all the jobs are assumed to be located. The city centre could be the site of a natural port or railroad terminal around which economic activity is organized.
3. There are N identical residents in the city. These residents all earn the same income. Each resident occupies one household (so you can consider these terms interchangeable). Each resident commutes to the city centre each day. There are no rivers or mountains to impede travel in the city. In fact, there aren't even any roads. Commuting occurs along a line connecting a household's residence and the city centre. All that matters in this model is how far you live from the city centre; direction is irrelevant. Distance to the city centre is denoted by d, measured in kilometres. Commuting cost is t per kilometre — so the round trip cost of commuting is t × d.
4. All markets are assumed to be perfectly competitive. As discussed in Chapter 5, this implies that land is rented to the highest bidder.

The simple geography of our monocentric city is illustrated in Figure 6.1.

Monocentric City

A simplified model of urban development where a city is assumed to have a single manufacturing-focused centre to which residents from surrounding areas commute

This monocentric model has a simplification from the similar concepts developed in Chapter 5 and that is where firms locate. In Chapter 5, firms chose locations at varying distances from a central market and shipped their goods to the market. In the monocentric city, we instead assume the firms are located in the central city and the workers choose household locations at varying distances from their employment. In effect, this is much the same model, with the key difference being each resident/household is acting like a firm and the product they are transporting to the "market" is his or her own labour!

---

[1] The assumptions that underlie the monocentric model are unrealistic. However, the simplifications are necessary to highlight the underlying principles. We will relax many of these assumptions and consider more complex problems later in the text.

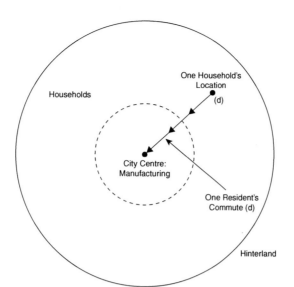

FIGURE 6.1

The Simple Geography of a Monocentric City

HOUSEHOLD LOCATION AND URBAN LAND RENT

Standard models of consumer behaviour focus on how people choose to consume various goods and services. In extending this to our residential land model, consumers must decide how much residential product they wish to "consume". However, they must also decide where to live. We are, in effect, extending the theory of consumer behaviour to include a household's location decision.

We assume that each consumer/resident/household has a fixed income from which to budget household expenditures and purchases of other goods. The consumer has to make choices between these two goods. If they want to occupy more land, it will cost them more (and for simplicity in this illustration we will assume that land prices are constant in all areas, so location does not matter for now ... we will relax this assumption shortly). The consumer's goal is to find the combination within this budget that maximizes overall *utility* or satisfaction. For example, a consumer may choose to have a large lot and have little money for other goods; or they may choose a small lot and have money left over to buy consumer goods.

This decision requires making economic trade-offs. To illustrate this thinking process in economic terms, we will apply two tools: budget line/constraints and indifference curves.

An *indifference curve* is a graph connecting bundles of consumption that the consumer finds equally desirable. Figure 6.2 illustrates the trade-off between lot size (ℓ) and consumption of other goods (x). On each curved line, the consumer is equally satisfied with any combination of goods that exist on that line. The curves extend outward for higher budget amounts, where the consumer can afford more of everything. Lines further right have greater satisfaction or utility. However, the budget will limit how high an indifference curve the consumer can reach.

Indifference Curve

A graph of the bundles of consumption that a consumer finds equally desirable; the curves extend outward for higher budget amounts

In economic terms, the consumer's utility is described by the utility function,[2] $u(\ell,x)$, where:

- u represents utility
- ℓ represents the amount of land that the household occupies (measured in acres, hectares, or some other area measure)
- x represents all other goods

The utility function $u(\ell,x)$ gives the level of utility that the household receives from the bundle (ℓ,x). Each indifference curve in Figure 6.2 illustrates one combination land versus all other goods that gives the same level of utility.

---

[2] We state this as: "u is a function of ℓ and x". This means that utility depends on the amount of occupied land and the consumption of other goods.

FIGURE 6.2

**A Household's
Indifference
Curves**

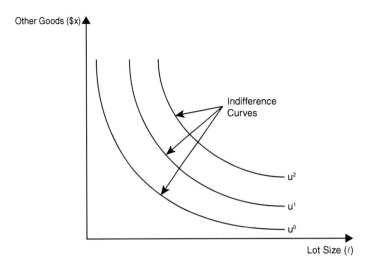

In theory, each individual has an infinite number of indifference curves for bundles of consumer goods and his or her satisfaction. Some key features of these curves are:

- Higher indifference curves represent higher utility (i.e., more is better)
- Indifference curves are downward sloping, which just means that when consumers give up some of one good, they need to be compensated with more of another good to maintain the same level of satisfaction. The slope of an indifference curve (often called the marginal rate of substitution) changes as one moves along the curve, but at any given point on the curve, the slope represents the ability of the consumer to trade off the consumption of one good for another and remain just as satisfied by the resulting bundle.
- Indifference curves are bowed inward, which can be interpreted as "consumers like variety". Notice that when our hypothetical consumer is already consuming a lot of land, he or she is willing to give up a lot of it in order to enjoy just a little bit more of the other goods; conversely, when the consumer is already consuming a lot of the other goods, he or she is willing to give up a lot of them in order to enjoy just a little bit more land.

Budget Line/Constraint

The fixed budget that limits the consumption bundles that a consumer can afford

As noted above, a consumer will choose the highest indifference curve possible, to achieve maximum highest satisfaction. However, being realistic, a consumer's choices will be constrained by limited income. Just as the indifference curves above show a trade-off between land and all other goods in terms of desirability, we also need to be able to represent that trade-off in terms of affordability. That is achieved with the *budget line/constraint*. For any given budget or income, this line shows:

- How much land could be occupied if no other goods are consumed;
- How much non-land goods can be consumed if no land is occupied; and
- All the possibilities in-between the above two extremes.

Like an indifference curve, a budget line shows a combination of land (ℓ) and other goods (x) that can be purchased. The difference is that instead of showing utility or satisfaction, the budget/line constraints shows possible combinations at a set level of income. This consumer could buy all land or all goods, or any combination of land and goods that lies along this line. The consumer cannot afford any combinations to the right of this line. Combinations to the left of this line would not spend all of the available funds, so would have less utility/satisfaction. Therefore, the consumer's purchasing choice must fall along this line.

The *budget line/constraint* in our case is given by the following equation:

EQUATION 6.1

$$(r \times \ell) + x = I - (t \times d)$$

Where:

- r is rent per unit of land and ℓ is the quantity of land consumed; therefore, r × ℓ equals expenditures on land
- x equals expenditures on other goods (to simplify matters, we assume that the price of the composite good x equals 1, so that we do not need to specify price in the equation)

- I is income
- t × d equals expenditures on commuting or transportation

The left side of Equation 6.1 gives expenditures on land and other goods and the right side provides income net of commuting costs. Thus, the budget line says that expenditures on land and other goods must equal income net of commuting costs. Note the intercepts of the budget line on the two axes. If the household consumes no land, then it can consume [I − (t × d)] dollars on other goods (x) – to find this amount, you could set ℓ = 0 in Equation 6.1. Conversely, if the household consumes no "other goods" (x = $0), then it can consume:

$$\frac{I - (t \times d)}{r} \text{ units of land}$$

The budget line connects these two points (as shown in Figure 6.3).

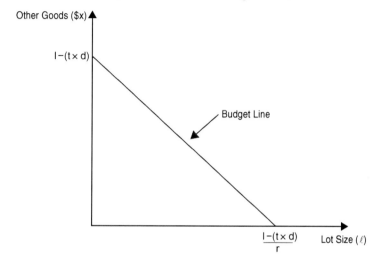

FIGURE 6.3

A Household's Budget Line

Now we combine the consumer's indifference curves and budget constraint onto one graph, as shown in Figure 6.4. The indifference curves are all about desirability and the budget constraint is all about affordability. The consumer's budget is set by his or her income; the consumer's choice is to select the bundle of goods that gives the highest possible level of utility or satisfaction. This is where our indifference curves prove their usefulness. The point on the budget line that gives the highest level of utility will be **the point that just touches the highest indifference curve that the consumer can reach**. At this point, this highest indifference curve and the budget line are tangent (parallel) and have the same slope.[3] The household's optimum choice is shown in Figure 6.4.

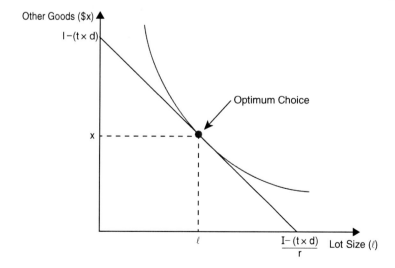

FIGURE 6.4

A Household's Optimum Choice

---

[3] A curve has a different slope at every point along it – picture holding a ruler alongside the curve to identify its slope, the ruler will have to be turned with any move along the curve. Tangent means the point on the curve where its slope is the same slope as the straight budget line.

Helpful Hint: What is "Optimum" Choice for a Household?

Households maximize their utility when they choose the bundle of land and non-land goods that:

1. is on their budget constraint; and
2. is located where the budget line and indifference curve are tangent.

Spatial Equilibrium

The section above highlights that consumers will make buying decisions based on maximizing their satisfaction when faced with scarcity — after all, we are all limited by a budget. The illustration demonstrated how a consumer will evaluate available choices and select his or her most satisfying overall combination of housing versus other goods.

However, this illustration was highly simplistic in a number of ways. Most notably, it assumed that location does not matter. The resident could locate anywhere in the city, with the same land cost and with no impact on the time and expense for commuting to work. Sadly, we can all recognize this is not realistic – shelter is first among our consuming choices, and all workers have to decide on the optimal combination of real estate costs versus commuting. For example, one person might choose to live in a house in the suburbs and spend an hour driving to work every day; another might choose a small condominium downtown and walk to work. Both reflect economic choices — and, theoretically, these choices could be mapped with indifference curves and budget constraints to find the optimal bundle for each individual. Location, and its impact on cost, is one more complication we must build into our model.

We have already established that a key principle of a competitive land market is that rent varies between locations to offset any advantage that one location may have over another. Based on the monocentric city model, land rent will decline with distance from the city centre. We will demonstrate this point in two ways: in an intuitive fashion, and then more precisely, using the indifference curves and budget lines introduced previously.

Figure 6.5 illustrates a basic relationship between land rent (r) and distance from the city centre (d). First, let's assume that equilibrium land rent is the same at every distance from the city centre, as shown by the dashed line $r(d)^0$ in the figure. Now compare two locations, d_1 and d_2. The land rent is the same in both locations, but the consumer living at d_1 pays less in commuting costs, since he or she travels a shorter distance to get to work. This means that this consumer's net income — what is left over after paying bid rent and commuting to work — is higher than that of a consumer living at d_2. Because land rent at the two locations is the same by assumption, the consumer living at d_1 must have more income left over to spend on other goods. This implies that the consumer living at d_1 is better off (can reach a higher level of utility) than the consumer living at d_2. As a result, the consumers living at d_2 will want to move to d_1; the initial situation cannot possibly have been an equilibrium.

FIGURE 6.5

Land Rent and Distance

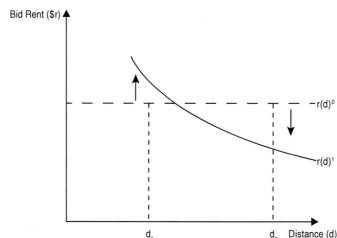

If consumers want to move from d_2 to d_1, this means more demand for something that has relatively fixed supply.[4] Unlike consumer goods like cars or cell phones, it is often difficult to supply

---

[4] As noted in earlier chapters, land supply can be somewhat flexible. Developers can drain swamps, shape terrain, and even infill ocean areas to make available more usable land for buildings.

more of the d_1 land to satisfy increased demand. That means the increased demand for land at d_1 will cause the price of land there to increase. Households face lower commuting costs at d_1 and they should be willing to bid at least these cost savings for land at d_1. If the rents at d_1 increase to a point that exactly matches the savings in commuting costs, then the consumer will have the same utility in either location. There is no cost advantage to d_1 and effectively no incentive to move.

At the same time, d_2 has become less attractive. Commuting costs are higher and people want to move to d_1 to save this expense. As people move away, the demand for d_2 land decreases and land rents will also drop in this location. Again, if land prices drop by the exact amount of the higher commuting costs, then households have the same utility in either location and no incentive to move. Therefore, we have arrived at spatial equilibrium.

In equilibrium in a monocentric city, land rents cannot be the same everywhere. Rather, to compensate for savings in commuting costs, households close to the city centre (d_1) will face higher land costs. Households farther from the city centre (d_2) will pay less for land. The bid rent line is the solid curve $r(d)$[1] shown by the solid line in Figure 6.5. This curve shows the equilibrium land rent. Equilibrium requires that identical households must reach the same level of utility in equilibrium. Otherwise, someone will have an incentive to change his or her behaviour.

This simple model highlights a basic urban land economic principle: controlling for other influences, the price of real estate declines as distance to the city centre increases in virtually all urban areas. We will explore this principle further in Chapter 7.

BID RENT, EQUILIBRIUM LAND RENT, AND CITY SIZE

We have now established that land near the city centre will be more expensive than land in the city's outskirts. The obvious follow-up question, for real estate professionals and market participants, is how much more expensive? What is the spatial pattern of equilibrium land rents?

The key determinant of land rents in different locations is the slope of the bid rent curve $r(d)$. The following sections examine bid rent and equilibrium land rent under different assumptions: fixed lot sizes, flexible lot sizes, and changes in the economic environment.

Key Concept: Bid Rents and "Residual"

Remember that bid rent functions are meant to describe the ability of a given user to pay for real estate. For both firms and households, bid rent is comprised of a leftover or *residual* after paying other non-real estate expenses. Households earn income, some of which is used to fund food, recreation, and commuting costs. Whatever amount remains after those expenses are satisfied can be used to bid for real estate.

Firms are similar – they earn revenues and pay production costs and pay transportation costs. The amount that is left over is the residual. That residual represents the maximum amount a firm could bid in an effort to move to a desirable location. The residual is the economic land rent in equilibrium and is the point where economic profits are reduced to $0 (though keeping in mind that the firm still makes normal profits as a part of its regular business costs).

Bid Rent with Fixed Lot Sizes

To begin our examination of land rents and location, we start with a simplifying assumption: lot sizes are fixed. No matter where a consumer lives, he or she consumes the same amount of land. In other words, the demand for land is perfectly inelastic (in contrast, in an elastic land demand market, cheaper land would mean you would want to consume more).

The variable ℓ^* will represent this fixed and common level of land consumption. Now, if each household consumes a fixed amount of land, then in order to achieve the same level of utility according to the utility function $u(\ell,x)$, each household must also consume a fixed quantity of other goods. Let x^* represent this fixed and common level of other goods consumption. Substituting ℓ^* and x^* into the budget line from Equation 6.1, we have:

EQUATION 6.2

$$(r \times \ell^*) + x^* = I - (t \times d)$$

We will follow a similar process to how we solved for r in Chapter 5. Similar to Equation 5.2, we find the following bid rent formula:

EQUATION 6.3

$$r(d) = \frac{I - x^*}{\ell^*} - \frac{t}{\ell^*} \times d$$

The equation for r(d) provides the consumer's bid rent function for land, under the assumption that lot sizes are fixed at ℓ^* (and other goods are fixed at x^*).

Figure 6.6 graphs the bid rent functions. Note that r(d) is a linear (straight-line) function of distance.

The Y-intercept of the bid rent function is the value of land at the city centre (d=0). Setting d to 0 in Equation 6.3 gives r(0) =(I − x*)/ℓ^*. This is noted on Figure 6.6 — again, this is the maximum amount that a household would be willing to bid for a unit of land located at the city centre.

FIGURE 6.6

Bid Rent with Fixed Lot Sizes

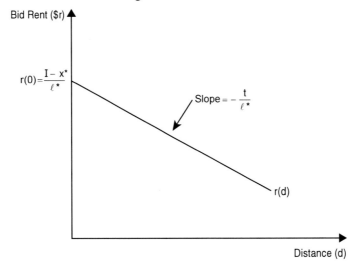

The slope of the bid rent function is:

EQUATION 6.4

$$-\frac{t}{\ell^*}$$

The slope of the bid rent function is negative — a logical result — since movement away from the city centre increases commuting costs, this will cause land rents to decrease by exactly this amount in equilibrium. The rate of decrease in land rents is t/ℓ^* — but with lot size constant, the rate of decrease will be directly related to t, commuting cost.

The bid rent at any point on this line represents the maximum amount that a consumer can pay for a unit of land at distance d and still achieve utility level u*. Bid rents vary across locations so that identical consumers get the same utility at every location. In this equilibrium state, no one has an incentive to relocate.

EXERCISE 6.1: Location and Bid Rent

Consider a monocentric city in which every household occupies 1/4 of an acre of land (ℓ^* = 0.25 acres). Assume that the cost of commuting for each household is $40 per kilometre per month, round trip (t = $40). This means that someone who commutes 10 kilometres to work, one way, incurs commuting costs equal to $400 per month, or $4,800 per year. In addition, assume that a lot 20 kilometres from the city centre rents for $1,000 per month. Finally, assume that lots sizes are fixed throughout the city region (meaning the resulting bid rent function is linear).

What is bid rent per acre at d = 10 kilometres?

continued on next page

Solution:

1. We know bid rent per lot is $1,000 per month at d=20. Let's scale up to bid rent per acre. If each lot takes up a quarter of an acre, then there must be room for four lots per acre. Therefore, we can multiply $1,000 by 4 to determine bid rent of $4,000 per acre per month at d=20.
2. We know that the cost of commuting per household is $40. Let's scale up to find the cost of commuting for the number of households that would occupy an acre, i.e., four. To do so, we just need to multiply $40 by 4, to obtain $160 per month (note that this is t/ℓ).
3. If all four households occupying an acre picked up and moved a kilometre closer to the city centre, they would collectively save $160 per month. Because people will bid up the price of real estate in order to avoid transportation costs, we know that the value of an acre one kilometre closer to the city centre must be $160 greater.
4. Therefore, if bid rent is $4,000 per acre at d=20, then bid rent per acre 10 kilometres closer to the city centre, at d=10, must equal $4,000 + ($160 × 10), or $5,600.

We can see from Equation 6.3 how changes in the parameters of the problem affect the bid rent function. For example, an increase in marginal commuting cost (t) will make the bid rent function steeper. An increase in income (I) will cause the entire bid rent function to shift outward in a parallel fashion — meaning land rents are higher at all distances from the city centre (and the outward boundary of our monocentric city expands).

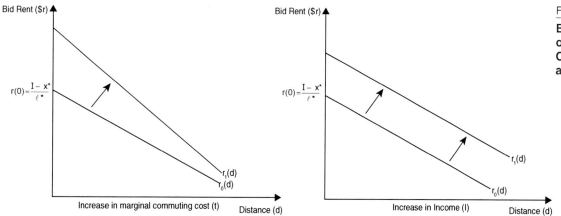

FIGURE 6.7

Bid Rent: Impact of Increases in Community Costs and Income

If the consumption of other goods (x*) changes, because land consumption is fixed, this changes the overall utility level (u*) of households in the city. This means an increase in spending on other goods (x*) will lead to lower bid rents. This makes intuitive sense: the only way consumers at a given distance can have more money to spend on other goods is if they spend less on land. A higher level of x* with the same amount of land, means higher overall utility (u*). Conversely, a decrease in u* from less spending on other goods (x*) would be associated with higher bid rents. This would have the same impact on bid rents as the increase in income (I) illustrated in Figure 6.7.

Equilibrium Land Rent and City Size

The slope of the bid rent function ensures that identical households are indifferent among locations. There are two additional conditions that determine the level of equilibrium land rents and the size of the city:

1. land is rented to the highest bidder and
2. everyone in the city must have a place to live

The demand for land and the supply of land must be in balance.

The first condition is the familiar requirement that land is rented to the highest bidder. There are only two competing land uses in this simple model: the urban use, with bid rent r(d) (varying with distance to the city centre) and the agricultural use outside city limits, with bid rent

r^a (not dependent on distance to the city centre). If land is occupied by the highest bidder, then the city will occupy all land where the urban bid rent is higher than what agricultural users will offer, or $r(d) \geq r^a$. Since bid rent declines with distance, and there are no impediments to urban development (like rivers or mountains), the area occupied by the city will be a circle of radius b. The boundary of the city, b, is where the city use ends and the agricultural hinterland begins. At this boundary b, the bid rent will be the agricultural rent, or $r(b) = r^a$.

The urban bid rent equation that accounts for these competing uses is derived as follows:

First we substitute $r(b) = r^a$ into Equation 6.3:

$$\frac{I - x^*}{\ell^*} - \frac{t}{\ell^*} \times b = r^a$$

This implies that:

$$\frac{I - x^*}{\ell^*} = r^a + \frac{t}{\ell^*} \times b$$

Substituting this expression back in Equation 6.3, we can rewrite the bid rent function for land as:

$$r(d) = r^a + \frac{t}{\ell^*} \times b - \frac{t}{\ell^*} \times d$$

By combining the like terms (t/ℓ^*), the equation simplifies to:

EQUATION 6.5

$$r(d) = r^a + \left(\frac{t}{\ell^*}\right) \times (b - d)$$

Equation 6.5 accounts for the competition for land between urban and agricultural uses. This is useful because it emphasizes that there are two components to bid rent in this model: agricultural rent and location rent. Agricultural rent (r^a) is the opportunity cost of urban land; this opportunity cost is effectively present at all locations in the city, because any location in the city could revert to agriculture if the urban bid rent is not high enough. Agricultural rent is the automatic default option for land use in this model. Therefore, r^a is added to bid rent for all locations in the city, as shown in Equation 6.5.

Location Rent

The premium that a household is willing to pay to live closer to the city centre

The other component of this bid rent equation, $[(t/\ell^*) \times (b - d)]$, represents *location rent*. This is the premium that households are willing to pay to live close to the city centre. At the city centre, where d=0, the location rent equals $(t/\ell^*) \times b$. At the boundary of the city, where b = d, the location rent falls to zero. There is no premium added to the agricultural rent r^a. These components of bid rent are shown in Figure 6.8.

FIGURE 6.8

Equilibrium Land Rent

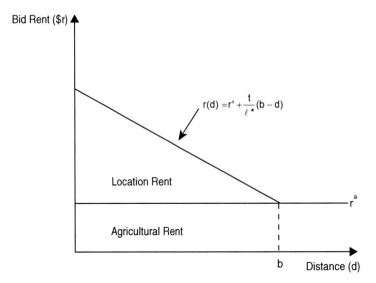

Key Concept: Opportunity Cost of Land

Equation 6.5 is a useful equation. To see why, recall the helpful tips for the commercial bid rent function and the first household bid rent function. Both allowed us to start from a maximum bid rent at the city centre (d=0), after which bid rent would decline with increasing distance. Equation 6.5 does something a little bit different. We start from a floor of agricultural bid rent, below which household bid rent cannot fall, and then we see bid rents increasing as the distance to the city centre declines. Another way to put this is that ra is the opportunity cost of land (the next best alternative land use after use as residential space). Bid rent for households cannot fall below that level – the value that farmers would be willing to bid for it keeps a floor under the price. Therefore, to determine land rents, start with the urban boundary, then move left, towards the city centre, adding the commuting costs that residents save at each location.

The second condition is that everyone in the city must have a place to live, or that the demand for land and the supply of land must be in balance. Since each household consumes ℓ^* units of land, the aggregate demand for land is $N \times \ell^*$, where N is the number of households in tthe city. If the urban boundary is b, then the aggregate supply of land within the circle of radius b is $\pi \times b^2$ (where $\pi \approx$ 3.14159 as previously defined). Thus, if land demand must equal land supply, then: $(N \times \ell^*) = (\pi \times b^2)$.

Rearranging this algebraically to solve for the urban boundary:

$$b = \sqrt{\frac{N \times \ell^*}{\pi}}$$

This is how large the radius of the city must be in order to supply each consumer or household with ℓ^* units of land. If we substitute the equation for b into Equation 6.5, the bid rent function becomes:

EQUATION 6.6

$$r(d) = r^a + \left(\frac{t}{\ell^*}\right) \times \left[\sqrt{\frac{N \times \ell^*}{\pi}} - d\right]$$

Equation 6.6 is useful because it shows how land rent depends on the population of the city. An increase in N will cause the rent function to shift up in a parallel fashion. We will use this fact in Chapter 8, when we examine how urban growth impacts property values.

EXERCISE 6.2: The Land Area of a City

Consider a monocentric city that contains 250,000 households, each of which occupies 0.25 acres of land.

Where is the boundary of the city?

Solution:

The total demand for land is $250,000 \times 0.25 = 62,500$ acres. We need to convert this figure into square miles or square kilometres, depending on how we measure distance. Let's follow our earlier example and measure distance in kilometres. Since there are 247.1 acres in a square kilometre, 62,500 acres equal $62,500/247.1 \approx 252.9$ square kilometres.

The supply of land in a circle of radius b is $\pi \times b^2 \approx 3.14159 \times b^2$.

Setting demand equal to supply implies $252.9 = 3.14159 \times b^2$, or $b^2 = 80.5$, therefore, $b \approx 9.0$ kilometres.

In this case, the area of the city is a circle with a radius of approximately 9.0 kilometres.

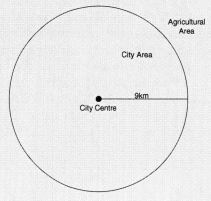

EXERCISE 6.3: Equilibrium in a Monocentric City

Continuing with the exercise given above, let's use Equation 6.5 to derive an expression for urban land rent.

Assume that the commuting cost is $50 per kilometre (t = 50), and agricultural land rent (r_a) = $1,000 per acre. Provide the relevant expression for urban land rent.

Solution:

Plugging this and the information given above (ℓ^* = 0.25 and b = 9.0) into Equation 6.5, the bid rent function for urban land is:

$$r(d) = r^a + [(\frac{t}{\ell^*}) \times (b - d)]$$

$$r(d) = \$1,000 + [(\frac{\$50}{0.25}) \times (9.0 - d)]$$

$$r(d) = \$1,000 + [\$200 \times (9.0 - d)]$$

At the city centre (d = 0), urban land rent r(d) equals $2,800 per acre. This is composed of $1,000 in agricultural rent plus $1,800 ($200 x 9.0) in location rent.

Urban rent declines with distance until at the boundary of the city, location rent equals zero, and urban land rent equals the agricultural rent of $1,000 per acre. Equilibrium land rent equals the urban rent inside the boundary and the agricultural rent outside the boundary.

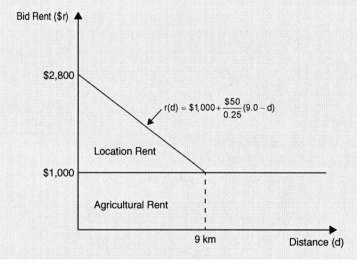

Bid Rent with Variable Lot Sizes

So far, the examples in this section have assumed that lot sizes were fixed: every household consumed ℓ^* units of land, regardless of its location. Allowing households the flexibility to vary the size of lot they demand complicates matters somewhat, but also makes the model more realistic. Clearly lot sizes do vary within a city. Since the demand for land slopes downward, consumers buy less land when the price is higher (smaller lots near city centre) and buy more land where the price of land is lower (larger lots near city's edge, the suburbs).

To emphasize this, we will revise the fixed lot size function ℓ^* to $\ell(d)$, in order reflect the fact that lot size will now vary according to the distance d from the city centre. If the household's indifference curves have the shape shown in Figure 6.2, then households living further from the city centre will consume more land.

Allowing variable lot sizes has two important consequences:

1. The bid rent function will no longer be a straight line. The slope is still negative, reflecting that bid rents fall with distance. However, the slope of the bid rent function is not constant. Rather, because of the commuting cost issues discussed earlier, the bid rent function is steeper near the city centre and gets flatter as one moves farther from the city centre. In other words, the bid rent function for land should be convex, like r(d)[1] presented in Figure 6.5. This convex curve reflects the lots size relationship in ℓ(d) — since land is more expensive near the city centre, households will demand less; and since land near the urban boundary is cheaper, households can afford larger lots.

2. If lot sizes are flexible, then the monocentric model predicts that population density will decline with distance. If each household at distance d consumes ℓ(d) units of land, then each unit of land at distance d will be home to $1/ℓ(d)$ households. Consider our fixed land scenario, with each household at a particular distance occupying 1/4 of an acre of land (ℓ(d) = 0.25), then each acre of land there will contain 4 households (1/0.25). The same relationship applies when land size is allowed to vary. Thus, $1/ℓ(d)$ is population density, the number of households or persons per unit of land. The more expensive land near the city centre will have higher population density, whereas the less expensive land near the urban boundaries has less. This population density relationship is a commonly observed North American urban phenomenon: high-rises downtown and large lot houses in the suburbs. We will present evidence in support of this claim in Chapter 7.

With the fixed lot size assumption removed, we now have a more realistic model of urban development to work with. In the next section, we will change the underlying assumptions to see what impacts these have on the form and structure of urban areas.

Changes in Commuting Costs

To start, let's examine the impact of a decrease in commuting cost (t) on a city with a fixed population and variable lot sizes. This example has relevance historically: consider how the introduction of motor vehicles reduced the cost of moving goods and people within cities during the 20th century. This obviously led to changes in the urban environment — these will be explored here.

Our analysis highlights two critical issues with a reduction in commuting/transportation cost (t):

1. The bid rent function gets flatter as commuting cost declines; this means proximity to the city centre becomes less important, since there are less savings in transportation costs by living closer. Similarly, land near the city boundary becomes more valuable, as the savings in commuting costs can contribute to higher bid rents. As well, the urban boundary will expand, as more urban area will be able to outbid agricultural uses in the hinterland.

2. Since lot sizes are flexible, the decline in land rent causes consumers to purchase more land; therefore, average lot sizes increase. This also means that the boundary of the city must move outward: the supply of urban land must expand to accommodate the increase in aggregate demand.

Figure 6.9 illustrates this impact. The light curve is the original equilibrium bid rent function. The original boundary of the city is labelled b_0. The bold curve is the new equilibrium bid rent function. The city's new boundary is extended out to b_1. As discussed above, the impact of this change on property values (land rents) depends on location. Properties near the city centre have a decrease in equilibrium land rent; properties near the urban boundary have an increase in equilibrium land rent; the point where this impact changes is b^* on the graph, where the old and new bid rent curves intersect. This makes intuitive sense: since it is now cheaper to commute, people should be willing to pay less to live close to the downtown and should be able to pay more to live in outlying areas.

FIGURE 6.9

**The Impact of a
Transportation
Improvement**

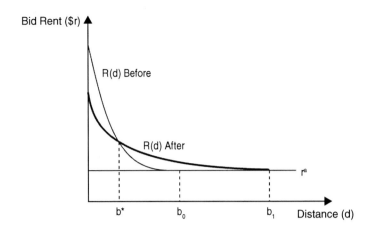

Two Types of Households

In this section, we relax the assumption that all households are identical. More specifically, we examine how differences in income affect bid rent and the spatial structure of a city. Each of these extensions removes a simplification towards making the model more realistic.

Imagine a city that contains two types of households: high-income and low-income households. For simplicity, let's assume that the number of households of each type is fixed, and that within each group, households are identical.

How does the bid rent function of the rich compare to that of the poor? There are several factors to consider. First, in our discussion following Equation 6.3, we showed that an increase in income (I) will cause the entire bid rent function to shift outward in a parallel fashion. Based on this logic, other things being equal, higher income households should be able to bid more for land at every distance. Land is a normal good, which roughly means the more income you have, the more you want to buy. Given this, high-income consumers will tend to demand more land than low income consumers. If we set ℓ_H as the lot size of a high-income household and set ℓ_L as the lot size of a low-income household, then $\ell_H > \ell_L$ at all locations in the urban area. Recall from Equation 6.4 that lot size is in the denominator of the slope of the bid rent function. Mathematically, this means that if the lot size is bigger, then the bid rent function will be flatter. Therefore, if higher income means larger lot sizes, then the bid rent function of the rich should be flatter than the bid rent function of the poor. This is illustrated in Figure 6.10 with the bid rent functions for high-income and low-income households, labelled $r_H(d)$ and $r_L(d)$, respectively.

FIGURE 6.10

**Bid Rents of the
Rich and Poor**

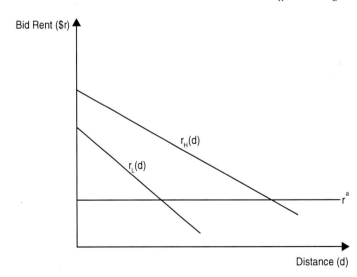

Another complication is the value of time. Time is an important component of the cost of commuting, and since the value of time rises with income, commuting cost per unit of distance should also rise with income. If we let t_H be the marginal commuting cost for a high-income household and t_L be the corresponding value for a low-income household, then $t_H > t_L$. Recall from Equation 6.4 that commuting cost is in the numerator of the slope of the bid rent function. This implies that, if indeed commuting cost rises with income, then the bid rent function of the rich should be steeper than the bid rent function of the poor.

Because each of these two factors (income and commuting costs) are pushing in opposite directions, and we don't know the magnitude of each factor, the net result is ambiguous. That is, since both the numerator and the denominator of the bid rent function rise with income, we cannot tell whether the bid rent function of the rich should be steeper or flatter than the bid rent function of the poor.

If we assume that the lot size effect is stronger than the value of time effect, the bid rent function becomes flatter as income rises, ast shown in Figure 6.10. The first thing you should notice is that something is terribly wrong with this picture: the poor have no place to live since the rich outbid them for land at every location. This means that the situation depicted in Figure 6.10 cannot possibly be an equilibrium — remember our assumption that everyone in the urban area must have a place to live. How can we correct the problem? The heights of the bid rent functions must adjust so that all the rich and all the poor households in the city can find a place to live.

Recall that the height of the bid rent function is related to the utility level that households achieve. This housing choice was illustrated back in Figures 6.2, 6.3, and 6.4, showing how a household will maximize his or her overall utility by purchasing the optimal combination of housing and other goods. However, for the poor household, this combination leaves them with nowhere to live.

Referring back to Figure 6.4, one option is for poorer households to increase the price per unit of land they are willing to pay at every location. This is shown in Figure 6.11, where the budget constraint of the poor rotates inward as they increase their willingness to pay for land, r, at every location. The new optimum — where the new budget constraint reaches the poor's highest possible indifference curve, labelled u_2 — involves a different consumption bundle. This particular consumption bundle has less land and more other goods. The poor now have lower utility, but given that the bid rent function of the poor was steeper than that of the rich, the shift upward in the poor household's bid rent function means that they can now outbid the rich for land near to the city centre.

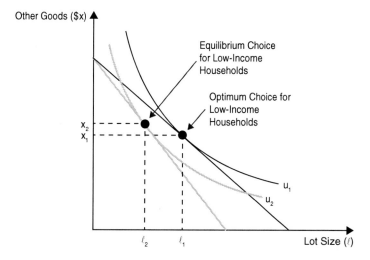

FIGURE 6.11

Equilibrium and Optimum Choices for Low-Income Households

The resulting equilibrium is shown in Figure 6.12. Since land is allocated to the highest bidder, the poor occupy all land between $d = 0$ and $d = b_1$, while the rich occupy all land between $d = b_1$ and $d = b_2$. The boundary between the poor and the rich, b_1, is the distance from the city centre at which $r_L(d)$ and $r_H(d)$ are equal. The outer boundary of the city is b_2, reflecting the distance at which urban uses can no longer outbid the agricultural land rent.[5]

---

[5]   An alternative scenario is that the bid rent function of the rich is steeper than that of the poor – a plausible result if the higher income households' wages mean that the opportunity cost of commuting is prohibitively high. In this case, when the poor increase their bid rent at every location, they will find that they outbid the rich only at the outskirts of the city. Again, their utility falls because they consume a different bundle of land and other goods than they would have chosen if they didn't have to compete with rich households for land.

To be an equilibrium, the area of the circle of radius b_1 must be sufficient to house all of the city's low-income families, while the ring of land between b_1 and b_2 must be sufficient to house all of the city's high-income families. As in Chapter 5, equilibrium land rent is the highest of the bid rents for any parcel. This is shown by the dark line in Figure 6.12.

FIGURE 6.12

A Monocentric City with Two Income Groups

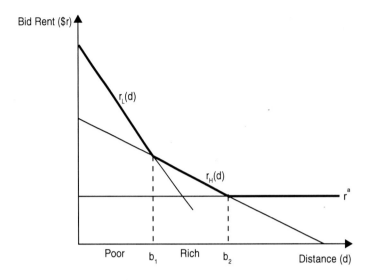

The location pattern shown in Figure 6.12 can be generalized to any number of income groups. Provided the slope of bid rent falls as income rises, and lot sizes are fixed within each income group, the different groups will occupy different rings around the city centre. The closest ring will be allocated to the lowest income group, the next ring to the second lowest income group, etc. In other words, the groups will be ordered in terms of their locations as they are ordered in terms of income. This is interesting because it is broadly consistent with income patterns observed in many metropolitan areas in North America, namely, that the lowest income neighbourhoods are located in or near the downtown, while higher income areas are located in the suburbs.[6] There are, of course, numerous counter examples — in those instances, it may be that the value of time effect overwhelms the lot size effect, i.e., the increased cost of commuting for higher income households restricts the amount of additional land they wish to occupy.

The Economics of Low-Income Housing

The discussion in the section above is based on an economic model with specific assumptions. Like all models, it simplifies reality to help us understand complex phenomena, but in this simplification it may only approximate reality. In truth, the issue of low-income housing is a lot more complex. Expanding our model leads to some interesting twists, complications, and possible explanations or solutions for the low income housing problem:

- A key assumption in this model is how rich and poor households value housing versus savings in commuting costs – or in other words, the income elasticity of housing demand versus the income elasticity of commuting distance. This varies by location; e.g., in European cities and increasingly in larger Canadian cities, you see luxury housing downtown, implying the rich prefer to increase spending on land to save on commuting cost. This is particularly important once congestion costs are considered, as commuting cost includes not just gas and car maintenance, but also the time and aggravation of dealing with traffic (this is explored in Chapter 9).
- Consider the possible impact of subsidized mass transit. If transportation cost (t) is reduced, this flattens the bid rent curve for the poor (as the rich probably prefer to drive), making locations further from the city more affordable. However, transit improvements will only help to a point, as even with efficient transit, eventually the

continued on next page

---

[6] This analysis ignores a number of other factors that influence the residential location decisions of households, including public safety, school quality, and the age and quality of the housing stock. We will discuss these issues later in the text.

commuting time will become excessive and unworkable – setting the boundary of that group's bid rent curve.

- The model does not consider assumptions about building cost. The rich can afford to build more at all locations, but the poor cannot. So the poor may have less interest in the larger lots in the suburbs if they cannot afford to build the large houses the larger lots allow. As well, considering the normal preference for new housing versus used – there tends to more vacant lots in the suburbs to build new housing and this may attract richer households.

- Some cities have less-than-desirable inner city neighbourhoods, with crime problems and lower quality amenities – the rich can afford to spend extra for suburban locations to avoid these issues (the "flight from the blight" problem is discussed in more detail in Chapter 7).

- Finally, consider relaxing the assumption on lot size, meaning more people can live on a lot closer to the city centre and less in the suburbs. In this way, higher density of use may allow the lower income households to pool their resources and afford housing. This is another form of reducing utility or satisfaction, as discussed in the section above. The invisible hand of the market takes care of this, as developers recognize the demand and offer real estate products to fill this need: consider the micro-housing trend! Density will be discussed in more detail in Chapter 7.

All of these issues are extensions of the basic monocentric city model and are hotly debated by urban land economists world-wide. The model provides the basic jumping off point for some very interesting discussions of the way cities form and how they might evolve in future.

Value Matters: Affordability and "Worth"

With ever-rising prices for housing in many cities comes growing debate over affordability. This is a political, social, and economic issue. However, appraisers do not typically get involved in such judgmental matters, as the appraiser's primary role is to act as an objective market observer, set apart from the action -- independent, uninvolved, and unbiased. Affordability discussions often centre on individual's highly subjective opinions on what houses are "worth" – as in "how can an 80-year old house possibly be worth $2,000,000?" An appraiser's answer might be: "its value is $2,000,000 because it sold in a competitive matter to prudent, knowledgeable buyers who were willing to pay that price". This sidesteps the awkwardness of trying to determine what something is "worth" to one person or another. But in this stance, the appraiser may also implicitly pass judgment on affordability: "clearly it's affordable if someone purchased it". In that sense, the appraiser's highly objective and somewhat detached role may be closer to an economist than anything else.

Firms and Households

Now we will relax the assumption that all land use in the city is residential. More specifically, we introduce manufacturing firms to the city and show how their location decisions lead to the formation of an industrial or commercial city centre. Again, this extension is intended to make our basic model more realistic, to see how bid rent allocates land among competing urban uses and how this shapes city development.

In the core-dominated cities of the 19th century, the city centre was occupied by manufacturing and commercial firms that provided jobs for the city's workers. Although we have focused on how commuting impacts residential location, land rent and land use, we have not discussed the size or structure of the commercial district in any detail. It is time to correct this omission, and specifically to revisit our unrealistic assumption that the area firms occupy is merely a point in space at the city's centre.

Imagine now that the city contains both firms and households. Assume that all households are identical (as in our earlier discussion) and that all firms are identical as well. Each firm produces a good that is exported from the city through the port, rail terminal, or airport at the city centre. Firms ship all their output to the export terminal. A firm produces the export good from two inputs, capital (K) and land (L), according to the production function Q = F(K,L). The capital variable K includes any machinery and equipment that the firm uses and the building that the firm occupies. The land variable L is the firm's lot size. The capital-to-land ratio, K/L, is particularly important in this context: in simple terms, it represents the height of the building that a firm occupies. For this reason, K/L is sometimes referred to as *structural density*. In general, each firm aims to maximize its profits by choosing:

1. how much to produce: a level of output;
2. how to produce: the investment in capital and land; and
3. where to produce: a location within the city, or better, a distance from the city centre.

Let P be the price that a firm receives for a unit of output once it reaches the terminal, and let T be the cost of shipping one unit of output one unit of distance. As in our earlier discussions, we assume that transportation cost depends only on distance; direction is irrelevant. To begin, assume that every firm produces the same amount of output Q from fixed amounts of capital and land.

Similar to the von Thunen agricultural model, the following equation shows the profit π of a manufacturing firm at distance d:

$$\pi(d) \ = \ [(P \times Q) - C] - [T \times Q \times d] - [L \times R(d)]$$

Where:

- (P × Q) is revenue
- C is non-land cost: expenditures on capital, assumed to be fixed
- [T × Q × d] is shipping cost
- [L × R(d)] is expenditures on land

Once again we set profit to zero, π (d) = 0, in order to find the equilibrium land rent at any location d from the city centre. Solving for R(d) in this equation gives the following bid rent function:

EQUATION 6.7

$$R(d) = \frac{(P \times Q) - C}{L} - \frac{T \times Q}{L} \times d$$

R(d) is the maximum amount that a manufacturer located d kilometres from the city centre is willing and able to pay for a unit of land. It is what is left over after all costs, including those for transportation (and normal profit), are subtracted from the firm's revenues.

Figure 6.13 illustrates this bid rent function for a manufacturing firm. Although the interpretation is somewhat different, this bid rent function is essentially the same as the agricultural bid rent function that was introduced in Chapter 5. Bid rent at the city centre is:

$$R(0) = \frac{(P \times Q) - C}{L}$$

The slope of the firm's bid rent function is:

$$-\frac{T \times Q}{L}$$

The slope is again negative, since bid rent will fall with distance from the city centre to offset the rising cost of shipping output to the export terminal. An increase in price of output P or a decrease in non-land cost C will result in more residual/leftover income that can be allocated to land — the bid rent function will shift upward in a parallel fashion. An increase in transport cost T will cause the bid rent function to get steeper — if shipping costs rise, then rent will fall faster as the firm moves away from the city centre, and land nearer the city centre becomes more valuable, reflecting the relatively less expensive shipping costs for nearby firms.

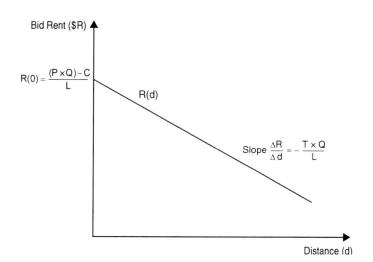

FIGURE 6.13

**The Bid Rent of
a Manufacturing
Firm**

Our assumption that the manufacturing firms must use fixed amounts of capital and land makes it easy to derive and illustrate the bid rent function. However, this is not realistic. Firms will choose the bundle of capital and land investment that maximizes profits. We touched upon this input substitution topic at the end of Chapter 5 and earlier in this chapter with regard to residential land use. It is worth reviewing and reinforcing the key points here. If we allow manufacturers to engage in input substitution, two things change:

- First, assuming that the price of capital is the same at every location in the city, the capital-to-land ratio will vary within the city. This will be reflected in the *structural density* of buildings and land use. Land near the city centre is expensive; therefore, firms who locate there will try to limit how much land they use. These firms will invest more capital to make the most productive use of their small parcel of land. For example, these firms will build taller buildings, so K/L will be high there. As we move away from the city centre, and the price of land decreases, there is less need to substitute capital for land, so the capital-to-land ratio will fall, as shown in Figure 6.14. This is one of the most basic characteristics of a city — most of the tall buildings are located near the downtown.

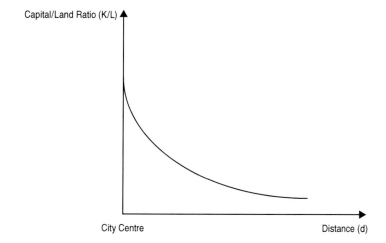

FIGURE 6.14

**Structural
Density and Input
Substitution**

- The second change caused by input substitution relates to the slope of the manufacturer's bid rent function. If the firm can substitute capital for land, then the bid rent function R(d) will not be a straight-line. Similar to the residential example earlier, R(d) will be steeper near the city centre and flatter further out — the manufacturer's bid rent function will be convex. The manufacturing bid rent function with input substitution is shown in Figure 6.15.

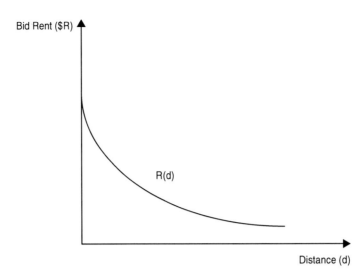

Input substitution leads to firms choosing larger lot sizes as distance to the city centre rises. If we specify L(d) as the lot size that a manufacturer chooses if located at distance d, then the slope of the bid rent function becomes:

$$-\frac{T \times Q}{L(d)}$$

Equation 6.8 is identical to our previous equation except that now L is a function of distance d.

EQUATION 6.8

$$R(d) = \frac{(P \times Q) - C}{L(d)} - \frac{T \times Q}{L(d)} \times d$$

Further from the city centre, where L(d) is larger, the denominator of Equation 6.8 is larger; therefore, the rent function is flatter. Conversely, closer to the city centre, where L(d) is smaller, the denominator of Equation 6.8 is smaller and the rent function is steeper.

Figure 6.16 combines all the ideas that we have discussed in the chapter; it shows the land market equilibrium in a monocentric city with both firms and households. In Figure 6.16, firms outbid households for all locations between d = 0 and d = b_1, and households outbid farms (and agriculture) for all land between d= b_1 and d=b_2. The change is land use is the point at which the bid rent functions intersect. The border of the city is at d=b_2, the point at which agricultural rent is higher than the household bid rent.

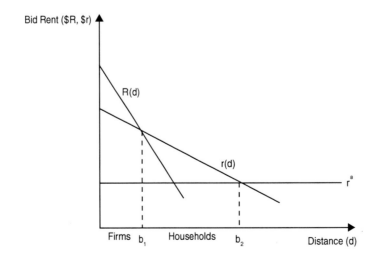

Thus we have a core-dominated city: firms at the centre, households in the periphery (suburbs), and agriculture in the rural hinterland. This conventional arrangement of activities occurs in our model only if the manufacturing firm's bid rent R(d) is steeper than the household's r(d). This reflects the reality of city formation in the 19th century, when the cost of shipping goods within cities (T) exceeded the cost of moving people within cities (t). The monocentric model shows exactly how this difference in transportation costs influenced the development of the large industrial cities that dominated the 19th century in North America, and largely still dominates today's urban landscape.

Much of the remaining chapters in this book will be spent exploring this model of urban development against contemporary reality. Our cities may have formed in the 19th century, but 21st century influences and pressures are reshaping them into new patterns. For example, today the cost of moving people — mostly the opportunity cost of high wages — may now outstrip the cost of moving goods. That may be one reason that office buildings now dominate the downtown core of many cities rather than factories. This is where the fun begins in urban land economics — with a fundamental explanatory model in hand, we can now begin to tweak it and play with its assumptions to see what happens — and try to offer some rational explanation for changing patterns in urban land use and, possibly, to predict future changes.

Value Matters: Evolving Appraisal

An old joke about appraisal is that it is like driving a car using only the rear view mirror. Because appraisers rely on historic events to predict future trends, they may be slow to react to changes in the fast-paced world of real estate. But consider one advantage of lagging the market a little: appraisers' slow reaction time also means they are less influenced by fads or wild market swings. A few notable trends in real estate valuation:

- Appraisers today are the "appraisers of the future" from the pre-internet age 30 or 40 years ago. No one fills in reports with a typewriter or uses film cameras any more. All appraisers, even the "old guys", now have a computer and an email address. Professionals rely on their cars as mobile offices. Yet many of the basic valuation processes and techniques remain much the same.
- The three primary appraisal approaches have not changed substantially in 50 years. However, an initial emphasis on cost-based methods has gradually shifted to market-based. This is also mirrored by accountants, who are evolving to fair market valuation of assets in new international standards.
- Early adopters yelled that computers would change everything in appraisal! Indeed, this computing power offers potential to dramatically increase the depth of analysis, e.g., discounted cash flow analysis for commercial properties. However, this sophisticated and complex analysis seems to have advanced beyond what the market actually wants – simple capitalization rate analysis still dominates.
- Yet in mass appraisal applications, such as for property tax assessment and mortgage finance, processes are unrecognizable from what was done decades ago. Clients demand valuations that are fast and economical, and are willing to accept the accompanying risks of less individual attention on properties. Appraisers prepare automated valuation models (AVMs) to meet this demand.
- The business model for appraisers is changing in response. The easy "bread and butter" work of days gone by is now automated. Appraisers have had to find a new competitive advantage to survive. Two responses dominate: (1) increased efficiency: same quality work, but done faster and cheaper; or (2) specialization: focus on more complex problems that require a deeper scope of work and more sophisticated analysis.

EXERCISE 6.4: Equilibrium in a Monocentric City with Two Land Uses

Consider a monocentric city with two land uses: manufacturing firms and households. Suppose that each manufacturing firm produces 1,000 units of output (Q), has total non-land costs of $500 (C), and occupies one acre of land (L = 1) and there is no input substitution (bid rent function is linear). The price of output is $2 per unit and shipping costs are $0.20 per unit of output per kilometre. The household or residential bid rent function is r(d) = $1,000 - $100d with $100 representing the commuting cost per kilometre.

continued on next page

1. Derive the firms' bid rent function for land, and show both this and the residential bid rent function on a diagram. Refer to Equation 6.7 in deriving the firm's bid rent function.
2. Calculate the sum of expenditures on land and shipping costs for a firm located at d = 1 and a firm located at d = 2.
3. Find the location of the border between the commercial and residential districts. How many firms does the city contain?
4. How would the size of the commercial district change as a result of each of the following:
    (a) an increase in the price of output?
    (b) an increase in shipping costs?

Solution:

1. $R(d) = [(P \times Q) - C]/L - [T \times Q]/L \times d$

With profit of zero,

$R(d) = (\$2 \times 1,000) - \$500 - [\$0.2 \times 1,000] \times d$

$R(d) = \$2,000 - \$500 - \$200d$

$R(d) = \$1,500 - \$200d$

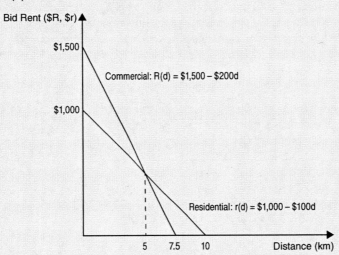

To graph the commercial and residential bid rent functions, we need two points of reference; we will use the vertical and horizontal intercepts of each. The commercial vertical intercept is $1,500 and the residential vertical intercept is $1,000 (from the equations).

If the vertical intercept = 0, solve for the distance to obtain the horizontal intercepts:

Commercial:

Set vertical intercept = 0: $1,500 - $200d = 0

Add $200d to both sides: $1,500 = $200 d

Divide both sides by $200: d = 7.5 kilometres

Residential:

Set vertical intercept = 0: $1,000 - $100d = 0

Add $100d to both sides: $1,000 = $100 d

Divide both sides by $100: d = 10 kilometres

2. At the city centre, total costs = $1,500 such that the economic profit = $0. For a firm located at d = 1, shipping costs = $200 ($0.2 × 1,000 × 1). Expenditures on land must equal $1,500 − $200 = $1,300 for a total of $1,500. For a firm located at d = 2, shipping costs = $400 ($0.2 × 1,000 × 2). Expenditures on land must equal $1,500 − $400 = $1,100 for a total of $1,500. This

continued on next page

illustrates the concept of a spatial equilibrium: rents change along the bid rent function so that identical firms earn the same level of profit (in this case zero) regardless of where they locate. Rents change along the bid rent function so that no one has an incentive to move.

3. The location of the border satisfies: $1,500 − $200d = $1,000 − $100d

> Add $200d to each side: $1,500 = $1,000 + $100d
>
> Subtract $1,000 from each side: $500 = $100d
>
> Divide both sides by $100: 5 = d

Therefore, the area of the commercial ring is π × b². Therefore, we have 3.14159(5²) = 3.14159(25) = 78.5 square kilometres or 19,398 acres. Since each firm occupies one acre, this is also the number of firms in the commercial district.

4. Refer to Equation 6.7: R(d) = [(P × Q) − C)]/L − [T × Q]/L × d

(a) If the price of output (P) increases, the y-intercept increases, i.e., the "P" in [(P × Q) − C] / L increases. The firm bid rent function would shift upward in a parallel fashion. The size of the commercial district would increase.

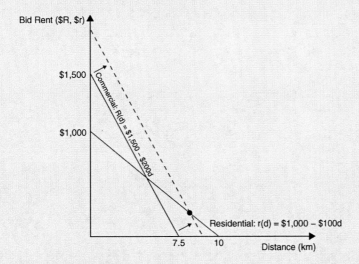

(b) If the shipping costs (T) increase, the slope increases, i.e., the "T" in [T × Q]/L × d increases. The firm bid rent function would become steeper, and the size of the commercial district would decrease.

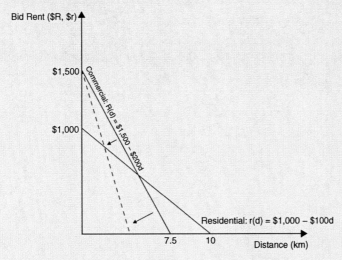

For both of the effects above, note that the urban boundary does not change, since P and T are not factors in the residential bid rent function in this example.

SUMMARY

This chapter introduced the monocentric model of a core-dominated city — the cornerstone of modern urban economics. The monocentric model explains:

- how urban land rents are determined;
- how land is allocated among competing uses;
- how the intensity of land use (population, employment, or structural density) varies within a city; and
- how the size of a city is determined.

The monocentric city model also lets us examine how cities and urban land markets respond to changes in the economic environment.

The simplest version of the model focuses on the residential location decisions of a population of identical individuals who work in the city centre. The basic insight, similar to von Thunen's agricultural model, is that equilibrium land rent will decline as distance to the city centre rises to offset the rising cost of commuting. If there is more than one land use in the city, then each use will occupy the land where it outbids all others. The boundary of the city occurs at the point where urban land rent equals the opportunity cost of land.

The next chapter examines how well the monocentric model approximates reality, and discusses ways that the model has been refined, extended, and applied.

Key Concept: Three Alternative Bid Rent Functions

The bid rent functions discussed in this chapter may be expressed in different ways. These end up with the same result, explaining the land rent in different locations in the urban area. However, each may be easier to apply in certain circumstances.

To summarize, the three bid rent ftunctions you should be familiar with are:

EQUATION 6.7

$$r(d) = \frac{(P \times Q) - C}{L} - \frac{T \times Q}{L} \times d$$

Why it is useful? Equation 6.7 uses the concept of land as the residual claimant (maximum bid rent is equal to revenues less costs) to calculate bid rent, r(d), for firms.

EQUATION 6.3

$$r(d) = \frac{I - x^*}{\ell^*} - \frac{t}{\ell^*} \times d$$

Why it is useful? Equation 6.3 uses the concept of land as the residual claimant (maximum bid rent is equal to income less expenses) to calculate bid rent, r(d), for households.

EQUATION 6.5

$$r(d) = r^a + \left(\frac{t}{\ell^*}\right) \times (b - d)$$

Why it is useful? Equation 6.5 expresses bid rent for households starting from the floor price of agricultural rent, then increasing as we get closer to the city centre, with saved commuting costs. Compared to Equation 6.3, this does not require estimating income (I) or expenditures (x^*).

CHAPTER 7

SUBURBANIZATION, SUBCENTRES, AND SPRAWL

INTRODUCTION

Real cities are much more complex than the cities that the monocentric model portrays. Like all economic models, the monocentric model suppresses the complexity of economic relationships and focuses on just a few key ideas. This is what makes it a model and also what makes it useful. Although the monocentric model is very simple, it captures some fundamental truths about cities. In this chapter we examine how well the monocentric model approximates reality and discuss ways that the model has been refined, extended, and applied. This leads us to examine the evolution of core-dominated cities. We will describe and analyze the economic forces that have transformed the relatively compact cities of the past into the expansive and multi-centred cities of the present.

The chapter begins with a review of the basic predictions of the monocentric model, examining how these have been tested and evaluating the mixed results of some of these tests. We then advance the discussion to consider *suburbanization*, or decentralization of population and employment, which is the dominant trend in urban development over the last century. We will define suburbanization, measure its extent in American and Canadian metropolitan areas, and discuss the economic forces that seem to explain this pervasive phenomenon. Along with residential suburbanization is a growing tendency for firms to cluster in the suburbs, leading to the formation of urban subcentres and *polycentric cities*.

The final section of the chapter discusses the negative aspects of suburbanization. Urban sprawl is a consequence of poorly planned suburbanization. We examine the causes and some of the policies that have been suggested to correct the excessive decentralization of cities.

TESTING THE MONOCENTRIC MODEL

The monocentric model generates a number of testable predictions. Recall that in a competitive land market, rent varies between locations to offset any advantage that one location may have over another. In a monocentric city, locations differ only in terms of their access to central city jobs; therefore, in equilibrium, land rent varies between locations to offset differences in commuting costs. Thus, the most basic prediction of the monocentric model is that land rent, or more generally, residential property value, will decline as distance to the city centre increases. Furthermore, since land rent declines with distance, we expect households located farther from the city centre to purchase more land, or live on larger lots, than households living near the downtown. As we noted in Chapter 6, this implies that population density should decline with distance in a monocentric city. Therefore, declining population density is another basic prediction. These predictions have been thoroughly tested; the results of these tests help us evaluate how well the monocentric model measures up against reality.

Land Prices and Distance

The relationship between residential property values and distance can be tested simply and on a small scale using basic appraisal comparisons of sold properties. For a more comprehensive and robust comparison, multiple regression analysis can be applied with property value as the dependent variable and distance to the city centre or some other measure of location as one of the explanatory variables, along with property characteristics like size, age of dwelling, neighbourhood quality, etc. Because of the necessity of controlling for differences in so many property characteristics, this conventional approach can be quite complex. Here we will report on one particularly simple study of land prices that sidesteps many of these difficulties.

Good data on urban land prices are hard to come by, especially in built-up areas with little or no vacant land. Sale prices for developed properties represent a combination of land value plus the value of the structure on the land — it can be very hard to separate the two. One method to overcome this problem is focusing on properties that were sold and then immediately redeveloped. Since the improvements on these properties were about to be demolished, they must have provided little economic value to the sale; the price of a property that trades just prior to redevelopment is essentially the value of raw land.

Using data on redeveloped properties in Vancouver in 1987, Rosenthal and Helsley [1994] estimated a land price function in which the price of a parcel was related to a few explanatory variables — basically lot size, date of sale, and commuting time to the central business district (CBD). The results indicated that commuting time was a significant determinant of land value — in this sample, the price of raw land fell by 2.6% with each additional minute of travel time. Figure 7.1 illustrates the relationship between land value and commuting time in this study. This plainly shows that the price of urban land in Vancouver varies with commuting time in a manner that is broadly consistent with predictions of the monocentric model.

Of course, commuting time and distance to the downtown core are not exactly the same. The monocentric city model focuses on distance from the CBD in concentric rings, not commuting time. However, commuting time is probably a better measure of a location's access to the city centre than is simple distance to the CBD. Consider two properties that are the same distance to downtown, but one is a direct drive on a near-freeway, while another has a series of heavily congested bridges to navigate. These properties face substantially different commutes and, theoretically, resulting differences in residential property value. If Figure 7.1 showed price versus distance, this would confound the relationship.

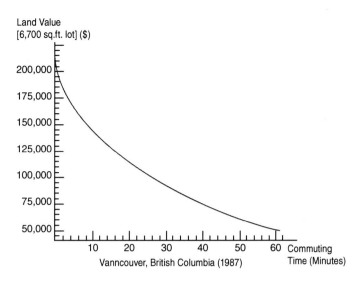

FIGURE 7.1

The Price of Land and Commuting Time to the CBD

Similarly, consider the impact of mass transit, which can move a lot of people longer distances much faster than cars. Mass transit is most effective for those who have easy access to the stations — either walking distance or with easy parking or efficient local transit. Again, consider two properties the same distance from downtown, with one located 200 m from a mass transit station, another in an opposite direction where there is no mass transit and a formidable commute. Once again, the model would indicate very different residential land values despite the same distance — showing commuting time is the better measure. Transportation economics are discussed in more detail in Chapter 9.

Value Matters: Mixed Value Impacts from Mass Transit

In cities with traffic congestion issues, rail transit improvements can offer a popular alternative. Not surprisingly, residential property values along the routes will increase, given easier access to jobs for commuters. The market's positive perception of this can be seen in the number of "Close to Subway" headlines in the sales listings in these cities. Property values tend to decrease with the distance from the stations, as you get away from comfortable walking distance. However, property values drop near the stations due to the noise, traffic, and potential for increased crime. If you needed to adjust for location, this might make for an interesting non-symmetrical relationship. If you graphed land values against distance from the CBD along this rail line, you might find a curve like Figure 7.1, but with a "blip" near each station — yet zooming in on each blip shows a volcano-shape with a value crater in the middle. This is not a straightforward location of adjustment of $x per kilometre!

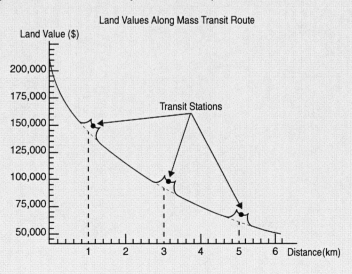

Population Density and Distance

Population density patterns within cities have been even more widely studied than the determinants of land prices. There is a great deal of research showing that the relationship between density and distance can be well-approximated by an exponential density function of the form:[1]

EQUATION 7.1

$$D(d) = D_0 \times e^{-gd}$$

Where:

- $D(d)$ is estimated population density at any given distance d — or the number of persons per unit area (e.g., square kilometre)
- D_0 is the implied density at the city centre (central density)
- e is the exponential function 2.71828 (the base of the natural logarithm)
- g is the rate in percentage terms at which density declines as distance increases (density gradient)

Central Density

The implied density of the city centre (D_0)

Density Gradient

Rate at which density declines as distance increases

For example, if a city has g = 0.3, and distance is measured in kilometres, then population density falls 30% per kilometre as one moves away from the city centre. Assume that this city has a central density, D_0 or density at the city centre, of 10,000 people per square kilometre. The estimated population density four kilometres away from the city centre is:

$D(4) = 10,000 \times e^{-0.3 \times 4}$

$D(4) = 10,000 \times 2.71828^{-1.2}$

$D(4) = 10,000 \times 0.30119$

$D(4) = 3,011.9$

This means that the density declined from 10,000 people per square kilometre to 3,012 people per square kilometre over four kilometres. Again, this is based on a 30% reduction per kilometre.

A large density gradient (g) indicates that density falls rapidly with distance, and that the city is relatively compact. A small density gradient indicates that density falls slowly with distance, and that the city is relatively dispersed. Figure 7.2 shows two exponential density functions. These show that London was denser in 1871 than in 1931 — among other reasons, the increased reliance on electric trams for transit led to a more dispersed suburban model. This technology-driven density change is clearly seen in North American cities with gas-powered vehicles: cars for personal use, buses for transit, and trucks for moving goods.

FIGURE 7.2

Exponential Population Density Functions for London

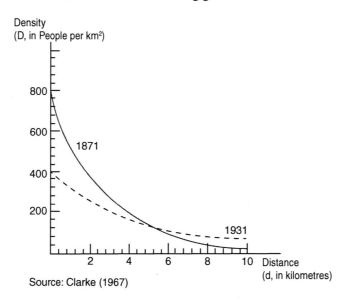

Source: Clarke (1967)

---

[1] Clark (1951) was apparently the first to undertake a systematic study of urban population density functions. Other early and important contributions include Muth (1969) and Mills (1972).

Exploring Exponential Density

What is e?

Like pi – which helps us relate the circumference of a circle to its radius – and c – the speed of light – e is a very special number. It is so useful that it is often put to work measuring things in the real world, like radioactive decay, interest earned on money, or a city's population growth.

It can be helpful to think of e like a natural speed limit on how quickly things can increase or decrease *depending on the frequency of compounding*. For example, if you received 100% interest per year on your savings, compounded *annually*, you would probably be pretty excited – that's a great rate of interest! Then, if the rate was the same, but instead compounded *monthly*, you would be even more excited, because now you would receive interest on some of the interest that you earned throughout the year. Nice!

Since compounding interest more frequently is better for you than compounding it less frequently, you might be wondering just how exciting this offer could get. What about compounding *daily*, *hourly*, or even every single *nanosecond*? This is where the speed limit comes into play – your excitement will max out when you receive 100% interest compounded *continuously* (which is even faster than every nanosecond, if you can believe it). In such a scenario, your balance at the end of the year will be 2.71828 times your initial savings. That number –2.71828 – which you might think of as the speed limit of 100% interest per year, is called e.

Great, so what does that have to do with Urban Land Economics?

Like pi or c, e is useful because it is flexible – it can be scaled to suit your purposes. While you may not be able to think of anything in urban land economics that is growing at 100% per year (that is a lot, after all), you may be able to think of things that grow by 2%, 5%, or 20%.

For example, suppose you think population growth is a continuous 2% in a particular city. To find out how many people will be in that city one year from now, you just need to multiply the starting population by $e^{0.02}$ (on the HP 10bII+ calculator, enter .02, then press the orange 🔶 (shift) key and then press e^x). The answer is 1.020201, which is just a little bit more than 2%. Because population growth has continuous growth characteristics, using e helps produce more accurate estimates.

To better understand population density gradients, let's see how this applies to Canadian cities. Table 7.1 illustrates the results of a historic study of central density (D_0) and density gradients (g) for selected Canadian cities. The last row of the table shows that the average central density in this sample was 8,193 and that the average density gradient was 0.31. This means that population density declined by 31% per kilometre on average in these metropolitan areas. However, there is obviously a great deal of variation between cities. Generally speaking, larger cities like Toronto, Montreal, and Vancouver tend to have higher central densities and smaller density gradients. This reflects the fact that larger cities have a more built-up downtown area and also more density in surrounding areas, in comparison to smaller towns.

Consider another example: Applying Equation 7.1, based on data in Table 7.1, Toronto's estimated population density function in 1981 was:

$$D(d) = 12{,}666 \times e^{-0.13d}$$

This means that the implied central density for Toronto was 12,666 persons per square kilometre, and that density declined 13% per kilometre as one moved away from the city centre. The estimated population density 5 kilometres away from the Toronto city centre was D(5) = $12{,}666 \times e^{-0.13(5)} \approx 12{,}666 \times 0.52 \approx 6{,}612$ persons per square kilometre. We could perform similar calculations for any of the cities listed in Table 7.1.

Table 7.1: Population and Employment Density Gradients for Selected CMAs, 1981				
	Population		**Employment**	
CMA	**Central Density D_0**	**Density Gradient g**	**Central Density D_0**	**Density Gradient g**
Calgary, Alberta	11,977.53	0.35	5,083.83	0.31
Chicoutimi-Jonquiere, Quebec	1,011.68	0.18	2,999.16	0.58
Edmonton, Alberta	9,107.39	0.28	5,771.78	0.31
Halifax, Nova Scotia	6,486.59	0.31	6,865.99	0.48
Hamilton, Ontario	7,312.23	0.26	4,634.22	0.32
Kitchener, Ontario	2,847.02	0.23	1,320.93	0.23
London, Ontario	11876.55	0.49	5,126.55	0.47
Montreal, Quebec	15,081.19	0.17	12,146.07	0.23
Ottawa-Hull, Ontario-Quebec	5,897.66	0.22	7,562.39	0.36
Quebec, Quebec	3,862.96	0.19	3,087.08	0.27
Regina, Saskatchewan	15,121.40	0.72	7,003.44	0.72
Saint John, New Brunswick	984.39	0.18	1,229.21	0.32
Saskatoon, Saskatchewan	9,020.63	0.56	5,593.96	0.68
St. Catharines - Niagara, Ontario	5,016.86	0.25	4,835.03	0.38
St. John's, Newfoundland	11,325.15	0.50	15,273.01	0.94
Sudbury, Ontario	1,073.00	0.20	873.62	0.29
Thunder Bay, Ontario	3,571.46	0.36	2,143.92	0.42
Toronto, Ontario	12,666.03	0.13	14,819.42	0.20
Vancouver, British Columbia	12,300.64	0.19	9,721.10	0.23
Victoria, British Columbia	9,861.18	0.36	15,876.97	0.69
Windsor, Ontario	9,537.82	0.39	6,257.90	0.50
Winnipeg, Manitoba	14,313.34	0.37	5,691.55	0.34
Maximum	15,121.40	0.72	15,876.97	0.94
Minimum	984.39	0.13	873.62	0.20
Mean	8,193.30	0.31	6,541.69	0.42

Notes: D_0 is the central density (estimated density, persons or jobs per square kilometre, at the city centre). g is the density gradient (rate at which density declines as distance to the city centre increases, was specified as in original study).

Source: Pratt (1993), Tables 4.3 and 4.5.

Other urban economic studies confirm that the size effect on population density functions seems consistent in both developed and developing countries — larger cities have higher central densities and smaller density gradients.[2] This result seems an intuitive and logical extension to our monocentric model.

Studies have also shown that population density functions tend to be flatter in higher income countries. In other words, cities in poorer countries appear to be more compact than cities of the same size in higher income countries. This is consistent with our ideal that land is a normal good (meaning the more you can afford, the more you prefer). Therefore, it is logical that land will be consumed in higher quantities in higher income areas, leading to relatively less dense cities.

"Wasteful" Commuting

The monocentric model does a good job of accounting for general patterns in the spatial behaviour of land prices and population densities. However, no economic model is universally successful; the monocentric model is no exception. In particular, the monocentric model does a poor job of predicting the level of commuting that occurs in cities.

The monocentric model assumes that every worker commutes along a line connecting the worker's home and job. No one in a monocentric city commutes across the CBD to a job on the

---

[2]　For example, Miles and Tan (1980).

other side of town, or commutes outward from the city centre toward a suburban job. Even if some employment is located outside of the city centre, the model predicts that the workers who hold these jobs should commute inward from homes located even further from the downtown. One variation of the model calculates the *mean optimum commute* as the average distance of all houses from the city centre minus the average distance of all jobs from the city centre.[3]

> **Mean Optimum Commute**
>
> Average distance of all houses from the city centre minus the average distance of all jobs from the city centre

Table 7.2 compares estimates of the mean optimum commute from the monocentric model with actual average commuting distances for a sample of US and Canadian cities. These figures suggest that the monocentric model under-predicts the amount of commuting that occurs in cities by a wide margin. For the US cities, actual commuting is about 8 times larger than the level that is predicted by the monocentric model. For the Canadian cities, actual commuting is seven times larger than the mean optimum commute. Interestingly, for both samples, the actual commuting distances are reasonably close to the distances one would observe if workers were just randomly assigned to houses.

Table 7.2: "Wasteful" Commuting

US Cities	Mean Optimum Commute (in miles)	Actual Commute (in miles)	Canadian Cities	Mean Optimum Commute (in kilometres)	Actual Commute (in kilometres)
Baltimore	0.68	10.20	Edmonton	0.51	10.49
Boston	1.82	9.00	Halifax	1.71	7.97
Columbus	1.01	8.10	Hamilton	1.09	15.63
Denver	0.85	8.50	Kitchener	0.02	12.09
Houston	1.57	10.50	Montreal	2.66	12.24
Milwaukee	0.69	7.10	Ottawa	2.79	10.39
Philadelphia	0.19	8.70	Quebec	2.07	11.29
Phoenix	0.94	9.50	Saskatoon	0.52	7.96
Pittsburgh	1.15	8.10	Sudbury	1.47	13.62
Rochester	1.87	7.80	Thunder Bay	0.47	10.13
Sacramento	1.78	8.50	Toronto	4.45	12.25
San Antonio	0.54	8.60	Vancouver	1.71	13.56
San Diego	2.08	9.90	Victoria	2.27	10.53
Wichita	0.35	7.90	Windsor	0.95	10.18
Sample Mean	1.11	8.74		1.62	11.31
Actual/Required		7.89			6.98

Sources: Hamilton (1982) – US Cities, Table 1, and Pratt (1993) – Canadian Cities, Table 5.1.

People have tried pretty hard to shield the monocentric model from these assaults.[4] Researchers have tried to identify factors that are obviously missing from the model and evaluate how these omissions might impact predictions about commuting. For example, one might allow jobs and houses to differ, or acknowledge that because it is costly to move, people may not adjust their home locations in response to changes in the locations of their jobs. Or one could incorporate a proper road network or urban employment subcentres into the model. However, Table 7.2 results have proven to be very robust. It seems to be a well-established fact that standard urban economic models are poor predictors of commuting behaviour.

The monocentric model does a very good job of explaining some aspects of cities, but a very bad job of explaining others — this is the nature of economic inquiry. Real economies are too complex to be understood without the benefit of a model of some sort, and too complex to be completely captured by any model. The monocentric model is actually an example of a very successful economic model. It has a solid foundation in microeconomic theory and makes a number of easily testable predictions. It helps us understand how market forces determine land rent, land use, and city size. As we will see, it also helps us understand how cities grow and change over time.

---

[3] Hamilton (1982).

[4] See Small and Song (1992) and the references given there.

SUBURBANIZATION

By far the most widespread and comprehensive change that has occurred in cities over the last century or so is that they have become more dispersed. This process is known as *decentralization* or *suburbanization*. In general terms, suburbanization can be defined as a gradual decline in the share of economic activity that is located in the city centre. More specifically, suburbanization can be measured by the flattening of urban population density functions over time.

Suburbanization

Gradual decline in the share of economic activity that is located in the city centre

In this section we will examine the nature and extent of suburbanization, focusing on North American cities. There are several facts about suburbanization that should be established:

1. Suburbanization seems to occur in all cities in all countries.
2. Suburbanization is not just a recent phenomenon. It has been occurring since at least 1800 in London (and probably for much longer than that).
3. Suburbanization is unavoidable. As cities grow, they inevitably expand outward, since most vacant land is found at the periphery.

The more difficult question is whether or not suburbanization is undesirable. Are cities too suburbanized in some sense? Does suburbanization represent an inefficient use of resources, as its pejorative *urban sprawl* seems to suggest?

Measuring Suburbanization

One simple way to measure suburbanization is by the declining share of a metropolitan area's population that resides in the *central city*. In this case, central city refers to the political jurisdiction that encompasses the downtown. For example, the City of Vancouver is the city centre of the Vancouver CMA. The average share of CMA population living in the central cities of Canada's three largest metropolitan areas was 67.1% in 1951 and 28.1% in 1981. For Vancouver alone, the central city population was 47% in 1961, 28.4% in 1996[5], 27.5% in 2001, and 26.1% in 2011. The historical evidence is clear: suburbanization is a steady and dominant feature of the cities of Canada.

Central City

The political jurisdiction that encompasses the downtown/CBD

The density gradient we defined above is another way of measuring suburbanization. If population density follows the negative exponential form given in Equation 7.1, then a city with a smaller g (a flatter density function) will have a smaller fraction of its population living within any distance of the city centre. A smaller value of g indicates a greater degree of suburbanization.

Table 7.3 shows historical estimates of D_0 and g for several cities worldwide. Notice that the gradient has decreased over time in each city; in most cases, the central density has fallen over time as well. This indicates that the cities grew less compact or more dispersed over time, as shown in Figure 7.2[6]. These data also show that suburbanization is not a recent phenomenon: London seems to have been decentralizing since at least 1800.

Table 7.3: Density Gradients and Suburbanization			
	Year	**D_0 (per hectare)**	**g (per kilometre)**
London	1801	1,040	0.78
	1841	1,080	0.58
	1871	865	0.38
	1901	660	0.23
	1921	443	0.17
	1931	475	0.17
	1939	320	0.14
	1951	240	0.12
	1961	205	0.09

continued on next page

---

[5]   The averages for Toronto, Montreal and Vancouver were calculated from the relevant Census of Canada volumes. The Vancouver data are from the Greater Vancouver Regional District (1999).

[6]   Figure 7.2 plots the implied density gradients for London for 1871 and 1931 from the data in Table 7.3. Therefore, the curve labelled 1871 is a plot of the equation $D(d) = 865e^{-0.38d}$ and the curve labelled 1931 is a plot of the equation $D(d) = 475e^{-0.17d}$.

Table 7.3: Density Gradients and Suburbanization (*continued*)			
	Year	**D_0 (per hectare)**	**g (per kilometre)**
Berlin	1885	1,120	0.68
	1900	1,580	0.59
Paris	1817	1,740	1.46
	1856	925	0.59
	1896	1,430	0.50
	1931	1,820	0.47
	1946	695	0.21
New York	1900	690	0.20
	1910	228	0.13
	1925	314	0.13
	1940	425	0.13
	1950	925	0.11
Chicago	1880	375	0.48
	1900	386	0.25
	1940	275	0.13
	1956	245	0.11

Source: Clark (1967), Table IX.4.

A bit closer to home, Table 7.4 reports average density gradients for US and Canadian metropolitan areas. The upper panel in the table shows that in the 1950s and 1960s, density gradients were larger in Canadian cities, but that by the 1970s, the slopes of the density functions were similar in the two countries. The lower panel reports average densities for 1975/76, disaggregated by the size of the central city. These data show that Canadian metropolitan areas whose central cities contained more than 500,000 people were considerably more compact than their US counterparts. The average density gradient for cities in this group was 0.30 in Canada and 0.19 in the US. The evidence shows that Canadian cities are historically less suburbanized than US cities. It is interesting to speculate about what factors could explain such a difference. However, first we must discuss the general causes of suburbanization. We will return to the apparent differences between Canadian and US cities at the end of the next section.

Table 7.4: Density Gradients in Canadian and US Metropolitan Areas		
	Average Gradient	
Year	**Canada**	**US**
1950/51	0.93	0.76
1960/61	0.67	0.60
1970/71	0.45	0.50
1975/76	0.42	0.45
	Average Gradient, 1975/76	
Central City Population, 1975/76	**Canada**	**US**
<100,000	0.41	0.95
100,00 - 500,000	0.43	0.48
500,000 - 1,000,000	0.43	0.26
>1,000,000	0.30	0.19

Notes: The gradients for Canada are averages over 20 CMAs. The gradients for the US are averages over 204 SMSAs.

Source: Edmonston, Goldberg, and Mercer (1985), Tables 1 and 6.

Explaining Suburbanization

Suburbanization appears to be a consistent phenomenon that occurs normally as cities age and grow. Economists have focused on a number of economic forces that seem to have contributed to the rapid decentralization of cities during the last century, particularly in North America. Three common explanations are natural evolution, the fiscal-social problem, and employment decentralization.[7]

Natural Evolution

According to the *natural evolution view*, the large industrial cities of the 19th century were gradually transformed by two fundamental economic events: rising incomes and falling transportation costs. As city residents became more affluent, they demanded more and better housing.

> **Natural Evolution View**
>
> The large industrial cities of the 19th century were gradually transformed by rising incomes and falling transportation costs

Larger and higher quality houses were built at the edge of a city, where vacant land is plentiful. This desire of high-income families for new and higher quality housing created pressure to move to new suburban neighbourhoods.

The introduction of streetcars, commuter trains, and eventually cars and highways made remote locations more accessible, reinforcing the tendency toward suburban residential development. Consider this account of how transportation improvements shaped the early development of Toronto:

> The growth of the built-up area after 1850 was characterized by the development or expansion of a number of high-income residential suburbs ... Their growth was in many cases linked to the introduction of the horse-drawn street railway in 1861 ... After the conversion to electric streetcars between 1892 and 1894 and the introduction of the radials (intercity electric railways), public transportation was extended to many suburban areas, creating a variety of streetcar suburbs ... (Nader [1976], Volume II, p. 209)

The natural evolution explanation of suburbanization is completely consistent with the predictions of a monocentric model of a city. If incomes rise and transportation costs fall, the model predicts that cities will expand outward and become less compact. This is another example of a useful prediction from the simple monocentric model.

Employment Decentralization

The monocentric model is predicated on the assumption that all employment is located around a central transportation terminal at the city centre. However, the evidence shows that this assumption is far from correct. For example, a study by Mills and Lubuele [1997] shows that only about 10% of total metropolitan area employment is located in the CBD in most modern US cities.

Employment decentralization can also be measured using exponential density functions. Table 7.1 gave density gradient data for both population and employment. Note that the employment density gradient is generally larger than the population density gradient, indicating that jobs are more centralized or less suburbanized on average than residences. For the sample of Canadian metropolitan areas listed in Table 7.1, the average employment gradient was 0.42, compared to an average population gradient of 0.31.

Table 7.5 illustrates historical employment gradients for different industries for a sample of US metropolitan areas. The data clearly shows the trend towards decentralization of employment; the employment gradients have declined over time in all of these industry groups.

Table 7.5: Employment Density Gradients by Industry in 18 US Metropolitan Areas						
Industry Group	**1948**	**1954**	**1958**	**1963**	**1970**	**1980**
Manufacturing	0.68	0.55	0.48	0.42	0.34	0.32
Retailing	0.88	0.75	0.59	0.44	0.35	0.30
Services	0.97	0.81	0.66	0.53	0.41	0.38
Wholesaling	1.00	0.86	0.70	0.56	0.43	0.37

Source: Mills (1972) and McCauley (1985)

---

[7] Mieszkowski and Mills (1993).

It is interesting to note the rankings of the industries by their density gradients over this period. The density gradients for the different industry groups seem to be converging over time, becoming less centralized (more suburbanized) in concert with the population trend towards suburbanization. However, the relative rankings of the industry types are relatively consistent.

For most of the study period, manufacturing was the least centralized (most suburbanized) sector. The key forces that are believed to account for the decentralization of manufacturing are improvements in transportation and technological change. In particular, the introduction of the truck made it easier for firms to move away from the export terminal at the city centre, and, once circumferential and interurban highways were developed, made it possible for manufacturers to export from suburban locations. The resulting tendency toward decentralization was encouraged by changes in production technology (e.g., continuous casting processes in the production of steel) that reduced manufacturing's optimal capital-to-land ratio. Furthermore, firms in many industries were also attracted to the suburbs by the growing population there, both for access to workers and customers. Thus, the suburbanization of population and manufacturing were complementary trends.

In contrast, the service industry was consistently one of the most centralized (least suburbanized) sector in this study period. The general view of this pattern is that firms in the traditional business services group (finance, insurance, and real estate) have maintained a relatively strong presence in downtowns because this gives them easy access to other, related businesses. The need for face-to-face contact is apparently an important centralizing force for many head office functions in a variety of industries. Of course, business service firms are also concentrated in downtowns because they can make efficient use of very tall structures, and can thus bid more for downtown land than other land uses.

Fiscal-Social Problem: Flight from Blight

The third historic explanation for suburbanization may be less economics-focused and more of a socio-political phenomenon. The *fiscal-social problem* explanation maintains that suburbanization has been hastened or encouraged by a number of fiscal and social problems that seem endemic to older US metropolitan areas. Central city problems that are thought to contribute to the flight of high-income families to the suburbs include high taxes, poor public services (especially poor inner city schools), racial prejudice, crime, congestion, and pollution. This explanation for suburbanization is also known as the *flight from blight* theory. The prevalence of gated communities is an example of this fear-driven motivation.

> **Fiscal-Social Problem**
>
> Suburbanization has been hastened or encouraged by a number of fiscal and social problems that seem endemic to older metropolitan areas (primarily US); also known as the *flight from blight*

The fiscal-social explanation has some popular, intuitive appeal, but it has not borne well under economic investigation. Two problems with it:

- Suburbanization appears to occur in virtually all countries, Canada included, but some of these central city problems are unique to the US experience.
- Even in the US, suburbanization appears to predate these fiscal and social problems by many decades.

Attempts to verify the fiscal-social problem explanation have not been very successful. Studies have found that differences in crime rates, educational attainment, and taxes did not help explain differences in the degree of suburbanization in US metropolitan areas. Interestingly, only the racial composition of the central city appear to have a strong impact on population decentralization.[8]

The information in Table 7.4 indicates that Canadian cities are more compact than cities of comparable size in the US. It is interesting to consider this difference in light of these explanations for suburbanization. With regard to the natural evolution explanation, Canada has fewer freeway miles per capita and much higher levels of public transit use. These observations are consistent with the hypothesis that auto commuting is more expensive in Canada, which is in turn consistent with the apparent differences in urban density patterns.[9] With regard to the fiscal-social explanation, rates of property crime are roughly equal in the two countries, but rates

---

[8] Mills and Price (1984).

[9] Goldberg and Mercer (1986).

of violent crime have been (and continue to be) multiples higher in the US. Similarly, fear of crime statistics are also much higher. This suggests that at least this one social problem is less acute in Canadian cities, which is also consistent with higher urban densities in Canada. These comparisons provide support for both the natural evolution and fiscal-social problems explanations of suburbanization.

Value Matters: Gentrification

The reverse of the so-called fight from the blight phenomenon occurs when higher-income individuals return to once blighted neighbourhoods. *The Appraisal of Real Estate, 3rd Canadian Edition* describes "urban pioneers" who "will tolerate higher crime rates and poorer services in exchange for lower housing prices and the potential for greater appreciation" (p. 4.12). This influx may improve the character of these neighbourhoods and increase property values – though at the cost of displacing lower-income residents or other urban uses that must be relocated.

SUBCENTRES AND CONTEMPORARY CITIES

Jobs and people are not spread evenly throughout suburban jurisdictions. Instead, much suburban economic activity is concentrated in just a few places in most cities. Modern cities are generally *polycentric*, consisting of an older, established downtown, and several newer and usually smaller downtowns spread throughout the suburbs. Suburban clusters of economic activity are generally known as *urban subcentres*.

Polycentric Cities

Consists of an older, established downtown, and several newer and usually smaller downtowns spread throughout the suburbs

Urban Subcentres

Suburban clusters of economic activity

Joel Garreau's book, *Edge City,* offered a fascinating view of the form and function of these new urban centres. Garreau's definition of an *edge city* is a place that:

- has more than 5 million square feet of office stpace;
- has more than 600,000 square feet of retail space;
- has more jobs than bedrooms;
- is perceived as one place; and
- was not urban (nothing like a city) 30 years ago.

This definition does a good job of capturing the theme that these subcentres are in many cases as large, diverse, and vibrant as any downtown. However, the book also touches on the controversy and contradictions that many people feel about modern polycentric urban areas. Edge cities are variously described as:

- "the crucible of America's urban future ... having become the place in which the majority of Americans now live, learn, work, shop, play, pray and die," and
- "plastic, ... and sterile", lacking "livability, civilization, community, and even a soul". (p. 8)

These edge cities are also called suburban activity centres, megacentres, and suburban business districts. The next sections explore the economic patterns that identify and form these subcentres.

What is a Subcentre?

There is no generally accepted definition of "subcentre". In common usage, this may be defined by geographic features or by political boundaries, such as CMAs that encompass a number of smaller legally independent municipalities. Urban land economists often identify subcentres by defining a threshold level of employment density. For example, Giuliano and Small (1991) classified an area as a subcentre if it contains more than 10,000 jobs and has an average employment density of more than 10 employees-per-acre. They estimate that there were 32 such subcentres in the Los Angeles metropolitan area in 1980. Each study will define its own threshold and thus its own form of subcentre.

Key Concept: Edge Cities

Garreau identified three distinct varieties of the edge city phenomenon:

- Boomers – The most common type, having developed incrementally around a shopping mall or highway interchange.
- Greenfields – Having been master-planned as new towns, generally on the suburban fringe.
- Uptowns – Historic activity centres built over an older city or town (sometimes a satellite city).

Most edge cities develop at or near existing or planned freeway intersections, and are especially likely to develop near major airports. They rarely include heavy industry. Spatially, edge cities primarily consist of mid-rise office towers (with some skyscrapers) surrounded by massive surface parking lots and meticulously manicured lawns. Instead of a traditional street grid, their street networks are hierarchical, consisting of winding parkways (often lacking sidewalks) that feed into arterial roads or freeway ramps. However, edge cities feature job density similar to that of secondary downtowns found in places such as Newark and Pasadena.

Edge cities may create a significant growth in sophisticated retail, entertainment, and consumer service facilities, which in turn leads to a rise in local employment opportunities. The edge city has a tendency to affect the surrounding areas by procuring more opportunities within the labour market. They are well-suited to an economy which is known for a service-orientated market as well as sustaining major manufacturing sectors.

Source: *www.wikipedia.org*

Highways and Subcentre Location

Garreau's edge cities are usually identified by, and sometimes named after, the suburban highways along which they have grown. Thus. there is the "Mass Turnpike and 128" subcentre in Boston, the "287 and 80" subcentre in Northern New Jersey, and the Seattle Interstate 405 north subcentre — "Technology Corridor". The tendency for subcentres to form along major suburban highways has been known for quite some time and fits very well with the themes that we have been discussing.

To see this, let's return briefly to our discussion of firm location in a monocentric city, from Chapter 6. However, let's now assume that firms can either export their products through the central transportation terminal located at d = 0 or through a circumferential highway or beltway located at d = s (illustrated on Figure 7.3). The idea is that this highway, which goes all the way around the city at distance d = s from the city centre, is connected to other cities through a national highway network. Firms who use the central terminal will bid for land according to the manufacturing profit. Firms who instead use the beltway to export their goods will earn profit based on the following modified equation:

EQUATION 7.2

$$\pi^{SE}(d) = [(P \times Q) - C] - [T \times Q \times |d - s|] - [L \times R^{SE}(d)]$$

Where:

- $\pi^{SE}(d)$ = Profit for the suburban exporting firm locating at any distance d from the city centre
- P × Q = Revenue
- C = Non-land cost
- T × Q × |d − s|= Firm's transport cost depending on how far their location (d) is from the suburban highway (s).[10] This is the only difference between the profit of a firm that exports through the central terminal (see Chapter 6) and the profit of a firm that exports through the beltway.
- L × $R^{SE}(d)$ = Lot size times land rent per unit at the location d

---

[10] Because a firm's location (d) may be on either side of the beltway (s), either closer to the city centre (d < s) or farther from the city centre (d > s), we have to use the absolute value |d – s| in the formula. Otherwise the transportation cost would be added instead of subtracted for firms located close to the city centre.

Just as with Equation 6.7, we set $\pi^{SE}(d) = 0$ (economic rent = $0) and solve for $R^{SE}(d)$ to find the suburban exporter's bid rent function for land:

EQUATION 7.3

$$R^{SE}(d) = \frac{(P \times Q) - C}{L} - \frac{T \times Q}{L} \times |d - s|$$

The suburban exporter's bid rent $R^{SE}(d)$ is highest if the first is located right at the highway (d=s), as this location minimizes their transport cost. This is the most attractive land from the suburban exporter's perspective. If the firm locates further from the highway, then |d − s| increases, their transport costs increase, and the firm's bid rent will decline.

FIGURE 7.3

Highways and Subcentre Location

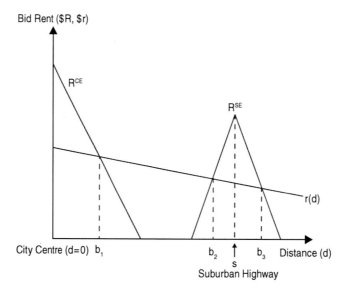

Figure 7.3 illustrates the bid rent function for this suburban exporter (labelled R^{SE}) and also a central city exporter (labelled R^{CE}).[11] Note that there are now two peaks in the firm bid rent function — one at the city centre and one at the suburban highway. The bid rents for a third competing use, residential land, is shown by the declining bid rent function r(d).

In this setting, competition for land generates an interesting land use pattern, again based on maximum bid rent at each location. Firms that export through the city centre will occupy sites between d = 0 and d = b_1. These firms will be surrounded by a ring of residential land use between d = b_1 and d = b_2. Then there will be another ring of employment concentrated around the suburban highway: firms that export through the highway will outbid all other land uses for sites between d = b_2 and d = b_3. Beyond b_3 is another residential ring, up to the point where the agricultural bid rent r_a outbids residential.

Thus, the city has both a downtown and an urban subcentre. This shows how the conventional relationship between access and bid rent can help explain where subcentres tend to arise.

Subcentre Formation

Why do subcentres form? At some level, subcentres must form for the same reasons that cities form — because it is advantageous to conduct economic activity in a spatially concentrated fashion. Recall back in Chapter 1 when we used the term *agglomeration economy* to describe the advantages of producing goods and services in a spatially concentrated fashion. It is reasonable to assume that agglomeration economies encourage clustering in the suburbs, in much the same way that they encourage clustering in downtowns. Looking at most larger cities with subcentres, it is clear that the various business and firms tend to congregate. The resulting higher employment densities show that agglomeration economies influence the location of suburban jobs.

---

[11] The figure assumes that the price that the firm receives is higher if it exports through the central terminal.

One study of subcentre formation, by Helsley and O'Sullivan [1991], explains how these subcentres form as part of a city's natural evolution. The basic idea behind this model is illustrated in Figure 7.4. The graph plots net marginal value (MV) of labour against the number of workers or labour (L). The right side shows the net marginal value of labour at the city centre (indicated by the superscript C) and the left side shows this labour value at a subcentre (indicated by the superscript S).

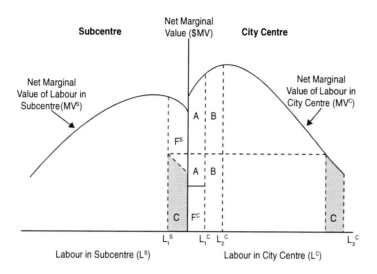

FIGURE 7.4

Subcentre Formation

So, for example, MV^C is the net marginal value of labour in the city centre. This represents the increment to output from adding one more job to the central city, minus the incremental costs of congestion, pollution, and other disamenities. The MV curves rise at first due to agglomeration economies — up to a certain point, the clusters become more productive as the number of workers increases. After this optimal point, the MV curves then fall as the costs of congestion and disamenities rise.

There is an implicit assumption that there is some productive advantage to the central city — after all, that is why it was developed in the first place. So we can assume that the $MV^C > MV^S$ for every given number of workers. For a start, we will focus only on the city centre (right side), since the subcentre will not form until the city reaches a certain size.

Assume that there is a fixed cost for the initial set up of the city centre as an employment location denoted by F. This might be the cost of the public infrastructure that is necessary in order for firms to produce at a particular place.

Now assume that the city is growing, adding n workers or jobs each time period. You, as the city's urban planner, allocate the first workers to the city centre (L_1^C), as this maximizes the net social value of the city's output. After paying the fixed cost F^c, this leaves the city with net benefit equal to the area labelled A.

The next workers should also be allocated to the city centre (L_2^C). You have already paid the fixed cost to establish the downtown, and placing these workers with their predecessors allows you to take advantage of agglomeration economies. The net benefit associated with these additional workers is equal to the area labelled B.

This pattern should continue for a while — since the cost of establishing the downtown is sunk, it is ideal to concentrate development there. However, the marginal benefit of each group of new workers gets less and less (the declining slope of MV_C). Eventually, the added costs of congestion and disamenities in the downtown increase to the point where it makes sense to establish another employment location. The subcentre should form when the value of the first workers in the subcentre (L_1^S) exceeds the combined fixed cost of establishing suburban infrastructure (F^s) and the lost benefit (or opportunity cost) from not having them work in the city centre (C). In the diagram, the subcentre forms when the value of workers in the central city (L_3^C) is only equal to the area labelled C, but their value in the subcentre is ($C + F^s$). At that point it makes economic sense to allocate additional workers to the subcentre — and after that point, with the fixed cost covered (F^s), it makes even better sense to send more. However, eventually the subcentre also becomes congested and its benefit wanes, until the net marginal value of labour at the two locations is equal. Thereafter growth may be split between the two locations (in a manner that equalizes the marginal value of labour at the two sites) or perhaps yet another more profitable subcentre may form.

The model mimics some of the stylized facts about subcentre development:

- The city initially enjoys an extended period of exclusive central city development. Cities are initially monocentric.
- The subcentre forms when the city centre becomes so large and congested that it makes sense to incur the fixed costs of establishing another employment location. Thus, in some sense, the subcentre forms when the city centre becomes an unattractive location for investment.

Once the subcentre is established, most of the growth occurs there, at least for a time. Therefore, the city's history features a prolonged period of monocentricity, followed by a period in which the city centre stagnates and most growth occurs in urban subcentres. In this way, the formation of subcentres is a natural feature of the evolution of an urban area.

Value Matters: Nodes

The Appraisal of Real Estate, 3rd Canadian Edition defines nodes as "a cluster of properties with the same or complementary uses" (p. 9.25). This includes office buildings downtown or retail stores along an uptown strip. Other nodes include industrial parks and office parks in suburban locations. Office parks are often located near airports, rapid transit routes, or post-secondary facilities, taking advantage of lower rent and ease of access. These parks may in turn generate a local service economy with restaurants, lodging, and recreation. And then housing may also develop nearby to accommodate workers. Thus, a sub-centre is born!

THE ECONOMICS OF URBAN SPRAWL

The term *urban sprawl* is pejorative, generally implying a negative city attribute. Urban planners have many contrasting visions for optimal or ideal development patterns. Some advocate more density in the downtown core, others want to see more effective subcentres, and others have grand plans for comprehensive mixed-use communities. However, one topic most contemporary planners seem to agree on is that urban sprawl, or the uncontrolled and inefficient dispersion of land uses, is not an ideal to strive for.

Sprawl

To be stretched or spread out in an unnatural or ungraceful manner

Source: *Dictionary.com*

From an economic perspective, our question is a relatively narrow one — whether or not market determined land use patterns are inefficient in the sense that they involve too much dispersion of economic activity in cities.

One way to approach this problem is to ask if there are systematic forces that cause developers to convert agricultural land at the edge of the city to urban uses too quickly or in excessive quantities. It turns out that there are.

1. It seems likely that there are external benefits associated with preserving open space in cities. For example, residents may value having access to undeveloped areas near the city for aesthetic reasons. Similarly, there may be social value in preserving prime agricultural land for local food production. However, these positive externalities tend to be ignored by individual property developers — leaving market mechanisms unchecked will tend toward preserving too little open and agricultural space (less than what society as a whole would find optimal).
2. It may be that new development does not pay a fair share of the costs that it imposes on municipal governments. Property taxes are the main source of revenue for most local governments, and property tax payments may not accurately reflect the costs of providing infrastructure and other public services to new residential development. Unless other charges or fees are levied on new developments, development costs may be too low. This would cause developers to convert too much land from agriculture to urban uses.

3. The most important source of land market failure, is related to the problem of traffic congestion.[12] Auto use generally involves a negative externality. When an individual chooses to travel on a congested road, he or she does not account for the impact of his or her choice on the travel times of other drivers. In the absence of congestion tolls, or some other policy designed to *internalize this externality*, the result is that auto travel in cities is underpriced — it is too cheap to travel by car — and consequently the level of auto travel in cities is inefficiently large.

This inefficiency also impacts the market for land. Of course, the cost of travel is an important determinant of land rent, land use, and city size. We know from our earlier analysis that a decrease in commuting costs causes a city to decentralize — the land rent function becomes flatter, and the boundary of the city expands. This implies that the inefficiently low cost of commuting by car causes our cities to be too spread out, just as the critics of urban sprawl suggest.

There are a variety of policies that could address these problems. Generally speaking, from an economic perspective it is best to address each problem directly. For example:

- To preserve open space, we could tax the conversion of land from agriculture to urban use.
- To correct the underpricing of infrastructure and public services, many jurisdictions impose additional fees (called impact fees or development cost charges) on new residential development.
- To correct the problem of traffic congestion, we could impose congestion tolls on travel on congested roads at peak times.

There are also a number of indirect approaches. For example, urban growth boundaries, which restrict development beyond a certain distance from the city centre, have been used to try to control urban sprawl. A general problem with indirect policies is that they do not correct the underlying problems — even with an urban growth boundary, travel within cities is still inefficient. Also, all of these policies may have other important effects. For example, both urban growth boundaries and impact fees undoubtedly increase housing prices in the cities where they are imposed. This poses a significant challenge for policy makers. Unless the corrective policies are carefully designed, their unintended consequences could easily outweigh the benefits of reducing urban sprawl.

SUMMARY

Although the monocentric model is very simple, it captures some fundamental truths about cities. This chapter reviewed the monocentric model's basic predictions, examining how these predictions have been tested and the different ways that the model's underlying principles have been applied in the real world. We showed, for example, that land prices and population densities generally fall with distance to the city centre, as the monocentric model predicts. However, the monocentric model is not perfect. In particular, it is a very poor predictor of the amount of commuting that occurs in cities.

The dominant trend in urban development during the 20th century was the suburbanization or decentralization of cities. We discussed how decreases in transportation costs will cause decentralization in a monocentric city. We also examined how suburbanization is measured and discussed the other economic forces that seem to contribute to this very general and broad phenomenon. An example of this is the emergence of subcentres or edge cities within existing metropolitan areas. Subcentres seem to form for many of the same reasons that cities form, in particular to take advantage of agglomeration economies in production. Not surprisingly, the location of subcentres seems closely tied to the location of transportation facilities in many cities. Finally, we introduced the problem of urban sprawl, or excessive decentralization. We discussed how positive externalities associated with open space, the pricing (or mispricing) of public services for new residential development, and transportation congestion may cause our cities to be too spread out.

The next chapter examines how the passage of time impacts the operation of land markets and the development of cities.

---

[12] We will discuss the economics of traffic congestion in detail in Chapter 9.

INTRODUCTION

Urban areas are constantly changing. City populations and boundaries expand, transportation systems evolve, property prices cycle, and structures are renovated, redeveloped, and in some cases, abandoned, as land use pressures rise and fall. To understand these issues, and the problems and opportunities that they raise, we must examine how the passage of time impacts the operation of land markets and the development of cities. Thus far our analysis has been largely static — we have basically ignored the passage of time. Obviously, this is not realistic, so in this chapter we will relax this assumption and examine the impact of time on urban development.

Cities are among the most durable of human creations. The physical assets that make up a city — its ports, commercial buildings, houses, and roads — provide services for many years after they are built. These assets are also expensive to modify or change. Consequently, most of the physical assets in a city were built long in the past and will be used for some time to come.

The durability of capital has important implications for cities. It means that decisions that were made in the past have important impacts on the present. For example, early decisions about the location and capacity of roads and bridges impact the current location of residential development. The durability of capital also means that decisions made today will have important impacts on the future. Current patterns of residential development patterns will affect the future location of commercial centres. In this chapter we examine how time, history, and the durability of capital affect the spatial growth of a city, property development patterns, and urban land and housing prices.

The chapter is organized as follows:

- First, we examine the durability of capital issue. We will see how the spatial growth of a city is an incremental process and that current population densities in cities are largely a product of historical factors established long ago.
- Next, we investigate another dynamic issue, property redevelopment, and its impacts on the spatial development of a city.
- A key issue flowing from this is how development decisions may change over time. Of particular importance is the insight that it can be efficient to withhold land from current development in anticipation of some more valuable future use.
- Finally, we consider the impact of urban growth on land and housing prices. Since the price of real estate equals the present value of future rents, and since rents rise with city size, current prices should be higher in cities that are expected to grow in the future. We present a diagram that summarizes this point, and analyze the relationship between growth and prices in a sample of Canadian CMAs.

Value Matters: Point-in-Time Appraisal

Appraisal assignments are nearly always focused on a moment in time – the value is estimated on a set date, which could be current or past (or, rarely, future). Changes over time such as urban growth may have limited impact in any given appraisal assignment. However, if you take a bigger view of the collection of valuation assignments over a career, the ever-changing, evolving market will have a major effect. Highest and best use analysis in particular is influenced by population density, spatial growth, and capital mobility.

THE SPATIAL GROWTH OF A CITY

Generally speaking, cities grow by converting land near the edge of the city from agriculture to urban use. Urban growth is an incremental process in which new development is added at the edge of the city as population increases.

Consider a growing, open monocentric city similar to those we studied in Chapters 6 and 7. The key difference is that this city is not static — it is growing. Our city is an open city, meaning its population can change by migration to and from other areas. If, for example, household income in this city rises over time, then individuals will be attracted from other areas, and the population of this city will increase.

One simplifying assumption for this model: assume that time can be broken into discrete time periods such that economic conditions do not change within any time period, but may change between time periods. For example, if we are measuring time in years, then incomes and commuting costs may change from year to year, but not from month to month. This is just a convenient way to keep track of time; the basic insights do not depend on whether the time periods are months or years or even decades.

Bringing forward the monocentric city model that we studied in Chapters 6 and 7, in period i identical households choose a lot size ℓ_i and a quantity of other goods x_i to maximize their utility subject to the constraint that their expenditures must equal their income. The budget constraint is written $(r_i \times \ell_i) + x_i = I_i - (t_i \times d)$, where x_i is expenditures on "other goods", r_i is land rent, I_i is income, and $(t_i \times d)$ is commuting cost from distance d in period i.

To properly examine this growth process, we must specify two additional assumptions: durability and households' expectations about the future. With respect to durability, we assume that once lot sizes are chosen, they are fixed for all time. In other words, the initial development of a parcel of land determines population density there for all future periods. In a more general model where people buy housing, and not just land, we would assume that the capital that is used to build the structures is durable — once you build a structure, it does not change. Our assumption about lot sizes is sort of a proxy for this more complicated process. We use the term *development* to refer to both population and structural density — the measures of the growth process that we discussed in the previous chapter.

The second new assumption relates to households' expectations about the future. To begin, we assume that households are unable to forecast what future economic conditions will be. This means that they base their decisions only on economic conditions as they are today. Decision makers who behave this way are commonly said to have *myopic expectations* about the future. How people perceive the future makes a huge difference in this context. The other extreme is to assume that households know the future and base their decisions on this *perfect foresight*. We will consider models in which decision makers have perfect foresight later in the chapter.

Myopic Expectations

An assumption that households are unable to forecast what future economic conditions will be and base their decisions only on the present day economic conditions

Perfect Foresight

An assumption that households have full knowledge of future economic conditions and base their decisions on this knowledge

Rent, City Size, and Density

To explore the growth of our stylized city over time, we need to solve for equilibrium land rent, lot size, and population density in each time period. The upper panel of Figure 8.1 shows the bid rent function in this city for one period, labelled "period 0". Similar to prior monocentric city examples, the land rent declines with distance in each period to offset the rising cost of commuting. The bid rents are once again based on households pursuing their maximum utility u. However, because of the openness assumption, the population of the city will adjust until all households living here achieve utility level u*, the utility level that is available in other cities in period 0.

The lower panel of Figure 8.1 shows the associated equilibrium population density function on newly developed land in period 0. Note that population density also declines with distance: households living further from the CBD purchase larger lots, other things being equal.[1]

Taken together, the two panels in Figure 8.1 show the initial development of the city during period 0. The initial border of the city is at the point b_0, where urban land rent in period 0, $r_0(d)$, equals agricultural land rent.

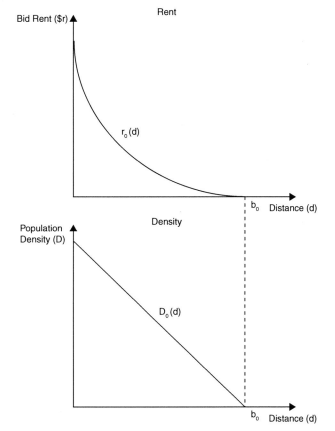

FIGURE 8.1

Initial Land Rent and Population Density

---

[1] Notice that population density is a linear function of distance in this case. This is not realistic (recall the density functions of Chapter 7), but it is a simplification we will adopt here for illustration purposes.

Incremental Growth

Now let's consider the next time period. Suppose that incomes are higher in period 1 than they were in period 0, but that all other factors are unchanged. An increase in incomes causes both the land rent and population density functions to shift upward, as shown in Figure 8.2.

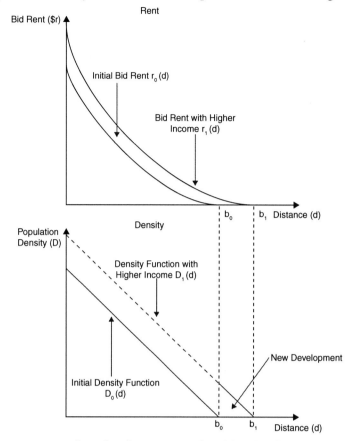

Because of our assumption that development is durable, the lot sizes inside the initial city boundary b_0 cannot change from their historical values from period 0. All new development will occur in the interval between the old border b_0 and the new border b_1. In other words, the city grows by adding a bit of new development at its edge. Inside b_0, nothing changes.[2]

If incomes continue to rise over time, then as the city expands, population density will follow a sawtooth pattern like the one shown in Figure 8.3. A similar pattern of urban growth would result in this model if commuting costs are decreasing. However, the increments to the density function will become flatter over time when falling commuting costs are the engine of growth. In either case, just enough new development is added at the edge of the city in each period to accommodate that period's population growth.

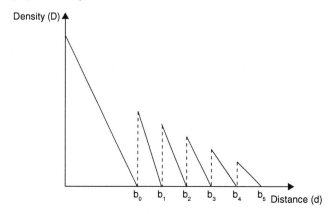

---

[2] This is not quite right. The rent on land inside b_0 changes. There are actually two rent functions in this case. One for new development, $r_1(d)$ as in Figure 8.2, and another rent function giving the maximum amount households are willing and able to pay for land inside b_0, given the historical lot sizes there. We will discuss the distinction between these two rent functions in greater detail in the next section.

This view of urban growth suggests that density is determined not so much by a long-run tradeoff between distance and housing consumption, but rather by an historical process that is heavily dependent on past economic conditions. In other words, the timing of development is a key consideration in the character of cities. Consider older cities like Boston and Toronto that are densely developed because they were largely developed when technologies were capital intensive, incomes were lower, and transportation costs were higher. Conversely, cities like Los Angeles and Vancouver are more sparsely developed because they are relatively young, and were largely developed when demanded structural densities were lower.

Table 8.1 provides some empirical evidence for this urban growth pattern. The 2001 Census showed that, across all CMAs, 59% of newly built housing could be found in low density areas, while the remaining 41% was in medium and high density areas. Furthermore, two-thirds of new housing stock across all CMAs was built at least 10 kilometres away from the city centre. However, the Census data show some variation among major cities. More than half of the newest housing in cities such as Toronto, Montreal, and Quebec were in low density areas, but Vancouver showed inverse development tendencies. Only 28% of Vancouver's newest housing stock was in low density areas.

Table 8.1: Distribution of housing stock constructed in 1991 and later, by type of neighbourhood											
	All CMAs[2]	Toronto	Montréal	Vancouver	Ottawa	Calgary	Edmonton	Québec	Winnipeg	Medium CMAs	Small CMAs
Density[1]											
High	17	17	26	33	13	3	7	25	5	9	12
Medium	24	19	19	39	39	10	16	21	10	24	27
Low	59	64	55	28	48	87	77	54	85	68	62
Total	100	100	100	100	100	100	100	100	100	100	100
Distance from city centre[3]											
0 - 9 km	34	13	18	36	36	25	31	48	50	59	69
10 km and more	66	87	82	65	64	76	69	51	49	42	31
Total	100	100	100	100	100	100	100	100	100	100	100

Source: Statistics Canada, 2001 Census.

Source: Turcotte, M. (2008). *The city/suburb contrast: How to measure it? Canadian Social Trends*, 85, Statistics Canada Catalogue no. 11-008-XWE.

[1] In low-density neighbourhoods, 66.6% or more of the housing stock is composed of single family dwellings, semi-detached dwellings or mobile homes. In medium-density neighbourhoods, the percentage is between 33.3% and less than 66.6%. In high-density neighbourhoods, these types of dwellings comprise less than 33.3% of the housing stock.

[2] Census metropolitan area.

[3] The city centre is defined as being the census tract that contains the city hall of the central municipality.

REDEVELOPMENT

As noted earlier, there are actually two distinct land rent functions lurking behind the density function drawn in Figure 8.2:

- the rent for newly developed land, $r_N(d)$, and
- the rent on previously developed land, given its historical characteristics.

If economic conditions change between the periods (as we have assumed) then these rent functions will differ. For example, older central city lots may be smaller than the lots that today's consumers prefer. After all, today's consumers have different incomes, and face different commuting costs and other variables than the consumers who initially purchased central city lots. An analogous issue may be that smaller inner city houses and lots are less attractive to current consumers than newly built houses. If this is true, then today's consumers will not be willing to pay as much for previously developed land as for a parcel that can developed to current standards.

It is as if there are two separate land uses in the city: old development and new development. Let's consider a simplified illustration of these two rent functions for a particular growing city. In Figure 8.4, the rent for previously developed land is labelled $r_i(d)\_old$ and new development is labelled $r_i(d)\_new$. The bid rent functitons are redrawn as straight lines to simplify the illustration.

<table>
<tr><td>FIGURE 8.4

Redevelopment</td><td>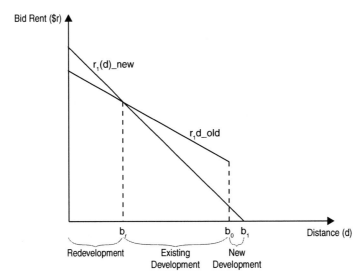</td></tr>
</table>

Based on these bid rent functions, we would conclude that new development should occur on parcels between b_0 and b_1. The basis of this conclusion is that, for these parcels, new development outbids all other land uses (in particular agriculture), and is the highest and best use of the land.

However, what about the land inside the point labelled b_r in the figure? New development is the highest bidder for this land as well, but we have assumed it to be frozen in its historical use. If we relax this assumption, then new development will occupy all land inside b_r as well. This, of course, is redevelopment: structures on older lots are demolished and replaced with newer, optimal ones.

There is a simple rule that governs whether and when a particular property should be redeveloped in this context: redevelopment should occur when the value of a new property (with its proposed optimal lot size and structure) exceeds the value of the existing property on a parcel (with its historical lot size and structure) by more than the cost of demolition. If this condition holds, then redevelopment must maximize land value, and be in the land owners' best interest. Generally speaking, redevelopment involves conversion to higher uses or higher densities — from small to large houses, in the simplest case.

Helpful Hint

Redevelopment should occur when the value of a new property (with its proposed optimal lot size and structure) exceeds the value of the existing property on a parcel (with its historical lot size and structure) by more than the cost of demolition.

Since older structures are generally redeveloped first, and since the age or vintage of development declines as one moves away from the city centre, this model predicts that redevelopment will gradually move outward from the city centre over time. Eventually, there may come a time when most central city properties have been replaced and redevelopment activity is concentrated in today's suburbs. However, we are not there yet: in most North American cities, redevelopment tends to be concentrated in central cities.

Key Concept: Redevelopment and Heritage Properties

The economic forces driving redevelopment will mean older properties are replaced with newer properties, when it makes economic sense to do so. The driver of this decision is profit-maximizing behaviour. Some people may not like this or agree with it, in wanting to preserve older buildings, but aesthetic preferences are not directly considered in economic decision-making. Society's desire to protect historically or culturally significant properties from redevelopment has led to political pressure for preservation of so-called heritage properties. The preservation of these properties may generate benefits for others that a land owner or developer would not consider. If left solely to market forces, private incentives would presumably lead to excessive redevelopment. Adding the external benefits of preservation to the market value of the heritage property would provide an economic test of whether or not redevelopment is warranted.

LAND DEVELOPMENT WITH FORESIGHT

The models thus far have assumed that decision makers do not look forward in time. The households or land owners in the growing cities make their decisions on current circumstances and assume that the future will be just like the present. For example, a land owner choosing how densely to develop a particular parcel does not consider the fact that commuting costs may be higher in the future than they are today. If the land owner considered this possibility, then he or she might choose to build a different structure now.

In this section and the remainder of this chapter, we will assume that decision makers are concerned with the future and use their knowledge about the future when making current decisions. Obviously the future is unknown, so the best we can do is use past and current events to make reasonable predictions of what might happen. This of course brings an element of uncertainty and risk that is difficult to factor into economic models.

So far, we have assumed perfect myopia: people act with no knowledge of the future whatsoever. To introduce forward-thinking into our models, we will make an extreme assumption: decision makers have perfect foresight. This means that they know the future with certainty. A land owner with perfect foresight knows what rent the property will earn in all future periods, depending on how it is developed. However, the reality is likely somewhere in between myopia and perfect foresight — people forecast the future and use these forecasts in their decisions, but real people are not omniscient. Myopia and perfect foresight are useful extreme cases for economic modelling: they are simple to analyze and capture elements of the truth, occurring somewhere in the middle.

A land owner with perfect foresight will choose the timing and form of current development and future redevelopment that maximizes the present value of future land rents. This might involve different land uses at different points in time. For example, it might be best to initially develop a parcel as housing and then later convert it to a commercial use. Or it might be best to subsequently redevelop low-density housing as high-density housing. Efficient development may also involve leaving the land vacant for some time.

Consider a simple example to illustrate these points.

- There are two time periods and assume that land owners can only develop in one of them, i.e., there is no redevelopment.
- You may choose the type of development (e.g., residential or commercial, and high- or low-density) and whether to develop in period 1 or wait until period 2.
- The future second period rent will be discounted to the present value by dividing it by (1 + i), where i is the one period discount rate. Assume that the discount rate is 10%.

The parcel of land you own has a highest and best use today for single-family housing. This use will earn you a net rent of $100,000 in period 1 and another $100,000 in period 2. The present value of this rent stream is:

$$\$100,000 + \frac{\$100,000}{1.1} = \$190,909$$

Alternatively, you can wait one period to develop the property. If the highest and best use of the land next period is the same as it is today, then waiting obviously won't make sense — you lose one period's return while the land is held vacant, and a future payoff is worth less than a payoff earned today. Waiting leaves you a present value return of:

$$\frac{\$100,000}{1.1} = \$90,909$$

Under these assumptions, it would never be desirable to hold the land vacant.

However, suppose that if you wait, the highest and best use of the land will change and this will increase the net rent substantially. For example, if the parcel's highest and best use one period in the future is high-density multi-family housing or even retail or office use, then the net rent may increase by enough to be worth waiting. Say the net rent increases to $225,000 in period 2, then the present value return is:

$$\frac{\$225,000}{1.1} = \$204,545$$

Since this is more than the return from immediately developing the parcel for residential use, it is optimal for you to hold the land off the market for period 1, and develop it in period 2 instead.

Keep in mind, though, that this conclusion is heavily dependent on the assumptions:

- A larger discount rate would mean future payoffs are worth relatively less today, making it less attractive to wait for some more valuable future use. In our example, an 18% discount rate leads to a $190,678 present value, which is a lower projected return than the immediate development option.
- A lower projected return for the future highest and best use also impacts its projected current return. Keep in mind too our unrealistic assumption of perfect foresight — the less certainty regarding this future earning, the more risk is involved in stalling immediate development. In effect, this decision involves a calculated risk — which is the real estate business equivalent of gambling!

EXERCISE 8.1 Which Development is Best?

Question 1

A developer owns a parcel of land and has to decide what to develop and when.

Option 1: Develop property immediately as mixed-use commercial space. This earns the developer $50,000 per year (with payments occurring at the beginning of each year).

Option 2: Leave the property vacant and pursue rezoning, such that it can be developed into condominiums. This will earn the developer $110,000 (paid at the beginning of period 2).

Assuming that the developer's discount rate is 5% per year (compounded annually, j_1) and that there are only two periods to consider, which is the preferred option?

Solution:

In order to make a reasoned decision, we need to find the present value of each option. Converting the two different payment streams into two present values allows us to consider each option as if all payments were occurring right now rather than some point in future.

Present Value of Option 1

$$= \$50,000 + \frac{\$50,000}{1.05}$$

$$= \$50,000 + \$47,619.05$$

$$= \$97,619.05$$

continued on next page

Present Value of Option 2

$$= \$0 + \frac{\$110,000}{1.05}$$

$$= \$0 + \$104,761.90$$

$$= \$104,761.90$$

Thus, Option 2 is superior having a higher present value.

Question 2

A developer has two development options to consider:

Option 1: a condominium that will return $10,000 in period 1 and $45,000 in period 2

Option 2: an office unit that will return $20,000 in period 1 and $30,000 in period 2

Assume there are only two periods and that all payments are made at the beginning of each period. Under what conditions would the developer prefer Option 1 to Option 2?

Solution:

It appears Option 1 generates more return in total, $55,000 versus $50,000 for Option 2. However, the timing of the cash flows is different, with Option 1 providing more return in future and Option 2 providing more upfront. Our task is to find out what discount rate would make Option 1 the preferred option. Expressing this algebraically, we would like to know what discount rate (r) would make the options equally satisfying:

PV of Option 1 = PV of Option 2

$$\$10,000 + \frac{\$45,000}{(1+r)} = \$20,000 + \frac{\$30,000}{(1+r)}$$

Using this equation, we now need to isolate and solve for r:

Subtract 10,000 from both sides: $\dfrac{\$45,000}{(1+r)} = \$10,000 + \dfrac{\$30,000}{(1+r)}$

Subtract $\dfrac{\$30,000}{(1+r)}$ from both sides: $\dfrac{\$15,000}{(1+r)} = \$10,000$

Multiply both sides by (1+r): $15,000 = \$10,000(1+r)$

Divide both sides by $10,000: 1.5 = 1+r

Subtract 1 from both sides: 0.5 = r

Our conclusion is that Option 1 is preferable to Option 2 only if the discount rate is higher than 50%. At a discount rate of less than 50%, the developer would prefer the more immediate cash flow from Option 1.

Note that just because we have found the condition where Option 1 is preferred to Option 2 does not make it likely. Developer's need to account for risk, opportunity cost, and time preferences within market realities. A discount rate as high as 50% is probably unrealistic.

Value Matters: Principle of Anticipation

The present value calculations briefly illustrated in Exercise 8.1 are the basis for appraisal's discounted cash flow techniques. When a commercial property or proposed development has a combination of upfront costs and income received in future, the value of the property can be calculated by discounting these positive and negative cash flows to present value terms. This is based on the appraisal principle of anticipation: value is created by the expectation of benefits to be derived in the future.

continued on next page

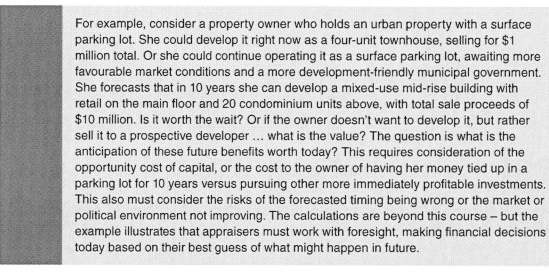

For example, consider a property owner who holds an urban property with a surface parking lot. She could develop it right now as a four-unit townhouse, selling for $1 million total. Or she could continue operating it as a surface parking lot, awaiting more favourable market conditions and a more development-friendly municipal government. She forecasts that in 10 years she can develop a mixed-use mid-rise building with retail on the main floor and 20 condominium units above, with total sale proceeds of $10 million. Is it worth the wait? Or if the owner doesn't want to develop it, but rather sell it to a prospective developer ... what is the value? The question is what is the anticipation of these future benefits worth today? This requires consideration of the opportunity cost of capital, or the cost to the owner of having her money tied up in a parking lot for 10 years versus pursuing other more immediately profitable investments. This also must consider the risks of the forecasted timing being wrong or the market or political environment not improving. The calculations are beyond this course – but the example illustrates that appraisers must work with foresight, making financial decisions today based on their best guess of what might happen in future.

It is common in land markets to withhold land from current development. The most common examples of this phenomenon are parking lots in the downtown. Why do surface parking lots exist on the busiest streets in the middle of a thriving city? Because the land is being reserved for some more valuable future use, presumably a very high density use. It is too expensive to build an alternative use in the short term and then demolish it once ready, so the best option is to hold the land vacant rather than develop it is some intermediate way. This is an example of land development with foresight. Yet land owners who delay development in this manner are often criticized for *speculating* in land. However, this type of speculation is essential for the efficient operation of an urban land market.

Speculation

Withholding land from current development in anticipation of some more valuable future use

This phenomenon also occurs in the suburbs, but there it can become more controversial. When suburban land is withheld from current development in anticipation of some more valuable future use, it often contributes to what is called *leapfrogging*. This occurs when current development jumps over the parcel being withheld, resulting in a discontinuous development pattern. One of the many criticisms of urban sprawl is that discontinuous development increases the costs of providing public services (roads, sewers, police and fire services, etc.). This may be true, but it does not necessarily imply that leapfrog development is economically inefficient. Efficiency generally requires that we reserve some land for more valuable future uses. The problem is that the market may reserve too much unless we charge appropriate prices for public services. We should certainly make new development pay the full costs that it imposes on local governments. However, even with properly priced public services, discontinuous development may still be warranted.

Leapfrogging

Occurs when current development jumps over the parcel being withheld, resulting in a discontinuous development pattern

PROPERTY PRICES AND URBAN GROWTH

We have shown that the passage of time has important impacts on the way that a city develops. In this section we examine the implications of urban growth for land and housing prices.

The monocentric model does a reasonably good job of explaining differences in land prices within a city. Generally speaking, the model implies that land near the city centre, or near some other concentration of commercial activity, should command a location premium relative to other land in the city. We now turn to a related question: what economic factors account for differences in land prices between metropolitan areas? All else equal, high real incomes or attractive physical or cultural amenities should increase the demand for land in a city, leading to higher aggregate or average prices. Again holding all else equal, government restrictions on the supply of developable land or high levels of agricultural productivity should decrease the supply of land to a city, leading to higher aggregate or average prices. However, in the context of the standard urban economic model, city size is the most important cause of intra-urban differences in land prices. Accessible locations are relatively scarce in large cities. Consequently, location premiums are larger in big cities than they are in small ones.

Figure 8.5 illustrates the relationship between house prices and city size in 31 Canadian census metropolitan areas in 2012. This figure suggests a positive relationship between average price and population, and this is confirmed by statistical analysis. Differences in population alone can account for around 27% of the variation in average prices in this sample. Further, with each increase in city size of 100,000, prices rise by roughly $10,200.[3] This estimated relationship is shown by the line drawn in the figure. Notice that the relationship between average price and city size is far from uniform. Although Quebec and Winnipeg are about the same size, the average price in Quebec ($252,171) is nearly one-half (56%) the average price in Winnipeg ($450,373) in 2012. Conversely, the average price in Montreal ($331,467) was about the same as the average price in Sudbury ($353,250), even though Montreal is almost 25 times larger in terms of population.

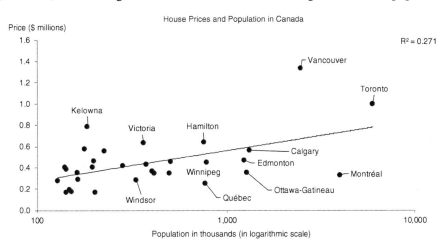

FIGURE 8.5

House Prices and Population in Canada

Source: Statistics Canada, Annual Estimates of Population (STC 91-212)

What could account for these differences? Look again at Figure 8.5. The cities above the regression line can be considered "over-priced" relative to their sizes; the cities below the line can be considered "under-priced" relative to their sizes. Now consider the data in Table 8.2, which gives population growth rates for Canadian census metropolitan areas (CMAs) from 1996-2001, 2001-2006, and 2006-2011. Many of the cities that are far above the line (Vancouver, Toronto, and Kelowna) had high population growth rates from 1996-2011 (each is in the 80th percentile or greater). Several cities that are far below the line (Quebec, Windsor, Montreal) grew much more slowly. These data suggest that population growth, in addition to size, has an impact on inter-metropolitan differences in land prices. However, there are some interesting counterexamples. For example, Calgary and Edmonton were the two fastest growing cities between 1996 and 2011, and yet they are both considered "under-priced" relative to their population size.

Table 8.2: Canadian Population Growth Rates (%)			
CMA	**1996-2001**	**2001-2006**	**2006-2011**
All census metropolitan areas	6.9	6.5	7.7
Abbotsford-Mission	7.2	7.2	7.7
Barrie	15.6	12.0	5.2
Brantford	4.4	5.5	3.2
Calgary	16.0	15.3	12.8
Edmonton	8.6	11.4	11.4
Greater Sudbury	−5.0	1.7	0.0

continued on next page

---

[3] The estimated relationship between the average unit price of unabsorbed single-detached and semi-detached homes is $p = \$369{,}368 + \$102.14 POP$, where p is price and POP is the 2012 Census Metropolitan Area population in 2012, measured in thousands. The coefficient of determination (or R^2) is 0.27.

Table 8.2: Canadian Population Growth Rates (%) *(continued)*			
CMA	1996-2001	2001-2006	2006-2011
Guelph	10.5	7.2	6.5
Halifax	5.0	4.2	6.5
Hamilton	7.1	5.8	4.2
Kelowna	8.6	8.4	9.9
Kingston	2.7	3.5	3.8
Kitchener-Cambridge-Waterloo	9.4	9.2	6.0
London	4.7	4.2	4.2
Moncton	3.8	5.4	8.5
Montréal	3.7	4.3	6.3
Oshawa	11.7	10.8	7.6
Ottawa-Gatineau	7.8	5.5	7.4
Peterborough	3.2	5.2	1.4
Québec	2.0	3.3	5.1
Regina	−1.3	1.2	9.5
Saguenay	−2.7	−3.1	−0.7
Saint John	−1.7	−1.1	2.8
Saskatoon	1.6	3.3	13.4
Sherbrooke	3.9	4.9	6.3
St. Catharines-Niagara	2.9	3.7	0.3
St. John's	−3.1	1.8	7.5
Thunder Bay	−3.5	−1.8	−0.1
Toronto	11.1	9.1	9.4
Trois-Rivières	D	1.0	3.7
Vancouver	8.9	5.6	10.8
Victoria	2.8	4.5	6.4
Windsor	8.4	4.7	−1.1
Winnipeg	1.7	3.0	6.9

Source: Statistics Canada

The intuition behind this positive relationship between growth and prices is straightforward. The price of land (or housing) should be a function of the present value of future rents. Earlier, we noted that as a city's population increases, land rent at every location rises. In other words, future land rents are higher in a growing city than in a stagnant one. This occurs because accessible locations grow increasingly scarce as city size increases. Since future land rents are higher, and the current price of land equals the present value of future rents, it follows that the current price of land should be higher in a more rapidly growing city. If the land market operates efficiently, then expected future rent increases are compounded into current prices. In other words, current land prices will include a growth premium equal to the present value of future rent increases.

Capozza and Helsley (1989) developed a simple model that illustrates these ideas. Their model focuses on the conversion of land from agriculture to urban uses in a growing city. The basic result in the model is that this conversion should occur when the marginal benefits and marginal costs of conversion are equal. In brief, this condition determines height of the rent function at the boundary the city.

Capozza and Helsley's model is summarized in Figure 8.6. The upper panel shows that land rent in a growing city has three logical parts:

1. location rent;
2. rent on the capital required to convert land from agriculture to urban use (servicing costs); and
3. agricultural rent.

The lower panel illustrates the four components of land prices. Three of these components are simply the present value of the rent components from the upper graph:

1. value of accessibility: the present value of location rent;
2. cost of conversion: servicing costs to convert land from agriculture to urban use; and
3. agricultural value: the opportunity cost of the alternative non-urban use.

The fourth component is the growth premium, or the present value of expected future rent increases. Notice that the price line does not drop directly to the agricultural value at the city boundary. The growth premium extends into the agricultural area. This helps explain why agricultural land at the edge of a growing city sells for a price in excess of the present value of agricultural land rent. The growth premium declines as one moves out beyond the boundary of the city because the expected conversion date moves further into the future; future rent increases on these parcels are discounted more heavily.

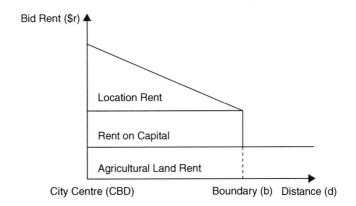

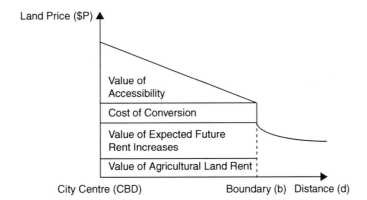

FIGURE 8.6

Land Prices and Rents in a Growing City

The growth premium becomes larger as the expected rate of population growth increases. Capozza and Helsley's study shows that with exponential population growth of 2% per year, the growth premium accounts for about 25% of the average price of land. With a population growth rate of 4%, the growth premium accounts for nearly 60% of the average price of land. This highlights the importance of the growth premium in estimating real estate value changes. If we return to the inter-metropolitan house price differences discussed in Figure 8.5, and incorporate urban growth into the analysis, we find that the population growth rate from 1996 to 2012 has a positive and significant impact on 2012 average prices, and that 1% increase in the rate of growth increases prices by approximately $6,000, controlling for differences in population. Urban growth and city size together account for roughly 36% of the variation in average house prices in this sample.[4]

Value Matters: Urban Growth and Appraisal

Appraisers rely on historic information as the basis for current estimates. In most cases, the market value of a given parcel of land or a building is based on the recent selling prices of similar properties. As long as sales occur close enough to the sale date, the appraiser is at least somewhat insulated from having to consider the larger, structural changes happening in his or her given market. That being said, the thoughtful appraiser is always on the lookout for patterns and systemic impacts that can help explain how real estate values are changing. A residential appraiser completing a single form report for financing purposes probably isn't going to comment on or adjust for the city's growth. However, in the course of completing hundreds of such appraisals over a given year, the appraiser may well observe this relationship and it may, directly or indirectly, begin to affect his or her value conclusions. Will prices continue to rise/fall? Has the rising market peaked or the falling market bottomed out and a turnaround is imminent? These are the questions an appraiser faces daily. Changes in the rate of urban growth may be a variable that can help foresee such trends and changes.

SUMMARY

This chapter examined how the passage of time affects the operation of land markets and the development of cities. There were several key ideas:

1. Since the capital that makes up a city is durable (buildings last a long time), a city's spatial growth is an incremental process in which new development is added at the fringe of the city over time. This implies that a city's variations in population or structural densities are largely determined by history. Changes in economic conditions over time may lead to a varied pattern of densities at different distances from the city centre.

2. Even though a building may still be physically useful, it may eventually be economical to demolish it and redevelop that parcel of land. Redevelopment should occur when the property's value redeveloped exceeds the property's value in its current use (given the current structure on the property) by more than the cost of demolition. Redevelopment patterns in Canadian cities seem to be broadly consistent with this simple rule.

3. Once we acknowledge that cities change over time, some spatial development patterns make more sense — for example, leapfrogging or discontinuous development. It can be efficient to withhold some land from current development, even in an area where all other land is developed, in anticipation of a more valuable future use (despite the potential political controversy this may cause).

4. City growth affects the price of land. The economic explanation for this is rents rise with city size, and since the price of land equals the present value of future land rents, cities that are expected to grow faster in the future should have higher current land (and housing) prices. This may help explain why average house prices in Toronto were 66% higher than average house prices in Montreal in 2012, even though Toronto was just 34% larger in terms of population — Toronto grew more than twice as fast as Montreal in the previous five years.

---

[4] The estimated relationship is P = $261,211+ $116,558GRTH + 80.68 POP, where GRTH is the compound annual growth rate of CMA population from 1996-2012, POP is measured in thousands. Both variables are statistically significant at the p<0.05 level. The coefficient of determination (R^2) is 0.37.

CHAPTER 9
TRANSPORTATION AND CONGESTION

INTRODUCTION

This chapter surveys the economics of urban transportation. Transportation influences every aspect of a city's internal structure. The cost of moving goods or people influence where firms and households choose to locate, how much they are willing and able to pay for commercial space and housing, and the type and density of development that the market will support. Prior chapters have illustrated how the form and character of our cities were shaped by historic transportation innovations. It stands to reason that this trend will continue in future, with cities evolving with changes in transportation costs and transportation conditions.

Urban transportation consumes resources, including land, capital, fuel, and, perhaps most important, time. Inefficient urban transportation wastes these resources. Automobiles are also a significant source of pollution; traffic can have dramatic impacts on neighbourhood quality.

Road congestion is a key issue. Some congestion is efficient, as we will see, but not when it becomes excessive. In peak periods, the decrease in travel speeds and the consequent increase in travel times are inefficient. There is a negative externality associated with road use — each driver ignores the fact that he or she causes travel times for others to increase — and this leads to excessive road use.

This chapter explores a number of issues and questions:

- Must congestion in cities continue to worsen, or are there policies that governments might pursue towards improving the efficiency of urban transportation systems?
- Should we build more roads, invest in rail rapid transit, or follow some alternative course?
- Is privatization an answer to the congestion problem? Should jurisdictions turn over the construction, maintenance, and operation of all or part of their transportation systems to private, profit-maximizing firms?
- Ultimately, how does transportation policy affect the markets for land and housing and the development of cities?

In this chapter, we will first present an overview of historic and current trends for travel and congestion in cities. We will then work towards a basic economic model of road use that can help us better understand the externality that is at the root of the congestion problem, as well as environment issues related to air pollution. As we shall see, one logical response to the congestion problem, from an economist's perspective, is road pricing. Another possibility is road privatization. Finally, the chapter will apply these transportation concepts to property markets, to see the impact of congestion on land value and urban land use.

Value Matters: Location, Transportation, and Property Value

Everyone in real estate knows the cliché that the three most important factors affecting real estate value are "1. Location, 2. Location, 3. Location". A property's location defines its attributes such as soil capability, topography, view, or waterfront. Or for a commercial property, the location features may include walk-by traffic and road visibility. In addition, consider that location also has a relative aspect, in defining a property's *distance* from work, from services or neighbourhood amenities, or from customers or competing businesses. These linkages are typically expressed in *travel time* for people, goods, and services. The efficiency of the transportation has an impact on real estate value, which appraisers must consider.

TRAVEL AND CONGESTION IN CITIES

This section examines the history of automobile use over time in major Canadian cities, then considers the state of their transportation conditions. The two key issues flowing from this are road congestion and the peak-load problem.

Dominance of Automobile Use

The salient feature of urban transportation over the past hundred years is the dominance of private automobile use. Our cities may have been transformed by the potential offered by the streetcar, but this influence has been left behind. Figure 9.1 illustrates that travel by transit (bus and rail) in Canadian cities has been roughly constant over the last half-century, while travel by auto has increased five-fold. Table 9.1 shows the distribution of work trips between cars, transit, and other modes of travel (commonly called the *modal split*) in Canadian CMAs in 2011. The propensity to travel by auto varies widely, from a low of 61% for the Ontario side of the Ottawa-Gatineau CMA to a high of 88% in Saguenay, Quebec. On average, for the CMAs shown, 77% of trips to work are made by people travelling as the driver in an automobile. A further 6% (on average) of trips to work are made by people travelling as passengers in vehicles. Public transit, walking, and cycling comprise a total of 15%.

Table 9.1: Proportion of workers commuting to work by car, truck or van, by public transit, on foot, or by bicycle, census metropolitan areas, 2011

Census Metropolitan Area	Car, truck or van (driver)	Car, truck or van (passenger)	Public transit	Walking	Bicycle
			%		
St. John's (Newfoundland and Labrador)	79.7	9.4	3	5.4	2.5
Halifax (Nova Scotia)	68.7	7.9	12.5	8.5	1.1
Moncton (New Brunswick)	78.8	10.1	3.3	6.1	0.6
Saint John (New Brunswick)	79.6	9.4	4.7	5.1	0.2
Saguenay (Quebec)	88	3.6	2.3	4.3	0.4
Québec (Quebec)	76.4	4.1	11.3	6.2	1.3
Sherbrooke (Quebec)	83.5	4	4.2	6.6	0.8
Trois-Rivières (Quebec)	87.5	3.4	2.3	5.1	1
Montréal (Quebec)	66.4	3.4	22.2	5.3	1.7
Ottawa - Gatineau (Ontario/Quebec)	63.8	6.7	20.1	6.3	2.2
Ottawa - Gatineau (Quebec side)	71	7.1	15.3	4.1	1.7
Ottawa - Gatineau (Ontario side)	61.2	6.5	21.8	7.1	2.4
Kingston (Ontario)	75.5	7.6	5.1	8.5	2.2
Peterborough (Ontario)	79.9	7	3.5	7	1.7
Oshawa (Ontario)	80.8	6.1	8.5	3.2	0.4
Toronto (Ontario)	64.5	5.4	23.3	4.6	1.2
Hamilton (Ontario)	77.8	6.7	9.3	4.5	0.7
St. Catharines - Niagara (Ontario)	83.2	7	2.9	4.8	1.2
Kitchener - Cambridge - Waterloo (Ontario)	81.4	6.7	5.4	4.3	1.1
Brantford (Ontario)	83.7	7.7	2.8	4.1	0.7
Guelph (Ontario)	79.1	7	6.2	5.1	1.5
London (Ontario)	78.6	6.7	6.9	5.4	1.5
Windsor (Ontario)	85.9	5.5	3	3.7	1.1
Barrie (Ontario)	82.7	7.1	4.6	3.7	0.7
Greater Sudbury (Ontario)	80.7	7	4.5	5.3	0.7
Thunder Bay (Ontario)	82.3	6.2	3.6	5	1.3
Winnipeg (Manitoba)	71	7.2	13.4	5.1	2
Regina (Saskatchewan)	81.7	6.8	4.8	4.7	1.2
Saskatoon (Saskatchewan)	80.5	6	4.4	5.1	2
Calgary (Alberta)	71.3	5.4	15.9	4.9	1.2
Edmonton (Alberta)	76.7	5.5	11.3	4.1	1.1
Kelowna (British Columbia)	81.6	5.5	3.4	4.9	2.6
Abbotsford - Mission (British Columbia)	84.6	7.6	2.5	2.6	0.8
Vancouver (British Columbia)	65.9	4.9	19.7	6.3	1.8
Victoria (British Columbia)	65.8	4.9	11.1	10	5.9

Source: Statistics Canada, National Household Survey, 2011.

FIGURE 9.1

**Automobile and
Transit Use
in Canada**

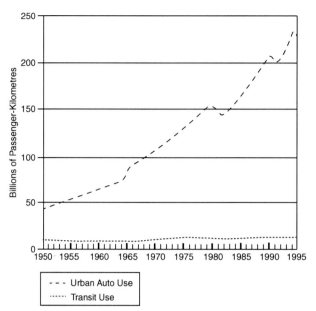

Source: Environment Canada, SOE Bulletin No. 98-5

The 2011 Canadian Census highlights the popularity of vehicle travel. Household surveys revealed that the average commute to work was 25.4 minutes, but that those travelling in cars cut that to 23.7 minutes. Those commuting via public transit took considerably longer — 42.9 minutes on average — in part because of the time spent either waiting at or walking to a bus stop, subway, or train station. The CMAs of Toronto, Oshawa, and Montreal had the longest average commute times, at 32.8 minutes, 31.8 minutes, and 29.7 minutes, respectively.

The dominance of the private auto raises the question of why transit has been unable to compete effectively. When considering direct monetary costs, the auto is certainly more expensive — including gas, insurance, maintenance, purchase price, and depreciation. However, when factoring in the indirect costs related to travel choices — convenience and comfort, plus the opportunity cost of time spent travelling — auto travel may actually be less costly than transit travel for most trips.

A key factor in the choice between auto and transit is the value of so-called out-of-vehicle time. For a bus trip, out-of-vehicle time includes time spent walking to the stop, waiting for the bus, and then walking to the destination at the conclusion of the trip. Transit trips involve more out-of-vehicle time than auto trips; studies show that consumers find the time walking and waiting to be much more onerous than time actually spent travelling. This is an inherent disadvantage to transit travel, and one that is apparently difficult to overcome. It appears consumers do not consider auto and transit travel as substitutes: lowering the cost of transit trips generally does not lead to large numbers of consumers switching from cars to buses or trains.

Cheaper Fares = More Transit Use?

A commuter faces three choices for how to get to work: rail transit, bus, or car. Assuming these are substitutes and that cost is a key consideration, then we expect a cost increase in one mode should increase demand for the others. The strength of this effect is measured by the cross price elasticity of demand: e.g., if bus fares increase, the cross price elasticity of rail demand is measured as the percentage change in the number of trips taken by rail divided by the percentage change in the cost of a bus trip.

When examining the cross price elasticity of auto demand with respect to the cost of a transit trip, studies of travel demand consistently find that this is a very small number, certainly less than 0.1, and perhaps less than 0.05. This implies that cutting the cost of a transit trip by 100% would decrease the number of auto trips by less than 10%. In other words, even making transit free would not have much of an effect on auto use! In an early and influential paper, Kraft and Domencich [1968, pp. 466] summarized the situation as follows: "These low cross-elasticities indicate that it will be very difficult to divert auto travellers to transit by lowering fares or improving service".

These economic considerations for auto versus transit use give rise to questions of what are optimal public policies for urban transportation. It seems that neither auto drivers nor transit users pay the full costs of urban transportation, as both are subsidized by government (though the general consensus is that the subsidies to bus and rail travel are significantly larger than the subsidies to auto use). As well, drivers impose additional external costs like pollution (e.g., air, water, and noise), accidents (both vehicle damage and health costs), traffic policing, and congestion. The subsidies and externalities distort the economic choices between auto and transit.

Key Concept: Transit Subsidies

Transportation planning in Canada relies on an interesting mix of politics and economics. There may be a sound economic basis for governments to subsidize transit providers: if there are scale economies in the provision of bus or rail travel, efficient trip prices (i.e., marginal cost prices) will not generate enough revenue to cover costs. However, subsidizing rail rapid transit in North America is questionable from an economic perspective. Scale economies in rail rapid transit are very strong, because of high capital costs, but travel densities in dispersed cities are too low to exploit them. The result is that commuter rail systems are extremely expensive relative to buses (and in many cities, even cars). This fact has been well-documented since at least the mid-1960s, yet tends to be ignored again and again by public officials.

Road Capacity and Congestion

Table 9.2 describes urban transportation conditions in Montreal, Ottawa, Toronto, and Vancouver in 2011 based on a report by the Transportation Association of Canada. These data show that there is a great deal of variation in the composition and capacity of the transportation systems in these cities. For example, Ottawa has almost three times the roadway capacity of Vancouver (measured by lane kilometres per capita), even though Vancouver has substantially more population.

Table 9.2: Urban Transportation Indicators for Selected Canadian Metropolitan Areas				
	Montreal	**Ottawa**	**Toronto**	**Vancouver**
Population in existing urban area	3,824,220	1,236,325	5,583,060	2,313,325
Supply				
Arterial lane-km per 1000 population	2.72	7.43	2.17	2.45
Expressway lane-km per 1000 population	0.83	0.83	0.68	0.27
Automobiles per capita	0.49	0.51	0.49	0.56
Demand				
Daily Trips per Capita (one-way)	2.1	2.82	2.25	2.73
Daily Transit Trips per Capita	0.39	0.32	0.34	0.29
Commuting to the CBD				
AM peak period auto share to/from CBD	27%	41%	25%	25%
AM peak period transit share to/from CBD	67%	45%	65%	60%
Commuting in the urban area				
AM peak period auto share overall	58%	61%	70%	69%
AM peak period transit share overall	23%	18%	19%	18%
Performance				
Median trip distance, home-work (km)	8.2	8.4	9.7	7.5
Annual injuries and fatalities per 1000 population	5.6	5.7	na	27.8
Costs and Finance				
Total road expenditures per capita ($)	628	468	335	254
Total transit expenditures per capita ($)	517	758	804	632

continued on next page

Table 9.2: Urban Transportation Indicators for Selected Canadian Metropolitan Areas *(continued)*				
	Montreal	**Ottawa**	**Toronto**	**Vancouver**
Transportation spending as % of regional GDP	na	0.93%	na	0.58%
Transit farebox revenue as share of operating & maintenance budget	49%	49%	67%	55%
Environmental Impact				
Fuel usage (litres per person per year)	862	1,119	1,037	813
Fuel usage per person trip (litres)	1.12	1.09	1.26	0.82

Source: Transportation Association of Canada (2016)

There is also considerable variation in the modal split between auto use and transit among the cities in this sample. For example, Ottawa has nearly twice as many peak period auto trips to and from the CBD than Toronto (41% versus 25%). The pattern is reversed for transit trips: Toronto, Montreal, and Vancouver have much higher transit use per capita than Ottawa. However, every city in this study shows transit use is highest for trips to and from the CBD than for other trips. These patterns are consistent with what we know about the demand for mass transit and mirrors observations from other countries. Cities with higher population and employment densities will have lower out-of-vehicle costs, especially for travel to and from the downtown. This lower cost, in effect reflecting less "wasted" time, appears to lead to higher transit patronage in larger and denser metropolitan areas.

Road congestion also varies in Canadian cities. Congestion occurs when road usage exceeds capacity, reducing speeds and increasing travel times. Transport Canada estimated the cost of congestion in Canadian cities in 2006 was between $3.1 billion to $4.6 billion[1] or roughly 0.3%-0.4% of Canadian GDP. This was measured as the cost of lost time (which could otherwise be spent for either work or private purposes), wasted fuel, and greenhouse gas emissions that result from overburdened roads. Canada's three largest urban areas — Toronto, Montreal, and Vancouver — accounted for almost 80% of the total estimated congestion costs: Toronto $1.3-2 billion; Montreal $0.7-0.9 billion; and Vancouver $0.5-0.8 billion.

An extensive study of 498 United States cities, by the Texas Transportation Institute (TTI) [2012]), found that congestion is a significant problem in US cities of all sizes and that it is growing worse. Despite the cities in the sample adding road capacity between 1982 and 2011, the Institute's roadway congestion index indicated rising congestion levels. On average, the TTI estimates that each commuter lost 38 hours in 2011 due to congestion, up from 15 hours in 1982. In other words, drivers spent the equivalent of a full work week sitting in traffic over the course of the year. Nationwide, an estimated 5.5 billion hours were lost due to congestion costs.

Traffic congestion not only consumes time, it also consumes fuel (and produces auto emissions, an issue that we will address momentarily). The TTI report estimates that, nationwide, nearly 2.9 billion gallons of fuel were "wasted" due to traffic congestion.[2] This works out to about 19 gallons per eligible driver per year. Holistically, the TTI estimates that the cost of lost time and spent fuel due to congestion was $818 per commuter in 2011, with the cost to the US overall calculated at $121 billion. That is a 23% increase over the prior decade and amounted to nearly 0.8% of GDP in 2011.

Key Concept: Work Trips vs. Non-Work Trips
Nearly all studies of urban transportation focus on commuting, or work trips, yet studies show that commuting accounts for only around 25% of total trips in US cities, and that non-work trips outnumber work trips even during peak periods. Commuting trips are seen as the engine that drives urban economies. However, transportation policies may benefit from also examining non-work trips (for shopping, entertainment, etc.) or of travel related to the movement of goods and services within cities.

[1] Urban Transportation Taskforce. 2012. "The High Cost of Congestion in Canadian Cities". This study considered three congestion scenarios, defining congestion as either 50%, 60%, or 70% of free-flow road speeds.

[2] TTI reports that 6.7 billion gallons of fuel were used by cars stopped in traffic. We should be careful about describing the resources consumed by congestion as "wasted", since some degree of road congestion is efficient.

Peak-Load Problem

Road congestion is not uniform throughout the day. Facilities that are heavily congested during the morning and evening rush hour may have excess capacity at other times. Thus, road use is a classic example of a *peak-load* problem. Where a public good has variable demand of this sort, economic efficiency generally requires that a higher price be charged for use during peak periods. We will examine road pricing in detail below.

> **Peak-Load Problem**
>
> Roads that are heavily congested in peak periods, then under-capacity in non-peak times; economic efficiency requires a higher price to be charged for usage during peak periods

Figures 9.2 and 9.3 show traffic volumes by time of day on Vancouver's Lions Gate Bridge and the south end of Oak Street Bridge during a particular day in December 2012. Traffic volume refers to the number of vehicles passing a particular point per hour — it is a measure of the flow of traffic. The figures clearly demonstrate the variation in demand by time of day. On the Lion's Gate Bridge, total traffic volume (in both directions) exceeds 4,000 vehicles per hour between 7:00 and 8:00 am and again between 4:00 and 5:00 pm. Between 8:00 pm and 6:00 am, traffic volume is less than 50% of this level. The peak periods at the south end of Oak Street Bridge are remarkably similar.

Generally speaking, the peak-load problem seems consistent on roads, bridges, and other urban transportation facilities throughout Canadian urban areas. A variety of economic solutions to this problem are proposed, including peak-load pricing and congestion tolls – the pros and cons of these are examined in the rest of this chapter. Another interesting proposed solution to this problem is to spread out the peak-load: for example, by varying work start times or by promoting work places other than the CBD, such as sub-centres or even telecommuting. However, as we will see, these appear to have limited success, because a fundamental (and unfortunate) principle of urban transportation seems to be that roads will always congest to just past their optimal load. Like many publicly provided goods, there is an unfortunate gulf between the equilibrium state and optimum state — this too may be tackled with economic policies, as we will see shortly.

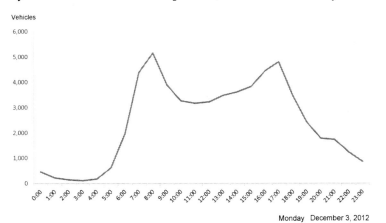

Monday   December 3, 2012

FIGURE 9.2

Traffic Volumes, Lions Gate Bridge

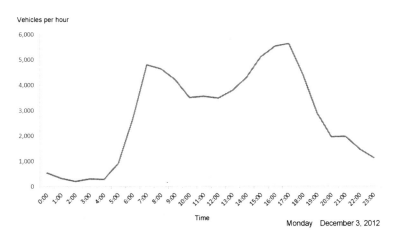

Time   Monday   December 3, 2012

FIGURE 9.3

Traffic Volumes, South End of Oak Street Bridge

Value Matters: Transportation Policy and Appraisal

When appraisers estimate market value, they typically rely on the most recent market evidence available, typically sales of similar properties. In applying appraisal techniques to analyze the data, the appraiser's focus tends to be more "micro", rather than directly analyzing bigger picture considerations like macroeconomics or politics. However, next to zoning, transportation may be the area of real estate that is most influenced by government policy. It is a combination of local, provincial, and federal governments that decide our system of roads, highways, railways, ports, and transit systems. Changes in these systems can have a profound impact on property value, ranging from a new highway interchange, an extension of light-rail mass transit, or to as simple a matter as snow removal policies for residential roads.

ECONOMICS OF ROAD USE

So far, the chapter has discussed problems with urban transportation, in particular road congestion. We now examine these problems from an economic perspective. By examining differences between equilibrium and optimal traffic volumes, we advance towards a policy recommendation — the use of differential road pricing, or congestion tolls, to help resolve road traffic problems.

Traffic Volume and Travel Time

We begin with some simple traffic engineering. Consider a two-lane road, one kilometre long, with no internal entrances or exits: vehicles enter at one end of the road and exit at the other. The amount of travel that is produced by the road is measured by traffic volume V per hour. As traffic volume rises, traffic speed eventually decreases — drivers tend to slow down for safety and other reasons. This is the essence of the *speed-flow model* of traffic congestion.

Figure 9.4 shows the relationship between speed S and flow V, or the speed-flow curve, for the beltway in Washington, DC. As expected, speed declines as flow increases. However, notice that the curve eventually turns back toward the origin. Along this portion of the curve there is hyper-congestion — somewhere in the system the capacity limit has been exceeded and traffic is at a standstill. From that point, an initial drop in demand will not speed up traffic, it will simply be less cars queuing. Obviously, this is horribly inefficient.[3]

FIGURE 9.4

A Speed-Flow Curve

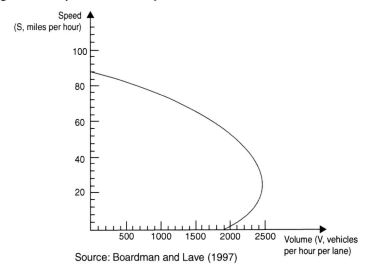

Source: Boardman and Lave (1997)

Road Capacity

The number of cars that can travel along a road without causing congestion, i.e., without increasing travel time above what would occur with just one car on the road

Since speed decreases as traffic volume rises, it follows that travel time must increase as traffic volume rises. Transportation researchers have estimated the relationship between travel time and traffic volume for road networks in a number of cities. The basic relationship is as shown in Figure 9.5: travel time is constant as long as volume is less than some critical level C, which represents the *capacity of the road*, or the capacity of a bottleneck if one is

---

[3]　Explained in Small, K.A. and Chu, X. 2003. "Hypercongestion". *Journal of Transport Economics and Policy*. 37. pp.319–3352.

present. As volume increases beyond C, congestion sets in, and travel time rises because speeds fall or because drivers are waiting in a queue. The relationship between travel time and traffic volume plays a central role in the analysis that follows.

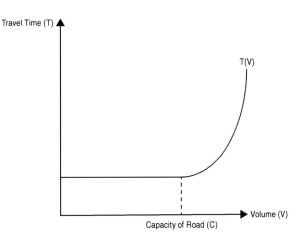

FIGURE 9.5

Travel Time and Traffic Volume

Key Concept: Bottleneck Model of Congestion

Another basic model of congestion focuses on the effects of a traffic bottleneck, like the entrance to a bridge or tunnel. Once traffic volume exceeds the capacity of the bottleneck, a queue forms, and subsequent vehicles must wait their turn before passing through. The details differ, but the basic outcome is the same: high traffic volume leads to longer travel times.

Costs of Auto Travel

The costs of auto travel to an individual driver fall into two categories: monetary costs and time costs. The monetary costs include the costs of owning or leasing a vehicle, maintenance, fuel, insurance, parking, taxes, licenses, fees, and any tolls that must be paid as part of a trip. The time cost is the opportunity cost of the time that a particular trip takes.

Studies of travel behaviour indicate that the opportunity cost of travel time tends to be measured against an individual's income or wage rate. For example, an individual seems to value in-vehicle travel time at about 50% of the gross wage, on average.[4] This means someone who earns $20 an hour will see the cost of travel time as roughly $10 per hour (this is an opportunity cost, i.e., what must be foregone to get something else).

Let w represent the value of travel time. An individual's private cost of auto travel is the sum of the monetary and time costs. Since travel time rises with traffic volume, the private cost of auto travel will rise with volume. Equation 9.1 outlines the private cost (PC) of auto travel per kilometre:

EQUATION 9.1

$$PC = M + [w \times T(V)]$$

Where:

- M represents direct monetary costs of auto use
- T(V) represents time cost, with time set as a function of traffic volume

The next sections will apply this model to identify the equilibrium and optimal levels of traffic as well as the cost of a congestion toll.

Equilibrium and Optimal Road Use

Individuals choose to drive on a road if the benefits they derive from the trip are at least as great as the costs. We will look at the benefits, costs, and equilibrium in turn.

---

4   Small (1992, pp. 42-45). Referring back to the point made earlier about out-of-vehicle time for transit use, travellers assign this more cost than in-vehicle time. If travel time is valued at 50% of gross wage on average, then out-of-vehicle time may be assigned more like 80%. In our example above, this means transit time is valued at $16 per hour – and hence the challenges of transit attempting to compete on cost.

Benefits of Road Use

The demand curve in Figure 9.6 outlines the benefits of travel. This line represents traveller's willingness to pay, showing how many trips will be taken at every price. Like all demand curves, this one can shift out in response to an increase in demand (which is likely to happen during rush hour) or shift in if demand for travel decreases (likely during off-peak periods).

FIGURE 9.6

Demand Curve for Travel

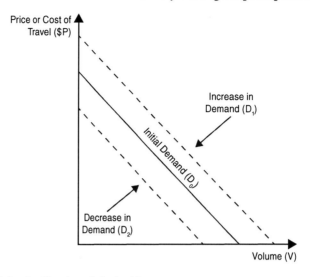

Congestion-Independent Costs

Costs largely incurred by drivers even before they get on the road; e.g., the cost of owning or leasing a vehicle, maintenance, insurance, taxes, and licensing fees (this also includes the time and fuel cost of travel absent any congestion)

Congestion-Dependent Costs

Costs that are a function of the amount of traffic on the road; e.g., increased travel time, increased fuel usage, etc.

Private Costs of Auto Use

The private costs of travel by car are summarized by the curve labelled PC in Figure 9.7. These costs have two components: congestion-independent and congestion-dependent. The congestion-independent costs are largely incurred by drivers even before they get on the road, such as vehicle ownership or leasing costs, maintenance, insurance, taxes, and licensing fees. These are shown as P_0 in Figure 9.7 (price of travel). The congestion-dependent costs are a function of the amount of traffic on the road: increased time to make a trip and increased fuel usage due to idling in traffic.

In Figure 9.7, the line's horizontal segment represents the distance where additional traffic does not add congestion, and thus no additional congestion-dependent costs are incurred. Once congestion costs start to have an impact, the slope of the cost line increases. This occurs at point C — similar to Figure 9.5, this is the road capacity, where congestion sets in.

FIGURE 9.7

Private Costs of Travel

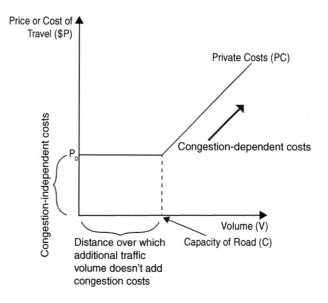

Road Use Equilibrium

The equilibrium level of road use by car occurs where the demand and private cost curves intersect. This is illustrated in Figure 9.8. However, remember that the demand curve will shift based on peak demands of rush hours and off-peak travel. Thus, the equilibrium volume of road use is V_0 during the off-peak period and V_1 during the peak period. Up until the point of road capacity (C), additional traffic volume is the same cost or price P_0. Note that the higher traffic volume in the peak period comes with a higher cost P_1. The costs of owning and maintaining the vehicle are the same for both times of day (congestion-independent costs); what varies in the figure on the right is the added cost from congestion.

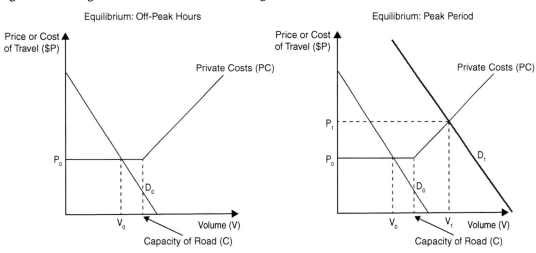

FIGURE 9.8

Equilibrium Level of Travel

Impact of External Costs

Unfortunately, an individual's auto use generates more than just private costs borne by that individual. When an individual makes the decision to drive to work, he or she adds to the road's congestion. This private decision effectively imposes an external cost on all drivers — namely, the additional congestions costs. Therefore, stepping away from the individual's personal outlook and instead looking at this decision from society's perspective, the total cost (TC) of vehicle use equals private costs (PC) + external costs (EC).

When an additional driver decides whether or not to use the road, his or her decision will typically be based entirely on private costs. This may seem inherently selfish, but keep in mind that one individual's impact is negligible — if an additional driver increases travel time on a road by 1 minute and there are 1,000 drivers who experience that cost, then the additional driver experiences one thousandth of the additional cost induced by his or her presence. As far as that driver is concerned, everyone else is the problem!

Because people tend to ignore external costs in their decision-making, they tend towards suboptimal decisions, at least in collective, global terms. For road use, drivers will choose to travel on the road as long as the private cost (PC) is no greater than the benefits they receive. With no consideration of external costs, the result is an equilibrium traffic volume of V_0 as shown in Figure 9.9.

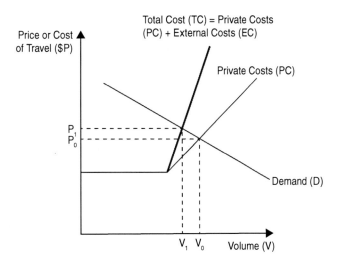

FIGURE 9.9

Impact of External Costs on Road Use Equilibrium

On the other hand, if drivers (and potential drivers) had to also take into consideration the external costs (EC) that they impose on others, the equilibrium traffic volume of traffic would drop to V_1. This lower level of traffic, with congestion costs built-in directly, is considered to be the socially optimal traffic volume.

Socially Optimal Traffic Volume

The equilibrium road use when individuals must consider both their own private costs of auto use as well as the external costs of congestion their use imposes on others

Interpreting this situation, the equilibrium traffic volume, V_0, means that if people consider only their own private costs then too many people choose to drive. This equilibrium economic outcome exceeds what is optimal for society as a whole, V_1. The area beneath the demand curve represents the total benefit that drivers receive from travelling the road. The area beneath the total cost curve represents the total cost of road use to society, including the costs of travel delay. Thus, the area beneath the demand curve minus the area beneath the total cost curve represents the net benefit of road use to society. The efficient traffic volume V_1 maximizes this net benefit. However, for all traffic volumes beyond V_1, total costs (private costs plus external costs) exceed the benefits of road use — this is another way of saying that road use is excessive in equilibrium.

Every vehicle on the road after V_1 imposes an additional cost borne by society as a while — a loss of welfare for drivers who experience too much congestion and everyone else who suffers from the noise, air pollution, and other detrimental effects. This cost is illustrated in Figure 9.10 as the area of the shaded triangle. It is quantified as the amount that total costs exceed benefits for every level of traffic volume above the optimal level.

? How Large Are the Costs of Travel Delay?

The Texas Transportation Institute [2012], in the study that we referred to earlier in this chapter, estimated that the total cost of travel delay in the 498 US urban areas in their sample was about $US 121 billion in 2011. If the same cost as a proportion of GDP were applied to Canada, we might expect the congestion cost in Canada in 2012 to be around $14.2 billion. That is just over $400 per individual in the country for the year. If we restrict this just to workers, it would easily be five times that amount — more than $2,000 per year per worker simply due to traffic congestion!

FIGURE 9.10

Society's Welfare Loss Due to Congestion

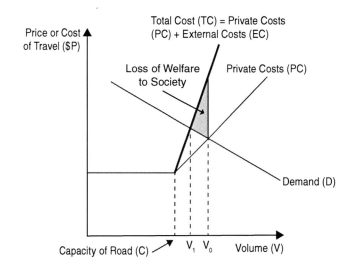

Key Concept: Environmental Cost of Auto Use and Congestion

The external costs of road use must also consider environmental impact. Motor vehicles are the major source of noise and air pollution in our cities.

Environment Canada notes that the transportation sector – including passenger, freight, and off-road vehicles – was the single largest contributor to overall greenhouse gas emissions in Canada in 2011.

- Transportation activities account for nearly one-quarter of Canada's greenhouse gas emissions.*
- Environment Canada reports that transportation and other vehicle use accounted for 25% of volatile organic compound (VOC) emissions from all human sources in 2012; VOCs contribute to smog formation, and are known to cause cancer in humans.
- Environment Canada reports that transportation and other vehicle use accounted for 54% of nitrogen oxide (NO) emissions from all human sources in 2012; NO contributes to respiratory problems in humans and is a significant source of acid rain.

Traffic congestion undoubtedly increases the environmental damage associated with auto use. An Environment Canada study found that a 16 kilometre trip in heavy traffic generated more than twice the VOCs as a light traffic trip. Research commissioned by Transport Canada has suggested that interurban passenger transport has an external air pollution cost of $0.00088 per passenger-kilometre, while intra-urban passenger transport has an external air pollution cost of $0.00842 per passenger kilometre (2002 prices, Canadian dollars)**.

Like the costs of congestion, these environmental costs are external to the choices of an individual driver. Individually each car makes little impact, so each individual driver has little incentive to consider environmental costs in auto use decisions. This reinforces excessive road use in equilibrium.

Efficiency requires individual drivers to consider environmental costs of vehicle use when making travel choices. One economic solution put forward is to incorporate a pollution tax into gasoline prices. This is analogous to the congestion tax to be discussed in the next section.

* Environment Canada. 2014. "Canada's Emissions Trends".

** Zhang, A. 2004. "Towards Estimating the Social and Environmental Costs of Transportation in Canada" Centre for Transportation Studies, Sauder School of Business.

ACHIEVING SOCIALLY OPTIMAL ROAD USE

What can we do to reduce road congestion? On the one hand, there seems to be widespread agreement that there is no one policy that will solve the problem. Some people have argued that it will be necessary to alter both transportation and land use practices to effect much of a change in road congestion levels. On the other hand, we know quite a bit about which policies are likely to work (or not work) and why. This section discusses alternative solutions to the congestion problem.

Capacity Expansion

One obvious approach is to increase the capacity of the road network. If the roads are congested, then let's build more roads! However, this simple approach will probably not work in this case.

In general, the capacity of the road system is efficient if the marginal benefit of increasing capacity and the marginal cost of increasing capacity are equal. Here the marginal benefit is the value of the decrease in total travel time that results from capacity expansion. The marginal cost is the additional capital cost that expansion entails. Attempting to build our way out of the congestion problem would be prohibitively expensive. As well, expanding the capacity of public transit systems is (as we noted earlier) unlikely to reduce road congestion significantly, and is also extremely expensive.

Furthermore, according to *Downs' law,* increasing the capacity of currently congested roads will likely see little or no improvement in congestion levels or travel times. In his *law of highway congestion,* Downs noted: "on urban commuter expressways, peak-hour traffic congestion rises to meet maximum capacity" (Downs [1962], pp. 393). Congestion deters some would-be drivers from using roads, leading to latent, pent-up demand for drivers. Capacity expansions that relieve congestion encourages some of these previously diverted drivers to use the road. These drivers were travelling by another mode, or at another time, or via another route, but now switch to the expanded road during the peak travel time. There are even well-documented cases of increases in highway capacity leading to increases in peak period travel (Small [1992], pp. 113).

Downs Law: Law of Highway Congestion

Traffic congestion rises to meet maximum capacity

Road Pricing

Clearly what is required is that we make more efficient use of the road capacity that we already have. The economic problem we face is that each individual driver is making his or her auto use decisions based on his or her own personal situation, without regard to impact on everyone else. But, oddly enough, when these individual decisions are aggregated, each driver is actually hurting his or her own personal situation too. If all drivers and potential drivers could coordinate and attempt to maximize their overall well-being, they would strive to achieve a total traffic volume of V_1. It is unlikely the drivers will coordinate on their own, so this is where government steps in to help steer the market's "invisible hand" toward a collectively optimal decision. From an urban economist's perspective, this is a primary function of local government — encouraging and motivating individuals to make collective decisions that are better for everyone (including themselves), despite personal incentives that would otherwise lead to a sub-optimal decision. However, private solutions are also possible, e.g., private toll roads.

One potential "market correction" here would be to implement a *congestion toll* on the road. If individual drivers are ignoring the additional time costs that they impose on others, and excessive road use is the result, then an economically optimal outcome can be achieved by making each driver pay the *total* cost of travelling on the road. In Figures 9.9 - 9.11, the equilibrium traffic volume (V_0) occurs because drivers can ignore these external costs. If a toll is imposed where drivers must pay the difference between the private cost and the total cost *at the socially optimal traffic volume* (as shown in Figure 9.11), this should lead to the socially optimal traffic volume (V_1) as the new equilibrium.

Congestion Toll

The difference between the private cost and the total cost at the socially optimal traffic volume

FIGURE 9.11

Congestion Toll

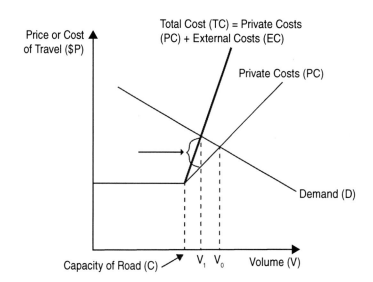

Note that traffic congestion begins in Figure 9.11 at point C. The road is still congested at the efficient solution: V_1 > C. Remember earlier when we said that some traffic congestion is economically efficient? Figure 9.11 illustrates this. Since it is costly to eliminate congestion, it is efficient to let some of it persist. The problem is that there is too much congestion during peak travel periods. The goal of a congestion toll is to reduce this to a socially optimal level. In economic terms, that point is where the benefit to society as a whole (the area below the demand curve) is equal to the combined private and external costs (PC + EC = TC).

The toll is only required during peak travel period. Since external cost equals zero when V < C, a toll need not be levied during the off-peak period.

Keep in mind that individual drivers may not like this solution, as they are the ones paying this toll. While they benefit collectively from reduced congestion, there may be a perceived disconnect between this direct out-of-pocket expenditure and the potential reduction in traffic volumes. A driver's perspective on this will be influenced by how they view their time among other considerations; their appreciation for the toll road may also depend in part on whether they have access to a free alternative. This highlights a second function of local government from an urban economist's perspective: hearing the individual complaints that result from acting in the collective interest!

Key Concept: Internalizing the Externality

Individuals acting in their own self-interest will only consider private costs. When these decisions affect others, and the resulting social costs are not considered, this leads to sub-optimal outcomes from society's perspective. Charging drivers a *congestion toll* for road use during peak periods makes these individuals take the full marginal cost of their decisions into account. By making the externality a part of the individual's internal or private costs, this should lead to more efficient travel decisions.

EXERCISE 9.1: Equilibrium and Optimum Traffic Volumes

Suppose we have a 10 kilometre road, with a capacity of C = 1,000 cars per hour. Assume that it takes 10 minutes to travel the road when it is not congested; therefore, the free flow speed is 60 kilometres per hour. Once volume exceeds capacity, speed falls, and travel time is given by 0.02V – 10.

Private Cost:

- Assume the monetary cost of a trip is M = $3 and travel time is valued at w = $0.2 per minute ($12 per hour)
- When the road is below capacity (V < 1,000), the private cost of a trip (in dollars) is PC = $3 + $0.2(10 minutes) = $5
- When the road is above capacity (V $ 1,000), then the private cost of a trip is PC = $3 + $0.2(0.02V – 10) = $1 + $0.004V

Total Cost:

- Assume external cost is EC = $0.004V
- Total cost is TC = $1 + $0.004V + $0.004V = $1 + $0.008V

For example, if V = 1,500, then the trip takes 20 minutes and PC = $7.

Suppose demand for travel along a stretch of highway is given by: V = 5,000 – (1,000/3)P

Where V = traffic volume and P = price of travel (from a demand perspective, drivers must get benefits at least as great as this price or they will choose not to travel. This is graphed in the figure below, along with the private cost and total cost curves.

continued on next page

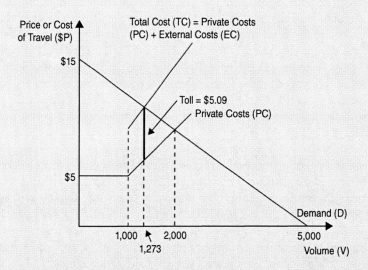

1. What is equilibrium traffic volume (the traffic volume that occurs in the absence of any intervention)?
2. What is the socially optimal traffic volume (the traffic volume a benevolent planner might impose)?
3. What toll amount would be required to achieve the socially optimal traffic volume?

Solution:

1. To find the equilibrium traffic volume, we first ignore external costs. Drivers will travel right up to the point where their private costs meet but do not exceed the benefits. We need to set demand, which is representative of the benefits of travel, equal to the private costs of travel.

Rearrange the demand curve to solve for P, the price of travel. Currently it is expressed as the number of trips as a function of the cost of travel:

$$V = 5,000 - (\frac{1,000}{3})P$$

Add $(\frac{1,000}{3})P$ to both sides: $(\frac{1,000}{3})P + V = 5,000$

Subtract V from both sides: $(\frac{1,000}{3})P = 5,000 - V$

Divide both sides by $\frac{1,000}{3}$: $P = \frac{5,000}{1,000 \div 3} - \frac{V}{1,000 \div 3}$

Therefore: $P = 15 - 0.003V$

This tells us what the private benefits are as a function of the number of trips. In equilibrium, the benefits must be equal to the costs: P = PC

And because $P = 15 - 0.003V$ and $PC = 1 + 0.004V$, we can express P = PC in an equation where the only variable is V:

$15 - 0.003V = 1 + 0.004V$

Add 0.003V to both sides: $15 = 1 + 0.007V$

Subtract 1 from both sides: $14 = 0.007V$

Divide both sides by 0.007

$V = 2,000 =$ Equilibrium traffic volume

continued on next page

2. Now let's find the socially optimal traffic volume, with external costs considered. This time, we will set the benefits equal to the total costs: P = PC + EC

    $15 - 0.003V = 1 + 0.008V$

    Add 0.003V to both sides: $15 = 1 + 0.011V$

    Subtract 1 from both sides: $14 = 0.011V$

    Divide both sides by 0.011

    $V = 1,273$ = Socially optimal traffic volume

3. To find the toll that will induce the socially optimal traffic volume, find the difference between the personal cost and the total cost at the optimal level of traffic.

We have an equation that describes the personal cost as a function of traffic volume:

    $PC = 1 + \$0.004V$

And we have a function that describes the total cost as a function of traffic volume:

    $TC = 1 + \$0.008V$

Thus, the toll is equal to: Toll = TC – PC

    $Toll = 1 + \$0.008V - (1 + \$0.004V)$

    $Toll = \$0.004V$

So now we simply need to plug the optimal traffic volume of 1,273 into the above equation:

    $Toll = \$0.004(1,273) = \$5.09$

A toll of $5.09 per car will force drivers to consider the external costs they impose on others by driving. By "internalizing" the negative externality, this toll should reduce driving demand from the equilibrium 2,000 cars to the socially optimal traffic volume of 1,273 cars. This means that 727 drivers will use alternative means of transportation, seek alternative routes, or cancel their trips.

Alternative Solution for Finding Equilibrium

First, recognize that we have an equation that specifies the demand for travel, or traffic volume, as long as we know the price. This is the demand curve, which is: $V = 5,000 - (1,000/3)P$

Next, we know that the private cost is equal to 1 + 0.004V, so we can find the equilibrium solution in which commuters only consider their private costs by plugging this value in for P in the demand equation. Thus:

$$V = 5,000 - (\frac{1,000}{3})(1 + 0.004V)$$

Expand the brackets: $V = 5,000 - 333.3333 - 1.3333V$

Add 1.3333V to both sides: $2.3333V = 5,000 - 333.3333$

Collect like terms: $2.3333V = 4,666.66667$

Divide both sides by 2.3333: $V = 2,000$, rounded

Similarly, to solve for the optimum traffic volume, start with the same demand curve:

$$V = 5,000 - (\frac{1,000}{3})P$$

and replace P with the total cost of 1 + 0.008V

Thus:

$$V = 5,000 - (\frac{1,000}{3})P$$

continued on next page

becomes

$$V = 5,000 - (\frac{1,000}{3})(1+0.008\,V)$$

Therefore, optimal traffic volume = 1,273

> Expand the brackets: V = 5,000 − 333.333334 − 2.666667V
>
> Add 2.666667V to both sides: 3.666667V = 5,000 − 333.333334
>
> Collect like terms: 3.666667V = 4,666.666667
>
> Divide both sides by 3.666667: V = 1,273, rounded

Road Pricing in Practice

Charging a price for the use of a road, bridge, or tunnel is not new. However, until relatively recently, tolls were intended primarily as means of generating revenue for transportation authorities, rather than a mechanism for controlling road use.

The first large scale system of congestion pricing was implemented in Singapore in 1975. Under the initial Singapore Area Licensing Scheme (ALS), motorists were required to purchase a pass (the initial fee was $S 3 per day) in order to travel to the city centre during peak periods. The ALS had significant impacts on vehicle use. Gomez-Ibanez and Small (1994) report that it reduced the number of vehicles entering the restricted area by 47% and reduced the number of single occupant trips by 60%. These reductions came from several sources. Some former drivers shifted to carpools and buses, while others rescheduled their trips or changed routes. The ALS increased travel speeds into and within the central area by 20%, but it also seems to have reduced speeds in other areas. Individuals who used to travel through the restricted area travelled around it after the imposition of the fee, which increased traffic volumes on circumferential routes. Paradoxically, the ALS did not result in a dramatic decrease in travel times. In fact, the ALS apparently caused travel times for bus riders to increase. However, the Singapore experience showed that a relatively simple form of congestion pricing can achieve large and sustained reductions in auto use.

Singapore's initial coupon-based system was replaced in 1998 by a fully electronic version called Electronic Road Pricing (ERP). Vehicles are fitted with small devices that can be pre-loaded with money for tolls; payment is made automatically upon passing under one of the many toll gantries straddling the city state's roads. The price varies by road, time of day, and local traffic conditions. The stated aim is to keep speeds at 20-30 km/h for major roads and 45-65 km/h for expressways.[5] One of the pricing scheme's innovations is *shoulder pricing* which gradually raises the toll prior to peak periods and gradually lowers it after peak periods. This helps to smooth traffic flows, rather than simply displacing congestion from one period to the next.[6]

London, United Kingdom, was the second major urban area to institute a large-scale congestion charging scheme. Implemented in 2003, London's congestion charge has been implemented to:[7]

- reduce congestion;
- improve bus services;
- improve journey time reliability for car users; and
- improve the efficiency of goods and services distribution.

The year it was put in place, Transport for London estimated that there was a 14% reduction in all vehicle traffic into the toll area, which spans 22 square kilometres in the centre of London. Unlike

---

[5] Menon, A P and Kian-Keong, C. 2004. "ERP in Singapore: What's Been Learnt from Five Years of Operation?" *Traffic, Engineering and Control magazine.*

[6] Xie, L and Olszewski, P. 2011. "Modelling the Effects of Road Pricing on Traffic Using ERP Traffic Data. Transportation Research". Part A. p.512.

[7] Transport for London. 2007. Central London Congestion Charging: Impact Monitoring, Fifth Annual Report.

the system in Singapore, London's congestion charge is a fixed amount that is chargeable between 7:00am and 6:30pm Monday to Friday. The scheme initially charged £5 per day to drive within the chargeable zone and has been raised twice since then. The first fee increase, to £8 per day, saw a further 2% decrease in vehicle traffic, while the second increase, to £10 per day, resulted in a 16% reduction in vehicle traffic within the chargeable zone.

Improvements in London's bus network have been instrumental in soaking up displaced car users. In the first year of congestion charging, bus ridership increased by 18%; in the second year, bus ridership increased by an additional 12%. The charges have also become a significant source of revenue — in 2012/13, congestion charges totalled £222 million.

Large scale congestion pricing of this sort has not been adopted anywhere in North America. Political impediments to road pricing remain strong — there seems to be resistance to the idea that voters should pay through tolls for facilities that they have already paid for through taxes. This may explain why congestion pricing in North America has been most successful on new, privately provided facilities.

Why Private Roads?

An interesting example of a private facility is the 407 ETR (electronic toll road), a 108 kilometre private highway that runs east to west just north of the city of Toronto. The 407 ETR is advertised by its owners as the world's first all-electronic open access toll highway.

The 407 was constructed by the Province of Ontario and subsequently sold to a private consortium for $3.1 billion. This consortium financed the acquisition of the highway through the issuance of over $2 billion in private bonds.

Tolls for travel on the highway are collected electronically using transponders mounted on the vehicle's windshield. Sensors at entrances and exits record the entry and departure of vehicles. A video image is made of vehicles that use the highway without a transponder. These users receive a bill for their travel (plus an additional billing fee) by mail. Prepaid accounts can be established to protect the anonymity of users.

There is congestion pricing of a sort on the 407. Tolls vary according to the time of day, vehicle type, and distance and section of the highway travelled. In 2013, the 407 was host to between 280,000 and 340,000 daily trips (depending on the month) and 2.4 billion vehicle kilometres.* The average revenue per trip in 2013 was $6.96, while total revenue for the 407ETR for the year was just over $800 million.

This type of privatization seems to make congestion pricing somewhat more palatable to road users. It is also attractive to cash strapped governments, and is increasingly common throughout the world. However, these automated highways are not necessarily a panacea for the ills of congestion:

1. If the additional capacity causes travel and trip lengths to increase, then auto emissions will presumably increase as well (Johnston and Rodier [1999]).
2. Like all additions to highway capacity, the effects of the 407 ETR depend critically on pricing. Trips must be priced at full marginal cost or consumers will end up making inefficient travel choices, no matter how technologically sophisticated the road pricing system.

* Source: Retrieved from ETR.com website: *www.407etr.com*

Alternatives for Road Use Control

Congestion pricing appears to be the most direct and effective means of controlling road use. However, it is not the only approach. Governments have tried a wide variety of policies to reduce auto use. Downs [1992, Table 11.1] analyzes 23 such policies and breaks them down as follows:

- *Supply side policies:* focus on the capacity of the transportation system
    - improvements in traffic control systems (coordinating signals, providing traffic information, etc.)
    - improving public transit service

- building new mass transit systems
- building new roads
- adding high occupancy vehicle (HOV) lanes to existing roads
- improving highway maintenance
- reducing the time that it takes to clear traffic accidents

- *Demand side policies:* focus on the demand for travel
  - controlling the growth and spatial development of metropolitan areas (encouraging the formation of subcentres, concentrating high density housing near transit stops, etc.)
  - staggering work hours and encouraging telecommuting
  - increasing licensing fees
  - gasoline taxes and parking charges
  - instituting congestion pricing on roads

Downs offers a number of general observations about the likely effectiveness of the different approaches:

1. He argues that very few of the policies have the potential to greatly reduce traffic congestion by themselves. In fact, he suggests that there are only two policies that could have much of an impact in isolation: peak-hour road pricing and a surcharge on parking downtown during the morning peak.
2. Supply side policies tend to be more costly to society as a whole than demand policies. Supply side policies often involve large scale public spending (new roads or transit systems, HOV lanes, etc.), which explains (in his view) why these policies receive strong support from certain industry groups. In contrast, demand side policies tend to raise the cost of travel to individual drivers.
3. Demand side policies have poor political acceptability, perhaps precisely because they will result in large changes in driver behaviour. Downs concludes (pp. 151) that "demand side tactics would be much more effective at reducing congestion, and less costly to society in general, than supply side tactics".

These views are consistent with other studies of transport control measures. For example, Hall (1995, pp. 96) notes that market based policies, "such as pricing parking, congestion pricing and gasoline taxes, ... have been shown to have the strongest influence" and that "parking pricing and gasoline taxes ... have the greatest influence on vehicle miles travelled and number of trips relative to any of the measures that might represent primarily time savings, such as high occupancy vehicle lanes and compressed work weeks".

CONGESTION AND LAND USE

At several points in prior chapters, we have discussed urban sprawl. In this section, we re-examine the monocentric model from Chapter 6 to see the links between transportation congestion and urban sprawl.

Recall that in the monocentric model, land rent declines as distance to the CBD rises to offset the rising cost of commuting. This led to a downward-sloping bid rent curve. In the simplest version of the model, for an open city with identical households and fixed lot sizes, the bid rent function for land is:

EQUATION 9.2

$$r(d) = r^a + \left(\frac{t}{\ell^*}\right) \times (b - d)$$

Where:

- r^a is the bid rent on agricultural land
- t is commuting cost per kilometre
- ℓ^* is lot size
- d is distance to the CBD
- b is the boundary of the city (refer back to Equation 6.5 and the surrounding text)

In terms of our current discussion, it is probably most natural to think of t as the private cost of a commuting trip. However, efficiency requires that households make their travel and location decisions based on the full marginal cost of commuting, including any external costs associated with road congestion. We will add the external costs (e) to find the efficient bid rent function:

EQUATION 9.3

$$r^e(d) = r^a + (\frac{t+e}{\ell^*}) \times (b-d)$$

These two bid rent functions will differ based on inefficiencies in the market for transportation. The failure to correct or internalize the congestion externality will distort the operation of the land market.

Let's see what the consequences of this distortion might be. Imagine that we have two cities. The first has transportation efficiently priced, with bid rent $r^e_0(d)$. The second has market-based inefficient pricing, with bid rent $r(d)$. Suppose further that the cities are open; therefore, each must offer the same exogenous utility level to its residents. The top chart in Figure 9.12 shows the bid rent functions in the efficient and inefficient cities from Equations 9.2 and 9.3 above. The only difference between them (at this -point) is that the efficient bid rent function is steeper — its slope is:

$$-\frac{(t+e)}{\ell^*} \text{ instead of } -\frac{t}{\ell^*}$$

Therefore, holding everything else fixed, rent in the efficient city is higher at every location.

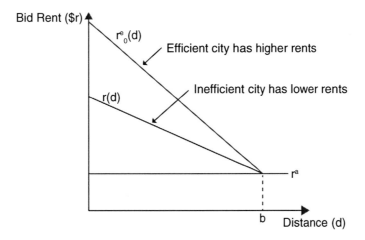

FIGURE 9.12

Congestion and Land Use

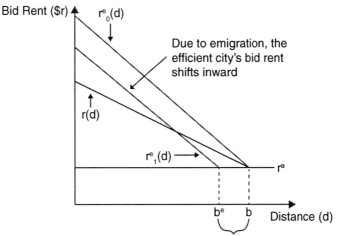

However, this implies that the utility of residents in the efficient city is lower than the utility of residents elsewhere in the economy (recall that higher rent is associated with lower utility); this cannot possibly be an equilibrium. If utility in the efficient city is lower, then we expect households to emigrate to other areas. This will cause the bid rent function in the efficient city to shift downward to $r^e_1(d)$. This consequently causes the boundary of the efficient city to move inward. If this emigration is beneficial to residents in the efficient city, then the process will stop when the bid rent functions look something like what is shown in the bottom chart in Figure 9.12. Land rent is higher near the city centre and lower near the periphery in the efficient city — reflecting the higher total cost of commuting. Most important, the efficient city's boundary moves inward to b^e. Thus, the efficient city is smaller and more compact than the market-based city. The market-based city's failure to properly price the congestion externality has led to it being too large. This illustrates how traffic congestion contributes to the problems and costs associated with urban sprawl.

SUMMARY

Land values, land development patterns, and city sizes all depend critically on the costs of transporting people and goods within cities. Unfortunately, much transportation within cities is inefficient because drivers do not pay the full social cost of road use. This underpricing arises from two types of externalities: congestion externalities and environmental pollution. Users of congested roads do not consider the impacts of their decisions on the travel times of other road users. This leads to excessive congestion during peak travel periods. In addition, cars and other vehicles are key contributors to urban air pollution. The costs of environmental damage are also external to the decisions of individual drivers, and these costs are exacerbated by traffic congestion. The mispricing of travel in cities also contributes to the problem of urban sprawl.

A number of policies and approaches have been suggested to deal with these problems. The traditional approach to the problem of traffic congestion has been to increase capacity, by building new highways, expanding existing highways or constructing new rail transit systems. It is now well understood that this is a bankrupt (and bankrupting) strategy. Building our way out of the problem is financially infeasible, and rail rapid transit is horribly inefficient at the population densities that one finds in most North American cities. Most important, in the absence of congestion pricing, adding capacity will not reduce congestion anyway C it just encourages more travel. It seems clear that effective solutions to the congestion problem will have to focus on the demand side of the market for urban travel. The policies that are typically favoured by economists focus on correcting the mispricing of transportation. For example, fuel taxes could be increased to internalize the environmental costs of motor vehicle use, and congestion tolls could be imposed on travel during peak periods. Although congestion pricing has not been widely adopted in North America, it has been implemented in other parts of the world. Private, tolled highways are another example of an urban transportation innovation that presents incentives for optimal use.

Beyond Profit – Do Real Estate Professionals Have Societal Obligations?

A key message in this chapter is that many of our transportation system problems flow from overuse of a common, public asset. The recommendation is to encourage (or force) users to "internalize the externality". This may raise a moral or ethical question for appraisers and other real estate professionals. In representing clients, their chief concern is maximizing their client's welfare, in terms of private costs and private benefits. But what if each individual pursuing his or her own personal benefit, when added together, leads to everyone losing collectively (including that client)? Does the professional have an obligation to inform the client of larger-scale social impacts of his or her actions? Does "market value" mean a profit-maximizing equilibrium outcome or a socially-maximizing optimum outcome?

CHAPTER 10
HOUSING AND HOUSING MARKETS

INTRODUCTION

Housing is the dominant land use in cities. Housing expenditures are the largest single item in the budgets of most households and housing equity is the largest item in many financial portfolios. New housing construction is a large and volatile component of national investment spending; changes in the level of new construction can have significant macroeconomic consequences. Thus, housing is an important commodity.

Housing is also a unique commodity:

- Like other forms of real estate, housing is both a consumption good and an investment good, and there are separate (but related) markets for the services that houses provide and the capital assets that houses represent.
- Housing is immobile and fixed in space. When you buy a house you also buy a large collection of location-specific goods and services, e.g., access to jobs, neighbourhood quality, school quality, and property taxes.
- A house is a bundle of characteristics and no two houses are exactly alike. This is partly due to the fact that houses can differ in so many ways (e.g., size, age, number of bedrooms, number of bathrooms, and quality of construction and fixtures), and partly due to the location issues mentioned above.
- Houses are durable in the sense that they provide services for many years after they are constructed. As a result, the supply of housing depends in important ways on the maintenance and renovation decisions of home owners.

- Housing consumption is a social issue; encouraging housing consumption is a public policy objective in most countries. The most severe of all housing problems, homelessness, is one of the most important social issues of our time.

Many commodities have some of the characteristics listed above; only housing has them all.

This chapter surveys the economics of housing markets. This is a huge topic, easily large enough to fill a text on its own. Our survey will, of necessity, be selective. We start by defining housing and exploring the housing consumption decisions of individual households, including moving decisions and the decision of whether to own or rent. Then, we take a more macro view of the market demand for housing, such as the controversial effects of the aging of the baby boom generation. This leads into a discussion of housing supply, linking to Chapter 6's monocentric city model, and specifically examining how housing prices vary with location. The chapter concludes by examining the filtering process and its implications for the operation of housing markets and housing policy.

DEFINING HOUSING: SUBMARKETS AND HOUSING SERVICES

Figure 10.1 illustrates demand and supply for housing. The curve labelled S_{SR} represents supply in the short run. The steep curve reflects that housing supply is slow to react to changes in demand, meaning demand increases lead to rising prices but not much more supply. The curve S_{LR} representing supply in the long run, where more houses can be built to meet increased demand.

FIGURE 10.1

The Housing Market

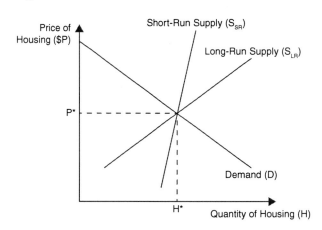

The demand and supply curves in Figure 10.1 implicitly assume that the housing market is competitive. A problem with this assumption is that perfect competition requires (among other things) that the good in question be homogeneous. For example, if we were to plot demand and supply curves for the economist's favourite commodity, widgets, there is an underlying assumption that buyers are indifferent between any given widget — they are perfectly interchangeable. If consumers have a preference of one type of widget over another, then we cannot rely on an assumption that competition is standardized or equivalent among the widgets.

Given the wide variations in house designs, it is clear that houses do not meet the requirement of homogeneity required for perfect competition. Yet at the same time, it is also clear that housing markets are indeed competitive, illustrated by the fierce battles for choice real estate assets. It seems that housing, despite its non-unique nature, can still be generalized sufficiently to allow economic comparison and analysis.

To see how this might work, first imagine that a city's housing market is composed of a number of relatively small submarkets for different types, sizes, and qualities of housing. The market for single-family housing in a particular neighbourhood is one example of such a submarket. Another submarket is for lower-priced town houses in another neighbourhood. The housing market may differentiate between studio, one-bedroom, or two-bedroom condominiums. It may also differentiate between houses that are ranchers, bungalows, or two-storey. If these submarkets are defined very narrowly, then the housing units in each one should be sufficiently homogeneous to be comparable.

Second, rather than focusing on the actual physical nature of the houses themselves, we can instead focus on the services that houses provide. Imagine that housing services are produced from the housing stock according to the following production function:

$$H = f(c_1, c_2 ... c_N)$$

Where:

- H represents housing services
- f stands for "is a function of"
- c_i's are the characteristics of a house, like its size, quality, location, etc.

This housing production function is increasing — larger, newer, and higher quality houses produce more services than smaller, older and lower quality houses.

For illustration purposes, let's assume that the only characteristics of a house that matter are lot size and structure size. The housing production function is then expressed as:

H = f(lot size, house size)

This housing production function is illustrated in Figure 10.2, with house size on the left axis and lot size on the right axis. The curves represent different combinations of land and structure that produce the same level of housing services (called an *isoquant*, which acts similar to an indifference curve). A buyer who can afford 100 units of housing services can choose any combination on the lower curve; e.g., 3,000 square feet of structure and 10,000 square feet of lot, or 1,000 square feet of structure and 30,000 square feet of lot, or any other combination along the curve labelled H = 100. Another buyer who can afford 200 units of housing services can choose any combination along the curve labelled H = 200. In principle, there is a curve associated with every conceivable level of housing services, where higher curves represent higher levels of housing services.

FIGURE 10.2

The Production of Housing Services

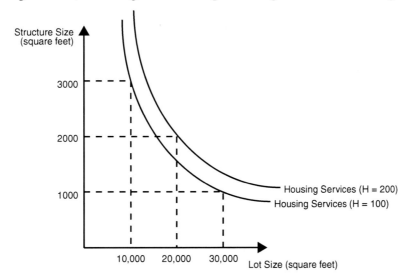

With these two assumptions in mind — differentiating submarkets within housing and focusing on housing services — this allows us to use demand and supply diagrams like Figure 10.1 without apology. Houses are not unique, but housing services can be defined in such a way that it meets the definition of a homogeneous good.

Value Matters: Uniqueness of Housing

Housing's uniqueness and lack of homogeneity has particular relevance in considering its market value.

1. The uniqueness of housing is a fundamental reason for why real estate brokers and appraisers are necessary. If housing was standardized, it would be a simple matter to price it. However, because each house is unique in both attributes and location, it requires market expertise to estimate the market value of any given property.
2. The unique attributes of housing present a valuation challenge. The market value of any particular house is found by comparing it to other similar properties that have recently sold. Yet if no other property is an exact replica, how can you be sure that the comparable sold properties are actually comparable? This is where real estate appraisal becomes more art than science: finding comparables that are as similar as possible to the subject and adjusting their sale prices to account for dissimilarities with the subject.

continued on next page

3. This notion of stepping away from the physical asset and instead considering the services or benefits it offers is the underlying basis for income methods of appraisal. Commercial properties tend to be so unique that it can be difficult to generalize their attributes to allow direct comparison. However, the financial benefit flowing from these properties can be relied upon to offer a consistent unit of comparison. Since buyers are primarily interested in the property's investment benefits, cash flow is the great equalizer. No matter what the property's physical attributes or location advantages, ultimately this is seen in the potential rents the property can generate and the expenses necessary to generate this revenue. Thus, market value is a function of expected future cash flows, capitalized to a present value.

EXAMINING HOUSE DEMAND

As noted above, the demand for housing comes from consumers making choices. They can choose among different combinations of land versus house, or any other feature or attribute, according to their personal preferences. They can also choose to spend their limited budget on combinations of housing versus other goods. This brings us back to the concept of utility maximization from Chapter 6.

Figure 10.3 illustrates a consumer's choice between two goods, housing services h, and other goods x. The consumer's budget constraint is defined as:

EQUATION 10.1

$$(p \times h) + x = I$$

Where:

- I = Income
- p is the price of housing, so $(p \times h)$ is total expenditure on housing
- x is the total expenditure on other goods, based on an assumption that the price of other goods is set to \$1 $(x \times 1)$

Utility maximization will generally occur at the point where the budget constraint is tangent to the highest possible indifference curve. At this optimal point, the consumer demands x_0 in goods and h_0 in housing services.

Key Concept: Utility Maximization

Recall from Chapter 6 the discussion of optimal choice. Budget constraints represent what is *possible*, while indifference curves represent what is *desirable*. Optimal consumption will occur at a point that lies along the budget constraint and tangent to the highest possible indifference curve.

FIGURE 10.3

Individual Housing Choice

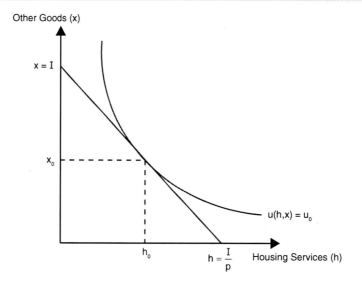

Impact of Moving Costs on Housing Demand

One of the unique features of housing is that it can be quite costly for a consumer to adjust his or her housing consumption. Adjustment costs for housing include the cost of moving, searching for a new home, and any transaction costs (e.g., broker fees, legal fees, security deposits) associated with changing accommodations. These adjustment costs can make housing demand "sticky" and unresponsive, meaning a change in a household's circumstances may not be directly linked to a change in its housing demand.

Consider a consumer with a growing family. Initially, before the change in family size, the consumer's preferences are represented by the indifference curve u_0 in Figure 10.3. The consumer maximizes utility by purchasing h_0 units of housing. Their equilibrium housing h_0 occurs at the tangency of the outer budget line and the indifference curve u_0.

The consumer's family now grows and this causes the consumer's preferences to change. The consumer's new indifference curves are shown in Figure 10.4, now labelled with a v instead of u, so v_0, v_1, and v_2. If the consumer faced no costs in adjusting housing consumption, then the consumer's new optimal housing consumption will increase to h_1. This new optimal housing demand h_1 occurs at the tangency of the budget line and the new indifference curve v_0.

However, this is not realistic, as it ignores the costs of changing housing consumption, which may include moving fees, for example. The consumer faces a cost C for adjusting his or her housing consumption. Figure 10.5 shows that the budget line shifts inward by the amount of C – given income I, the consumer can now afford less of both housing h and other goods x. The y- and x-axis intercepts for this budget line reflect incurring this cost C, as $x = I - C$ on the left axis and $h = (I - C)/p$ on the right axis.

When these moving costs are factored in, the consumer's optimal housing choice becomes h_2, where the indifference curve v_2 is tangent to the inner budget line. This point means that the consumer can afford not only less other goods x, but also less housing h too – the consumer's utility level decreases overall by this move. When adjustment costs are factored in, the consumer is better off staying put in this case, ignoring his or her changed preferences for housing. If the consumer stays in his or her current accommodations h_0), based on the new indifference curve, the consumer can achieve a utility level of v_1 (given by the indifference curve that goes through the initial consumption point). This utility level is higher than the highest level the consumer can achieve by moving.

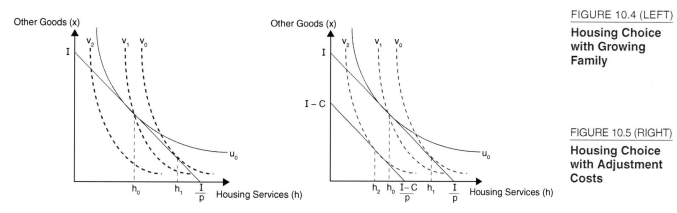

FIGURE 10.4 (LEFT)
Housing Choice with Growing Family

FIGURE 10.5 (RIGHT)
Housing Choice with Adjustment Costs

Even though the consumer would like to increase his or her housing consumption, adjustment costs make it uneconomical to do so. The high cost of moving is presumably one of the factors that makes home renovation attractive to many home owners: renovation allows the consumer to change his or her housing consumption, but avoid the adjustment costs.

Tenure Choice: Renting versus Owning

In addition to choosing how much housing to consume, households can also choose between owning and renting. This is known as tenure choice, since it refers to a choice between two different ways that property can be "held" by the consumer.

Consumers will seek to maximize utility by choosing the optimal level of housing services and mode of tenure. If we hold the level of housing services constant, with only mode of tenure varying, then the consumer will maximize utility by choosing the tenure with the lower total economic costs.

The *user cost of housing ownership* is the cost to an owner of occupying a particular housing unit for a given time period. The user cost of housing ownership includes mortgage interest payments, the opportunity cost of any equity invested in the house, property taxes, maintenance expenditures, the costs of depreciation, and any capital losses on the property over the time period in question (and offset by any capital gains, of course). The user cost of housing ownership (UC) is represented by this equation:

EQUATION 10.2

$$UC = iM + r(V - M) + (t + m + d - g)V$$

Where:

- V is the property value and M is the size of the mortgage on the property, so V − M is equity invested in the property
- i is the mortgage interest rate
- r is the opportunity cost of equity (the rate of return on non-housing assets)
- t is the property tax rate (expressed as a percentage of initial property value, V, ignoring impact of depreciation or capital gains)
- m is maintenance expenditures (expressed as a percentage of property value)
- d is the rate of depreciation on the building (in general, land does not depreciate)
- g is the rate of capital gains on the land (or possibly capital losses)

Notice that capital gains (g) reduce the user cost of housing – alternatively, if there is a capital loss, this would add to the cost of housing (a negative number multiplied by a negative in the equation).

In contrast, consider that an owner may instead choose to avoid all of these expenditures and simply rent. The cost of renting a particular housing unit for a given time period is simply the market rent R. Thus, for a given level of housing services, we expect a consumer to own if UC < R and rent if R < UC.

EXERCISE 10.1: Rent or Own?

You face the choice of either buying a $250,000 house or renting it for $2,000 per month.

Housing costs: the down payment is $70,000, the opportunity cost of equity is 10% per year, the mortgage interest rate is 8% per year, the property tax rate is 1% per year, annual maintenance expenditures are 0.25% of property value, and assume that depreciation and capital gains offset each other to 0% (for now, assume that the house is not expected to appreciate).

Are you better off to rent or own?

Solution:

Applying Equation 10.2, the user cost is:

UC = 0.08($250,000 − $70,000) + 0.1($70,000) + (0.01 + 0.0025)($250,000) = $24,525 or $2,044 per month. Housing costs are lower if you rent at a cost of $2,000 per month.

How might your answer change if you expect the property to appreciate at 1.5% per year (net of depreciation)?

UC = 0.08($180,000) + 0.1($70,000) + (0.01 + 0.0025 − 0.015)($250,000) = $20,775 or $1,731 per month. Now, housing costs are lower if you own.

Suppose that you are expecting to be transferred to another city in 12 months. The house will appreciate 1.5% over this year, but it will cost 6% of its value to sell it (assume this is in current dollars). Does this change your tenure choice?

UC = $20,775 + 0.06 t($250,000 × 1.015) = $36,000 or $3,000 per month. Housing costs are now much lower if you rent.

In a perfectly competitive market without barriers or impediments, landlords face exactly the same costs (including taxes) as owners, so market rent and user cost should be equal. This would mean consumers are indifferent between owning and renting. The idea here is that under competition, market rent should equal the marginal cost of supplying a unit of housing services. If landlords and home owners face exactly the same economic costs, then marginal cost and user cost should also be the same, implying R = UC.

However, in practice there are a number of reasons why this equivalence may fail.

- Potential owners may not be able to borrow enough to buy the desired level of housing services. This forces a sub-optimal choice: reduce housing consumption or rent rather than own.
- Owners have greater security of tenure than renters — e.g., since rental contracts can generally be terminated by landlords with notice, consumers who are concerned about tenure security may prefer owning to renting even if the economic costs are the same.
- Owners have better incentives to care for and maintain their properties than renters, since the benefit of any upkeep that a tenant does accrues to the landlord. This *rental externality* helps explain why owner-occupied housing is generally of higher quality than rental accommodations. This quality difference also contributes to the attractiveness of owner occupancy.

Tax policy differences between renting and owning may also distort the equation:

- The tax deductibility of mortgage interest in the US decreases the user cost of housing and favours owning over renting for many families.
- In Canada, capital gains on principal residences are tax-exempt.
- Rental income for landlords is fully taxed (and presumably built into rents), while home owners do not pay any tax on what is called *imputed rent*, or the rent they pay to themselves to live in their own homes.
- In a progressive income tax system (where t rises with income), the value of the deductions will be greater for a higher income consumer.

Table 10.1 describes the size and characteristics (including tenure) of the housing stock in Canada and the provinces in 2012. These data show that ownership is the dominant form of tenure in Canada, with approximately 67% of occupied private dwellings owned and the remaining 33% were rented. It is unclear how much this rental versus ownership tenure decision may be skewed by the factors outlined above. It appears that tax benefits, legal advantages, and aesthetic preferences all contribute to tipping the balance towards home ownership.

Rent or Own?

Sauder School of Business associate professor Tsur Somerville, discusses the rent versus own question in the paper "Are Renters Being Left Behind? Homeownership and Wealth Accumulation in Canadian Cities". Somerville and his colleagues examine the potential for wealth accumulation for owners and renters, comparing households that buy a home and pay down the mortgage versus a renter who invests the difference. The research shows that only renters who are highly disciplined, savvy investors are able to match the wealth that owners can accumulate simply by making their mortgage payments. "In the best scenario for renters, they can accumulate over 24 percent more wealth than owners in Edmonton, Halifax, Montreal, and Regina, and they can accumulate at least as much wealth as owners in Ottawa, Vancouver, and Winnipeg. In Calgary and Toronto renters cannot on average over our study period match the wealth achievable through homeownership". However, they suggest this ideal investment scenario may be unlikely in practice, as it "demands a level discipline that most North American households have shown themselves unable to achieve". In the end, their research affirms that "homeownership offers a unique opportunity for households to accumulate wealth … A tremendously significant benefit of homeownership for individuals is that the constraint of mortgage payments effectively forces home buyers to save by building equity through the repayment". In other words, for a typical Canadian household, a primary benefit of home ownership may be its impact in forcing savings … in effect, a home equity retirement plan!

Table 10.1: Dwelling and Household Characteristics, Canada and the Provinces, 2012

	Canada		British Columbia		Ontario		Quebec		Alberta		Saskatchewan		Manitoba		Nova Scotia		New Brunswick		Prince Edward Island		Newfoundland and Labrador	
	000s	% of Total	000s	% of Total	000s	% of Total	000s	% of Total	000s	% of Total	000s	% of Total	000s	% of Total	000s	% of Total	000s	% of Total	000s	% of Total	000s	% of Total
Total occupied private dwellings																						
Owned dwelling with mortgage(s)	4813	35.6	594	32.6	1846	36.7	1137	33.8	597	41.2	131	31.6	174	36.9	131	33.4	113	36.4	20	34.1	71	33.5
Owned dwelling without mortgage	4220	31.2	655	36	1540	30.7	897	26.7	445	30.7	155	37.4	150	31.8	150	38.4	119	38.6	19	32	91	42.9
Rented dwelling	4481	33.2	571	31.4	1638	32.6	1331	39.6	408	28.1	128	31	148	31.3	110	28.2	77	25	20	33.9	50	23.6
Type of dwelling																						
Single detached dwelling	7610	56.3	919	50.5	2930	58.3	1519	45.1	944	65.1	295	71.4	317	67.3	271	69.3	218	70.4	39	66.3	159	75.1
Single attached dwelling	1526	11.3	250	13.7	698	13.9	313	9.3	134	9.2	36	8.6	24	5.1	25	6.5	22	7.3	5	8.2	19	9.1
Apartment	4141	30.6	577	31.7	1381	27.5	1515	45	293	20.2	73	17.7	124	26.3	82	21	56	18.1	12	20.7	29	13.5
Other dwelling	237	1.8	75	4.1	N/A	N/A	N/A	N/A	80	5.5	N/A	N/A	N/A	N/A	13	3.3	13	4.2	N/A	N/A	N/A	N/A
Number of bedrooms																						
Dwelling with 1 bedroom	1715	12.7	301	16.5	569	11.3	528	15.7	124	8.5	45	11	62	13.1	41	10.5	28	9	5	9	13	6.2
Dwelling with 2 bedrooms	3262	24.1	464	25.5	1139	22.7	942	28	283	19.5	86	20.8	118	25	88	22.4	79	25.7	15	26.5	48	22.6
Dwelling with 3 bedrooms	4929	36.5	552	30.3	1916	38.1	1164	34.6	565	38.9	152	36.9	170	36.2	160	40.8	127	41.1	24	41.1	99	46.7
Dwelling with 4 bedrooms or more	3388	25.1	477	26.2	1316	26.2	652	19.4	465	32	126	30.6	111	23.5	101	25.8	74	24	14	23.3	52	24.4
Condition of dwelling																						
Major repairs needed	1216	9	168	9.3	436	8.7	247	7.3	149	10.3	49	11.9	49	10.3	45	11.4	45	14.6	5	8.9	23	10.9
Minor repairs needed	2269	16.8	258	14.2	890	17.7	516	15.3	257	17.7	72	17.4	99	21	77	19.7	55	17.9	10	17.4	36	16.9
No repairs needed	10029	74.2	1394	76.6	3698	73.6	2603	77.3	1045	72	292	70.7	324	68.7	270	68.9	208	67.4	43	73.7	153	72.2

Source: Statistics Canada

N/A = Too unreliable to be published (Statcan determination)

MARKET DEMAND FOR HOUSING

The prior section focused on individual households and the influences on their housing decisions. If the demands of all these individuals are aggregated, the result is a market demand curve like the one shown in Figure 10.1. The quantity demanded should be negatively related to the price (or user cost) of housing, meaning a downward sloping demand curve. The position of the demand curve will depend on a variety of characteristics such as income, the number of consumers, and demographic variables like the age profile of the population.

The general consensus is that housing demand is slightly inelastic with respect to both price and income. When we say that housing demand is inelastic with respect to both income and price, this means that the quantity of housing demanded does respond to changes in household income or prices, but at a lesser or slower rate. We will see why this may be the case below.

Recall that elasticity measures the sensitivity of one variable to changes in another. The price elasticity of demand for housing is defined as the percentage change in the quantity of housing demanded divided by the percentage change in housing prices:

EQUATION 10.3

$$E_{H,P} = \frac{\%\Delta H}{\%\Delta P}$$

The income elasticity of housing demand is defined as the percentage change in the quantity of housing demanded divided by the percentage change in household income:

EQUATION 10.4

$$E_{H,I} = \frac{\%\Delta H}{\%\Delta I}$$

The price elasticity of demand must be negative, since the demand curve slopes downward. If the elasticity is higher in absolute terms, the stronger the behavioural response to changing household income. Alternatively, the closer to 0, the weaker the behavioural response — changes in income or price have little or no impact on the quantity of housing demanded.

Studies have shown the price elasticity of demand for housing tends to be about –0.7. Using the definitions given above, $E_{H,P}$ = –0.7, meaning a 10% increase in price should be associated with a 7% decrease in the quantity of housing services demanded, other things being equal.

Research into housing demand and price elasticity are complicated by the fact that it can be difficult to measure the price of housing. When a property is sold, we know its sale price or market value. However, this value is a product of its price and the quantity sold — i.e., larger houses will sell for more at least partially due to their added size. To isolate the price of housing independently, we must control for differences in the quantity and quality of housing services in different houses. We will discuss how this is done later in this chapter.

For the income elasticity of housing demand, studies show it tends to be about 0.8. If $E_{H,I}$ = 0.8, this means a 10% increase in income should be associated with an 8% increase in the quantity of housing services demanded, other things being equal. Because consumption rises with income, housing is considered a normal good. However, the ratio of housing consumption to income tends to fall as income rises — more income leads to less and less housing in proportionate terms. For example, if someone earning $30,000 demands 1,000 square feet of living area, someone else earning $3,000,000 probably demands something less than 100,000 square feet (and similarly, a third person earning $3,000 needs more than 100 square feet).

Small variations in income from one year to the next probably do not have much effect on housing demand. There is time and cost involved in adjusting one's housing consumption, so people are unlikely to move in response to a minor income change. In other words, the income elasticity of housing demand with respect to current income is probably very small. Some measure of lifetime or "permanent" income is likely more important than income in any particular year in determining the level of housing that people choose. For example, wealth may be more important than income in determining house purchase decisions.

Wealth versus Income

The terms *wealth* and *income* are sometimes used synonymously in modern culture, but they do have differing meanings. If someone has a high income, it does not mean they are wealthy. Wealth can be defined by net worth – an individual's assets minus their liabilities. If someone has a lot of assets, it doesn't mean they are wealthy either – if the assets were entirely purchased with debt.

Consider a professional hockey player who receives an income of $2 million dollars per year. At the same time, his yearly expenses amount to $1.95 million, i.e., maintaining his mansion, servicing his fleet of sports cars, keeping his Olympic-size pool clean, and servicing the debt that paid for all of these assets. By year end, the hockey player has only $50,000 to store away in his savings. The hockey player has a very high income of $2 million, but has only accumulated wealth of $50,000 for that year. If next year the hockey player retires from professional hockey, he may receive an income of $0 and have wealth of $50,000.

On the other hand, consider a software engineer at a successful start-up company who is only paid $2,000 per month, but is given stock options that can be sold in future. When her company is eventually bought out by Google, she will retire with wealth in the billions. In contrast to the hockey player, she has low income but great wealth.

Housing demand is also influenced by demographics, especially the *headship rate* and the age profile of the population. The headship rate is defined as the number of *households* per 100 persons in the population (where a household is all of the individuals occupying a housing unit). The headship rate is essentially the ratio of households-to-population. The headship rate is also the inverse of average household size — e.g., if there are 20 households among 100 people, then there are 5 people per household and the headship rate is 20/100 or 1/5. Rearranging the headship equation provides a helpful measure for estimating housing demand. If we know the population and the headship rate, then the number of households is equal to population times the headship rate.

Headship Rate

The number of households per 100 persons in a population

Household

All of the individuals occupying a housing unit

Headship rates are influenced by a variety of social and economic factors. For example, overall headship rates were relatively stable from post-World War II to 1960, but past that point there was dramatic growth in headship rates among so-called *non-family households* (individuals living alone or with unrelated persons). This change in North America's "family unit" had an important impact on the level and composition of housing demand during this period.

Headship rates are also sensitive to economic conditions: more households form when incomes are high relative to housing costs, and fewer households form when incomes are low relative to housing costs. This highlights the danger of extrapolating demographic trends into the future without accounting for changes in economic conditions.

Consider the effects of the baby boom generation on housing markets as an example of extrapolating demographic trends. The standard pattern for housing consumption over the life cycle is that new households start out as renters; they switch to home ownership when their income and wealth is sufficient to meet the debt coverage and down payment requirements of mortgage lenders, trade up to larger houses during the child rearing years, and subsequently trade down to smaller houses in retirement. The net result is that the per capita demand for housing tends to increase up to about age 40 and then decline thereafter.

The baby boom is a massive demographic group with a massive impact on all aspects of our society and economy, real estate included. As the baby boom generation started their families, it is logical to expect an increase in housing demand — and this has coincided with huge growth in North American cities, in particular the suburbs. It seems logical that the aging of the baby boom generation should lead to significant decreases in housing demand as they approach retirement. Intuitively, the argument is quite simple: if housing demand per person tends to rise until about age 40, and then declines slowly thereafter, then as an especially large segment of population exits the prime home buying years, housing demand will fall. Based on baby boom demographics, some economists predicted that house prices in the US and Canada would decrease by up to half in the early 2000s.

However, this has proved false. Figure 10.6 shows a steady increase in real housing prices in Canada from 1981 onward. In fact, it appears price increases have accelerated through the 2000s.

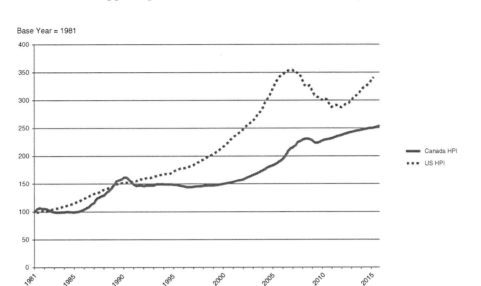

FIGURE 10.6

Trend in Real Home Price Index (HPI)

As intuitively appealing as the baby boom demographic theories may be, clearly there is more to the housing demand story than just demographics. Equilibrium house prices depend on countless variables: incomes, interest rates, taxes, construction costs, exchange rates, GDP, immigration, business cycles, etc. For example, in Canada, consider the impact of historically low interest rates from the mid-2000s onward on real estate prices. Or, for another confounding variable in some markets, the significant increase in foreign capital from China may be elevating the market. In the US, the price crater in 2008/09 in Figure 10.6 is related to the sub-prime crisis — with an ensuing decade of slow recovery.

Consider too that the price effect of a change in demand (due to the aging of the baby boom, a change in interest rates, or any other factor) also depends on supply conditions. The supply of housing may be very elastic in the long run, meaning changes in demand will lead to increased housing consumption (and perhaps new construction). However, it seems doubtful that these demand changes alone can explain changes in housing prices. The general consensus among housing economists seems to be that while demographics are important and the aging of the baby boom is significant, analysts must exercise caution in attempting to link demographics with housing demand and housing prices.

HOUSING SUPPLY

Most research on housing supply treats the residential construction industry as if it is perfectly competitive, with a typical upward sloping supply curve and downward sloping demand curve. Under this assumption, the level of new construction or housing starts should be a function of housing prices and construction costs. Studies show that new construction does indeed rise with the price of housing, as expected, but housing starts do not appear to respond to construction cost changes in any consistent manner. In some cases, increased construction costs appear to reduce new housing starts, as common sense would suggest. In other cases, increases in costs precede increases in supply, which seems to defy common sense; however, in such cases the likely explanation is that other factors — such as strong demand growth — are more than offsetting the effect of the cost increase in terms of influencing developers' choices.

One defining characteristic of housing supply that differentiates it from other commodities is that the stock of housing is essentially fixed in the short run, leading to the nearly vertical supply curve S_{SR} illustrated in Figure 10.1. This means the short-run supply of housing is very inelastic, so the price of housing is largely determined by changes in demand. Conversely, in the long run, the supply of housing is more elastic; given enough time to build new houses, the supply can be responsive to price and cost changes.

Consider an extreme case of supply elasticity — in Figure 10.7 the short-run supply curve S_{SR} is vertical, or perfectly inelastic, while the long-run supply curve S_{LR} is horizontal, or perfectly elastic. An increase in demand in the short run causes no change in the quantity of housing, but a very large increase in price (from P_0 to P_1). However, in the long run, when the stock of housing can change, this price increase elicits new construction and, under the assumption that long-run supply is perfectly elastic, the price ultimately returns to P_0, while the quantity increases from H_0 to H_1. This general pattern is probably realistic in most circumstances. In the short run, demand changes should primarily affect the price of housing, while in the long run, demand changes should primarily affect the quantity of housing.

FIGURE 10.7

Extreme Assumptions about the Elasticity of Supply

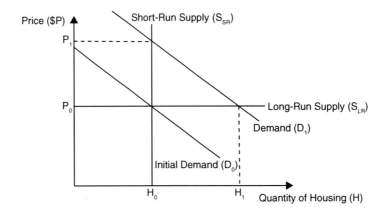

The extreme case in Figure 10.7 is useful to illustrate how elasticity affects the quantity and price of housing, but it is unlikely to occur in practice. The graph in Figure 10.1 is probably more realistic, with degrees of elasticity in the short and long run, and therefore mixed results on the drivers of housing quantity and prices. For example, the Organization for Economic Cooperation and Development (OECD), in a cross-country study published in 2011, found that the price elasticity of new housing investment in Canada for the period 1980 to 2000 was 1.19.[1] Other studies show price elasticity of housing starts ranging from 1.0 in the short run and 3.0 in the long run, or as high as 6.0. It seems clear that the supply of housing is at least somewhat elastic, but this seems to vary significantly over time.

A rough rule of thumb for any given Canadian market in any given year is that new construction averages about 3% of the stock of housing. However, new construction varies a great deal over time. Figure 10.8 shows new housing starts in Toronto over the 1980-2012 period. The jagged pattern in this figure is partially due to seasonal variation in starts — in cold climates, most construction activity occurs in the third and fourth quarters of any year. Smoothing out this seasonal variation with a four-quarter moving average brings out a strong cyclical trend. Total housing starts increased from 3,070 in the first quarter of 1980 to nearly 14,000 in the second quarter of 1987; then plummeted to 2,300 in the first quarter of 1991, eventually rising again to 13,000 in the second quarter of 2005. There were further sharp downswings in 2007, 2009, and 2010, while there were large upswings in 2008, 2011, and 2012. The general business cycle appears to be a confounding external influence that messes up our neat and tidy housing demand and supply curves!

FIGURE 10.8

Housing Starts in Toronto

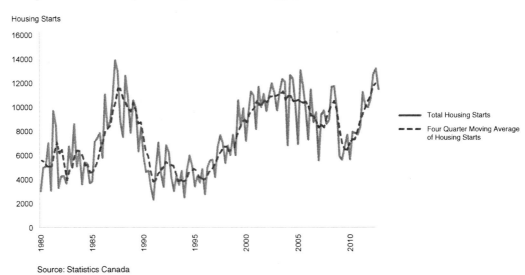

Source: Statistics Canada

[1]   Caldera Sánchez, A. and Å. Johansson (2011), "The Price Responsiveness of Housing Supply in OECD Countries", OECD Economics Department Working Papers, No. 837, OECD Publishing. This study is discussed in greater detail in Chapter 12.

The durability of housing presents a further confounding variable in examining housing supply. The stock of new housing changes slowly over time as new houses are added. But once built, housing provides services for many years. The stock of housing also changes when older houses are altered and improved. In fact, with most housing services supplied from the existing housing stock, these renovations and alterations present a major influence on housing supply.

Figure 10.9 plots expenditures on alterations and improvements and the value of new residential construction (in real terms) in Canada over the 1990-2011 period. The average ratio of new construction to alterations and improvements was about 1.4 over this period, meaning every $1.40 in new construction saw $1.00 spent on renovations. Canada Mortgage and Housing Corporation (CMHC) reports that in the first three months of 2013, expenditure on new construction in Canada amounted to $57.4 billion. Over the same time, expenditure on renovations in Canada totalled $46.6 billion. New construction is an obvious driver in our economy, but the impact of renovations is surprisingly large.

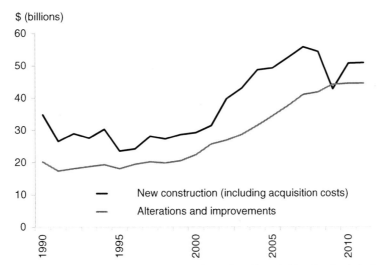

FIGURE 10.9

Construction Spending in Canada

Source: CMHC, *"Housing and Market Information: Monthly Housing Statistics"*, 2013

Looking more closely at the renovation issue, it is interesting to note how property owners must make economic decisions regarding maintenance, alterations, and improvements to their properties. The property owner must weigh the pros and cons of investing additional capital in the property, considering the conflicting factors of depreciation of improvements, potential price appreciation, the cost of alternative new housing, and the added transaction costs of moving (travel, sales costs, etc.).

To examine this decision in a simple fashion, assume that housing services are produced from capital and land, and that the amount of land that a particular property occupies is fixed. Then we can write the production function for housing services in period t as $H_t = f(K_t)$ — meaning housing services in period t is a function of the stock of capital K_t. In any given period, the stock of capital K_t may increase if the owner decides to invest in the property via maintenance, alterations, and improvements. This increases the amount (or value) of housing services H_t. However, at the same time, depreciation is constantly eating away at the value of improvements. If the level of new investment in period t is represented by k_t and depreciation on the property in period t is represented by d_t, then the change in the stock of capital in period t is $\Delta K_t = k_t - d_t$. This means that for any given period, if new investment is greater than depreciation, then the level of the stock of capital will rise, and the level of housing services provided by the structure built on the land will increase (meaning the house contributes to an increase in the supply of housing for the market). Alternatively, if new investment is less than depreciation, then the stock of capital and the level of services will fall.

Each time period, the property owner faces a decision on how much additional capital to invest in the property. Figure 10.10 illustrates this decision in economic terms. To maximize the value of his or her holdings, the owner should choose to make capital investment k_t up to the point where the marginal benefit of investing and the marginal cost of investing are equal.

- The marginal cost of investing another unit of capital in the property is simply the opportunity cost — i.e., the cost of foregoing the next best use of these funds, which could be investment in your RRSP, buying a ski season pass, or a trip to Hawaii.
- The marginal benefit of investing is given by the value of the marginal product of structural capital: $MB = p_H \times MP_K$. The marginal product of capital here means the benefit from investing one more unit of capital. This is multiplied by the price of housing, p_H, to find the overall benefit of this housing investment.

FIGURE 10.10

Housing Maintenance and Improvement Decision

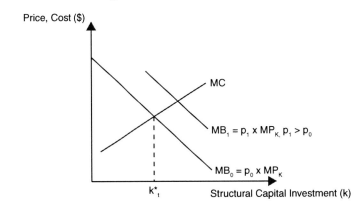

The optimal choice in period t is labelled as k^*_t. This is the point at which the investment in maintaining or updating the house is worthwhile economically. Above that point, investments will not return enough in value to be worthwhile; below that point, the owner is not keeping up with necessary maintenance and eroding the value of the house.

If the marginal cost and marginal benefit curves in Figure 10.10 were stable over time, then k^*_t would be a constant amount, say k^*, and the contribution of renovations and upgrading to the housing stock would be easy to estimate. However, reality is generally not as simple as our neat and tidy economic charts. In housing markets, prices are constantly changing, and depreciation also varies over time.

- Depreciation: we generally expected d_t to rise over time, so older houses will have more depreciation than younger ones. Under these conditions, depreciation will eventually overtake new investment, such that $d_t > k^*$, and the level of housing services will decline.
- Price: an increase in the price of housing will cause the optimal capital reinvestment k^*_t to rise over time; if this is sufficient to overcome depreciation, then structural capital will increase and the property will be improved. This is one component of the process of *gentrification*, or the renewal of inner city neighbourhoods in many cities. If older neighbourhoods become more attractive, and the price of housing in that location rises, then this may encourage home owners to improve the quality of their older structures.

Gentrification

The process of renewal and rebuilding of deteriorating neighbourhoods

Value Matters: Do Renovations Pay Off?

This capital reinvestment decision faced by owners, whether or not it's worthwhile to spend money on renovations, upgrading, or even basic maintenance, can serve to illustrate several of the guiding principles of real estate appraisal.

Principle of Contribution: the value of an addition is measured by its contribution to the whole of the property's value or by the amount that its absence detracts from the whole; e.g., renovation may add the value of the capital reinvested – or, alternatively, deferring maintenance may reduce property value.

Principle of Balance: real estate value is created and maintained when contrasting elements are in a state of equilibrium; e.g., the overall benefit of renovations will vary depending on the situation, comparing marginal benefit (value increase) to marginal cost – replacing a kitchen in an older house may be a big improvement, whereas adding a second kitchen to a new house would likely be a waste of money.

continued on next page

Law of Decreasing/Increasing Returns: investments up to a certain point will add more than their cost, and then past that point will return less than their cost; e.g., owners should reinvest in their property as long as the value increases by at least as much as the investment – beyond this tipping point, investment is not worthwhile (at that point, it would be considered *incurable depreciation*).

Appraisal Questions: For each of the following home ownership decisions, consider if it is worthwhile to:

- Repaint the exterior wood siding and soffits?
- Reshingle the cedar roof?
- Update an outdated, functionally obsolete bathroom?
- Repair a sloping kitchen floor in a historic, heritage house?
- Raise the house to convert the basement to liveable space?
- Convert the house to energy efficient and sustainable building systems?

Answer: It depends! You must analyze the marginal benefit versus marginal cost for each of these capital reinvestment decisions in that particular situation. Every situation is different and navigating this ever-changing landscape is what makes appraisal more of an art than a science.

HOUSING IN A MONOCENTRIC CITY

Now that we have investigated the peculiarities of housing demand and supply, we can revisit the monocentric city model introduced in Chapter 6 and adapt this basic model to consider housing specifically. Listed below are the assumptions that will underlie our monocentric housing model:

1. The basic monocentric city assumes a flat, featureless plain, with all jobs concentrated in the city centre. All households in the city are identical, with the same preferences and the same incomes; one member of each household commutes to the city centre once each day.

2. Rather than assuming that households consume land directly, we now consider the more realistic case where households consume housing services that are produced by a competitive building or construction industry. This allows us to see the relationship between the price of housing and the price of residential land. It also allows us to explore the concept of density, where land use may be more or less concentrated, e.g., high-rises downtown and houses with big yards in the suburbs.

3. All housing locations vary only by distance to the centre. Because housing is fixed in space, the price of housing varies with location within a city. Residential locations are completely described by their straight-line distance to the city centre, which is represented by the variable d. The round trip cost of commuting is (t × d), where d is distance from the city centre and t is cost of commuting another unit of distance (the marginal commuting cost).

4. Households make housing decisions based on maximizing overall utility (u) by spending their fixed income (I) on a basket of housing (h) and other goods (x). Housing h is measured, for simplicity, in square feet of floor space; the price per square foot of housing will be denoted by p. The price of other goods x is set to $1.

5. All markets are competitive and the city is open in the sense that migration to other urban areas is free. Competition implies that all residents or households must achieve the same level of utility in equilibrium. Since the city is open, the equilibrium utility level (u*) will equal the level that is available in other cities.

The Housing Price Function

Given households can choose to spend their income I on a combination of housing h and other goods x, the household's budget constraint says that expenditures on housing and other goods must equal income net of commuting costs. This is expressed as follows:

EQUATION 10.5

$$(p \times h) + x = I - (t \times d)$$

We now want to rearrange this equation to isolate the price of housing services. To do so, we assume that every household consumes the same amount of housing h* (which we will measure in number of square feet), regardless of price – this is equivalent to assuming that the demand for housing is perfectly inelastic. Further, assuming that every household must achieve the utility level u*, it follows that every household must also consume the same quantity of other goods x*.

Substituting h* and x* into the budget constraint and solving for p gives:

EQUATION 10.6

$$p(d) = \frac{(I - x^*)}{h^*} - \left(\frac{t}{h^*}\right) \times d$$

Where:

- p(d) is price of housing per square foot at a given distance from the city centre (this is very similar to r(d) or bid rent from Chapter 6); this is the equilibrium housing price function, illustrated in Figure 10.11.
- (I–x*)/h* is the expenditure on housing (I–x*) divided by the amount of housing (h*); this is the vertical intercept in Figure 10.11.
- –t/h* is the travel/commuting cost (t) divided by the amount of housing (h*); this is the slope of the price function in Figure 10.11.
- d is the distance from the city centre; this is the x-axis or horizontal axis in Figure 10.11.

P(d) can be measured as a purchase price, an annual price, a monthly price, or even a weekly price. Whichever one chooses, it is important that all variables are measured using the same unit of time. If the housing price function is used to measure the monthly price, for example, then Income I should be monthly, consumption of other goods x should be monthly, and commuting costs should be monthly.

The equilibrium housing price function p(d) is interpreted much like the bid rent functions from Chapter 6. It says that in order for households to achieve the same level of utility everywhere in the city, the price of housing must decline with distance to offset the rising cost of commuting. Houses at desirable locations (closer to city centre jobs) must command a premium relative to other houses in the city.

Given our assumption that households have the same utility in all locations, and because the price of housing will adjust by location according to our price function, this means no household has an incentive to move. Just like bid rents in our monocentric city model, there is a spatial equilibrium.

FIGURE 10.11

The Housing Price Function

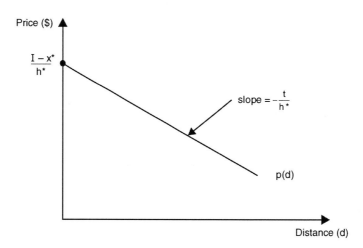

EXERCISE 10.2(a): Housing Prices and Distance in a Monocentric City

Consider a monocentric city in which all houses contain 1,000 square feet of floor space. The cost of commuting is $50 per kilometre per month, round trip.

At a distance of 10 kilometres from the city centre (d = 10), the price of housing is $0.75 per square foot per month.

    1. Determine the housing price function.

    2. What is the price of housing at five kilometres from the city centre (d = 5)?

Solution:

    1. We know that, in this case, the housing price function is a straight line with a slope of:

$$-\frac{t}{h^*} = -\frac{\$50}{1,000} = -\$0.05$$

Therefore, the housing price function has the form p(d) = a – ($0.05 × d), where a is the vertical intercept.

If p(10) = $0.75, this means:

    $0.75 = a – $0.05(10)

Therefore, a = 1.25, and the housing price function is:

    p(d) = $1.25 – ($0.05 × d)

    2. Since the housing price function is $1.25 – ($0.05 × d), if we substitute d = 5 into the equation:

    p(5) = $1.25 – ($0.05 × 5) = $1.25 – $0.25 = $1.00

The price of housing at d = 5 is $1 per square foot per month.

As we have previously discussed, the monocentric model may be abstract and unrealistic, but it can be useful in highlighting basic truths about cities. One basic truth is that the price of housing varies with access within a city. From that basic truth comes many jumping off points for researchers to study: the specifics of the transportation system, the importance and nature of non-commuting travel, the locations of subcentres within a city, and many others. The basic point that housing prices vary with access remains, but these additional factors help to determine and define the access characteristics of different houses within a city — and thus attempt to decode some of the mysteries of residential price relationships in our cities.

Builders and the Bid Rent Function for Land

The prior section spoke to household demand for housing. But as we know, demand is just one side of an economic equilibrium. We must also consider the mechanisms for housing supply.

    We assume that housing is supplied by a competitive building industry, motivated by pursuit of profit π. The market price function determines a price p(d) for housing at various locations in the city. Builders decide how much they are willing to pay for land in these varied locations in order to profitably build housing.

    In the simple monocentric city model, developers were only concerned with units of land ℓ*. However, we now must add another layer of complexity (and realism) by considering the construction costs that builders face. For simplicity, we will assume that structural density is fixed, meaning buildings are the same height for every house in the city. The builder needs to spend k* units of capital on ℓ* units of land.[2]

---

[2] In building more realism into this model, the first assumption that might be discarded is to consider that developers may construct buildings with varying degrees of structural density, e.g., high rises downtown and houses on large lots at the urban boundary. This means developers must also be concerned with the atmount of capital investment k* per lot, with this varying throughout the city region. This greatly complicates the calculations – but approaches the realism of pricing urban residential properties on a value per buildable foot basis.

The profit of a builder who supplies housing at location d is:

$$\pi = \big[p(d) \times h^*\big] - \big[p_K \times k^*\big] - \big[r(d) \times \ell^*\big]$$

Where:

- p(d) is price of housing at a given distance from the city and h* is the amount, measured in square feet, of housing services demanded
- p_K is the price of capital (interest on borrowed funds; rate of return on equity invested)
- k* is the amount of capital (building cost) required for construction on that lot
- r(d) is land rent at location d and ℓ^* is the amount of land (lot size)

All variables should be measured using the same unit of time, e.g., if we measure profits on a monthly basis, then housing prices, capital prices, and land rent should all be measured on a monthly basis, too.

Competition forces economic profits to zero in the long run.[3] Solving for π = 0 for r(d) gives the builder's bid rent function for residential land:

EQUATION 10.8

$$r(d) = \frac{(I - x^*) - (p_K \times k^*)}{\ell^*} - \left(\frac{t}{\ell^*}\right) \times d$$

Note that this expression is very similar to Equation 6.3 from Chapter 6, the bid rent function for land. Equation 10.8 says that bid rents for residential land are based on distance from the city centre. The bid rent function has a negative slope of $-t/\ell^*$, or travel/commuting cost divided by lot size.

We are now at the point where we can use this bid rent function for land in concert with the housing price function, to see their common equilibrium.

Equilibrium Housing Prices and Land Rents

Housing prices provide the revenue for housing builders/developers, which in turn helps to determine how much they are willing and able to pay for land at different locations. To illustrate the relationship between the housing price and land rent functions, it is useful to add just a bit more structure to the model. Let's bring back our familiar assumption about the rent land earns in agriculture, ra. This is considered the opportunity cost of urban land, in that land not used for housing will be used for agriculture at the rent ra. Competition for land will then determine the boundary of the city (b) where the bid rent for residential land equals ra. This boundary is illustrated in Figure 10.12.

We revisit the builder's bid rent function from Equation 10.8, specifying the distance d as location b, the boundary of the city:

$$r^a = \frac{(I - x^*) - (p_K \times k^*)}{\ell^*} - \left(\frac{t}{\ell^*}\right) \times b$$

By rearranging this, substituting in common terms, and simplifying, we find the following equilibrium residential land rent function and the equilibrium housing price function:

EQUATION 10.9

Equilibrium Land Rent: $r(d) = r^a + \left(\dfrac{t}{\ell^*}\right)(b - d)$

EQUATION 10.10

Equilibrium Housing Price: $p(d) = \dfrac{(p_K \times k^*) + (r^a \times \ell^*)}{h^*} + \left(\dfrac{t}{h^*}\right)(b - d)$

These equilibrium functions are drawn in Figure 10.12.

---

[3] Keeping in mind the point from Chapter 6 that a normal entrepreneurial profit is included within the building costs k*, because without a profit incentive no developer would go to all this trouble. What the economic equilibrium does is eliminate *excess profits* or *economic profits*.

In considering equilibrium housing prices, two points of note:

1. Point b on the graph is the city boundary; beyond this point, no houses will be built. In Equation 10.10, if d and b are equal, this means the second term is equal to zero, and the resulting price of housing is $= [(p_k \times k^*) + (r^a \times \ell)]/h^*$. This is the opportunity cost of the resources that are needed to build a unit of housing, noted as p(b) on Figure 10.12.
2. The slope of the housing price function is $(t/h^*)(b - d)$. This is the location premium (per square foot of housing) that households are willing to pay to occupy housing that is close to their city centre jobs. At the boundary of the city (where b = d), the location premium is zero. The location premium reaches its maximum of $(t/h^*) \times d$ at the city centre.

Similarly, in considering equilibrium land rents, two points of note:

1. At the urban boundary b, the bid rent of land r(d) drops below the agricultural rent, r^a. This means land beyond this point is more valuable in agricultural use than urban. This means r^a is the opportunity cost of urban land.

The slope of the land rent function is $(t/\ell^*)(b - d)$. This is the location premium that a builder is willing to pay for land near the city centre. This occurs because consumers are willing to pay more for housing there. At the boundary of the city (where b = d), the location premium is zero. The location premium reaches its maximum of $(t/\ell^*) \times b$ at the city centre.

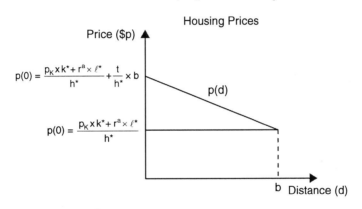

Housing Prices

$$p(0) = \frac{p_K \times k^* + r^a \times \ell^*}{h^*} + \frac{t}{h^*} \times b$$

$$p(0) = \frac{p_K \times k^* + r^a \times \ell^*}{h^*}$$

Price ($p) / p(d) / b / Distance (d)

FIGURE 10.12

Equilibrium Housing Prices and Land Rents

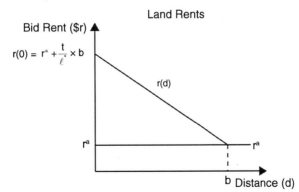

Land Rents

$$r(0) = r^a + \frac{t}{\ell} \times b$$

Bid Rent ($r) / r(d) / r^a / b / Distance (d)

EXERCISE 10.2(b): Housing Prices and Land Rents in a Monocentric City

We can expand the example given in Exercise 10.2(a) to include the market for residential land.

This monocentric city has houses with 1,000 square feet of floor space and a cost of commuting is $50 per kilometre per month, round trip. We showed that if the price of housing (per square foot) is $0.75 per month at a distance of 10 kilometres from the city centre, then the equilibrium housing price function, again per square foot and per month, is p(d) = $1.25 − ($0.05 × d).

Now assume that every house in the city occupies $\ell^* = 0.25$ acres of land (4 units per acre) and requires capital/construction funds with a cost of $p_K \times k^* = \$500$ per month.

What is the bid rent for residential land at d = 10? d = 5?

continued on next page

Solution:

The price of housing at d = 10 is $0.75 per square foot per month. Since each house contains 1,000 square feet of space, the revenue of a builder at that location is $750 per month ($0.75 × 1,000). If construction cost is $500 per month, then the residual per housing unit is $250 ($750 – $500). Since there are 4 units per acre, the bid rent for residential land must be $1,000 per acre ($250 × 4).

The bid rent at d=5 can be solved using the slope of the residential bid rent function = – t/ℓ* = $50/0.25 = –$200.

Therefore, if d changes by –5 km, then multiplying this by the slope implies a change in bid rent = –5 × –$200 = +$1,000. The bid rent on land 5 kilometres from the city centre is $2,000 per acre.

EXERCISE 10.3

Consider a monocentric city in which all houses contain 1,000 square feet of floor space (h*).

The cost of commuting is $50 per kilometre per month, round trip. Agricultural land has a bid rent ra = $1,000 per acre per month starting at the urban boundary b=40 kilometres from the city centre. Every house in the city occupies R* = 0.25 acres of land (4 units per acre).

Capital/construction costs: interest rate is p_K =0.5% per month, capital is k* = $100,000 per house ($100 per square foot of house). Therefore, p_K × k* = $500 per house per month.

1. What is the monthly land bid rent per acre and monthly price of housing per square foot at the city centre? (Y-intercept)
2. By how much does land bid rent and housing price change with each kilometre from the city centre? (slope)
3. What is monthly land bid rent per acre and monthly housing price per square foot at five kilometres (d = 5) or ten kilometres (d = 10) from the city centre?
4. Briefly explain how the land bid rent and housing price functions are related. Why do they need to be analyzed together to find equilibrium? t(or some other question that explains why/how these are linked)

Solution:

This exercise requires analysis of the equilibrium residential land rent function and the equilibrium housing price function:

Equilibrium land rent: $r(d) = r^a + (t/\ell^*)(b - d)$

Equilibrium housing price: $p(d) = [(p_K \times k^*) + (r^a \times \ell^*)]/h^* + (t/h^*)(b - d)$

1. Finding monthly land bid rent and monthly price of housing at the city centre requires solving for the Y-intercept in both equations – set d=0 km and solve for r(0) and p(0).

   $r(0) = r^a + (t/\ell^*)(b - d)$ = $1,000 + ($50/0.25)(40 – 0) = $9,000 per acre per month ($2,250 per quarter acre per month)

   $p(0) = [(p_K \times k^*) + (r^a \times \ell^*)]/h^* + (t/h^*)(b - d)$

   p(0) = [($500) + ($1,000 × 0.25)]/1,000 + ($50/1,000)(40 – 0) = $0.75 + $2.00

   p(0) = $2.75 per square foot per month ($2,750 per month for a 1,000 square foot house)

   This is the amount needed to break even after the developer pays for the land (bid rent) and the cost of capital (interest rate on loans).

2. Solving for the slope of the housing price and land bid rent functions requires solving for the function in front of (b-d), i.e., t/R* and t/h*.

   Land rent slope = t/R* = $50/0.25 = $200. The land rent for a quarter acre lot increases by $50 per kilometre per month; therefore, for an acre (with four lots), land rent increases by $200 per kilometre per month. This is the amount that four households would be willing to pay to avoid commuting one extra kilometre per month.

   Housing price slope = t/h* = $50/1,000 = $0.05. The price of housing increases by $0.05 per kilometre on a square foot per month basis ($50 per kilometre per month for a 1,000 square foot dwelling).

continued on next page

3. Monthly land bid rent per acre and monthly housing price per square foot at d=5 and d=10:

   r(5) = $1,000 + ($50/0.25)(40 − 5) = $8,000 per acre per month

   p(5) = [($500) + ($1,000 × 0.25)]/1,000 + ($50/1,000)(40 − 5) = $2.50 per square foot per month ($2,500 per month for the house)

   r(10) = $1,000 + ($50/0.25)(40 − 10) = $7,000 per acre per month

   p(10) = [($500) + ($1,000 × 0.25)]/1,000 + ($50/1,000)(40 − 10) = $2.25 per square foot per month ($2,250 per month for the house)

4. The equilibrium for the housing market must consider two sub-markets concurrently: the price and supply of land that underlies housing (the developers' concern) and the price and supply of the dwellings on the land (the concern of households). These two sub-markets are entwined and mutually dependent. For example, if land becomes so expensive that the resulting housing prices are not affordable, or if housing prices are so low that it's not economically feasible to develop housing, then the market does not produce any new housing services. The equilibrium solution is where both sub-markets are in balance, reaching an optimum that satisfies the needs of both developers and households, given the costs involved in that market. You can see that this is a lot more complicated than the simple monocentric city introduced in Chapter 6 − and it highlights how complex real estate markets are, with a constant interplay of a multitude of complementary and competing variables.

Substitution and Density

In the interests of simplicity, we have assumed that consumers cannot substitute housing for other goods, and that builders cannot substitute capital for land in housing production. Under these assumptions, the housing price and residential land rent functions are straight lines. This makes it easy to derive and illustrate the functions.

A downside of these assumptions is they are completely unrealistic. Most importantly, they imply that both population and structural density are constant throughout the city, which ignores the true nature of nearly every city in the world! If households can substitute housing for other goods (and the demand for housing is elastic), they will attempt to reduce their housing consumption where the price of housing is high — i.e., at locations near the city centre, households are willing to live in smaller dwellings. This will cause the housing price function to be convex — steeper near the city centre and flatter near the boundary of the city.

Similarly, if builders can substitute capital for land in housing production, then they will try to economize on their use of land where the rent on land is high — again, at locations near the city centre. This will cause the land rent function to become convex as well, and will lead to higher population and structural densities near the city centre than near the boundary of the city.

These are, of course, some of the most basic characteristics of cities: the tallest buildings and the highest density neighbourhoods are always in or near the downtown (recall our earlier discussion of population density functions). This pattern of development will occur in equilibrium in a monocentric city if we allow consumers and producers the flexibility to respond to changes in the prices of housing and land.

EXERCISE 10.4

Consider a monocentric city in which the cost of commuting is $50 per kilometre per month round trip. A household located 10 km from the city centre (d = 10) occupies a dwelling with 1,000 square feet of floor space at a monthly price of $800. Non-land cost per dwelling ($p_K \times k$, paid by the developer) is $400 per month. Housing demand is perfectly inelastic. Residential developers are flexible (i.e., they engage in factor substitution between land and capital), and the number of housing units per acre ($1/\ell^*$) is given by 20 − (8/5)d.

1. How many units per acre are built at d = 5, 10, 12?

2. What is the monthly price per square foot of housing at d = 10?

3. What is the monthly bid rent per acre for residential land at d = 10?

4. What is the monthly price of housing at the city centre?

5. What is the monthly bid rent for residential land at the city centre? (per unit and per acre)

continued on next page

6. Derive and graph the housing price function on a monthly, per square foot basis.

7. Derive and graph the bid rent function on a monthly, per acre basis.

Solution:

1. The number of units per acre at 5 km: $20 - 8/5(5) = 12$; 10 km: $20 - 8/5(10) = 4$; 12 km: $20 - 8/5(12) = 0.8$ (i.e., each housing unit occupies 1.25 acres)

2. $p(10) = \$800/1{,}000 \text{ ft}^2 = \$0.80$ per ft^2 per month

3. The residual is $r(10) = 4(\$800 - \$400) = \$1{,}600$ per acre per month

4. The slope of the housing price function $= -t/h = -\$50/1{,}000 \text{ ft}^2 = -\$0.05$ per ft^2.
   Since $p(10) = \$0.80$ (from part 2), then the housing price function at 10 km is:
   $\$0.80 = a - \$0.05(10)$
   Solve for the Y-intercept (a):
   $a = \$0.80 + \$0.5 = \$1.30$; the price of housing at the city centre or $p(0)$, the vertical intercept.

5. Since the density function for land $= 20 - 8/5d$, if $d = 0$, there are 20 units per acre at the city centre. The total price per unit is \$1,300 per month ($\$1.30 \times 1{,}000 \text{ ft}^2$). Since non-land cost is \$400 per month, bid rent is \$900/unit/month ($\$1{,}300 - \$400$) or \$18,000 per acre per month ($\$900 \times 20$).

6. From part 4, with a slope of $-\$0.05$ and vertical intercept of \$1.30, the housing price function is $p(d) = \$1.3 - \$0.05d$. In this case, because we have assumed that housing demand is inelastic (that is, households do not change the amount of space they occupy as the price of that space varies), the graph of the housing price function is a straight line and resembles Figure 10.11.

7. Developers will earn $P(d) = \$1.3 - \$0.05d$ per square foot for each dwelling they build, and their non-land costs are \$0.40 per square foot (or \$400 per 1,000 square foot dwelling). A developer's profit before land costs per dwelling will be:

$$p_i = p(d) \times h^* - p_K \times k^* = 1{,}300 - 50d - 400 = 900 - 50d$$

We can then multiply that by the number of dwellings that a flexible developer will build per acre depending on distance from the city centre, which is $20 - 8/5d$. The result is:

$$(900 - 50d)(20 - 8/5d) = 18{,}000 - 1{,}440d - 1{,}000d + 400/5d^2$$

Simplifying further, this becomes $r(d) = 18{,}000 - 2{,}440d + 80d^2$

We can enter various values to test this bid rent function. For example, if we set $d = 0$, we find that bid rent per acre per month is \$18,000 (the value we found in part (5) of this exercise). And if we set $d = 10$, we get \$1,600 per acre per month (the value we found in part (3) of this exercise). The graph below shows all possible values up to a distance of 12.5 kilometres from the city centre. The graph does not show distances farther from this, as beyond this distance, developers choose not to build anything, i.e., $1/l^*$ falls below zero.

The housing price function here was linear, given our assumption of price inelasticity of housing demand, but the bid rent curve is a convex curved line. Properties near downtown can earn higher bid rent, because of the input substitution by developers: less land, but more capital, and more density of housing. This reverses as we approach the city boundary, where land is less expensive, the lots bigger, and the living less dense.

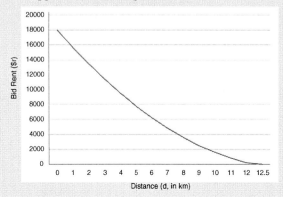

PRICING RESIDENTIAL REAL ESTATE

Suppose you are a real estate consultant and a client has hired you for a simple assignment: carry out a market analysis to determine if the price of housing in a certain residential area, Hamilton Heights, is greater than the price of housing in another area, Strange Lanes, and if so, by how much.

You gather data on the sale prices of different properties in the two areas, and find out that the average price of a single-family home in Hamilton Heights is $400,000, while the average price in Strange Lanes is $300,000. You dutifully report to your client that the price of housing is about 33% higher in Hamilton Heights. Unfortunately, your client lives in Strange Lanes and she knows that all the houses there have much smaller lots than the houses in Hamilton Heights. "You are comparing apples and oranges," she says, "maybe you should look for work in the produce industry".

A simple comparison of mean or median prices is not going to give an accurate picture of how the price of housing varies across space or over time. The average house in one area may be very different than the average house in another. Further, there may be trends in housing quality that make changes in average prices a misleading measure of changes in the price of housing services. To accurately measure the price of housing services, you have to control for the fact that the houses in Strange Lanes are different than the houses in Hamilton Heights.

Houses are complex bundles of characteristics. The value-influencing characteristics of a house may include the following:

- Physical characteristics of the structure, e.g., size, age, and quality
- Lot size and shape
- Location relative to jobs, shopping, parks, and other destinations
- Property taxes and local public services, such as schools, policing, fire protection, etc.
- Social and economic characteristics of neighbours, e.g., their income, education, or ethnicity
- Quality of the local physical environment, e.g., amenities like views or disamenities like noise or air pollution
- Neighbourhood effects, including the density and the appearance of neighbouring properties

Different houses will offer different bundles of these characteristics — uniqueness is a defining characteristic of real property.

If you want to find the value of real property, you can look to recent sales of similar types of properties. However, a problem is that each of these sales is a bundle of characteristics. The individual characteristics are not traded on a market and therefore do not have market prices. The market price of the bundle gives us a measure of expenditures on housing – of the product of price and quantity – but it does not give us an independent measure of either price or quantity. What we need is some way to isolate the contribution of each characteristic to property value.

One method for doing this is *hedonic pricing*. It estimates the marginal value or *implicit price* of each characteristic of a property. This information allows us to construct a measure of the price of housing in different areas or at different points in time where the characteristics of the houses are held constant. Such constant quality price indices can then be used to make correct inferences about how housing prices vary across space or over time.

Hedonic Pricing

The decomposition of price into its constituent parts; each characteristic of the good is assigned a monetary value according to its contribution to the overall price

Key Concept: Repeat Sales Index

If you are primarily interested in measuring how prices have changed in a particular area over time, you can avoid the difficulty of controlling for property characteristics by focusing on changes in the prices of properties that have sold more than once. The characteristics of these properties presumably have not changed; therefore, differences in value are purely differences in price. The resulting measure of price change is called a *repeat sales index* – or in real property appraisal, a *sale/resale analysis*. This is a very useful tool in real estate economics for studying the informational efficiency of residential real estate markets and other problems in real estate investment.

Hedonic prices are generally estimated by thorough statistical analysis of prices and property characteristics — specifically, linear regression using ordinary least squares. A typical example of the estimated equation might be:

EQUATION 10.11

$$p_j = a + \left(b_1 \times c_{1j}\right) + \left(b_2 \times c_{2j}\right) + \; \dots \; + \left(b_n \times c_{nj}\right) + e_j$$

Where:

- the subscript j identifies a particular property
- c_i is the value-influencing characteristics of the properties
- b_i are the implicit hedonic prices estimated for each characteristic (called *coefficients* in the regression equation), with n characteristics considered
- a and error e_i are amounts showing the variations in prices that remain unexplained by the model's coefficients (e_j is generally assumed to follow a normal distribution with a mean of zero and constant variance)

Let's see how hedonic pricing can help us solve the problem of comparing housing prices in Hamilton Heights and Strange Lanes. Assume that the houses in these areas differ in terms of three characteristics: lot size (L, measured in square feet), number of bedrooms (B), and the age of the structure (A, measured in years). We now examine the database of sale prices and property characteristics and use this to estimate separate hedonic price equations for Hamilton Heights and Strange Lanes. The results are:

P_{HH} = \$320,000 + (\$3 × L) + (\$20,000 × B) − (\$500 × A)

and

P_{SL} = \$180,000 + (\$10 × L) + (\$25,000 × B) − (\$600 × A)

These equations give the estimated hedonic prices of the various characteristics in the two communities.

- An additional square foot of lot size is worth \$3 in Hamilton Heights and \$10 in Strange Lanes.
- A bedroom is worth \$20,000 in Hamilton Heights and \$25,000 in Strange Lanes.
- A year of age reduces value by \$500 in Hamilton Heights and \$600 in Strange Lanes.

Now suppose that the average values for the characteristics in the two communities are L = 10,000 square feet, B = 3 bedrooms, and A = 20 years in Hamilton Heights, and L = 6,000 square feet, B = 3 bedrooms and A = 25 years in Strange Lanes. To compare prices in the two areas, we evaluate the hedonic price equations at a common set of property characteristics. For example, we could ask how much a typical Hamilton Heights home would sell for in either area. Plugging the characteristics of an average Hamilton Heights structure into our two regression equations, we find that the predicted price is \$400,000 in Hamilton Heights and \$343,000 in Strange Lanes. This tells us that prices vary by 17%, if we hold constant the characteristics of the structures. This is considerably less than the 33% differential we found by simply comparing the mean prices in the two communities. By controlling for differences in property characteristics, we can more accurately compare housing prices in two different areas or in the same area at different points in time.

Value Matters: Hedonic Pricing

Hedonic pricing involves splitting the price of real estate assets into bundles of services, such as the number of bedrooms, the number of square feet, the number of bathrooms, the age of the building, etc. This is also the basis for appraisal's direct comparison approach — in particular the process for making adjustments to the sale prices of comparables. The appraiser must use market analysis techniques to determine the value impact of a bedroom, bathroom, or view, for example.

Statistical analysis is a powerful tool for this type of appraisal process. With a large enough database of sales and statistical software like SPSS or NCSS, the appraiser can identify the value contribution of a square foot of living area, a year of age, or a percentage improvement in quality, among many other variables. These forms of statistical estimation techniques are most commonly used by property tax assessment agencies, as well as by firms offering automated valuation models (AVMs).

For more information and examples of how hedonic pricing can combine with statistics to improve appraisal procedures, see the BUSI 344 course, *Statistical and Computer Applications in Valuation*.

One final note on our simple regression model. The model's "error" is $320,000 in Hamilton Heights and $180,000 in Strange Lanes. This amount is not error, as in making a mistake; this is the variation in prices that is unexplained by the three variables specified in this model. Comparing this to the predicted values, the unexplained variation here is quite large. If this was a real-world application, you might want to return to the sales database and see if other value-influencing characteristics can be identified: perhaps lot size, view, and construction quality may help explain more price variation and reduce the prediction error. More variables in a hedonic price regression are helpful, but only to a point — once variables start to overlap in attempting to explain price variations, then the coefficients start to become untrustworthy. Say we included all of total square feet of living area, first floor area, second floor area, bedrooms, and total rooms as variables in the model — the model would have difficulty differentiating or isolating these duplicate variables. This modelling problem is known as multicollinearity.

FILTERING IN HOUSING MARKETS

It is often helpful to view the housing market as a collection of related submarkets for different housing qualities. Most new construction occurs at the high end of the market, that is, at the higher quality levels. There is generally less new construction of low quality housing. Rather, most of the demand for lower quality housing is fulfilled by used housing. This process is known as *filtering*.

The filtering process works as follows: as houses age, they generally move down the quality hierarchy. Furthermore, since housing is a normal good, as the quality of a house declines, its price declines as well, making it available to occupants with lower income. Thus, as houses age, both housing quality and the income of occupants tends to decrease. Houses tend to filter down from the high-income market participants to the low-income market participants over time.

> **Filtering**
>
> Household mobility changes the availability of housing stock, because when some households move up to newer housing, older housing becomes more affordable; i.e., the housing stock "filters down"

Filtering has some important (and somewhat controversial) implications:

1. It should not be surprising that there is limited new construction of low-income housing. Given the durability of houses, it is generally more efficient to meet the housing needs of low-income families through the used housing stock than to construct new, affordable housing for them. Low-income families can obtain a higher level of housing services more economically through the filtering process.

2. Events in one part of the quality hierarchy may affect outcomes in other parts. For example, an increase in the supply of medium-quality housing may be beneficial to consumers with lower incomes. The logic is simple: an increase in supply in the medium-quality submarket will cause the price of existing medium-quality housing to fall, which will discourage investment in maintenance and improvements, and cause some of this housing to filter down. This increases the supply of used housing in the lower-quality submarket, which will increase the quality of housing at the higher-end of this lower submarket, and also reduce the price of housing already in this submarket. Therefore, consumers in the lower submarket will be better off. In contrast, without this addition of medium-quality housing, some middle-tier buyers may compete for lower-quality houses due to a shortage of medium-quality housing; this increased pressure raises the cost of lower-quality housing for the lower-income consumers.

3. Filtering has implications for housing policy: to improve housing consumption of low-income families, it may be that the best approach is to subsidize construction of medium-quality housing rather than to try to construct new, affordable low-income housing. As counter-intuitive as it may seem, supplying housing to lower-income groups via filtering may be the most economically efficient solution.

4. Regulations that restrict the supply of housing in higher-income and higher-quality submarkets (like zoning regulations and urban growth controls) may have the perverse effect of worsening housing conditions in lower quality submarkets. Supply restrictions tend to raise prices, encouraging housing maintenance and improvement, and thus discouraging downward filtering. We will discuss these and other policy issues in greater detail in Chapter 12.

SUMMARY

Housing is an important and unique commodity. It is the dominant land use in cities and the largest item in the budgets and portfolios of many families. Housing also has a number of features, like heterogeneity, durability, and a fixed location, that make it unusual if not unique among consumer durables. These features also complicate the study of housing markets, especially the measurement of housing prices. There are a number of unique issues that arise in studying the housing choices of individuals, the most important of which is the choice between owning and renting. Demographic factors like average household size and the age structure of the population have important effects on the aggregate or market demand for housing.

Most housing services are supplied from the existing stock. This implies that in the short run, the supply of housing is very inelastic. The housing stock changes through new construction, demolitions and retirements, and through expenditures on alterations and improvements. Alterations and improvements may represent a surprisingly large component of investment in the housing stock — for Canada, these expenditures are nearly as large as the value of new construction in some years. Most new construction occurs toward the higher end of the range of housing qualities, and is therefore targeted at higher income consumers. Over time, as houses age and their quality lessens, they filter down to lower income occupants. The filtering process has interesting and important implications for the operation of housing markets. The next chapter shifts the focus to examine the macroeconomics or aggregate performance of urban real estate markets.

CHAPTER 11

MODELLING REAL ESTATE MARKETS

INTRODUCTION

Up to this point, we have focused largely on microeconomic decisions. For example, we have examined how individual firms and households make location decisions, and how these decisions influence land rents at different locations in a city. We have also explored the implications of individual location decisions for broad characteristics of cities, including city sizes and the development of subcentres. In this chapter, we will adjust our focus slightly to macroeconomics or the aggregate performance of an urban area's real estate market.

This chapter examines three important issues:

1. *Uniqueness*: what is unique about real estate and real estate markets? How are these markets different from the textbook markets that we commonly study?
2. *Economic Forces*: how do real estate markets operate. Specifically, how are rents, prices, and construction levels determined? What are the economic processes or forces that tie rents, prices, and construction levels together?
3. *Responsiveness*: how does a real estate market respond to changes in the economic environment, including regional economic growth or decline, variations in operating and construction costs, and changes in interest rates and the returns on other investments.

The chapter focuses on rent and asset price determination, real estate capitalization rates and their determinants, and new construction and changes in the stock of space. Putting together these various pieces of the model, we see how rents, prices, and construction levels are jointly determined in a long-run equilibrium. This leads to a unified framework for real estate market analysis that can be used to examine how the market responds to changes in the economic environment. The examples in the chapter examine the operation and performance of office markets in Toronto, Montreal, and Vancouver over the past few decades.

CHARACTERIZING REAL ESTATE MARKETS

In comparison to other assets and financial markets, real estate markets have a number of unique characteristics:

- Real estate is both a commodity and a financial asset.
- There is generally some excess supply of space or vacant real estate.
- Buyers and sellers of real estate have market power.
- Quantities and prices adjust slowly to economic conditions.

Each of these is examined in the following sections.

Real Estate as a Commodity and Financial Asset

Characterizing real estate as a commodity refers to the services it offers. Residential structures provide housing services to their occupants. An office or store provides commercial real estate services to its resident businesses. The market in which real estate services are traded is often referred to as the market for real estate space, or the *space market*. The main actors in the space market are the households and firms who purchase, rent, or lease space to have a place to live and work.

Space Market

The market in which real estate services are traded, with the primary concern being the *use* of real estate space

At the same time, the buildings themselves are financial assets, bought and sold for investment purposes. The market in which land and buildings are traded is often referred to as the *asset market*. The main actors in this market are investors (including home owners) who purchase land and/or build structures with the intention of earning investment income. For example, mutual funds, pension funds, and real estate investment trusts (REITs) are important participants in the market for office buildings, shopping malls, hotels, and other types of income-producing property.

Asset Market

The market in which land and buildings are traded, with the primary concern being the *buying and selling* of real estate assets

In some cases, there is a clear distinction between the space and asset markets, such as a property owner who leases space to other independent businesses. In other cases, this distinction is blurred — consider someone who both owns and occupies a house or condominium (or, alternatively, if a car manufacturer buys land and builds a plant). This owner-occupant is simultaneously participating in both the space and asset markets. Most of the examples in this chapter focus on the office market, where there is usually a clear distinction between the space and asset markets. However, the analysis can be more complicated when the division is not clear.

Excess Supply of Space

A second unique characteristic of real estate markets is that there is generally an excess supply of space, or a positive level of vacancies, even in the long run. Figure 11.1 illustrates vacancies over time in downtown office markets in Toronto, Montreal, and Vancouver. The dark shaded bars show net construction of office space in each year, or the change in the stock of space. This is a measure of the change in the quantity supplied. The lighter bars show *net absorption*, which is defined as the rate at which rentable space is filled. Net absorption is a measure of the change in the quantity demanded, accounting for vacated space and newly constructed space, against the rate of rental take-up. The figure clearly shows that new demand and new supply are almost never in balance; for example, look at conditions in Toronto in 2010. The line in the figure shows the *vacancy rate*, the percentage of the stock that is unoccupied, in each year.

Net Absorption

The net change in occupied space, accounting for space vacated and newly constructed space, against the rental take-up during the specified time period

In commercial leasing, the rate at which rentable space is filled; in residential sales, the rate at which homes sell in a given area over a given time period

Figure 11.1 illustrates the somewhat erratic and highly cyclical nature of office markets. It is not uncommon for net construction or net absorption to increase or decrease dramatically from one year to the next. It also appears that each market is at least somewhat independent;

Vacancy Rate

The percentage of rental stock that is unoccupied

for example, vacancies may be increasing in Vancouver but decreasing in Toronto, depending on local rental demand and, in particular, on local construction. Though keep in mind, too, that local market trends are also influenced by regional and national factors, like employment, inflation, interest rates, and the economic business cycle.

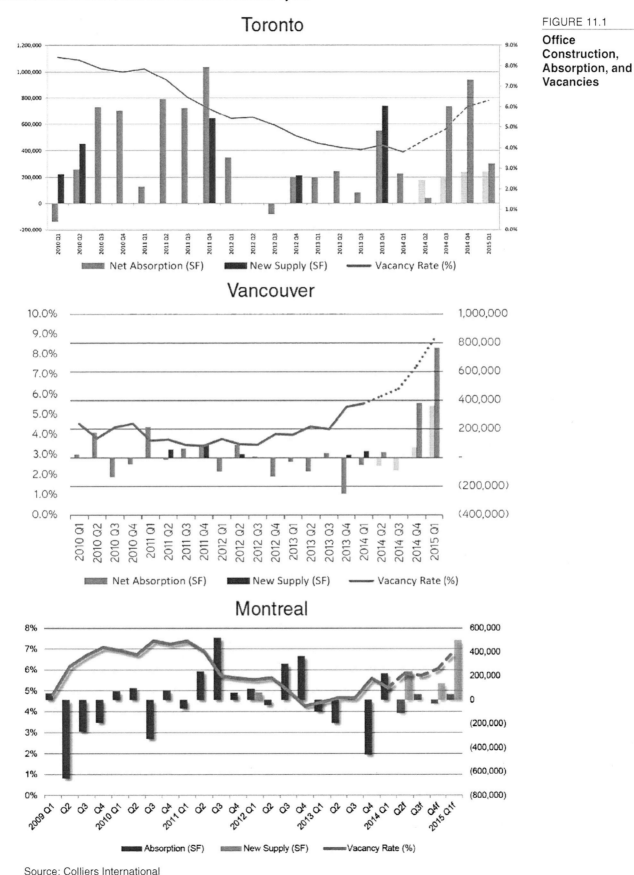

FIGURE 11.1

Office Construction, Absorption, and Vacancies

Source: Colliers International

The owner of a commercial building will obviously prefer to have as much space as possible leased out. Empty space means lost rental revenue and reduced profits. However, there are some benefits to maintaining some degree of vacancy in commercial properties.

- Vacancies facilitate the search and match process through which buye rs and sellers meet. Because the preferences of buyers and the characteristics of properties are all different, finding a suitable match can require an extensive search of the available stock. Without an inventory of available unoccupied space in the market, the prospective tenant will be unable to find and match suitable premises.
- Vacancies provide a "buffer" for unexpected changes in demand. Building new real estate space on short notice is generally impossible, or at best very costly. This is especially true for office space in or near the CBD. By adding extra space to buildings, beyond immediate needs, this leaves an inventory of unlet or unsold space to meet future growth in demand. This buffer allows building owners to quickly accommodate new demands for space.

To an individual owner, vacant space and the resulting lost profit may seem like a property management failure. However, with the above two considerations in mind and viewing this from a market-level perspective, having some vacant inventory over the long term is both expected and desirable. As well, even in a very tight rental market with close to zero vacancies, there will always be some space vacant just due to transitions between tenants.

Value Matters: Vacant Space

Valuing a commercial property using the income approach to appraisal requires first specifying gross *potential* revenue, or the maximum revenue the building can earn if fully occupied at market rents. Then an allowance for vacancy is deducted to find gross *realized* revenue. The vacancy deduction is required to account for the fact that there will ALWAYS be some amount of vacancy space for any given property in any commercial real estate market. A common mistake for newcomers to commercial property valuation is to rely on the currently vacant space in the subject building. Instead, the income statement must be "normalized" or "stabilized" by applying a vacancy rate that reflects the typical market experience for properties similar to the subject.

Market Power of Buyers and Sellers

A third characteristic of real estate markets compared to other types of commodity markets is the market power of both buyers and sellers. The uniqueness of real estate means having to first match buyers and sellers. Once matched, they must negotiate and bargain to reach an agreed upon price. The likely outcome of this bargaining depends on a number of factors, including the patience of the two parties, the values that they place on the good, and the other alternatives that are available to them. For example, when there are many similar properties on the market, so that the buyer has several other options, it is likely that buyers will have more bargaining power than sellers — it will be a *buyers' market*. In contrast, in a *seller's market*, when there are limited properties for sale, the seller may be able to stay closer to his or her asking price, or even more, as there are competing buyers.

Buyer's Market

Buyers have more bargaining power than sellers, due to many similar properties on the market offering purchase alternatives

Seller's Market

Sellers have more bargaining power than buyers, due to limited similar properties for sale or other market constraints

The power that buyers or sellers may have implies that real estate markets are not perfectly competitive in an economic sense. An economically competitive market has a homogeneous product, buyers and sellers act as price takers, and the equilibrium price occurs where the quantity demanded and the quantity supplied are equal. In a real estate market, products are heterogeneous (unique) and buyers or sellers may have the ability to influence the sale price — neither party acts as a price taker. Furthermore, in order to facilitate the search and match process, it is necessary that there be an inventory of unoccupied properties, or excess supply, in equilibrium.

Notice that these departures from the perfectly competitive paradigm are exactly the features of real estate that give rise to brokerage. From an economics perspective, the primary functions of real estate brokers are to facilitate both the search and match process and the bargaining between potential buyers and sellers.

Value Matters: Market Inefficiencies

If the benefit of real estate brokers is largely due to a lack of perfect competition, so too is the role of real estate appraisers. The uniqueness of real property, in a particular location, makes it very difficult for non-experts to understand the market value drivers and nuances in any given market. Another feature of economic competition is perfect information about products and prices – this is certainly not the case for real estate, where market data can be notoriously difficult to acquire. These highlight the role of appraisers: helping clients navigate the uncertainty and unknowns inherent in a risky marketplace.

Adjusting Quantities and Prices

A fourth unique characteristic of real estate markets is that quantities and prices tend to adjust slowly to changes in economic conditions. Several factors contribute to this, including the fixed nature of real estate supply, difficulties in changing rents, and long-term leases.

The supply of real estate, or the stock of space, changes very gradually over time. Most real estate space is supplied from existing structures. New construction adds to the stock, while the deterioration, demolition, and even abandonment of older structures subtracts from the stock. The net change in supply in any period, illustrated in Figure 11.1, equals new construction minus the subtractions listed above. However, the stock of existing structures is much larger than net construction in any time period, and as a result, the stock tends to change relatively little in any year. Consider that some types of real estate may have a time lag of five to ten years between the start and finish of a construction project. These construction lags mean that even a quick response by developers to demand changes or other economic conditions cannot immediately provide more supply.

Rent adjustments for real estate space also present lags. In a textbook competitive market, a shift in demand leads to an immediate change in the market price. In a real estate market, a shift in demand will generally result in price changes that are spread over several time periods. The reason is that a rapid adjustment in rents would cause vacancies to deviate from their desired levels, leaving too large or too small a buffer of unsold units. This implies that the size and speed of rent or price adjustments depends on the level of vacancies in a market. For example, if the vacancy rate in a market is high, then it may not be in the owners' interest to raise rent in response to a demand shock. Doing so would just cause vacant units to be unoccupied for a longer time. Conversely, when vacancy rates are low, and thus time on the market is short, an increase in demand should be followed by significant rent increases to keep vacancies from falling below their desired level. Figure 11.2 shows the relationship between rents and vacancy rates in the Calgary market over the 2012-2015 period. This figure shows that vacancy rates and rents are inversely related: high rents tend to be associated with low vacancy rates, and vice-versa.

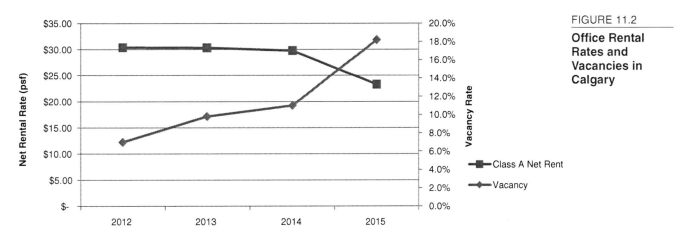

FIGURE 11.2

Office Rental Rates and Vacancies in Calgary

Another factor contributing to slow rent adjustment is the presence of long-term leases in some real estate markets. Although many leases contain clauses that allow owners to change the rent at specific times and under specific circumstances, long-term leases cause rents to adjust more slowly than they would if rents were set every month or even every year.

Our goal in outlining these unique characteristics of real estate has been to highlight the complications in attempting to define real estate markets using a simple economic model. With so many complementary and competing impacts all acting concurrently, the real estate market is much too complex to be modelled with a simple, static demand and supply graph. In the next section we will introduce a four-quadrant model that attempts to explain the dynamic relationships between space and asset markets in the long run. This model was largely developed by DiPasquale and Wheaton; the discussion in the following sections closely parallels their work.

FOUR-QUADRANT MODEL OF REAL ESTATE MARKETS

The four-quadrant model for describing and explaining real estate markets is presented in Figure 11.3. The left side outlines four quadrants, each of which represents a distinct component of real estate markets:

1. Asset market: investors
2. Space market: tenants
3. New construction: developers
4. Stock adjustment: depreciation and demolition

Each of the quadrants has its own specific relationships and all of the quadrants are also interrelated. The right side of Figure 11.3 illustrates these relationships. For example:

- in the space market, a demand curve shows the rents that tenants will pay given a particular stock of space;
- in the asset market, the line shows the price that investors are willing to pay in order to receive the cash flows generated by any given level of rents;
- in the new construction market, the line shows the quantity of new construction that developers will undertake given the prices buildings can be sold for; and
- in the stock adjustment quadrant, the line shows the relationship between the flow of new construction and the resulting stock of space — this measures the overall gain or loss of stock when considering the additions from new construction against losses of existing stock due to depreciation and demolitions of older buildings in the existing stock.

The dashed line passing through the four quadrants represents the starting equilibrium in the market. This establishes a starting point for the four key variables: rents, prices, level of construction, and the stock of space. We then examine various scenarios that move the four markets away from their initial equilibrium position and see the impact on the variables — and ultimately on how real estate markets change and evolve over time.

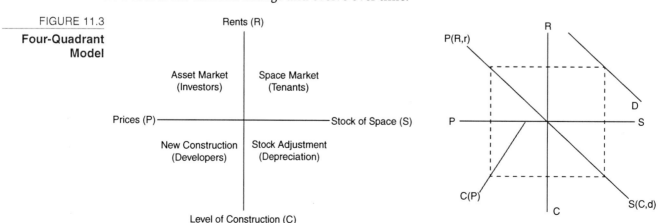

FIGURE 11.3

Four-Quadrant Model

Keep in mind too that each of the four quadrants can be "snapped off" and analyzed on its own. That is our plan for the next four sections of this chapter, starting with the space market.

The Space Market

The space market is illustrated in the top right quadrant of Figure 11.3. It shows how much space tenants choose to occupy and at what rent, depending on the interaction of demand and supply in the space market.

Figure 11.4 illustrates demand and supply in the space market. In the short term, the stock of space is fixed and consequently the supply of space is perfectly inelastic. This means a vertical supply curve, since space cannot increase or decrease in response to price. The current fixed stock of space is S_0 in Figure 11.4.

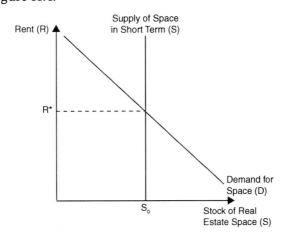

FIGURE 11.4

The Space Market

Value Matters: Rent Analysis

Rent is a payment for the use of real estate services for a given time period. Generally speaking, rent refers to the actual cost of occupying a property for a given time period, say, a month or a year. Rent is commonly described on a per unit of space basis, e.g., rent per suite for multi-family residential or per square foot or square metre for commercial or industrial properties. Residential rents may be complicated by the inclusion of heat, hot water, electricity, parking, or other attributes. Commercial rents may specify complex arrangements for the owner's recovery of property taxes, utilities, and certain maintenance costs. For new tenants, commercial leases may also include a period of free rent and the owner paying the costs of modifications and improvements to the space. Calculating the true rent that the tenant pays involves accounting for all of these contingencies over the term of the lease.

The market demand for a particular type of real estate space in a city or region depends on the overall level of economic activity there. For commercial real estate, a key indicator of market demand is the health of industries that are heavy users of commercial space, e.g., office markets depend on finance, insurance, and real estate industries. Figure 11.5 illustrates the close relationship between office space absorption and the employment growth rate in Calgary over the 2012-2015 period.

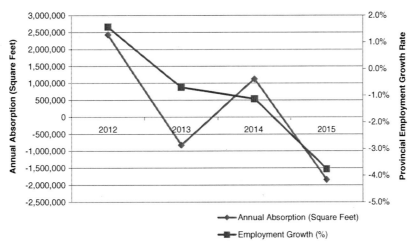

FIGURE 11.5

Office Absorption and Employment Growth in Calgary

The demand for space comes from the profit maximizing decisions of firms. Consider a firm that uses real estate space S (measured in square feet or square metres) and other inputs to produce some commodity. In principle, the demand for space is just like the demand for any other input. If R is rent per unit of space, and VMP_S is the value of the marginal product of space (the increment to revenue from employing an additional unit of space), then the firm should choose S so that R = VMP_S. VMP_S = p × MP_S, where p is the price of the firm's output, and MP_S is the marginal product of space, the firm's demand for space will depend on the price of its output (just as in our earlier discussion of the demand for labour in Chapter 3). In other words, rent is dependent on the productivity of the space for the tenant and the profit this can achieve. The market or aggregate demand for space is the sum of the individual firms' demands in the market.

Equilibrium rent is determined by the intersection of the demand and supply curves. Since the stock of space is fixed at S_0, the equilibrium rent in Figure 11.4 is R*. If the demand curve depends on employment, an increase in employment will cause the demand for space to shift to the right, leading to an increase in the equilibrium rent. This parallels our earlier discussion of the relationship between economic growth and real estate markets. A favourable event in the market for the basic or export goods that a region produces will cause production there to rise, which will in turn increase the demand for labour, real estate, and other inputs — all other things being equal, this will cause the prices of these inputs to rise. We will return to this issue a little later in the chapter, examining the implications of economic growth for real estate values and construction levels.

The Asset Market

In investment terms, the value of an asset equals the present value of the stream of future income that the asset will provide. For real estate investments, the relevant income stream is the net operating income or net rent from the property. This is one of the essential links between the space and asset markets: the rent on real estate space comprises the income stream that determines the value of real estate assets.

There are several ways to illustrate the relationship between real estate rents and real estate asset prices or asset values (we will use the terms asset price and asset value interchangeably). Consider a risk-neutral investor who is considering purchasing a real estate asset. The investor may anticipate earning a return through rent and/or from price appreciation (capital gains).[1]

In a competitive real estate market, equilibrium real estate values will be a function of future rents. The current value of a real estate asset can be estimated as the present value of future rents. With an infinite time horizon, or rents received in perpetuity, this can be expressed as:

EQUATION 11.1

$$Price = \frac{Rent}{Capitalization\ Rate} \quad or \quad P = \frac{R}{r}$$

Where:

- r is the capitalization rate (expressed as a decimal or percent)
- R is the rent[2]
- P is the price

Capitalization (Cap) Rate

The ratio of rent to the price of the asset

This is the simplest form of the asset market equilibrium condition that links real estate rents and prices; it is the form that is commonly used in practice for both commercial property buyers and sellers as well as appraisers. This *capitalization rate*, or simply the *cap rate*, is a simple form of rent-to-price ratio — rearranging Equation 11.1 as follows:

EQUATION 11.2

$$r = \frac{R}{P}$$

---

[1] Estimating market value with capitalization rates implies that all future price appreciation is directly related to rental income. This assumes a rational marketplace where investors work with perfect information, where buyers do not act irrationally in speculative over-heated bidding wars and, by the same token, where sellers do not give away bargains in under-pricing properties. In other words, the basis for capitalization rates assumes a perfect market and is therefore unrealistic! However, despite the imperfections in real estate markets, cap rates serve as a very useful form of economic modelling that is commonly used in commercial property valuation. Cap rates are less useful, though, if the market shows signs of appreciation unrelated to income (speculation) or where a property's future value is expected to rise or fall out of sync with comparable properties. So, for now, we ignore capital gains and losses and use cap rates with these simplifying assumptions.

[2] Capitalization analysis should rely on rental income after subtracting expenses incurred by the owner in operating the rental property – called net operating income or NOI. For simplicity, we will assume the renter pays all operating expenses, so Rent = NOI. Also, for simplicity we will ignore the issue of rent being paid in advance, as this complicates the mathematics a little.

Our risk-neutral investor finds a commercial property that is expected to produce rents of $800,000 per year every year into the foreseeable future. Based on sales of other similar properties, with their expected rents, the prices that investors were willing to pay implies a capitalization rate of 10%. Given our investor expects to earn no better than this market rate of return (investors set their capitalization rate according to their next best alternative investment opportunities) then the property's price is estimated as:

$$\text{Price} = \frac{\$800,000}{0.1} = \$8,000,000$$

Figure 11.6 illustrates how the capitalization rate equation can describe the market equilibrium condition for the asset market. The line in the figure depicts the relationship, $P = R/r$, and shows how a given rent is converted into an equilibrium asset price. The slope of the line is $1/r$, the inverse of the capitalization rate. An increase in the cap rate (an increase in the required rate of return) decreases the slope of the line, and decreases the asset price associated with every level of rent. Intuitively, if investors are to earn a higher rate of return, then they must pay less for a property with a given income stream. This is illustrated later in this chapter in Figure 11.15.

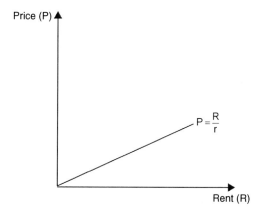

FIGURE 11.6

The Asset Market

Value Matters: Gross Rent (Income) Multiplier

The slope of the asset price function in Figure 11.6 is $1/r$ or the inverse of the capitalization rate. In commercial real estate markets, this $1/r$ measure is useful - called the *gross rent multiplier* or *gross income multiplier* (GRM or GIM). Thist is a direct measure of the rent to price relationship. For example, if the cap rate is 10%, then the GIM is 10. Value = Gross Income × GIM = $800,000 × 10 = $8,000,000. This multiplier also presents another helpful investment measure, the *payback period*; e.g., a GIM = 10 means this real estate asset requires 10 years of rents to pay back the $8,000,000 upfront capital investment.

Figure 11.7 shows how the space market influences the asset market. The right half of the figure shows the space market from Figure 11.4, where employment determines the demand for space, which in turn determines the equilibrium rent, given the fixed stock of space. Then on the left half of the figure we see that the equilibrium rent R* from the space market directly influences the equilibrium price P*.

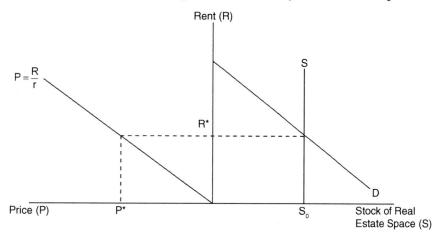

FIGURE 11.7

The Space and Asset Markets

Note that the asset market function is rearranged in Figure 11.7 to have rent R on the vertical axis and price P on the horizontal axis. This is simply Figure 11.6 rotated 90 degrees counter-clockwise. The asset market equilibrium remains P = R/r or Price = Rent/Capitalization Rate. The slope of the line in this figure remains at R/r. An increase in the cap rate will cause this line to shift right, as this will decrease the price that investors are willing to pay for a given income stream R.

EXERCISE 11.1: Calculating Equilibrium Rents and Prices

Suppose the demand for space takes the form R = 0.1E – 0.004985S, where E is employment and S is the stock of space. The capitalization rate is r = 0.06. If employment equals 50,000 and the stock of space equals 1,000,000 square feet, what is the equilibrium asset price of real estate space?

Solution:

Equilibrium rent is R* = 0.1(50,000) – 0.004985(1,000,000) = $15 per square foot per year

The equilibrium asset price of real estate is:

P = R/r; therefore, P = 15/0.06 = $250 per square foot

You should be able to draw the diagram that illustrates these calculations (it should look similar to Figure 11.7).

Capitalization Rates and Discounted Cash Flow

The asset market equilibrium condition P = R/r is widely used in practice as a kind of rule of thumb for valuing real estate investments. Dividing an estimate of the stabilized net operating income of a property by an appropriate cap rate gives a very simple estimate of property value.

Figure 11.8 shows capitalization rates on commercial properties in Vancouver over the 2002-2015 period. Figure 11.9 shows capitalization rates for the commercial property types in several Canadian markets in 2015. A few general trends are evident:

- The capitalization rates in Vancouver decreased markedly for all the property classes, associated with decreasing interest rates and rising property values over this time frame.
- The capitalization rates in Vancouver vary by property type, with multi-family lowest, industrial highest, and retail and office in between. This reflects the fact that property types seen as riskier by market participants will have higher yields in the market place.
- The capitalization rates in the four Canadian cities in 2015 show a similar variation between these property types, demonstrating this risk/yield continuum is generalizable to all commercial real estate markets (though the specifics will vary by market).

FIGURE 11.8

Cap Rates vs. Five Year Bond Rate, Greater Vancouver Area

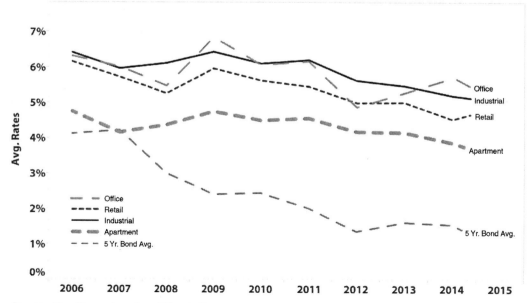

Source: Altus Group. Investment Trends Survey.

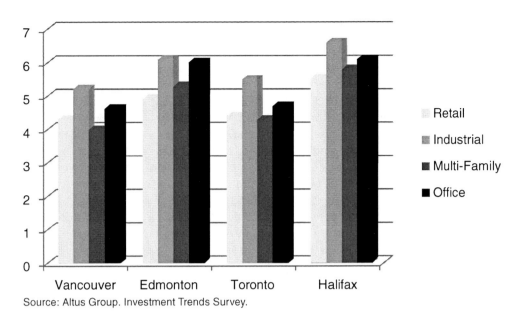

FIGURE 11.9

Canadian Capitalization Rates

- Retail
- Industrial
- Multi-Family
- Office

Source: Altus Group. Investment Trends Survey.

There are two ways to view the cap rate:

1. We can view the cap rate as an investment measure that is primarily determined by the level of interest rates in the economy (and other factors that we will discuss shortly). From an economist's point-of-view, we would say that rents and prices are *endogenous* (that is, determined within the model), while the cap rate is *exogenous* (that is, determined outside the model).

2. We can also view the cap rate endogenously, determined as part of the $P = R/r$ function that relates price, rent, and yield (r). A change in any two of these variables then determines a change in the third. For example, if rents are rising and prices are stable, then yields must rise as well, so that the condition $P = R/r$ continues to hold. Conversely, if yields are falling and rents are stable, then prices must be rising. This view is common in professionally-oriented real estate research.

There are three basic determinants or components to the capitalization rate for real estate:

1. Capitalization rates should be related to the overall level of interest rates in the economy. If interest rates rise, then, other things being equal, we expect the yield on real estate investments to rise as well. By the same token, the capitalization rate should also depend on the yields on other, comparable investments. For example, a stock market boom should put upward pressure on real estate yields, and therefore put downward pressure on prices, assuming that rents remain unchanged.

2. Capitalization rates should reflect the risk associated with a particular property class or location. Generally speaking, properties or locations that are perceived to be riskier should have higher expected yields and therefore higher capitalization rates than other properties — meaning investors will expect to pay less to take on properties that have higher risk. Otherwise, investors will not be willing to bear the additional risk involved in holding these properties.

3. Capitalization rates should reflect the rate at which rents are expected to grow in the future. For example, if rent, is expected to grow at the compound rate g, then the equilibrium asset price becomes:

EQUATION 11.3

$$P = \frac{R}{r - g}$$

The capitalization rate is now the difference between the discount rate r and the expected growth rate of rents g. The faster rents are expected to grow, the smaller the cap rate, and therefore the higher the asset price for any given initial level of rent. This parallels our earlier discussion of the relationship between growth and residential land and housing prices.

In practice, this introduction of the rent growth variable g proves unnecessary in the endogenous cap rate model described above. If cap rates are found by observing market sales, then rent growth is already considered implicitly in this market data – assuming the market is efficient at factoring future earnings expectations into prices. A key assumption, though, is that the expected rate of change must be consistent between the comparable properties relied on to derive the cap rate and the subject property being appraised. If this consistency is true, then the expression "a rising tide floats all boats evenly" applies — as long as all properties are rising and falling at the same rate, then all of this information and future expectation will be captured in the capitalization rate. This means rental growth is accounted for (and future price appreciation is similarly accounted for).

In cases where a property is anticipated to have unstable cash flows relative to other properties, or where the cash flows are not perpetual, then capitalization will not be effective. The value of a property remains the present value of expected future cash flows — but these unstable cash flows must each be considered independently and each separately discounted to their present value. This form of discounted cash flow (DCF) analysis uses the following formula:

EQUATION 11.4

$$\text{Value} = P_0 = \sum_{t=1}^{n} \frac{R_t}{(1+r)^t}$$

Where:

- P_0 is the price today, or the value where $t = 0$
- $\sum_{}^{n}$ means summing the present value of each individual cash flow from one time period from today ($t=1$) to n time periods in future ($t=n$); i.e., substitute 1 for t, then 2 for t, then 3 for t, etc., up to the final value n, adding up each individual present value result as you go along[3]
- R_t is rent in period t
- r is the discount rate for converting cash flows to the present value; represents a competitive rate of return for similar (substitute) real estate investments; in effect, this is the opportunity cost of capital
- $(1+r)^t$ in the denominator means discounting each cash flow by t periods, back to the present value today.

Furthermore, the assumption of holding a real estate investment in perpetuity is probably not realistic. Most investors have an anticipated holding period, at the end of which they intend to sell the asset. If the end of the holding period is time n, then the final cash flow, P_n or the sale price of the property n periods in future, must also be discounted back to the present value:

EQUATION 11.5

$$\text{Value} = P_0 = \frac{R_1}{(1+r)} + \frac{R_2}{(1+r)^2} + \frac{R_3}{(1+r)^3} + ... + \frac{R_n}{(1+r)^n} + \frac{P_n}{(1+r)^n}$$

Just as in capitalization, the current equilibrium price of the asset equals the present value of the stream of cash flows that it generates during the holding period. The difference here is that the holding period is not indefinite, so we must add the present value of the price the investor can sell the asset for at the end of the holding period.

EXERCISE 11.2: Calculating the Value of a Property with DCF

Consider a commercial real estate property that will be held for n = 4 years. The rents that the property will generate in each of the four years are R_1 = $100,000, R_2 = $150,000, R_3 = $100,000, and R_4 = $120,000, where each is paid at the end of the year. In the fourth year, the property can be sold for P_4 = $500,000. The discount rate (opportunity cost of funds) is 12% per year, compounded annually.

What is the value of the property today?

continued on next page

---

[3] Though here, with the assumption of perpetual rents, n=infinity. This unrealistic assumption is to be revisited shortly.

Solution:

Using Equation 11.5:

$$P_0 = \frac{\$100{,}000}{(1.12)^1} + \frac{\$150{,}000}{(1.12)^2} + \frac{\$100{,}000}{(1.12)^3} + \frac{\$120{,}000}{(1.12)^4} + \frac{\$500{,}000}{(1.12)^4} = \$674{,}064.03$$

This present value represents the value of the commercial property today. This can be considered the equilibrium price of the asset under these conditions.

Value Matters: Capitalization and Discounted Cash Flow Formulas

The capitalization and discounted cash flow formulas presented here are the two main methods for estimating the value of commercial properties.

- The capitalization method is the simpler method, requiring an estimate of only a single year's rent (income) and the market capitalization rate.
- The discounted cash flow (DCF) method allows for more precision, because it can accommodate rent changes over the holding period and directly accounts for assumptions regarding sale price at the end of the holding period.

If a property has "upside" due to low rents or high vacancies, or if it can be renovated or upgraded to increase its value, the DCF method is preferable. Yet, in market practice, the simplistic capitalization method is much more common. Reasons for this:

1. The longer the holding period, the smaller the present value of the sale price. Say the property in Exercise 11.2 is sold for $100,000,000 in 100 years ... this only adds $1,197 in present value terms. Mathematically, beyond approximately 60 years, the present value of any amount of money adds virtually nothing.

2. Capitalization cannot directly accommodate rental growth, but indirectly it can – as long as the rental growth in comparables is forecasted to be similar to the subject property, it remains an "apples to apples" comparison.

3. Where a property has below-market rate leases or requires immediate expenses, this can be accommodated by a subsequent adjustment to the value found by capitalization.

Consider that appraisal methods are a form of economic modelling, which attempt to approximate buyer behaviour. Appraisers must be cautious not to over-complicate the analysis, or risk becoming the proverbial "cart leading the horse". What has shown time and again is that real estate market participants seem to prefer the simplicity of capitalization to the additional precision, sophistication, and complication of DCF. Discounted cash flow tends to be used mostly for investment analysis to find the justified investment price for one specific owner rather than for market value appraisal.

This topic is discussed in detail in the BUSI 331 course: *Real Estate Investment Analysis and Advanced Income Appraisal.*

New Construction

So far, we have focused primarily on how conditions in the market for real estate space influence real estate values through the capital market equilibrium condition P =R/r. However, there is another link between the asset and space markets. As noted earlier, new construction adds to the stock of existing space; as the stock of space changes, so too will equilibrium rent in the space market. The level of new construction is primarily determined by the price of real estate assets — builders make their production decisions based on how much buyers or investors are willing to pay for new space. This section discusses how stock of real estate evolves as a result of builders' production decisions.

For the purposes of this exercise, assume that the construction industry is competitive. For residential real estate, this is probably a reasonable assumption. Home builders tend to be relatively small, local firms. It is also reasonable to assume that residential construction firms are price takers — the production decisions of an individual builder have little or no impact on the price of housing. For commercial real estate, the assumption of perfect competition is more challenging to accept. Office builders and developers, in particular, tend to be larger, national firms, and, of course, markets with a few large firms are less likely to operate in a competitive fashion. Unfortunately, a more realistic treatment of the construction is beyond the scope of this discussion. We will assume that the construction industry is competitive.

More specifically, we will imagine that the construction industry is a competitive, increasing cost industry. This means that there are many small producers, each of whom acts as a price taker, and that it is easy for firms to enter or exit the market. Most important, we will assume that some inputs into the building process are scarce in the sense that their prices rise as more and more firms enter the industry. For example, skilled trades like carpenters, electricians, plumbers, and masons could become scarce as the level of construction in a city or region increases. Under these conditions, the cost curves of each firm in the industry will shift upward as the level of new construction rises, and there will be a positively sloped long-run supply schedule for the industry, like the one shown in Figure 11.10.

In Figure 11.10, C(P) represents new construction and the long-run supply curve of the industry. A higher price (P) in the asset market will result in an increase in the level of new construction (C). Notice that there is no construction until a minimum price level is reached, i.e., the supply curve crosses the vertical intercept at a point <0. This occurs because developers face a number of fixed costs, and they require a price greater than or equal to those fixed costs before they can begin any development project.

FIGURE 11.10

The Supply Curve for New Construction

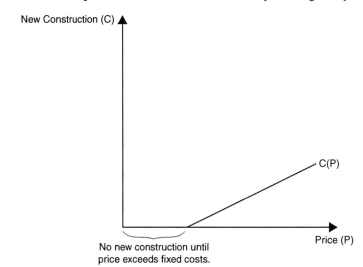

Stock Adjustment: Depreciation and Demolition

Stock Adjustment: Depreciation and Demolition

As we previously stated, new construction adds to the stock of space, while depreciation and demolitions subtract from the stock of space. If we assume that depreciation and demolitions occur at a constant rate d, the amount of the stock lost to these forces is $d \times S$ in any period, where S is the size of the stock at the beginning of the period.

The change in the stock of space in any given period is expressed in the following equation:

EQUATION 11.6

$$S_{t+1} = S_t + C_t - (d \times S_t)$$

Where:

- S_{t+1} is the stock of space one period in future
- S_t is the current stock of space
- C_t is addition to the stock from current construction
- $d \times S_t$ is the rate of loss of the current stock due to depreciation or demolition

In other words, the stock next period equals the stock this period plus new construction minus depreciation and demolitions. The change in the stock of space next period can be expressed as:

EQUATION 11.7

$$\Delta S_{t+1} = C_t - (d \times S)$$

This equation means that the net change in the stock of space in any period equals new construction minus depreciation and demolitions.

Figure 11.11 illustrates the relationship between new construction (C) and the stock of space (S) in the long run, or steady state. The slope of this line is based on 1/d, where d is the rate of loss of stock due to depreciation and demolition. Depreciation/demolition (d) varies between 0 and 1 or 0% to 100%. The inverse relationship, 1/d, means that:

- a lower rate of d leads to a steeper line — i.e., a lower rate of depreciation/demolition means that new construction > loss of stock, so the stock of space is growing.
- a higher rate of d leads to a flatter line — i.e., a higher rate of depreciation/demolition means that new construction < loss of stock, so the stock of space is contracting.

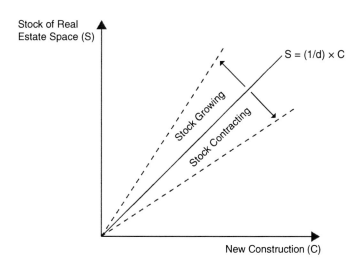

FIGURE 11.11

Changes in Stock of Space

FOUR QUADRANT EQUILIBRIUM

We are now in a position to examine how rents, prices, and construction levels are jointly determined — we are going to put everything we have discussed into a single diagram. It is important to emphasize that although the model we have described is implicitly a dynamic model, we are going to focus on an equilibrium in which rents, prices, construction levels, and the stock of real estate space are stable. If we think of rents, prices, and construction levels as evolving over time, then eventually, so long as there are no shocks to the system, they should all settle into stable or *steady state* values — this will greatly help in simplifying our analysis.

In a steady state, the stock of space will be held constant, or at least pause for a moment to let us observe the equilibrium condition. During this pause, assume there is no change in the stock of space, $\Delta S = 0$, and new construction simply replaces depreciation and demolitions. From Equation 11.7 this implies:

$$C = d \times S$$

EQUATION 11.8

Note that this does not mean the stock of space won't change over time. We can still examine how the market responds to changes in the economic environment by examining successive steady-state equilibriums. The real estate market is dynamic and ever-changing — we are simply stopping momentarily so we can examine the variables.

The four-quadrant diagram shown in Figure 11.12 (initially shown in Figure 11.3(b)) puts all the pieces of the model together and illustrates a long-run or steady-state equilibrium.

- The northeast quadrant shows the space market, where demand and the existing stock of space combine to determine the level of rents.
- The northwest quadrant shows how this rent is converted into an asset price using the capitalization rate.
- The southwest quadrant shows the long-run supply of new construction, and how level of new construction is determined by the asset price of real estate.
- The southeast quadrant shows the relationship between new construction and depreciation/demolition that must hold in order for the stock of space to be constant.

Notice that the values of the equilibrium variables in Figure 11.12 are all consistent, as they must be in equilibrium, i.e., the stock of space (S*) generates a rent (R*) that in turn generates a price (P*) that elicits just enough new construction (C*) to maintain the stock of space (less depreciation/demolition) at its equilibrium level.

Our next step is to modify a market factor and see how this influences the equilibrium for the four variables. For simplicity, our solutions will apply graphical techniques, drawing the new "rectangle" through the four quadrants. These models can also be solved using algebraic techniques, but the mathematics are overly complex for this book.

FIGURE 11.12

Four-Quadrant Diagram

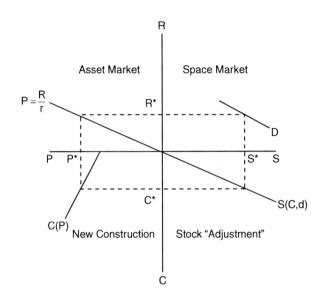

Changes in the Economic Environment

The dashed line in Figure 11.12 represents the starting equilibrium in the four quadrants. In this section, we will analyze scenarios that will change this starting equilibrium, where a new equilibrium is reached. Our focus will be in the direction of change[4] of the four key variables: rents, prices, new construction, and the stock of space.

EXAMPLE 11.1: A Shock in the Space Market

The space market quadrant is affected if the demand curve shifts. For any given level of stock, the price that tenants are willing to pay for space increases or decreases. Figure 11.13 illustrates shifts of the space market demand curve.[5]

FIGURE 11.13

Shifts in the Space Market

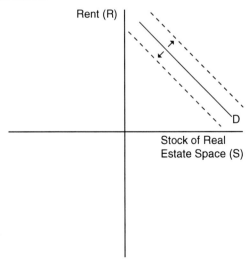

---

[4] Note that we might also be interested in the magnitude of change. However, this model is not sophisticated enough to provide insight in that regard.

[5] The space market demand curve can also rotate. For example, an increase in the availability of substitutes may cause tenants to become more price sensitive, with the curve becoming flatter (i.e., price elasticity of demand increases).

Scenario: Widespread adoption of computers makes professional service firms more productive, which increases the marginal product of space for these firms, i.e., renting the next unit of floor space increases profitability.

Analysis: Because renting another unit of floor space is more attractive now than it was before, professional service firms will be willing to pay more for space at any given level of stock. Therefore, the demand curve shifts outward from D_0 to D_1. The new equilibrium is found as follows:

1. Focus on the quadrant that is directly affected. In this case, the space market.
2. Consider the clockwise variable within the affected quadrant. For example, the quadrant identified in Step 1 is the space market, so the variable located on the axis directly clockwise is S, the stock of space.
3. Assume for the moment that the clockwise variable is held constant, then consider how the curve in the quadrant should shift or rotate such that the effect on the *counterclockwise* axis variable is congruent with the shock. In our scenario, the stock of space is held constant for now, and the other variable in the space market is rent. The demand curve will shift outward and lead to an expected increase in rent.
4. Consider how the shock in the first quadrant will impact the remaining quadrants, and carry out this change. In doing so, keep in mind that effects are transmitted through this model in a counterclockwise direction. For our scenario:
    (a) Rents are determined by the stock of space in conjunction with a demand curve; here, rents increase.
    (b) The price of real estate assets is then determined by the present value of the stream of net rents that the asset will generate; here, higher rents lead to higher sale prices.
    (c) Then, new construction depends positively on the price of real estate assets; here, higher prices means more new construction.
    (d) Finally, the stock adjustment moderates or counter-acts new construction with losses due to demolition and depreciation and brings the increase in the stock of space to an equilibrium level.

The new equilibrium, represented by the lighter dashed line in Figure 11.14, is an increase in rents, prices, construction, and the stock of space ($R \uparrow, P \uparrow, C \uparrow, S \uparrow$).

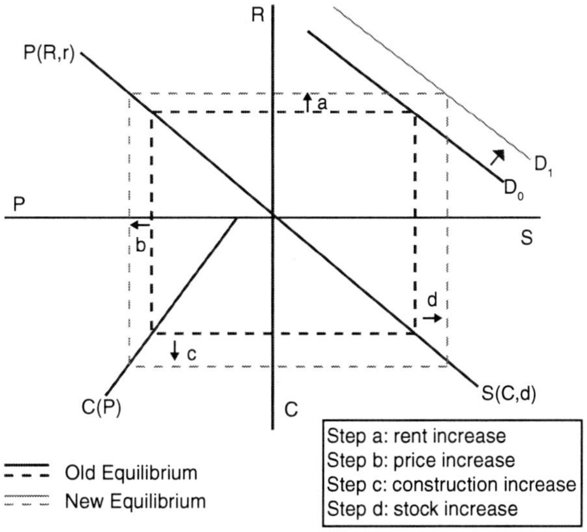

FIGURE 11.14

Improved Space Productivity

Step a: rent increase
Step b: price increase
Step c: construction increase
Step d: stock increase

- - - Old Equilibrium
⋯⋯ New Equilibrium

Helpful Hint!

When you are drawing the new equilibrium line (the lighter dashed line in the examples shown here), it can be difficult to get the four corners of the new equilibrium line to form a closed rectangle.

Here is a handy tip to overcome that when the change initially occurs due to a shift in demand in the space market quadrant: Start the first corner of the new equilibrium rectangle at approximately 45 degrees from the corner of the starting equilibrium rectangle.

EXAMPLE 11.2: A Shock in the Asset Market

Scenario A: Perceived real estate investment risk increases, raising investors' required discount rates.

Analysis: First, consider if the asset market quadrant is affected. We can answer yes if for any given level of rents, investors are willing to pay more or less to capture a particular income stream. If investors are willing to pay more, the curve will rotate to the left; if less, the curve will rotate to the right. Keep in mind that the curve representing the relationship between prices and rents always begins at the origin, i.e., investors do not need to wait for a certain level of rents before assigning a value to them. Therefore, the curve is only capable of rotating in this quadrant (rather than shifting).

FIGURE 11.15

Rotation of Asset Market Curve

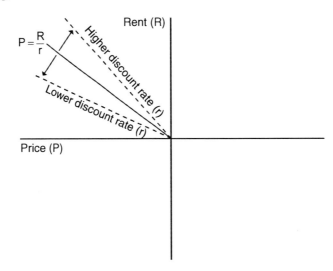

Investors who are less sure of the reliability of their income streams will have a high discount rate that reflects this increase in risk. In other words, investors will be willing to pay less for any given level of rents. Therefore, the asset market curve rotates upward to reflect this, from $P_0(R,r)$ to $P_1(R,r)$. This leads to lower prices (and ultimately higher rents, which we will see shortly).

Consider effects on other quadrants, in a counterclockwise direction, as illustrated in Figure 11.16:
(a) asset market: higher cap rate means lower prices
(b) new construction: lower prices mean less new construction
(c) stock adjustment: less new construction, considered with an ongoing stable rate of depreciation/demolition, means less stock of space
(d) space market: less space with unchanged demand means higher rents

The new equilibrium: R↑, P↓, C↓, S↓

FIGURE 11.16

Scenario A: Increased Investment Risk

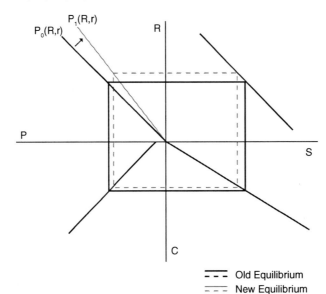

- - - Old Equilibrium
- - - New Equilibrium

Scenario B: Investors' expected return from investing in the stock market falls.

Analysis: Capitalization rates are a function of real estate investors' next best alternatives (opportunity cost), so a decline in alternative assets would mean increased competition for real estate investments. Thus, investors would be willing to pay more for any given level of rents, implying lower discount rates.

    (a)   asset market: curve rotates downward from $P_0(R,r)$ to $P_2(R,r)$ (lower cap rate means higher prices at any given level of rent); prices increase

    (b)   new construction: higher prices mean more new construction

    (c)   stock adjustment: more new construction, considered with a stable rate of depreciation/demolition, means more stock of space

    (d)   space market: more space with unchanged demand means lower rents

Therefore, R↓, P↑, C↑, S↑ as shown in Figure 11.17.

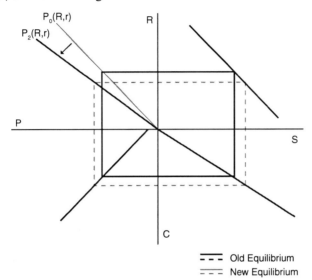

FIGURE 11.17

Scenario B: Investors' Expected Return Falls

—— Old Equilibrium
—— New Equilibrium

 Helpful Hint

Here is a handy tip to help close the rectangle when the change initially occurs in the asset market — though the same logic applies for initial changes in the new construction or depreciation quadrants too:

1. For the old and new curves in the affected quadrant, find the vertical height separating the old and new curves (the length of the vertical dashed, initial-equilibrium line that connects them).

2. Then, on the new curve, move away from the original equilibrium price (P) by one-half of the distance in step 1, to start the new equilibrium rectangle.

3. Draw the new rectangle through all four quadrants, with this new line ending at this starting point, closing the outside boundaries of the new rectangle.

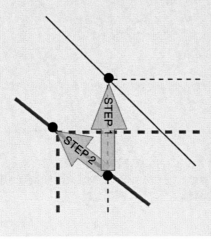

EXAMPLE 11.3: A Shock in the New Construction Market

Is this quadrant affected? We can answer yes if for any given price level, developers are willing to build more or less than before. If developers will build more, the curve will shift or rotate to the right; if less, the curve will shift or rotate to the left. Shifts occur because of changes to fixed costs that developers face, while rotations occur because of changes to variable costs.

FIGURE 11.18
(LEFT)

Construction Curve Shifts Due to Altered Fixed Costs

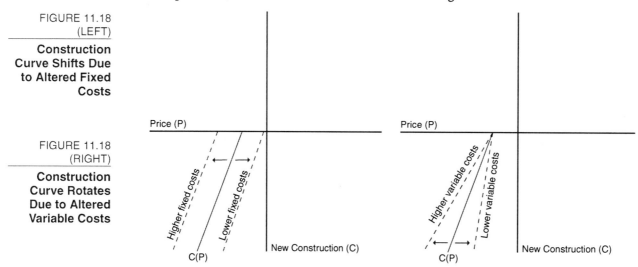

FIGURE 11.18
(RIGHT)

Construction Curve Rotates Due to Altered Variable Costs

Scenario A: The market price of concrete falls.

Analysis: The cost of concrete is a variable cost for developers, and a decrease will mean that for any price purchasers might offer them, developers will be more willing to build than before. Therefore, the curve in this quadrant will rotate to the right, from $C_0(P)$ to $C_1(P)$. This shock involves a rotation rather than a shift because the decrease is to variable costs rather than fixed costs. The result is $R\downarrow$, $P\downarrow$, $C\uparrow$, $S\uparrow$ as shown in Figure 11.19.

(a) new construction: lower variable costs lead to more new construction
(b) stock adjustment: more new construction, considered with a stable rate of depreciation/demolition, means more stock of space
(c) space market: more space with unchanged demand means lower rents
(d) asset market: lower rents with unchanged cap rates mean lower prices

FIGURE 11.19

Scenario A: Market Price of Concrete Falls

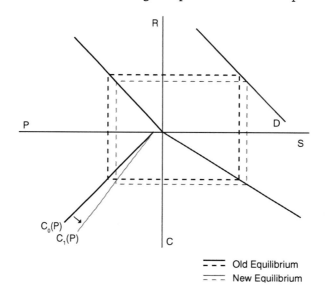

Scenario B: Suppose developers' permits must be purchased before construction can begin and, once purchased, the cost does not vary depending on the number of units actually constructed. The cost of obtaining a developer's permit increases.

Analysis: Under the circumstances described, a developer's permit can be considered a fixed cost. The increased cost means that for any given price that purchasers might offer them, developers are going to be less willing to build than before. Therefore, the curve in the construction quadrant will shift to the left from $C_0(P)$ to $C_2(P)$. This shock involves a shift rather than a rotation because it is a fixed cost component of construction that has changed (rather than a variable component). This means developers now need a greater incentive to consider starting a project. Therefore, R↑, P↑, C↓, S↓ as shown in Figure 11.20.

  (a) new construction: higher fixed costs lead to less new construction
  (b) stock adjustment: less new construction, considered with a stable rate of depreciation/demolition, means less stock of space
  (c) space market: less space with unchanged demand means higher rents
  (d) asset market: higher rents with unchanged cap rates mean higher prices

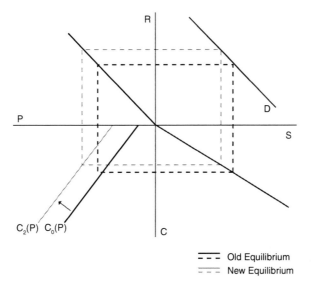

FIGURE 11.20

Scenario B: Cost of Developer's Permit Increases

--- Old Equilibrium
--- New Equilibrium

EXAMPLE 11.4: A Shock in the Stock Adjustment (Depreciation) Quadrant

Is this quadrant affected? We can answer yes if, for any given level of construction, buildings are lasting longer than before or wearing out more quickly. If buildings are lasting longer, the curve will rotate to the right (for any given level of construction, the stock of space will be greater); if buildings are wearing out more quickly, the curve will rotate to the left, i.e., the stock is reduced. The relationship between new construction and the stock of space always starts at the origin; therefore, the curve only rotates, i.e., depreciation doesn't wait for some minimum level of construction before acting on the world.

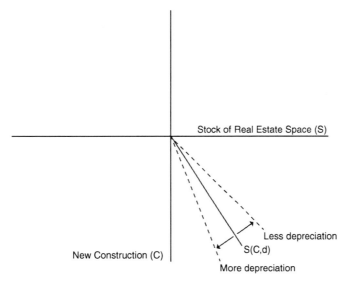

FIGURE 11.21

Rotation in Stock of Space (Depreciation)

Stock of Real Estate Space (S)

New Construction (C)

Less depreciation

S(C,d)

More depreciation

Scenario A: The building codes are updated, requiring more stringent seismic engineering in older buildings.

Analysis: The cost associated with more seismic engineering in older buildings will lead to more rapid depreciation and more demolitions (when the cost of repair is not economically justified). The increased rate of depreciation means that the stock of space will be lower for any given level of construction. This necessitates a rotation to the left for the curve in this quadrant, from $S_0(C,d)$ to $S_1(C,d)$. Therefore, R↑, P↑, C↑, S↓ as shown in Figure 11.22.

    (a) stock adjustment: increased rate of depreciation/demolition, means less stock of space

    (b) space market: less space with unchanged demand means higher rents

    (c) asset market: higher rents with unchanged cap rates mean higher prices

    (d) new construction: higher prices means more construction

FIGURE 11.22

**Scenario A:
Building Codes
Updated**

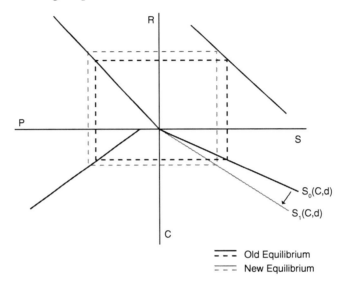

Scenario B: ACME Roofing Inc. develops a new, longer lasting, less expensive roofing system.

Analysis: For any given level of construction, the stock of space is going to be greater because this lower cost, higher quality improvement will contribute to extending the economic life of buildings for which it is installed (both new installations and renovations). This suggests that the curve in this quadrant should rotate to the right from $S_0(C, d)$ to $S_2(C, d)$. Therefore, R↓, P↓, C↓, S↑ as shown in Figure 11.23.

    (a) stock adjustment: reduced rate of depreciation/demolition, means more stock of space

    (b) space market: more space with unchanged demand means lower rents

    (c) asset market: lower rents with unchanged cap rates mean lower prices

    (d) new construction: lower prices means more construction

FIGURE 11.23

**Scenario B:
Less Expensive
Roofing System**

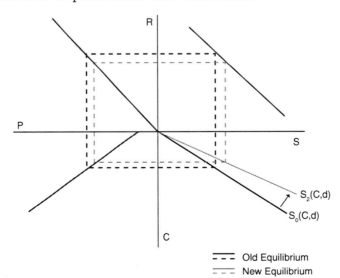

Value Matters: Linking Depreciation and Highest and Best Use

The rate of depreciation/demolitions (d) in the stock adjustment quadrant highlights some important issues for real estate value.

Highest and Best Use: as noted earlier, estimating market value requires first considering the property's most profitable legal use. For existing properties, this means considering if the improvements contribute to value or if the property would be worth more if vacant and ready for redevelopment. In other words, the question is how close d is to 100% -- at which point the improvements are fully depreciated and ready for demolition.

Cost Approach: in this valuation method, the appraiser estimates the cost of replacing the building with a substitute, then subtracts estimated depreciation to account for the existing building's age and condition. In estimating depreciation, *curable* items are those that are economically worth fixing or replacing, in order to bring the building to its cost or value as if new. Incurable items cannot be repaired economically – the cost of repair is less than the value added, so they are not worth fixing. As these incurable items add up, the rate of depreciation d grows, until eventually, depending on market conditions, the improvements are no longer the highest and best use and are demolished in favour of some new more valuable use.

SUMMARY

The competitive market defined in economics textbooks presents a model that helps illustrate market behaviour. However, this model requires simplifying assumptions that make it unrealistic in practice. This departure from realism is particularly the case for real estate markets because of the following characteristics:

- Real estate is both a commodity and an asset, and there are separate but related markets for real estate space and real estate assets.
- Because houses and other buildings are heterogeneous (an issue that we discussed at some length in Chapter 10), real estate buyers must generally undertake a time-intensive search process. In order to facilitate this *search and match* process, it is efficient for the real estate market to always have some inventory of unoccupied units, or a positive level of vacancies. This also helps accommodate unforeseen changes in demand.
- Real estate prices are generally determined through bargaining between buyers and sellers — neither party acts as a price taker.
- Real estate markets tend to adjust slowly to changes in economic conditions. The rate of price adjustment depends on the level of vacancies in the market. When vacancies are high, an increase in demand may have little or no immediate impact on rents.

DiPasquale and Wheaton developed a very useful long-run equilibrium model of real estate markets that captures many of the unique features listed above. The four-quadrant model defines the relationship between the market for real estate space and the market for real estate assets. The price of a real estate asset (a building) is largely determined by the present value of the stream of net rents that the asset will generate. In the simplest case, this asset market equilibrium condition takes the form P =R/r, where P is asset price, R is space rent, and r is the cap rate. Concurrent with these market impacts is the rate of new construction (net of the losses in space due to depreciation and demolitions of existing buildings). The rate of new construction depends positively on the price of real estate assets, and new construction adds to the stock of space, which in turn affects the rent on space. Thus, rents, prices, construction, and the size of (or changes in) the stock of space are all interrelated. The four-quadrant model allows us to sort out the interactions among these sectors in a relatively simple manner. For example, the model shows that, in the long run, an increase in employment should lead to higher rents and asset prices, an increase in new construction and an increase in the stock of space. The model is thus useful for studying how changes in the economic environment will likely affect real estate market performance.

The next chapter, the final chapter in this book, examines how the actions of local government affect this complicated and interrelated real estate market equilibrium. Of particular concern is the impact of land use controls, technically a form of market inefficiency, but also the main tool that local governments use to steer real estate market outcomes towards socially — or perhaps politically — desirable outcomes.

CHAPTER 12

LOCAL GOVERNMENT AND LAND USE REGULATION

INTRODUCTION

Our focus in most of the book has been on how market forces influence the development of cities. However, in many cases the actions of governments are at least as important as the power of markets. The operation of land markets may be best viewed as a collaboration (sometimes unwilling) between the private and public sectors. Government policies for taxation and spending directly affect quality of life, and these effects are reflected in land values and land development patterns. Furthermore, nearly every parcel of urban land in North America is subject to the regulation of at least one level of government. These regulations have profound impacts on the ways that land is used and priced.

This chapter examines the impact of local government and land use controls in real estate markets. In particular, this chapter discusses the following:

- defines the basic concepts in public finance, including the economic justification for government, the problem of public goods, and the roles of different levels of government;
- examines municipal tax and spending policies, particularly the property tax;
- presents the Tiebout model of local government; and
- explores the economic justifications for zoning laws and growth controls, seeing how these impact real estate markets.

GOVERNMENT INVOLVEMENT IN REAL ESTATE

From an economic perspective, there are three essential justifications for the existence of government:

1. *Property Rights*: establish and provide for the enforcement of laws, especially those dealing with property rights. Clearly defined and well-protected property rights are required in order for a market economy to function.

2. *Equity and Fairness*: take actions that promote an equitable distribution of income. Leaving market economies to be governed by the "invisible hand" of competition may lead to efficiency, but with ruthless disregard for fair or just outcomes. Concepts of fairness or equity vary between people, across cultures, and over time, but virtually all governments take actions that are designed to assist poor and disadvantaged individuals. This assistance comes in a wide variety of forms, such as progressive taxes (tax rates that rise with income) and programs that subsidize health care, housing, and education for lower income individuals.

3. *Correct Market Failures*: as discussed in Chapter 2, market failure occurs when the outcome of a market is inefficient in the sense that it does not maximize welfare, which we have defined as the sum of consumer and producer surplus. Common examples of market failure include imperfect competition (which is the basis for anti-trust regulation), externalities like congestion and pollution (which, as we will see, are the basis of much land use regulation), and the problem of –s. We have discussed externalities at several points in the text, but we have not discussed the problem of public goods in any detail. This is the subject of the next section.

Defining Public Goods

The two defining characteristics of public goods are:

1. *non-excludable*: people cannot be prevented from using or benefitting from the good; and
2. *non-rival*: one individual's use of the good does not diminish another person's ability to use it.

Public Good

Good that is *non-excludable* (people cannot be prevented from using or benefitting from the good) and *non-rival* (one individual's use of the good does not diminish another person's ability to use it)

Free Riders

Individuals who receive the benefits of a good, but avoid paying for it

Examples of public goods may include national defence, tornado/hurricane/tsunami sirens, or uncongested public roads. Perhaps up to 100 years ago we might have added ocean fishing and forestry to the list, but less so today — as these illustrate the inherent problem with public goods, the tendency towards over-use.

Let's examine the components of the public good definition in more detail. Efficient provision of a pure public good requires that the good be provided at the level where the sum of the marginal benefits to all consumers equals the marginal cost of provision. This in turn implies that each of us should contribute to the provision of a public good (through prices or individual taxes) an amount equal to the marginal benefit that we receive. Such payments are called benefit taxes. However, since the public good is *non-excludable,* it is difficult or impossible to prevent people who do not pay from consuming the good – people have little incentive to reveal how much the good or service is actually worth to them. In fact, most people will probably choose not to pay for the program at all. They will likely try to become *free riders*, i.e., individuals who receive the benefits of a good, but avoid paying for it.

As an illustration of the non-excludability problem of a pure public good, suppose a private firm decided to provide national defence privately. Assuming a private firm could take on such a large task, it will be impossible for the firm to adequately charge for the service because it cannot exclude consumers who choose not to pay. Each individual gets to enjoy the benefits of a safer country regardless of whether or not that individual contributes to the good's provision.

There is another problem associated with private provision of this pure public good: how much does it cost to protect one more person under a national defence program? The answer is that it doesn't cost anything — once the program is in place, the cost of providing the service to another person is zero. This means the consumption of a pure public good is *non-rival* in the sense that one person's consumption does not detract from another person's consumption; it is as if we all consume the same units of a pure public good.

From an economic perspective, efficient provision requires that price equals marginal cost; therefore, if the marginal cost is zero, then the price should be zero as well. Thus, even if one can charge for a pure public good, it may be inefficient to do so.

These non-excludable and non-rival issues mean that private markets cannot efficiently provide pure public goods.[1] If public goods are to be provided, it must be done collectively, where all beneficiaries pay for their use and free riders are precluded. This is typically achieved through government, which has the power to levy coercive taxes. As noted above, efficiency generally requires that each consumer pay a tax equal to the marginal benefit that he or she receives; the level of provision of the public good should then be set so that these benefit taxes add up to equal the total cost of that provision.

There are two important caveats to this traditional account of the efficient provision of a public good:

1. Non-excludability and non-rivalry are matters of degree. Most goods, even those provided by governments, are excludable in some way, and very few goods are completely non-rival. There are very few examples of pure public goods. Think of policing, parks, or fire protection, all of which have been cited as public goods — it is certainly possible to exclude non-contributors, and consumption is clearly rival. Or returning to our earlier example citing roads as public goods: in fact, these are non-rival only to a point, as increased congestion eventually means new users diminish the enjoyment of existing users. Exclusion from roads is difficult, but not impossible. Therefore, partially rival and partially excludable goods can in some situations be provided by private markets, e.g., toll highways.

2. Despite the failures of market mechanisms to provide optimal levels of public goods, we must be careful not to assume that government intervention is a panacea or cure-all. It is certainly possible that government intervention will increase efficiency and there are many demonstrations of these successes — but there are also situations where government intervention does not increase efficiency. Casual observation suggests that most governments are at least as fallible as markets are. For example, rent controls are a form of government intervention in real estate markets that seem to begin with the good intention of keeping rents "fair" (for tenants, if not for landlords). But they also tend to restrict new construction, take away incentives to maintain existing buildings, and prevent the efficient allocation of housing among tenants. Think of a couple living in an apartment with three extra bedrooms because their kids have left for college — someone else might be able to make better use of those bedrooms, but the couple may be reluctant to leave because their current space is rent-controlled. Assar Lindbeck, an economist (who was also a socialist), famously said, "In many cases rent control appears to be the most efficient technique presently known to destroy a city — except for bombing."[2]

Government Provision of Public Goods

Canada has three levels of government, federal, provincial, and municipal, with each providing a variety of services. The provision of public goods by each level of government varies depending on constitutional jurisdiction and the nature of the good or service.

Pure public goods that affect the entire country, like national defence, are generally provided at the federal level. Provincial and municipal governments tend to focus on public goods that are excludable and rival to some degree ("less pure"), and whose benefits are restricted to a particular geographic area. Common expenditures of this sort include primary and secondary education, roads, streets and public transportation, policing, fire protection, and sanitation. These are known as local public goods or local public services.

Despite this rough separation of duties, there is still considerable debate about the responsibilities of each level of government and what is more efficient or optimal for providing public goods. In particular, at the municipal level, there are ongoing debates about proximate municipalities duplicating local services and whether it would be more efficient to band together for regional provision. For example, Greater Victoria, BC has 13 distinct municipalities, each with its own council and its own provision of policing, garbage collection, and fire protection. Yet the region as a whole has unified bodies to provide public transit, water, and sewage removal (though provision of a communal treatment facility remains a hotly debated topic!). These discussions may often lead to the question of consolidating neighbouring municipalities — a further hot topic of political debate.

---

[1] At least for firms organized around the profit motive. There are certainly examples of volunteer or charity-based organizations providing public goods — fire brigades and lighthouses are examples.

[2] *www.econlib.org*

From an economic perspective, much of this debate can be summarized in the question: what is the optimal jurisdiction size for provision of local public goods? There are number of considerations in answer to this question.

Scale Economies

Studies of local governments have generally shown that the per capita cost of providing most local public goods is approximately constant. In other words, there do not appear to be large, unexploited scale economies in the provision of local public goods and services. This means that from a cost perspective, it would not make sense for a provincial government to take over garbage collection.

For provision of many goods and services, the optimal jurisdiction size is probably no larger than a metropolitan area — e.g., the Greater Vancouver Regional District or the Greater Toronto Area can offer the most cost effective public transit throughout the larger metropolitan region. Other services may have little benefit from this aggregation, meaning lower levels of government can provide the services in a cost effective manner.

Local Diversity

Some areas may have considerable diversity in demand for local public goods, with some individuals wishing to consume large quantities and others less. In this situation, provision in smaller jurisdictions is advantageous because it gives people a choice.

Local provision seems to have some inherent political advantages. Politicians in small jurisdictions may better understand the needs of the electorate and democratic control of public officials may be more effective. This principle of "keeping it local" is very important idea in the theory of local government, and one we will explore in greater detail later in the chapter when we discuss the Tiebout model of local government.

Efficient Taxation

Since local taxes are more direct than other taxes, the costs of public decisions may be more accurately perceived at the local level. Principles of fair taxation say that everyone who is affected by a local public good or service and its funding should ideally have a say in its provision.

- If a good that is provided in one jurisdiction benefits individuals who live, vote, and pay taxes in another jurisdiction, then the good is likely to be under-provided since some of the benefits are not counted when the funding decision is made.
- Conversely, a good that is provided in one jurisdiction that has negative consequences for individuals in other jurisdictions will likely be over-provided since some of the costs are not counted when the funding decision is made.

The benefits and costs to individuals in other jurisdictions are called *spillovers*. Thus, another principle that might influence the choice of a jurisdiction for the provision of a particular public good is that the jurisdiction should include all affected parties — that is, spillovers should be minimized wherever possible. Transfer payments between different levels of government (where a province gives municipalities money earmarked for, say, policing) are one way to counteract some spillover effects.

However, local provision and taxation can also be abused with destructive effects. The classic example involves attempts by local economic development authorities to lure industry to their jurisdictions by relaxing regulations, granting tax breaks, or providing other subsidies. The effectiveness of so-called enterprise zones is mixed. They clearly displace employment and other economic activity from nearby localities, which may benefit the municipality, but be inefficient in a larger economic sense. Some regions or countries may overbid in order to attract firms and investment, and the result is inefficient location of firms and a net loss to the region that won the additional economic activity.[3]

---

[3] See the following for more on enterprise zones:

Mayneris, F and Py, L. 2013. "The Efficiency of Enterprise Zone Programs: Some Conflicting Results?" Discussion Papers (IRES – Institut de Recherches Economiques et Sociales) 2013025, Université catholique de Louvain, Institut de Recherches Economiques et Sociales (IRES).

Furusawa, T and Hori, K and Wooton, I. 2010. "A Race beyond the Bottom: The Nature of Bidding for a Firm," CESifo Working Paper Series 3049, CESifo Group Munich.

Key Concept: Metropolitan Consolidation

In metropolitan areas with numerous independent municipalities, there are arguments for and against consolidation into one large legally-defined entity.

Advantages:

- A unified metropolitan government means offering public goods and services collectively, with the potential for scale economies for costs and improvement in overall fiscal situation.
- Spillovers are internalized, with payment for public services applied more fairly among beneficiaries. This counters a common claim by central city governments that suburban residents use the central city's streets and other facilities, but (usually) pay no central city taxes.

Disadvantages:

- There is a loss in diversity and therefore choice.
- There appear to be few (if any) cost savings associated with metropolitan area wide government, reducing the potential for scale economies.
- Equalization of tax rates and public expenditures are beneficial to some communities and harmful to others: communities with relatively low tax bases and expenditure levels will generally find that equalization causes taxes to fall and expenditures to rise, while communities with relatively large tax bases and expenditures levels will have the opposite experience.

Many public good issues can be addressed through other mechanisms, such as the creation of regional authorities with jurisdiction over goods and services where spillovers are important.

LOCAL GOVERNMENT

As noted earlier, the federal government tends to fund pure public goods, while provincial and municipal governments tend to control public goods whose benefits are restricted to a particular geographic area. Tables 12.1 and 12.2 describe expenditures and revenue sources for local governments in Canada. Local government expenditures are dominated by education, at nearly 40% of total spending. Other relatively large expenditure categories include roads and streets (13%); water, sewerage, and garbage collection (10%); policing, firefighting, and courts of law (10%); and recreation and culture (8%). Notice that all of these categories correspond to local public goods and services for which exclusion is possible, at least in principle, and where consumption is rival — they are not pure public goods.

Table 12.2 shows that local government revenues are dominated by two sources: transfers from other levels of government, often earmarked for elementary and secondary education (40% of total revenue), and the real property tax (38%). Thus, local governments raise a substantial amount of funds locally to pay for locally beneficial public goods.

This focus on local services and local fundraising is reflected in the model of governance. Local government is often characterized as the most participatory of Canada's multiple levels of government. For example, it is standard practice for the voting public to be afforded an opportunity to directly address their concerns with elected officials. As well, voting referendums for key policy issues are more common than at the provincial or federal government levels. Interested parties are able to get more directly involved in the machinations of government.

That being said, it is important to recognize that local governments in Canada are not completely autonomous. Municipalities are a creature of provincial legislation and these rules establish guidelines for the extent of local decision-making authority. Education provision is one example where local autonomy is limited. Local school boards are technically independent — some have the authority to seek surcharges to property taxes to provide additional school funding. However, broadly speaking, the provinces control the educational process — they set the taxes that support the schools, they determine the curriculum, and they make all educational expenditures. Yet it is interesting to note that this lessened local autonomy is associated with lessened local funding requirement, since provincial and federal transfer payments cover much of the cost of education. The result is a somewhat standardized curriculum with a relatively uniform quality of provision — though with a loss of local diversity and choice. In contrast, consider the US model, where local school districts tend to have more autonomy but also are more reliant on self-funding. All too often it appears this greater diversity and choice comes at the cost of substantial inequality in the calibre and content of education provision, based largely on the wealth of the community.

There is no "right" answer for which system is better; ultimately it is a political debate regarding the appropriate degree of government intervention. The policy questions are:

1. What are the optimal expenditures for local services?
2. What is the optimal level of property tax to fund these services?

The next section explores this question of optimal property taxation.

Table 12.1: Local Government Expenditures, Total for Canada, $ millions (2012 prices)

	1990		2000		2008		Change in share 1990-2008	Annual average growth rate
	$millions	% of total	$millions	% of total	$millions	% of total		
Total expenditures	95,211	100	100,643	100	131,036	100		1.8
General government services	5,274	5.5	4,895	4.9	7,672	5.9	0.32	2.1
Executive and legislative	406	0.4	367	0.4	578	0.4	0.02	2.0
General administrative	4,278	4.5	4,065	4.0	6,500	5.0	0.47	2.4
Other general government services	590	0.6	463	0.5	594	0.5	0.17	0.0
Protection of persons and property	7,725	8.1	9,178	9.1	12,930	9.9	1.75	2.9
Courts of law	90	0.1	134	0.1	354	0.3	0.18	7.9
Policing	4,471	4.7	5,428	5.4	7,615	5.8	1.12	3.0
Firefighting	2,590	2.7	3,005	3.0	4,071	3.1	0.39	2.5
Regulatory measures	405	0.4	445	0.4	548	0.4	−0.01	1.7
Other protection of persons and property	169	0.2	165	0.2	342	0.3	0.08	4.0
Transportation and communication	11,536	12.1	11,377	11.3	16,896	12.9	0.78	2.1
Road transport	9,467	9.9	9,160	9.1	13,733	10.5	0.54	2.1
Snow removal	934	1.0	1,193	1.2	1,633	1.2	0.27	3.2
Parking	303	0.3	169	0.2	315	0.2	−0.08	0.2
Other road transport	8,230	8.6	7,797	7.7	11,784	9.0	0.35	2.0
Public transit	1,921	2.0	2,087	2.1	2,664	2.0	0.02	1.8
Other transportation and communication	148	0.2	131	0.1	500	0.4	0.23	7.0
Health	1,101	1.2	1,167	1.2	2,055	1.6	0.41	3.5
Hospital care	234	0.2	77	0.1	77	0.1	−0.19	−6.0
Medical care	10	0.0	0	0.0	1	0.0	−0.01	−13.5
Preventive care	670	0.7	620	0.6	983	0.8	0.05	2.2
Other health services	187	0.2	470	0.5	994	0.8	0.56	9.7

continued on next page

Table 12.1: Local Government Expenditures, Total for Canada, $ millions (2012 prices) (*continued*)

	1990		2000		2008		Change in share 1990-2008	Annual average growth rate
	$millions	% of total	$millions	% of total	$millions	% of total		
Social services	4,492	4.7	7,058	7.0	7,128	5.4	0.72	2.6
Social assistance	2,549	2.7	4,781	4.8	4,407	3.4	0.69	3.1
Other social services	1,943	2.0	2,276	2.3	2,721	2.1	0.04	1.9
Education	40,982	43.0	42,664	42.4	51,206	39.1	−3.97	1.2
Elementary and secondary education	40,982	43.0	41,853	41.6	50,298	38.4	−4.66	1.1
Other education	-	-	811	0.8	908	0.7	0.69	N/A
Resource conservation and industrial development	1,214	1.3	1,199	1.2	1,628	1.2	−0.03	1.6
Environment	8,212	8.6	8,671	8.6	13,679	10.4	1.81	2.9
Water purification and supply, sewage collection and disposal	6,336	6.7	6,271	6.2	10,023	7.6	0.99	2.6
Water purification and supply	3,227	3.4	3,363	3.3	5,465	4.2	0.78	3.0
Sewage collection and disposal	3,109	3.3	2,907	2.9	4,558	3.5	0.21	2.1
Garbage, waste collection and disposal	1,748	1.8	2,198	2.2	3,377	2.6	0.74	3.7
Other environmental services	128	0.1	202	0.2	279	0.2	0.08	4.4
Recreation and culture	6,421	6.7	7,065	7.0	9,800	7.5	0.73	2.4
Recreation	4,796	5.0	5,248	5.2	7,331	5.6	0.56	2.4
Culture	1,580	1.7	1,789	1.8	2,399	1.8	0.17	2.3
Other recreation and culture	45	0.0	28	0.0	69	0.1	0.01	2.4
Housing	1,005	1.1	1,890	1.9	2,973	2.3	1.21	6.2
Regional planning and development	1,170	1.2	996	1.0	1,474	1.1	−0.10	1.3
Debt charges	5,783	6.1	4,050	4.0	3,437	2.6	−3.45	−2.9
Other expenditures	296	0.3	432	0.4	158	0.1	−0.19	−3.4
Surplus (+) / deficit (−)	−2,007	−2.1	897	0.9	−1,148	-0.9	1.23	−3.1

Source: Statistics Canada

Table 12.2: Local Government Revenues, Total for Canada, $ millions (2012 prices)								
	1990		2000		2008		Change in share 1990-2008	Annual average growth rate
	$millions	% of total	$millions	% of total	$millions	% of total		
Total revenue	93,204	100	101,541	100	129,888	100		1.9
Consumption taxes	116	0.1	106	0.1	124	0.1	−0.0	0.4
General sales tax	55	0.1	87	0.1	102	0.1	0.0	3.5
Other consumption taxes	61	0.1	19	0.0	22	0.0	−0.0	−5.4
Property and related taxes	37,967	40.7	41,267	40.6	49,242	37.9	−2.8	1.5
Real property taxes	28,444	30.5	34,246	33.7	42,115	32.4	1.9	2.2
Lot levies	1,037	1.1	1,250	1.2	2,365	1.8	0.7	4.7
Special assessments	1,624	1.7	836	0.8	883	0.7	−1.1	−3.3
Grants in lieu of taxes	2,416	2.6	2,188	2.2	1,796	1.4	−1.2	−1.6
Other property and related taxes	4,446	4.8	2,747	2.7	2,084	1.6	−3.2	−4.1
Land transfer tax	139	0.1	242	0.2	538	0.4	0.3	7.8
Business taxes	3,706	4.0	1,633	1.6	649	0.5	−3.5	−9.2
Miscellaneous property and related taxes	601	0.6	872	0.9	898	0.7	0.0	2.3
Other taxes	510	0.5	655	0.6	1,003	0.8	0.2	3.8
Miscellaneous taxes	510	0.5	655	0.6	1,003	0.8	0.2	3.8
Sales of goods and services	11,495	12.3	15,430	15.2	19,561	15.1	2.7	3.0
Investment income	3,655	3.9	3,115	3.1	3,578	2.8	−1.2	−0.1
Other revenue from own sources	548	0.6	875	0.9	1,232	0.9	0.4	4.6
General purpose transfers from other government subsectors	2,643	2.8	1,486	1.5	2,641	2.0	−0.8	0.0
Specific purpose transfers from other government subsectors (5)	36,270	38.9	38,605	38.0	52,507	40.4	1.5	2.1

Source: Statistics Canada

The Property Tax

Property taxes are important to local governments; however, they can also be controversial with voters. It appears that Canadian property owners generally accept the notion that ownership of real estate comes with an obligation of fund the provision of local services. While no one especially likes to pay taxes, it appears Canadian property owners do not overly object to property taxation as long as it is seen to be reasonable and fair. However, when owners perceive that this taxation is unreasonable or unfair, then they loudly demand changes to the methods and levels of property taxation. These issues have led to tax policy changes in Vancouver and Toronto in response to rapidly rising property values. At the extreme, property taxation has been the genesis of tax revolts in California and Massachusetts during the 1990s and the target of tax limitation movements in many other US jurisdictions. Consider the "Boston Tea Party" and the American War of Independence as extreme examples of public responses to unpopular taxes!

There are a wide variety of property taxation schemes around the world and throughout history. These may range from evaluating the productive capacity of farmland to simply counting the number of coconut trees on each parcel. All of Canada has adopted an *ad valorem* taxation system, where property taxes are based on the value of property held. In past, personal property may also have been taxed, but today property taxation is generally limited to real property.

For property tax to be accepted by the general public and be successful, the taxation system must be established with this ideal of perceived fairness of taxation in mind. Property taxes are levied based on the market value of real property. For properties that have recently sold, market value is obvious, but the larger majority of unsold properties must be regularly appraised to find their market value. The more frequent and more accurate are these appraisals, the better the quality of the tax assessments. However, more frequent and more comprehensive appraisals are also more expensive, and this increased cost must be funded with increased property taxes. Clearly it is not ideal to spend a lot of money assessing tax bills — so tax assessment offices often try to find a middle ground solution, an optimal point where the taxation system is sufficiently accurate to ensure an adequate level of fairness, while at the same time is cost effective to administer.

The amount of the tax burden in any given municipality is based on the government's desired tax revenues. The local government establishes the nominal tax rate, or *mill rate*, based on the desired taxes divided by the total assessed values in the municipality. For example, if the municipality wishes to raise $50,000 in taxes and the assessed values of all properties totals $10,650,000 (tax base), then the mill rate is calculated as follows:

Mill Rate = Total Taxes Desired/Tax Base (Net Taxable Value, in thousands)

= $50,000/$10,650

= 4.6948357 or $4.69 in taxes per $1,000 of property value

For example, if Mr. Smith owns a $500,000 property, he will pay property taxes of $2,347 ($500 × 4.6948357).

A common misconception with property taxes is that rising property values invariably mean rising property taxes. Say all properties increased in value by 10%, but the municipality still only needs $50,000 in total taxes. The increased property value causes the mill to drop to 4.27, but Mr. Smith's net taxes payable would remain the same (with a minor difference due to rounding).

Value Matters: Property Tax Assessment and Market Value

A property's assessment and property taxes payable can be linked to market value considerations:

- In jurisdictions with a market value assessment standard and annual reassessments, market participants may perceive the values to be accurate enough to be reliable for appraisal purposes. Sales listings that promote "below assessed value!" as an incentive to buyers offer evidence for this – if assessments bear no resemblance to market value, this would not likely be emphasized. In this situation, the assessment may directly or indirectly influence perceived value for buyers and sellers.
- A property that is subject to lower taxes than competing properties may have a competitive advantage and this may translate into market value differences (and vice versa for a property with higher taxes). This is particularly notable for commercial properties, where property taxes represent a significant proportion of operating expenses.

As well, properties that have inaccurate or inequitable assessments may warrant pursuing an appeal. The ease of pursuing assessment appeals varies by jurisdiction. Appeals are a source of professional specialization for many appraisers, which may entail working with either property owners or the assessment agency. UBC's BUSI 443 course "Real Property Assessment" is focused on the efficiency and effectiveness of property tax systems.

In evaluating the efficiently and fairness of property taxation, the first consideration is examining accuracy from a valuation perspective. An efficient tax is one that results in little excess burden and has a small welfare cost. Assuming an intention to assess properties at their market values for tax purposes, how well is this standard being met, both for individual properties (the concern of individual taxpayers) and for the system as a whole (the concern of government)?

Property assessment is a specialization within real property appraisal, with its own systems, processes, and commonly accepted benchmarks for success. The accuracy of assessment will depend on processes for both data gathering and valuation analysis.

- A more complete and up-to-date property inventory is important, but this requires inspections, which is one of the most expensive aspects of assessment.
- If relying on market-based valuation methods, then the quality of comparable data is crucial.
- If relying on cost-based valuation methods, then the link between cost and market value must be critically explored — and a realistic evaluation of depreciation is key.

Assessment practices are important; sudden changes in assessments can have dramatic impacts on tax liabilities. Further, assessment errors can cause identical properties to have different tax liabilities. This violates one of the basic principles of equitable taxation.

Equity is the second consideration in evaluating the fairness of property taxation. Put simply, this means taxpayers should expect to receive similar taxation treatment. If two people have the same welfare before any taxes are imposed, then under a tax system that obeys the principle of equity, they will have the same welfare after any taxes are imposed.

Equity is often measured in terms of the level of assessment relative to market value, in comparison to other properties. This is called the *assessment ratio* or A/V, which is calculated as assessed value divided by market value. If properties are assessed at their market values, then the assessment ratio equals 1 or 100%. If properties are assessed at less (more) than their market values, then the assessment ratio will be smaller (larger) than 1 or 100%.

The effective property tax rate is given by the ratio of tax paid to property value:

EQUATION 12.1

$$\frac{T}{V} = t \times \frac{A}{V}$$

Where:

- T/V is the effective tax rate
- t is the nominal (stated) tax rate
- A is the assessed value
- V is the market value
- A/V is the assessment ratio

Properties assessed at market value have an assessment ratio of 100% and the nominal and effective property tax rates are the same. If properties are assessed at less (more) than their market values, then the effective tax rate will be smaller (larger) than the nominal rate.

Two sub-categories of equity:

- *Horizontal equity* means that the tax system should treat equals equally — properties that have similar market value should be taxed similarly. An example of horizontal inequity would be properties that have identical market values, but are located in different neighbourhoods — properties in one neighbourhood are on average assessed at market value, while properties in the other neighbourhood are assessed at only 75% of market value. Equity says that if one group of taxpayers is afforded a privilege (in this case, being taxed at only three-quarters of property value), then this privilege should be extended to all consistently.
- *Vertical equity* means that unequals should be treated unequally – higher value properties should be subject to higher taxes than lower value properties. That could mean both are charged the same percentage of value, in which case the level of the tax will be higher for the higher value property in direct proportion to the value differential (proportionate tax). It could also mean that the higher value property is subject to a higher percentage rate (progressive tax), in which case the level of the tax levied on the higher value property is disproportionately more than would be suggested by the value differential itself.

An early form of property taxation was a *head tax* or *poll tax*, where taxes were set as a fixed amount per person living on the feudal estate. Unless all taxpayers are identical, this is vertically inequitable, since poorer people would pay a much larger proportion of their income than richer people. This is one of the arguments presented in favour of *ad valorem* property taxation. No taxation system is perfectly fair or efficient, but the market value basis appears to be the best available option at the moment.

Key Concept: Efficient and Equitable Taxation

Economists use two criteria when evaluating taxes:

1. Efficiency: a good tax is one that results in little excess burden or has a small welfare cost. The accuracy of assessment is crucial, but the optimal system must also weigh improved accuracy against the higher cost of administering the system.
2. Equity: a good tax is one that is applied fairly and consistently. Horizontal equity means that the tax system should treat equals equally. Vertical equity means that unequals should be treated unequally.

In urban land economics, a key question is property tax *incidence*: who ultimately bears the burden of the property tax? The registered property owner is legally obligated to transfer funds to the municipality, but one of the findings of economics (perhaps counter-intuitive) is that the person who remits a tax does not necessarily bear the burden of that tax. Knowing who truly foots the bill for property taxes, and thus the provision of local public goods, is an important consideration in tax policy.

The burden of any tax depends on the relative ability of market participants both "upstream" and "downstream" of the taxed item to change their behaviour. Inflexible consumers and producers (those with relatively steep supply or demand curves) will bear a high burden of any tax. People who are flexible (those with shallow supply or demand curves) will bear little of the burden of any tax. This is true regardless of who physically sends the cheque or money transfer to the government. Furthermore, taxes levied on goods or services where both the producers and consumers are highly flexible result in large welfare losses and low tax collections. If market participants choose not to buy or sell things in order to avoid taxes, the result is a loss of consumer and producer surplus in the market, and the government also loses the associated tax revenue.

Governments are attracted to land taxes, partly because they can be harder to avoid than taxes on other goods and services. Economists have often noted that because the supply of land is relatively fixed,[4] such taxes are efficient. Recall our discussion of Henry George and the single tax in Chapter 2.

Many people want to use land because of the structures they can build on it. Structures are the result of capital investment, and it is much harder to argue that this is fixed. Each person involved in producing or using the structure can be affected by a tax on the structure. Builders may be paid less for their work, lenders may earn a lower rate of return, and buyers of goods and services produced in the structure may pay more; these people will bear the burden in inverse-proportion to their relative ability to change their behaviour and produce or consume other, less taxed items.

Figure 12.1 illustrates the economic effects of the land portion of a property tax, assuming that the supply of land is fixed. We will separate the land and building (capital) portion of the tax by using L/V to represent the land portion of the tax and S/V to represent the building (capital) portion. Adding L/V and S/V together equals 1 or 100%.

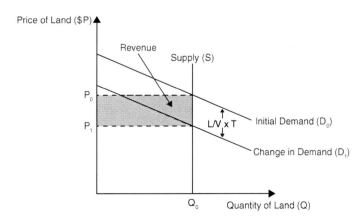

FIGURE 12.1

The Land Component of the Property Tax

---

[4] Land fit for buildings must be cultivated too. Trees must be cut, land shaped, and swamps drained before buildings can be constructed. Therefore, to an extent, the supply of usable land can increase or decrease based on market forces.

Assuming the supply of land is fixed, the quantity of land remains Q_0 no matter what taxes are imposed. With no property tax, the land owner received land rent of P_0. After the property tax is imposed, the demand curve shifts down from D_0 to D_1 by the amount of the land tax, $L/V \times T$. Since supply is fixed, the rent that the land owner receives falls by the full amount of the tax, or from P_0 to P_1 per unit. Notice also that the land component of the tax creates no excess burden: revenue (the shaded area in the figure) is exactly equal to the decrease in producer surplus. Since there is no way for land owners to alter their behaviour to avoid the tax, the land tax is non-distortionary. Thus, the land portion of the tax is paid entirely by land owners.[5]

In contrast, Figure 12.2 illustrates the economic effects of the capital/improvement portion of the tax. The supply of capital curve is horizontal, reflecting an assumption of infinite price elasticity for the supply of capital. Funders demand a fixed return of P_0 per unit of capital invested and will move their capital elsewhere if they face earning less than this. Under these conditions, if a tax on structures is imposed, owners must be fully reimbursed for this tax in order to continue their investment. This means the price that capital owners receive has to rise by the full amount of the tax, $S/V \times T$, from P_0 to P_1. This results from a shift in this supply curve by the full amount of this tax. This shows that the portion of the property tax that falls on capital improvements is passed forward to consumers. Notice also that there is a welfare cost or excess burden associated with this component of the property tax. Intuitively, the excess burden arises from the higher price discouraging some demand. From a tax policy perspective, the property tax raises some revenue, but at the cost of lost consumer surplus.

FIGURE 12.2

The Capital Component of the Property Tax

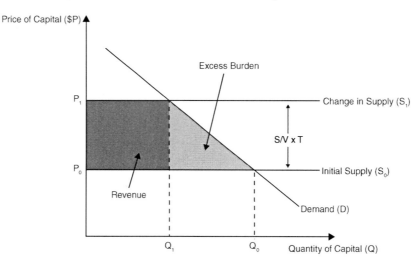

If the land portion of the tax is paid by land owners, this implies a tendency towards progressive taxation. Since land ownership rises with income, this likely means higher income owners tend to pay higher taxes.

In contrast, if the capital portion of the tax is passed forward to consumers, this may be regressive, as this tax will represent a higher proportion of income for lower income consumers.

The consequences of property tax incidence will vary by property type:

• Owner-occupiers absorb the land component of the residential property tax, and shoulder some of the burden of the capital component, sharing the latter with "upstream" suppliers (including builders and lenders) and "downstream" consumers (for households, a downstream consumer is an employer).

• Landlords may be able to pass at least a portion of the structure part of the tax forward to renters in the form of higher rents, a fact that is often addressed through property tax relief programs for low-income families and elderly individuals.

---

[5] Economists debate various perspectives on property tax incidence. The traditional view (sometimes called the "old view" in literature on the topic) is taxes on land fall to the owner and taxes on capital improvements are shifted to consumers; this follows from the assumption that land supply is fixed while capital is highly mobile. An alternative view (sometimes called the "new view") expands the perspective beyond a specific municipality to see the economy wide consequences of property taxes. This model assumes that the nation-wide supply of capital is fixed, so, taken as a whole, the property tax must depress the overall return to capital and consequently the entire property tax is paid by capital owners. In reality, these assumptions won't hold perfectly – for example, capital can not only cross municipal borders, but international ones, so capital supply at the national level is unlikely to be fixed – but the implications drawn from them can be helpful either as rough rules of thumb or thought experiments that illustrate different elasticity scenarios.

- In the case of commercial property, higher rents result in higher costs for businesses, which are at least partly passed on to their own suppliers in the form of lower prices paid for goods received as well as consumers in the form of higher prices for goods sold.

This last point raises a key issue for tax policy: it seems that part of the burden of the property tax can be shifted to consumers in other jurisdictions who consume the products that a high tax jurisdictions exports (this is sometimes called *tax exporting*). This may partially explain why many jurisdictions impose higher property tax rates on commercial properties than on residential properties.

> **Tax Exporting**
>
> When a high-tax jurisdiction exports products to other jurisdictions, effectively passing on the local property tax burden to non-locals

As noted earlier, no one prefers to pay tax. But given the need to raise funds to pay for local public goods, the *ad valorem* property tax has evolved as the optimal means of doing so. Local governments need a tax base that is relatively immobile – otherwise local taxes will simply push economic activity into other areas. The immobility of the tax base is also what makes the land portion of the property tax efficient. However, care must be taken to avoid promoting tax regressivity.

Towards Optimal Taxation: The Tiebout Model

As previously noted, a problem with government provision of local public goods is the incentives it provides for free riders. These are people who benefit from the local amenities, but who do not contribute to them. Beyond being unfair, this presents a policy challenge, because it can potentially lead to local governments under-providing services. Governments need to know the true demand for local public goods in order to both provide the necessary service levels and establish adequate property taxes to fund them.

In 1956, Charles Tiebout presented an economic model that resolves this free rider problem. He suggested that, under specific conditions, consumers will reveal their preferences for local public services through their choice of a residential community. They "vote with their feet" for the bundle of taxes and public services that they prefer.

The conditions required for Tiebout's model:

- There are a large number of independent jurisdictions in a metropolitan area offering different combinations of public services and taxes.
- Consumers are perfectly mobile and fiscal variables dominate community choice. This implies that residents don't have to worry about their job locations when choosing where to live. Note that this assumption is a departure from the models that we have considered previously.
- Community populations and public service supplies are optimal, in the sense that local public services are produced at minimum cost, that is, where average cost (AC) and marginal cost (MC) are equal.
- Public services are financed through head taxes or poll taxes (taxes that are a constant amount per person) and local budgets are balanced. So, if N is the population of a jurisdiction, and T is the tax per person, then total revenue is $T \times N$. If total cost is TC, then the budget is balanced when $T \times N = TC$. Since the communities produce at minimum cost, $T = AC = MC$.

Tiebout argues that the provision of local public goods is likely to be efficient as long as consumers or residents have sufficient choice among jurisdictions offering different packages of public spending and taxes. When each household chooses the community offering its most preferred combination of public services and taxes, they effectively equate the tax they pay to the marginal benefit that they receive, that is, where $T = MB$. This leads to efficient provision of local public services. $T = MB$ and $T = AC = MC$ imply $MB = MC$, i.e., people are consuming public services up to the point where the marginal benefit that they receive equals the marginal cost of provision. This is the basic requirement for efficiency in this context.

However, like all economic models, Tiebout's assumptions and conditions simplify reality — and critics question if it is over-simplified to the point of irrelevance.

- Are there enough jurisdictions for the Tiebout sorting mechanism to work? Probably not — in order for the model to produce the efficient outcome, there would have to be a very large number of jurisdictions in a metropolitan area.

- Is there enough local autonomy to provide residents with this kind of choice? Perhaps not, especially in Canada, where many of the activities of local governments are controlled by the provinces.
- What about local politics? The Tiebout model seems to view the behaviour of local governments as if they are cost-minimizing or profit maximizing firms.
- Do local governments use head or poll taxes to finance their activities? No, as noted above, they rely on a variety of revenue sources, the most important of which is the property tax.

The Tiebout model would probably have remained an obscure footnote in the field of local public finance were it not for one thing: there is overwhelming evidence that the model is basically right.

This evidence comes from the land market, where countless studies have shown that local public services and property taxes are capitalized into land values. In other words, other things being equal, properties in jurisdictions with high levels of public services and low taxes are more valuable than properties in jurisdictions with low levels of public services and high taxes. Similarly, properties in areas with a large fiscal differential (high taxes but low social benefits) are less valuable, other things being equal, than properties in more balanced jurisdictions. Unless consumers were shopping among jurisdictions as Tiebout's model suggested, these results would not hold. At minimum, the demand side of the Tiebout model seems correct — people choose jurisdictions based, in part, on the bundle of public services and taxes that they represent.

Value Matters: Principle of Balance

Balance is a guiding principle in evaluating real estate value. *The Appraisal of Real Estate, 3rd Canadian Edition* states: "The principle of balance holds that real property value is created and sustained when contrasting, opposing, or interacting elements are in a state of equilibrium" (page 3.7). This principle most commonly refers to an optimal blend of land and capital improvements, but it equally applies to any element or consideration that is important to buyers and sellers. People shopping for real estate care about local amenities, including schools, transportation, recreation opportunities, etc. They also view property tax as a big part of the annual operating expense. Tiebout's model says that buyers will shop among neighbourhoods and communities to find the combination that best suits them. Areas with overly high taxes and poor amenities are out of balance and thus less desirable. (And presumably areas with great amenities and low taxes would be highly desirable, but may not be sustainable in the long term.)

ZONING

Zoning is the division of a community into districts or zones in which certain activities are prohibited and others are permitted. In the simplest case, a zoning plan specifies admissible

Zoning

The division of a community into districts or zones in which certain activities are prohibited and others are permitted

land uses and densities for all land in a city. However, zoning in modern cities usually encompasses a complex maze of regulations that may specify site setbacks, building heights, minimum lot size, maximum lot coverage, minimum or maximum building areas, parking rules, environmental protections, development cost charges, etc. Furthermore, the zoning may be discretionary, with variances permitted by decisions of local government, and also ever-changing and evolving.

Zoning is a limitation on the rights of a property owner in favour of the municipality. Consider that the property rights for land ownership in Canada are limited by definition. Individuals in Canada cannot "own" land in an absolute sense. When someone purchases a fee-simple interest in land, the closest to absolute ownership in Canada, that individual acquires the right to use the land in specific ways, but ownership remains with the Crown. Further, the Canadian Charter of Rights and Freedoms, like its predecessor, the British North America Act, grants no federal or constitutional protection to property rights. Thus, there is no legal basis to challenge zoning or other land use regulations in a Canadian court.

Zoning can be separated by its two primary motivations: zoning for exclusion and zoning for separation of conflicting land uses. From an economic perspective, zoning (like other forms of regulation) may be justified by inefficiencies in private land markets. We want to consider whether or not zoning is the best way to deal with these inefficiencies.

Zoning for Exclusion

The idea behind exclusionary zoning is to keep certain groups out of certain areas, usually because of concern that their presence will decrease property values. The first zoning laws in North America were exclusionary in nature, e.g., Modesto, California from the turn of the 20th century.[6] Modern exclusionary zoning laws are more subtle in their construction, but the effect is the same: they are designed to keep certain groups (usually low-income families) out of certain areas. As Fischel (1992, pp. 171) wryly noted: "The family of eight that wants to rent part of a lot in Scarsdale (an exclusive suburb of New York City) and park two house trailers on it and send their kids to Scarsdale's fine schools is apt to find a few regulations in the way".

Modern exclusionary zoning laws have an important fiscal motivation, one that is related to our earlier discussions of property taxation and the Tiebout model. Consider a community with N total households, separated into two types of households, N_L low-income and $(N-N_L)$ high-income. The low-income households have house values V_L and high-income households have a higher house value V_H. Suppose that the annual cost of providing public services is a constant C per household, and that the community must balance its budget using market value assessment with a uniform property tax — that is, each property is assessed at its market value, with a consistent property tax rate levied on all property. The required property tax rate (t) is:

EQUATION 12.2

$$t = \frac{NC}{N_L V_L + (N - N_L) \times V_H}$$

Where:

- t = Property tax rate
- N = Number of total households
- C = Cost of public services per household
- N_L = Number of low-income households
- $N-N_L$ = Number of high-income households
- V_L and V_H = House values of low- and high-income households

This is the rate that balances the community's budget. For example:

- Assume there are 10,000 households (N) and a need to raise $4,500 per household (C).
- There are 2,000 low income households (N_L) with a value of $50,000 ($V_L$) and 8,000 high income households with a value of $100,000.
- The total taxes needed to be raised is NC = 10,000 × $4,500 = $45,000,000.
- The total assessed value of the community's real estate is [(2,000 × $50,000) + (8,000 × $100,000)] = $900,000,000.
- Dividing these values gives a tax rate t = 0.05 or 5% ($45,000,000/$900,000,000). Or, applying the mill rate formula provided earlier, a mill rate of $50 per thousand dollars of value.

Now suppose we change the proportions of high and low income families, say, N_L = 5,000. Then, performing the same calculation, we get t = 0.06 or 6%. The larger the number of low-income households, the higher the property tax rate. Assuming these property tax differences are capitalized into land values, this implies that property values will fall with greater numbers of low-income households in the community. Suddenly we have a fiscal motivation for excluding low-income families. Of course, the community cannot write a law that directly excludes low-income families. However, it may prohibit multi-family housing, or mandate lots so large that low- or moderate-income housing cannot be constructed. These indirect exclusionary measures are just as effective.

---

[6] The Modesto statute made it "unlawful for any person to establish, maintain, or carry on the business of a public laundry ... within the city of Modesto, except for that part of the city which lies west of the railroad tract and south of G street." (Goldberg and Horwood [1980], pp. 11) The public laundries in question were operated by Chinese immigrants, and the unstated intent of the law was racial or ethnic segregation – to prevent individuals of Chinese descent from living and working in certain areas of the city.

Key Concept: Exclusionary Zoning - Is it Bad Public Policy?

Exclusionary zoning is controversial and often characterized negatively in public policy discussions. However, from an economic perspective, the fiscal impacts of this type of zoning can facilitate the efficient provision of local public goods. Exclusionary zoning tends to make an area more homogeneous in terms of desired level of public services and ability to pay taxes, and it limits the potential for one group of residents to be subsidizing another through property taxes. Combining exclusionary zoning with full capitalization of these differentials allows the property tax to function as a benefit tax (users pay for benefits received) even in mixed communities.

Zoning for Separation of Conflicting Land Uses

The idea behind this form of zoning is to create exclusive land use zones to limit or prevent interactions between conflicting land uses. Most of the conflicts in question arise from negative externalities like industrial air pollution, traffic congestion from retail activities, and neighbourhood externalities from low-income, high-density housing. The apparent rationale is that when there are negative externalities, a private land market places conflicting land uses too close together. In other words, left to its own devices, the market equilibrium will not adequately segregate conflicting uses.

Consider a standard monocentric model with two land uses, firms and households, and suppose that the bid rent functions take the familiar forms shown in Figure 12.3. The bid rent function of the manufacturing firms that occupy the land closest to the city centre is shown as $R^M(d)$. The bid rent function of the households that occupy the land at the periphery is shown as $R^H(d)$. b_1 is the boundary between the firms and the households, while b_2 is the outer boundary of the urban area. Beyond b_2 are agricultural uses. The resulting locations of uses are shown with the highlighted curve in Figure 12.3.

FIGURE 12.3

A Monocentric City

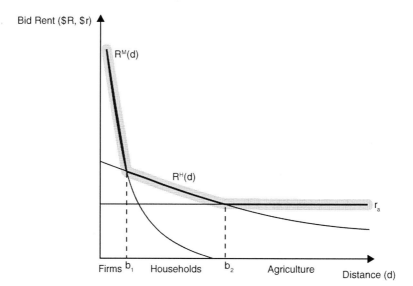

Now add a negative externality to this city. The easiest way to do this is to assume that the manufacturing firms generate air pollution that is harmful to households who live nearby. Assume that the pollution impact is worst right at the firm/household border b_1, and dissipates as ones moves further away toward the city's edge. This externality means that household bid rent now depends on two factors: as usual, the distance to the city centre, d, but then also its distance to the firm-household border $\{d - b_1\}$. This bid rent function could be written as $r(d,\{d - b_1\})$.

This revised bid rent function means that households are willing to bid less for land located at or near the border b_1, because these locations expose them to higher pollution levels. Stated differently, households who live where pollution is high must be compensated for this through lower land rents (and lower housing prices).

The pollution will cause the household's bid rent function $R^H(d)$ to shift downward by the amount of the pollution externality. This is illustrated in Figure 12.4 as the new household bid rent function $R^{H'}(d)$. This shift causes the b_1 firm/household transition point to move outward to b'_1, as land that was formerly demanded by households is now too polluted to be desirable housing, but manufacturing firms are not impacted by pollution.

But an interesting thing happens at point b'_v — at this distance from the city centre the manufacturing firms' bid rent $R^M(d)$ falls below agricultural rent, r^a. At this point, it is no longer economically viable for manufacturing firms to outbid agricultural uses. However, household bid rent is also depressed by the pollution externality, meaning household bid rent is also below r^a. So, at this point, the most economic use of this inner city land is to remain vacant (or, alternatively, perhaps some kind of holding use like parking lots or storage facilities or an agricultural use that is not impacted by the pollution). The pollution has its maximum impact where the distance between the old residential bid rent curve and the new one is the greatest.

Because the manufacturing stops at point b'_v it means the pollution impact lessens as we move further from the city centre. As the pollution impact subsides, the household bid rent $R^{H'}(d)$ begins to recover towards its unpolluted values — notice how the bid rent curve briefly has a positive slope as the depressed household bid rents recover.

Households emerge as the highest bidders for land once the pollution impact has lessened substantially. When the household bid rent curve $R^{H'}(d)$ reaches point b'_1 it means that households are once again able to outbid agricultural/holding uses (household bid rent $> r_a$).

Eventually, the rising cost of commuting should dominate the clean air effect, causing the household bid rent function to be downward sloping once again. This is the logic behind the curving shape of the household bid rent function in Figure 12.4. The portion of the polluted housing bid rent curve $R^{H'}(d)$ that is above the original no-pollution curve $R^H(d)$ is due to the pent-up demand that now cannot be satisfied close to the city centre.

The location of land uses are as shown by the highlighted curve. Household uses continue as long as the residential bid rent exceeds r^a, beyond which agricultural uses take over. Point b'_2 is the new city limit. Note that the pollution has caused the household uses to extend further than before, displacing agricultural uses.

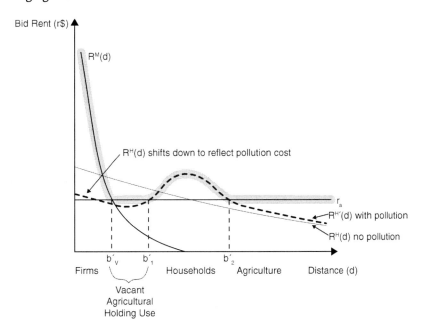

FIGURE 12.4

A Monocentric City with a Pollution Externality

This is obviously a highly stylized model of the problem, but it does make the point that a private land market will, under some circumstances, separate conflicting land uses when there are negative externalities. However, it may do so inefficiently, with too little separation. This private market failure in optimally separating conflicting uses is an argument for zoning.

Value Matters: Conflicting Uses in Practice

There is strong evidence that the effects of environmental externalities, like air and noise pollution, are capitalized into property values. However, for externalities between conflicting land uses, the evidence is ambiguous. Casual observations say there should be a strong link between the presence of undesirable activities on a block and residential property values. As Fischel [1995, pp. 220] notes: "For those who doubt whether the average nonconforming store affects neighbouring home values, I urge them to attend a zoning hearing at which a prospective store owner seeks a variance to locate in an otherwise residential neighbourhood."

However, urban land economics studies of such conflicting uses have shown little or no systematic effect on market values. The undesirable activities that have been studied include high-density housing, parking lots, light industry, wholesaling and retailing, and railroad lines. Furthermore, zoning changes that allow higher densities or different uses also seem to have little or no systematic effect on sale prices of single-family homes.

Several possible reasons are cited to explain this:

- The externalities are small relative to market value.
- Nonconforming land uses, like stores in residential areas, impose some cost but also present some benefits. Perhaps the negative and positive effects of proximity to nonconforming land uses are offsetting.
- Zoning is doing the job that it was intended to do – allowing nonconforming uses only when they do not have large negative impacts on welfare.

Source: Mark and Goldberg (1986)

Internalizing Urban Externalities

Recall from Chapter 2 that the traditional economic solution to an externality problem like this is to impose a pollution tax on the firms to internalize the costs of the pollution that they create. We illustrated the determination of such an efficient pollution tax in Figure 2.25 from Chapter 2. The basic result is that to achieve an efficient level of production when firms generate a negative externality, we should impose a pollution tax per unit of output equal to the level of marginal external cost at the efficient level of production. From an economic perspective, this is an optimal solution to the problem of air pollution.

The problem in Figure 12.4 is that the land market does not adequately separate firms and households because firms do not have to consider their true social cost. The household bid rent curve shifted in response to the added cost, when it really should be the firms producing the cost who should pay. Unless the firms are forced to consider these extra costs they are imposing, then they will be able to bid too much for land.

If we internalize the externality by imposing an efficient pollution tax, this will shift the firms' bid rent $R^M(d)$ inward. This is the social, rather than private, bid rent for land, illustrated in Figure 12.5. When faced with the true social cost of their operations, the firms cannot afford to bid as much for land. The pollution tax reduces the size of the manufacturing district to a more efficient level, lessening exposure to pollution. This may have the effect of reducing the vacant space on the industrial/residential margin or perhaps eliminate it altogether.[7]

Once again, the highlighted curve shows the location of land uses according to maximum bid rents — as noted above, the vacant area has been eliminated.

The example highlights that private markets have a tendency to provide too little separation of conflicting uses. Zoning regulations and pollution taxes are two forms of government intervention that may address this problem. A third is direct regulation of the polluting firms.

---

[7] This is a simplified scenario. For example, if the size of the business district decreases, then both the level and location of pollution in the city will change. This will affect the household's bid rent function. Further, the imposition of a congestion tax will also likely affect the number of jobs in the city. Incorporating these issues is beyond the scope of this example – the simplification should suffice to illustrate the impact of a pollution tax.

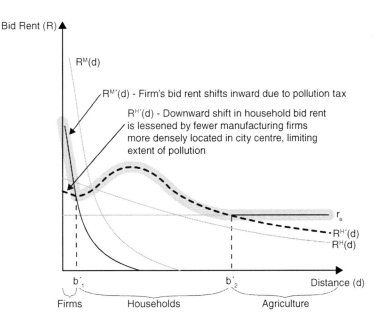

FIGURE 12.5

Internalizing the Externality in a Monocentric City

Therefore, if a private market failure justifies government intervention, which option is optimal? Political constraints or information requirements may impede the feasibility of all of these. For example, calculating an efficient tax requires accurate measurement of the damage from air pollution. As we saw in Chapter 9 with auto air pollution, this is not an easy task. Zoning is certainly easier to apply. Though creating an efficient amount of separation between firms and households with zoning also requires substantial information.

Yet the fundamental issue with zoning as a policy toward addressing externalities is that it does not directly tackle the problem, i.e., there are still excessive amounts of pollution, congestion, or neighbourhood externalities under zoning. Consider the following critique of using zoning to remedy externalities:

> The most basic evaluation of land-use controls to control externalities is that they are fundamentally defective for the simple reason that they control the wrong variable. … If noise is the offensive externality, it is much better to formulate government programs to control noise than to control land use. Land-use controls merely move the noise around. Although that may be better than nothing, it cannot be more than a peripheral contribution to solving the problem.[8]

There are potentially other ways to solve externality problems like those posed by nonconforming land uses. Consider that the city of Houston, Texas, has no comprehensive zoning laws. What it has instead are private covenants that govern land use. These covenants are voluntary agreements between land owners that specify how property rights can be exercised. In contrast to public zoning, under a private covenant, a price is paid to exercise control over the use of property. Changing a covenant generally requires the unanimous consent of, and compensation to, affected parties.

This is an application of the *Coase Theorem*: with well-defined property rights, perfect information, and zero transactions costs, private bargaining can lead to an efficient allocation of resources in the presence of externalities. For example, if existing land owners have the right to prevent retail shops from locating in a particular area, then shop owners will have to bribe the land owners to gain their consent before moving in. If the value of the nonconforming use is so large that all land owners can be compensated in this way, then the project should go ahead since everyone will be better off. Furthermore, the outcome does not depend on who has the property right, as long as it is clearly defined. In the example, if the shop owner has the right to move in, land owners will have an incentive to bribe the shop owner to stay out. If these voluntary bribes are successful, the shop owner will withdraw his or

Coase Theorem

With well-defined property rights, perfect information, and zero transactions costs, private bargaining can lead to an efficient allocation of resources in the presence of externalities

---

[8]   Mills (1979), p. 528

her proposal, and everyone will once again be better off. The distribution of resources depends on the assignment of the property right, but the outcome of the bargain does not.

This kind of bargaining is generally considered impractical on a large scale. The difficulties of reaching private agreement over land use conflicts can be considered another argument in favour of zoning. As well, should highly restrictive land use controls be deemed necessary, governments do not have to compensate property owners for the effects of zoning regulations.

With zoning's effectiveness described as somewhere between "fundamentally defective" and offering at best a "peripheral contribution" to resolving externalities, this does not speak well to zoning as an optimal solution. However, amidst political and information constraints, and the impracticality of other alternatives, it may well be that zoning is the "least worst" choice — not a perfect solution, but the optimal solution in the circumstances.

Value Matters: Principle of Conformity

Conformity is another key principle for real estate market value. *The Appraisal of Real Estate, 3rd Canadian Edition* states: "Conformity holds that real property value is created and sustained when the characteristics of a property conform to the demands of its market" (page 3.9). This conformity is established through shared preferences by owners and users of properties. To some extent it is enforced by economic pressures, but is also shaped by local governments regulating land use through zoning. Consider too that standards of conformity set by the market are subject to change – land use preferences evolve and zoning regulations are not necessarily permanent.

Growth Controls

Rapid population growth can bring negative consequences such as congestion, pollution, crime, and the loss of open space. Growth can also cause severe fiscal pressure on local governments, necessitating reductions in services or increases in taxes, especially if new residents do not "pay their way".

Growth controls are local government policies that are designed to halt, or at least slow, the growth of urban areas. Growth controls come in a variety of forms. Some attempt to limit population growth directly. These include limitations or moratoria on building permits, and reductions on allowable densities for new development. Others restrict growth by raising development costs. The most important of these are fees such as development cost charges or impact fees imposed on builders of new housing. However, any policy or policy change that delays or prolongs development will increase costs and reduce supply growth. For example, a city can increase the cost of development by simply lengthening the permit approval process.

One way to see the effects of various regulatory environments is to measure the price elasticity of supply — that is, the responsiveness of developers to increase the supply of housing when the price rises — across countries. We presume that developers everywhere are motivated by profit and would like to increase their supply when prices rise (all else equal) but that their responsiveness can be dulled by growth controls, increased time to obtain permits, and other regulatory burdens.

One study examining the elasticity of supply across countries was done by The Organization for Economic Cooperation and Development (OECD).[9] The study compared the flow of residential investment across a group of 21 countries, including Canada. Using a regression approach, the study estimated the long-run responsiveness of residential investment to price changes.[10] Table 12.3 presents the results of this estimation process.

---

[9] Sanchez, (2011), "The Price Responsiveness of Housing Supply in OECD Countries".

[10] The technique is known as *error correction modelling*, which includes both long-run and short-run adjustment components. We are primarily interested in the long-run component – the tendency of supply to respond to changes in prices in the long-run – but the short-run component is also interesting because it tells us how quickly the system reverts to the long-run if it gets "off track".

Table 12.3: OECD Estimates of Housing Supply Responsiveness to Price Changes		
Country	**Price Responsiveness**	**Standard Error**
Australia	0.528	(0.054)*
Austria	0.234	(0.057)*
Belgium	0.315	(0.028)*
Canada	1.187	(0.198)*
Denmark	1.206	(0.053)*
Finland	0.988	(0.037)*
France	0.363	(0.055)*
Germany	0.428	(0.172)**
Ireland	0.631	(0.045)*
Israel	0.379	(0.185)**
Italy	0.258	(0.050)*
Japan	0.993	(0.074)*
Netherlands	0.186	(0.061)*
New Zealand	0.705	(0.145)*
Norway	0.486	(0.024)*
Poland	0.442	(0.122)*
Spain	0.452	(0.051)*
Sweden	1.381	(0.193)*
Switzerland	0.146	(0.055)*
United Kingdom	0.395	(0.029)*
United States	2.014	(0.376)*

* denotes significance at the 1% level
** denotes significance at the 5% level

Source: OECD

Price responsiveness in this table is a measure of the price elasticity of supply, or how directly residential construction changes with housing prices. The United States, with a price elasticity of supply estimated at just over 2, was the most responsive to changes in prices over the time period studied. An elasticity of 2 suggests that, in the long run, if prices were to increase by 10% there would be a 20% increase in the quantity supplied. Sweden, Denmark, and Canada are also considered relatively responsive, as each shows a supply response in percentage terms that is greater than the price change.

On the other hand, some countries are estimated to have particularly low price elasticities. For example, Switzerland, the Netherlands, and Austria, with price elasticities of 0.1-0.2, have steep supply curves, where a 10% increase in price would yield a mere 1% or 2% increase in the quantity supplied.

This OECD study also considers the number of days required to obtain necessary building permits and the impact of legislation that may act to steepen the supply curve. This timing delay is a constraint on development — and can be used intentionally by local governments as a form of growth control.

The OECD study uses World Bank figures for the number of days required to obtain the necessary permits to build a basic commercial warehouse, including the time cost of connecting the warehouse to water, sewerage, and a fixed landline.[11] Figure 12.6 shows the price elasticities linked to the number of days required to obtain necessary building permits.

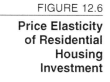

FIGURE 12.6

Price Elasticity of Residential Housing Investment

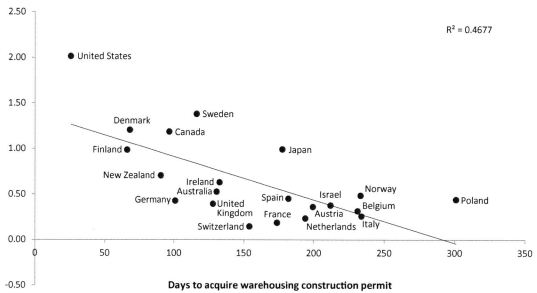

Source: OECD and World Bank

The chart shows a strong relationship between price elasticity of supply and faster permitting. It appears that development restrictiveness explains nearly half ($R2 = 0.47$) of the variation in how real estate supply changes with price in the countries under study. In other words, slowing down real estate development is an effective form of growth control. Whether or not this is desirable is a matter of political preference!

Growth controls are often justified as necessary for preserving environmental quality. For example, they may be imposed to protect agricultural land from urban encroachment, to maintain sensitive habitats, or simply to promote green space. However, growth controls may also play a self-serving role in protecting and preserving the property values of existing residents. Studies have shown that growth controls increase housing prices in the cities that adopt them, by as much as 9% to 38%.[12]

There are two competing views of why growth controls should raise housing prices:

1. Growth controls improve amenities in the controlled city and these amenity effects may be capitalized into land values.
2. Controls simply decrease the supply of developable land, resulting in higher land rents and prices.

By virtue of preserving the value of some developed properties, growth controls may at the same time decrease the value of undeveloped land near the edge of the city. Thus, the controls may act as a mechanism for transferring resources from the owners of undeveloped land to the owners of developed land.

---

[11] World Bank, (2013), Doing Business 2013. Because the OECD's elasticity estimates are for residential housing while the World Bank's estimates of supply restrictions are for commercial warehouse construction, this analysis should be treated with some degree of caution. It would be preferable to have available a common measure of the ease or difficulty of obtaining permits to build residential assets, but a lack of cross-country comparable data prevents this. However, the permitting process required for new warehousing construction may work as a useful proxy for supply restrictions in general. Indeed, the chart provides some support for the OECD's estimates of the price elasticity of supply.

[12] Fischel (1990)

Returning to the OECD data, Figure 12.7 shows price elasticity of supply on the x-axis and the average percentage increase in house price to income ratios (y-axis) over a 15-year period and across 16 countries.[13]

This chart shows a somewhat convincing relationship between inelastic supply and a tendency for house prices to rise faster than incomes (R^2 = 0.17). This suggests that in countries that experienced rises (on average) in the house price to income ratio between 1997 and 2012, about 17% of this increase can be explained by the capacity or incapacity of developers to effectively respond to price increases.

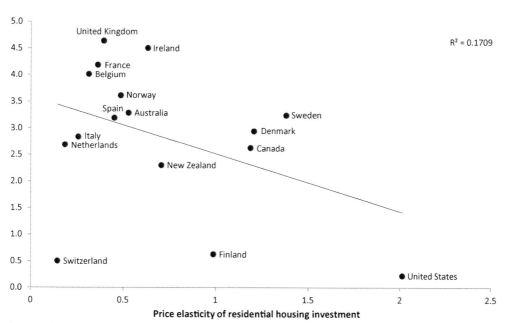

FIGURE 12.7

Average % increase in house price to income ratios, 1997-2012

Source: OECD and World Bank

In addition, some growth controls have an explicit spatial element. An urban growth boundary (UGB) is a boundary beyond which development is prohibited, at least up to some given future date. An UGB controls the earliest date at which land at the fringe of the city can make the transition to urban use. An urban service boundary (USB) is a boundary beyond which urban public services (especially hard services like sewer lines, drainage, and roads) will not be extended. Land outside the USB is much more expensive to develop than land inside the USB; this has the effect of deterring some development and encouraging more compact development patterns.

There may also be a strategic element to the adoption of growth control policies. If some communities in a metropolitan area impose growth controls, there is pressure on others to follow, since growth will be diverted from controlled to uncontrolled areas. This may help explain why growth controls are widely adopted in some areas, but completely absent in others.

SUMMARY

From an economic perspective, the failure of private markets offers a justification for government intervention. The most common sources of market failure include imperfect competition, externalities, and public goods. Public goods are goods that, by their nature, cannot be provided privately. The most important problem in the provision of public goods is the difficulty of excluding individuals who do not want to pay for the good from consuming it. This in turn leads to the problem of free riding.

---

[13] Austria, Germany, and Japan are unique in experiencing both falls in their house price to income ratios between 1997 and 2012 together with very low or even negative population growth. Removing these three outliers offered more significant results, clarifying the relationship between growth controls and prices.

All countries have more than one level of government. The appropriate size and scope of the providing jurisdiction for a particular public good depends on economies of scale, the diversity of demand, and whether or not the benefits of the good are confined to a particular geographic area, which is the defining characteristic of a local public good.

Municipal governments in Canada derive much of their revenue from provincial grants (largely earmarked for education). Elementary and secondary education is the largest single spending category for Canadian local governments by a wide margin.

The next largest funding source for Canadian municipalities is property taxes. This important source of revenue can be controversial, as to their economic impact and who ultimately "foots the bill". The traditional view is that the land portion of the residential property tax is paid by land owners, while the capital or improvements portion of the tax is passed forward to housing consumers or consumers of the products and services from firms occupying the land.

Municipal governments regulate land use in a variety of ways, principally through zoning and growth controls. Some zoning laws are designed to exclude certain individuals from certain areas, while others are aimed at controlling externalities between conflicting land uses. While zoning has its drawbacks, it appears to be the most effective response available to address these issues. Growth controls are imposed to limit the harmful environmental consequences of rapid population growth. However, these policies also serve to protect the property values of existing residents at the expense of the owners of undeveloped land.

INDEX

A

Agglomeration
    clustering, 1.3
Agglomeration economies, 1.3, 1.11
Agricultural land rent, 8.13
Asset market, 11.2, 11.8
Autos, 9.13

B

Bid rent, 1.3, 1.4, 1.11, 5.1, 5.7, 5.15
    economic profit, 5.2, 5.7
    fixed lot sizes, 6.7
    function, 5.9, 10.17
        for land, 9.20
        shape of, 5.19
    input substitution, 5.19
    land rent and location, 5.9
    rent and economic profit, 5.2

C

Capacity expansion, 9.13
Capitalization rate, 11.8
Capitalization rates, 11.11
Central places, 1.6
Characteristics of real estate markets, 11.2
Cities, 4.2
    economic cities, 4.4
    political, 4.2
    statistical, 4.2, 4.4
    systems, 4.13
City size, 1.3, 6.7, 6.9, 8.3
Classical location theory, 3.19
Clustering, 1.3
    localization economy, 4.7
    urbanization economies, 4.7
Comparative statics, 2.14
Concentration, 4.4, 4.7
Conflicting land uses, 12.16
Congestion and land use, 9.20
    monocentric model, 9.20
Congestion, 9.2, 9.18, 9.20
    in cities, 9.2
    out-of-vehicle time, 9.4
    solutions, 9.13
    transit, 9.2, 9.4
Construction, 11.13
Consumer and producer surplus, 2.17
Core-dominated cities, 7.1
Costs of auto travel, 9.9
Cumulative causation, 3.22

D

Decentralization, 7.8
Demand, 2.2
    demand curve, 2.3, 2.5, 2.8
    price takers, 2.2
Density, 8.3
Depreciation, 11.14, 11.21
Developed land, 8.3
Durability of capital, 8.1
Dynamics, 1.4

E

Economic
    environment, 11.15
    geography, 3.21
    profit, 5.2, 5.7
Economics of road use, 9.8
    speed-flow curve, 9.8
    traffic volume, 9.8
    travel time, 9.8, 9.9
Efficiency, 9.13
Elasticity, 10.9
Equilibrium, 2.12, 5.6, 11.15
    city size, 4.7, 4.9
Equilibrium land rent, 5.1, 5.9, 5.16, 6.7, 6.9
Exclusion, 12.15
Exclusionary zoning, 12.15
Export industry, 3.5
External cost of travel, 9.11
External economies, 4.5, 4.7, 4.9
External scale economy, 3.3, 3.22
Externalities, 12.18

F

Filtering, 10.25
Firm location, 3.19
    classical location theory, 3.19

G

Government and jurisdictions, 12.2
    public goods, 2.26, 12.3
    levels of government, 12.3
    spillovers, 12.4
Growth, 8.2, 8.4, 8.10
    premium, 8.11, 8.12

H

Hedonic pricing, 10.23
Highest and best use, 8.2
Household location, 6.3
Households and the housing price function, 10.15
    household's budget constraint, 10.15
Housing
    consumer choice and individual demand, 10.4
    costs of adjusting housing consumption, 10.5
    housing supply, 10.11
    market demand, 10.9
    monocentric city, 10.15
    supply, 10.11
    tenure choice, 10.5
Housing Market, 10.2
    monocentric city, 10.15
    submarkets and housing services, 10.2

I

Income elasticity, 10.9
Increasing returns, 3.21
    cumulative causation, 3.22
    external scale economy, 3.3, 3.22
Incremental growth, 8.4
Input substitution, 5.19, 5.20